René Girard's Mimetic Theory

Studies in Violence, Mimesis, and Culture

SERIES EDITOR

William A. Johnsen

The Studies in Violence, Mimesis, and Culture Series examines issues related to the nexus of violence and religion in the genesis and maintenance of culture. It furthers the agenda of the Colloquium on Violence and Religion, an international association that draws inspiration from René Girard's mimetic hypothesis on the relationship between violence and religion, elaborated in a stunning series of books he has written over the last forty years. Readers interested in this area of research can also look to the association's journal, *Contagion: Journal of Violence, Mimesis, and Culture.*

René Girard's Mimetic Theory

Wolfgang Palaver

Translated by Gabriel Borrud

Michigan State University Press · *East Lansing*

Copyright © 2013 by Michigan State University
René Girards mimetische Theorie © Lit Verlag, 2011

♾ The paper used in this publication meets the minimum requirements of ANSI/NISO
Z39.48-1992 (R 1997) (Permanence of Paper).

 Michigan State University Press
East Lansing, Michigan 48823-5245

Printed and bound in the United States of America.

19 18 17 16 15 14 13   1 2 3 4 5 6 7 8 9 10

LIBRARY OF CONGRESS CATALOGING-IN-PUBLICATION DATA
Palaver, Wolfgang, 1958–
[Reni Girards mimetische Theorie. English]
Reni Girard's mimetic theory / Wolfgang Palaver ; translated by Gabriel
Borrud.
p. cm.—(Studies in violence, mimesis, and culture series)
Includes bibliographical references (p.   ) and index.
ISBN 978-1-60917-365-4 (ebook)—ISBN 978-1-61186-077-1 (pbk. : alk. paper)
1. Girard, Reni, 1923– 2. Imitation. 3. Mimesis in literature. 4. Philosophy, Modern. I. Title.
B2430.G494P3513 2013 2003
203'.4—dc23
2012028780

Book design by Charlie Sharp, Sharp Des!gns, Lansing, Michigan
Cover design by David Drummond, Salamander Design, www.salamanderhill.com
Cover photograph of René Girard by Herlinde Koelbl is used with permission.
All rights reserved.

Visit Michigan State University Press at *www.msupress.org*

Contents

Preface

The fox knows many things, but the hedgehog knows one big thing.

—Archilochus

A ccording to Roberto Calasso, René Girard is one of the "last surviving hedgehogs."[1] With this thesis, the Italian philosopher makes use
of Isaiah Berlin's interpretation of Archilochus's dictum in order to
describe the founder of the mimetic theory more closely. Berlin differentiates "hedgehogs" such as Plato, Dante, Hegel, Dostoyevsky, or Proust from
"foxes" such as Aristotle, Shakespeare, or Goethe. While the former authors
attempt to trace all phenomena back to one single insight or principle, the
latter take on an array of ideas and inquiries. We must agree with Calasso
here: Girard's work is that of a hedgehog. In his own words, the mimetic
theory lives from one "single intuition" (*Quand ces choses commenceront*,
190).[2] Whereas for Calasso the "one big thing" around which Girard's work
revolves is the scapegoat, I believe the crux of Girardian thought is found
in the more encompassing concept of the *mimetic cycle*. In his most recent
systematic book, Girard uses this concept to summarize the central core of
his thought.[3]

The mimetic cycle is composed of three different components. In the first place, one finds the crisis brought about by mimetic rivalry, which we will examine at length in the third chapter of this book. Our analysis will focus on Girard's articulation of mimetic desire—the anthropological core of his entire theory. The second component concerns the collective violence of the scapegoat mechanism, which transforms the chaos of the mimetic crisis into a new social order. This is the crux of Girard's theory of the origin of culture, which we will address in the fourth chapter. The third component is based on the religious veiling of the scapegoat mechanism, which begins with the divinization of the sacrificed victim and forms the origin of archaic religion. In its analysis of this final component, the mimetic theory shows itself as a theory of religion that explicates the origins of archaic myth and discovers in Christianity a form of religion that differs fundamentally from paganism. While mythical religions are based on texts that are told from the perspective of persecutors, the biblical writings show solidarity with the victims of sacrificial persecution. The fifth chapter of this book presents Girard's interpretation of biblical scripture.

In these central chapters, the three main elements of the mimetic theory will be discussed at length. Examples from literature will help to illustrate my presentation of Girard's thought, and a comparative analysis with other philosophers and cultural thinkers will attempt to provide an intellectual positioning of the mimetic theory. These chapters build the center of a project that can be viewed as a kind of triptych: Two chapters on either side serve to complement this main middle section and can be viewed as the side panels that both refer to the center and must be understood through the concepts discussed therein. The first chapter of the left panel introduces the life and work of René Girard and stresses above all that his exclusive focus on the mimetic cycle is due to a personal conversion that he experienced while working on his first major study of mimetic desire: "It all began for me in 1959. I felt that there was a single whole there that I had penetrated little by little. It was there in its entirety from the beginning, all parts together in one" (*Quand ces choses commenceront*, 189). The second chapter of the left panel examines Girard's mimetic theory in the context of the contemporary debate on secularization. In a world in which the topic of religions has once again become a virulent part of political debate, all theses that had proclaimed the "death of God" in the modern world have proved inadequate. The mimetic theory, meanwhile, has taken a completely different path with regard to the topic of religion; since it never adopted any naive theory of secularization, it is able to explicate the complex relation of religion and modernity in a convincing fashion.

The two chapters of the right panel reflect on additional applications of the mimetic theory. The sixth chapter examines volatile political topics that include the origin of political power and the death penalty, as well as that of friend/enemy relations and war. Just as with the topic of religion, these phenomena are of increasing relevance in our world today; the mimetic theory can offer insight into the deeper connections of contemporary manifestations of crisis such as civil wars, terror, and wars against terror. The concluding seventh chapter discusses the relation between the genders [tr. *Mann und Frau*] in order, on the one hand, to reject any theses that propose a fundamental difference between male and female desire and, on the other hand, to explicate the cultural tendency to stamp women as the preferred victims of collective persecution. At the end of the book, one finds an index of names and the central concepts of the mimetic theory, as well as a chronology of the significant events in Girard's life and work.

As clear and as simple as the core of the mimetic theory presents itself, the more broad and all-embracing its spectrum of application becomes. Although this book pursues many questions and insights opened by Girard's theory, it also excludes many significant areas in order to avoid transcending its own context. For example, there already exist interesting studies of the mimetic theory in the field of economics, which, however, this book only refers to bibliographically.[4] The same goes for film, which like literature offers an array of connecting points for Girard's theory.[5]

Originally, a chapter had also been planned in which critical objections to the mimetic theory were to be addressed. However, I decided instead to address and discuss these criticisms within my presentation of the theory itself; the most frequent objection brought against Girard, that his theory represents an ontologization of violence, i.e., that it posits a principle of inexorable violence, is discussed in several of the following chapters and clearly rejected. Even if no explicit criticism of Girard can be found in this book—because my intense study of his writings was continually able to answer my questions and provide ever deeper insights, the scope of which remains unforeseeable—the mimetic theory must of course also be exposed to critical analysis. In the part of this book devoted to biblical understanding—in particular the chapters pertaining to Original Sin, grace, and sacrifice—one will see that Girard himself even revised and redeveloped his theory where he was forced to recognize inherent errors and ambiguities.

My work on this book lasted exactly ten years. Many people accompanied me during this time and supported my work, and I would like to take this opportunity to thank some of them here: First and foremost, I would like to thank Raymund Schwager, who made the mimetic theory known in the German-speaking realm and brought it above all to Innsbruck, where I was first introduced to it as a student. Schwager supported my work in many ways. Particularly significant was his advice—following a reading of a first draft of this book—to incorporate Augustine into my presentation and analysis of the mimetic theory. This delayed the eventual completion of the book, but it enabled a much deeper understanding of Girard's work. I also received valuable help from friends and colleagues of the *Colloquium on Violence & Religion*. In particular, I would like to thank James G. Williams for the encouraging help he gave to a young colleague, and Robert G. Hamerton-Kelly, who made my one-year research fellowship at Stanford University possible. Martha and René Girard also contributed greatly to my—and my family's—year at Stanford. Girard's Shakespeare lecture and his Aeschylus seminar were crucial for me on the way to writing this book; after my return from Stanford, I offered an annual lecture on Girard's mimetic theory for ten consecutive years at the University of Innsbruck. The core of the present book is based in large part on these lectures. Conversations and discussions with students prompted me time and again to make revisions and additions, for which I am very thankful. Many friends and colleagues were kind enough to read through significant parts of this book. Constructive feedback from Sonja Bardelang, Alexander van Dellen, Hans Dollfuß, Jürgen Kühnel, Józef Niewiadomski, Barbara Ostermann, Petra Pösel, Willibald Sandler, Peter Tschuggnall, and Richard Weiskopf contributed greatly to the book's present form. I thank Maria Hahnen and Elfriede Landauer for their proofreading, and Klaus Giesriegl and Michael Rainer from the two German publishing houses for their patience in waiting five additional years for a book originally scheduled to be finished in 1998. I would like to thank my colleagues at the Institute of Systematic Theology in Innsbruck for a pleasant working atmosphere, and of course my family—especially my wife Andrea—for their enduring support of an undertaking that seemed for a long time to have no end. I dedicate this book to our three children, Stephan, Jakob, and Anna, because I firmly believe that the significance of the mimetic theory extends beyond the realm of academia, and that its deep insights can help establish the true meaning of a Christian life.

Preface to the English Edition

Since this book was first published in 2003, the worldwide acceptance of Girard's mimetic theory has expanded significantly. What was once an insiders' tip among cultural theorists and scholars of literature and religion now finds itself increasingly in the focus of academic attention. This can be seen most clearly in the numerous honorary doctorates Girard has received in past years, and above all in his induction into the Académie française in 2005.[1] The awarding of the Dr. Leopold Lucas Prize by the Eberhard Karls Universität in Tübingen underlines the recognition that Girard has meanwhile gained in Germany.[2]

In the realm of the natural sciences, representatives of the mimetic theory have been engaged in dialogue with empirical researchers over the past years in mutual study of the mimetic behavior of humans and animals.[3] Research focusing on imitation among young children, as well as the discovery of mirror neurons have both underlined the importance of mimesis in social life. In a similar way to Girard, modern neuroscience stresses the importance of imitation in acquisitive behavior, even if the latter underestimates the conflictual dimension of mimesis in comparison to Girard.

Looking ahead to the near future, the mimetic theory is faced with the crucial and difficult task of taking into consideration religions other than

Judaism and Christianity. In Girard's work there are two possible paths hinted at for the future direction of the mimetic theory. One of these could pursue the thesis that only Christianity—and to a slightly lesser extent, Judaism—enables the ultimate exit from the world of the scapegoat mechanism. In an interview conducted in 2005 by Nathan Gardels, Girard emphasizes the singularity and superiority of Christianity among all other religions: "All of my work has been an effort to show that Christianity is superior and not just another mythology. . . . This revelation of collective violence as a lie is the earmark of Christianity. This is what is unique about Christianity. And this uniqueness is true."[4] While this position does rightly reject the danger of relativism, it is also perhaps too narrow, because it limits the universal potential of the mimetic theory too rashly. In response to Girard's interview, the Indian essayist Pankaj Mishra expressed his admiration of Girard's insight into the nonviolent message of the Gospels, in which he also recognized a significant source of inspiration for Mahatma Gandhi's political-spiritual vision and method. With the reference to Gandhi, however, Mishra was quick to criticize Girard's emphasis on the superiority of Christianity: "I wonder if it is not more relevant to try to find traditions—in Buddhism, Hinduism, Islam—which chime with the truth of the Gospels."[5] Similarly, some younger Girard scholars also claimed that the mimetic theory should be taken into interreligious dialogue.[6] A first step in this direction was taken at the annual gathering of the "Colloquium on Violence and Religion" in Boston in 2000, with the talks and discussions of this conference printed in the journal *Contagion*.[7] In 2011, the American theologian and Dominican Richard Schenk and I convened a symposium at the Graduate Theological Union in Berkeley on the topic "René Girard and World Religions," in which we delved into the relationship of the mimetic theory and religions outside the Judeo-Christian tradition.

These two symposiums pursued the second path suggested by Girard's mimetic theory, namely, the notion that—as Mishra claimed—religions other than Christianity and Judaism can offer potential ways out of the world of the scapegoat mechanism. In 2002, Girard gave a lecture at the Bibliothèque nationale de France in Paris on the topic of sacrifice in the ancient Indian Vedas and different forms of transformation within this archaic sacrificial culture. In the same year, he relativized his position on the absolute superiority of the Bible in an interview with Sandor Goodhart: "I don't want to privilege the Bible absolutely."[8] With regard to Eastern religions, Girard names the *Vedānta*, certain *Upanishads*, Jainism, and Buddhism as particular examples that display parallels to the biblical exodus from sacrificial order.[9]

A particularly important question today is the interpretation of Islam from the perspective of the mimetic theory. Girard himself has only offered a few remarks on Islam, most of which are combined with the wish for more comprehensive studies.[10] Other mimetic theory scholars, as well, have until now addressed the issue in a merely isolated and marginal way.[11] A research group at Innsbruck University, working to apply and develop the mimetic theory through the interdisciplinary research platform "Politik—Religion—Kultur" [tr. politics, religion, culture], published a first collection of articles in 2009 aimed at an understanding of Islam from the perspective of mimetic theory.[12] Plans already exist to incorporate Muslim colleagues directly in future research.

For the English edition of this book, I would like to thank Gabriel Borrud, who translated the text from German with great care; Martina Pamer for the Index of Names; Bill Johnsen, who included this volume in the Michigan State University Press series Studies in Violence, Mimesis, and Culture; Kristine M. Blakeslee, managing editor of MSU Press, who carefully shepherded this book through the production process; and the organization Imitatio, which provided financial support for the translation.

CHAPTER 1

Life and Work
of René Girard

Girard is a phenomenon. Many in the world see him as one of the greatest thinkers of our time—of the stature of a Freud or Marx, with, what's more, truth.

—Jean-Pierre Dupuy, "Le Christ et le Chaos: Entretiens avec René Girard"

René Girard refers time and again in his analysis of literature to the correspondence between the lives of authors and their work. From the perspective of the mimetic theory, the existential connections between biography and work are not to be overlooked. In his first book, *Deceit, Desire and the Novel*, Girard bases his central thesis on the observation that Cervantes, Flaubert, Stendhal, Proust, and Dostoyevsky arrived at their insights into human nature by going through a personal conversion themselves.[1] Only after seeing through their own romantic search for autonomy and authenticity were these authors able to perceive the truth about human life. In the case of Proust and Dostoyevsky, Girard underlines the connections between biography and work most distinctly, as can be seen in the introduction to a collection of essays on Proust (*Mimesis and Theory*), as well as in his book on Dostoyevsky, *Resurrection from the Underground*.[2]

As he traces Dostoyevsky's descent into hell through the psychology and metaphysics of the underground to resurrection, he describes not only the personal path of the Russian novelist, but also the development of his novelistic creation. Distinct parallels can be seen here to Dante's *Divine Comedy*. According to Girard, Dante's trilogy already contains—similar to Augustine's *Confessions*—the literary structure of conversion that likewise characterizes the works of the great modern novelists.[3] This same insight regarding the connection between biography and work can be found in Girard's essay on Camus, "Camus's Stranger Retried."[4] *The Fall*, Girard stresses, must be understood as Camus's attempt at self-criticism.

Girard is of course aware that his emphasis on the connection between the life and work of these authors makes him vulnerable to being accused of naive biographism. For this reason, he frequently points out that he posits no direct identification of the authors with their literary figures, but rather that he is merely interested in their insight into the "existential" or "spiritual" form of autobiography that reveals a deeper connection between author and literary work, one that transcends any merely superficial correlations between the two.[5]

In his book on Shakespeare, *A Theater of Envy*, Girard addresses the relationship of biography and literary creation most extensively. In no way, especially in this case, does Girard fall victim to the temptations of approaching Shakespeare's work via purely biographical speculations.[6] However, this does not imply that Girard gives in to the reverse danger of advocating a complete separation of life and work. He argues, rather, for an existential connection between the great works of literature and the lives of the authors that created them. In both, one finds insights into the mimetic relationships that constitute human life: We are not autonomous, self-sufficient individuals, but rather beings that are formed through the imitation of models, especially with regard to desire. In reference to Shakespeare, Girard shares James Joyce's insights into the mimetic nature of the English playwright.[7] It was precisely because Shakespeare's own life was so formed by mimesis, Girard and Joyce argue, that he was able to create works that depict the mimetic dimensions of humanity—above all, envy, jealousy, and rivalry—in such detail. Joyce expresses this in *Ulysses* through his character Stephen Dedalus, who presents a biographical approach to Shakespeare in a literary circle in Dublin.[8] Dedalus's audience reacts with coarse confusion. For them, such a biographical approach represents mere "speculation of schoolboys for schoolboys."[9] This "peeping and prying into the family life of a great man," this "living," is "interesting only to the parish clerk" and can be done by the "servants."[10] According to Girard, the inability to comprehend the connection between an author's life and work is typical for many scholars of literature, which he argues is due to their repression of the complex problem of mimesis. In contrast, Girard praises Joyce's allusion to the interconnectedness of biography and work, for in the end this is itself a reference to the mimetic lives of these authors. Even if Dedalus's presentation is not historically accurate, Girard argues that he has completely understood the mimetic core of Shakespeare's life. This comprehension, of course, has its deeper roots in Joyce's life; Dedalus bears several of Joyce's traits, and the propensity to imitate others is central among these. These biographical elements appear most distinctly in *Ulysses*, where Joyce's compulsive jealousy—a mimetic phenomenon, par excellence, which can be found throughout the letters to his wife, Nora[11]—becomes visible.

That which Girard observes systematically in the great works of literature also takes on meaning for his own work. Just as the great novelistic authors based their works on insight—obtained in a kind of conversion—into their own mimetic desire, Girard's mimetic theory, too, is also formed by such an experience of conversion. The following biographical sketch will therefore place particular emphasis on Girard's own conversion.

A Biographical Sketch

René Girard was born in Avignon on December 25, 1923.[12] After graduating from high school, he studied medieval handwriting—paleography—at the École des Chartes in Paris from 1943 to 1947. Under the influence of his parents during World War Two, he supported the Résistance, the French movement against the German occupation of France. In 1947, he earned his PhD with a dissertation entitled "Private Life in Avignon in the Second Half of the 15th Century" ("La vie privée à Avignon dans la seconde moitié du XVe siècle"). Faced with the decision of becoming an archivist like his father or taking a completely different path, he decided in 1947—at the age of twenty-four years—to pursue a teaching career in the United States. He accepted an offer to teach French at Indiana University in Bloomington, where he simultaneously started work on a dissertation project on the subject of contemporary history. In 1950, he earned his second doctorate with a work entitled "The American Opinion of France in the Years 1940–1943."

The experience of greater intellectual freedom at American universities eventually led him to emigrate completely from France and establish his career in the United States. Girard was denied tenure at Indiana for insufficient publication; he moved on to Duke University in 1952. Seven articles—among them studies of Saint-John Perse, Malraux, and Kafka—which he published in 1953, were enough to gain him a position as assistant professor at Bryn Mawr College in Pennsylvania. Four years later, he was appointed professor of French literature at Johns Hopkins University in Baltimore (1957: associate professor; 1961: full professor). Gradually, his first works began to receive attention in the academic world. In October 1966, toward the end of his first professorship in Baltimore, Girard organized an important international symposium, "The Languages of Criticism and the Sciences of Man," in which leading thinkers such as Roland Barthes, Jacques Derrida, Lucien Goldmann, Jean Hyppolite, Jan Kott, Jacques Lacan, Georges Poulet, Tzvetan Todorov, and Jean-Pierre Vernant took part.[13] Derrida's lecture at the conference, "Structure, Sign, and Play in the Discourse of the Human Sciences," is regarded today as one of the classical texts of deconstruction.[14]

From 1968 to 1976, Girard was a professor of literature at the State University of New York in Buffalo, before returning to Johns Hopkins for another four years as professor of French literature and the humanities. From 1980 until his retirement in 1995, he was the Andrew B. Hammond Professor of French Language, Literature, and Civilization at Stanford University in California. In March 2005, he was elected into the Académie française. He has been married to Martha McCullough since 1951 and is the father of three children. He currently lives in Palo Alto, California. As a literary scholar, one could say that Girard "lacks the professional training required in his field" [tr. *Quereinsteiger*]. Many scholars also accused him of deserting the realm of literature when he later expanded his mimetic theory in the direction of anthropological and biblical analysis. Such criticism led to the observation that, as a trained historian, he was just as unqualified in the field of comparative literature as he was in the disciplines that he later pursued (anthropology and New Testament exegesis). It was precisely this unconventional approach to literary analysis, however, that enabled him to develop a theory that went far beyond the field's narrow realm. With that being said, Girard claims he never consciously intended to develop any interdisciplinary theory, admitting rather that his research simply led him to pursue analyses in diverse areas. The mimetic theory, in turn, has become a topic of discussion in several academic disciplines today. The international and interdisciplinary "Colloquium on Violence and Religion"[15] founded in 1990 publishes an annual journal, *Contagion: Journal of Violence, Mimesis, and Culture*, aimed at exploration, criticism, and development of the mimetic theory.

The connection between Girard's personal development and his conception of the mimetic theory is particularly interesting. As a French teacher at Indiana University, he received an offer to also teach literature. At the time, Girard was familiar with Cervantes (whom he had read in an abridged French edition for children) and Proust (whom he had been reading since he was 18 years old), but he was forced to read the works of Stendhal, Flaubert, and Dostoyevsky for the first time during his preparations. He gradually discovered similarities between these authors and came to the realization that their great works were based on a personal conversion. The discovery of conversion among the great novelists of European literature went along with Girard's own experience of conversion.[16] He began to turn away from his own pride and to see himself as a puppet of his own mimetic desire. Just as with Dostoyevsky, this reversal was accompanied by a turning towards Christianity, as his intellectual work led him to a new understanding of the Gospels. From the age of ten to thirty-eight years, Girard was an agnostic. As a child, he went to church with his mother, a devout Catholic; however, his interest in the Christian religion declined, and he appeared to follow in his father's footsteps, an anticlerical person and opponent of the Church. Girard saw himself in his young years as a left-leaning atheist. He sympathized with the intellectual, revolutionary avant-garde and the surrealists. Girard's intense study of the novelistic authors eventually led him back, after decades of distance, to the Christian faith and the Catholic Church. At first, this applied merely to his intellectual stance, but Girard eventually returned to the Catholic Church and began once again to practice his faith. He described the decisive moments of his conversion in an interview in the mid-1990s; given the vital importance of this conversion for Girard's life and the development of the mimetic theory, I have decided to reprint major parts of this interview here:

> In the autumn of 1958, I was working on my book on the novel, on the twelfth and final chapter, "The Conclusion." I was reflecting on the analogies between the religious experience and that of the novelist, who discovers in himself a systematic liar, a liar for the benefit of his ego, which in the end is composed of a thousand lies that have amassed over a long period of time and perhaps been carried around for an entire life.
>
> I finally understood that I was going through an experience of the exact type I was attempting to describe. The religious symbolism embryonic to these novelists began in my case to function on its own and caught fire inside me spontaneously. I was no longer able to give in to illusions about what was happening within me, and I was completely discountenanced, for I took pride in my skepticism. I could not see myself going into the church, genuflecting, et cetera. I was akin to a windbag, full of that which the old catechisms call the "fear of man" [*respect humain*].
>
> Intellectually, I had converted, but I remained incapable of bringing my life in accord with my thoughts. Over a period of a few months, faith became for me a delicate enjoyment that also heightened my other pleasures, a type of candy in a life that had nothing criminal about it, but consisted merely of *self-indulgence....*
>
> During the winter of '59, I was already teaching at Johns Hopkins but still giving lectures at Bryn Mawr College where I had spent four years, and every week I rode back and forth between Baltimore and Philadelphia in the old squeaking and rocking cars of the *Pennsylvania Railroad*. A landscape passed before my eyes that consisted mostly of scrap iron plants and vacated terrain—typical of the old industrial regions of Delaware and to the south of Philadelphia—but my mental state transfigured everything, such that even the smallest rays of the setting sun aroused veritable ecstasy within me. It was in this train one morning that I discovered a small pimple in the middle of my forehead that didn't want to go away—one of those forms of skin cancer which, in reality, are not very dangerous. My doctor, however, whom I consulted and who listened to my inquietude, forgot to inform me of this, perhaps because he was worried that I could cross the Atlantic at any time and escape paying my fees. Thankfully, I had medical

insurance, and everything possible was done to remove my little pimple forever. . . .

[But then], shortly thereafter, abnormal aftereffects appeared in the exact place where the miniscule operation had been performed. This seemed to trouble the serenity of my doctor, and my peace of mind was now completely shattered. It was clear to me that the cancer had begun to grow anew and that this time it could be fatal. . . .

My period of anguish lasted a rather long time. It began in the week after Septuagesima. Prior to the liturgical reforms of the last Council, the two weeks following Septuagesima Sunday functioned as a preparation for the forty days of Lent, during which the disciples, in imitation of Jesus and his forty-day fast in the desert, do penitence *in cinere et cilicio*, "in ash and in penitential robe."

My preparation for this Lent was excellent, of that I can assure you, and the ensuing fast was also exemplary, for I was so full of worry that I endured sleepless nights until the day these worries, as suddenly as they began, disappeared from the world during a final visit to my medical oracle. After all the necessary tests had been carried out, the good man declared me healed, precisely on the Wednesday of Holy Week, which precedes the Passion—properly speaking—and Easter, the official conclusion of penitence.

Never before had I experienced a celebration that could be compared with this deliverance. I saw myself as already dead, and, all of a sudden, I was resurrected. The most miraculous part for me was that my intellectual and spiritual conviction, my true conversion, had occurred before this great fear during Lent. If it had come thereafter, I would have never truly believed. My natural skepticism would have persuaded me that my faith was the result of fear. This fear, however, could never have been the result of faith. The duration of my dark night coincided exactly with the period prescribed by the Church for the penitence of sinners, with three days of grace left over—the most important of all—perhaps to allow me to reconcile with the Church in peace before Easter.

God had called me back to my senses with a bit of humor, which, given the mediocrity of my case, was well merited. In the days following Easter, I had my two sons baptized, and I married my wife in the Catholic Church. I am convinced that God sends people many signs, which for the wise and learned may not objectively exist. Those for whom they are not intended see them as imaginary, but those for whom they are destined cannot deceive themselves, for they experience them from inside. I understood immediately that the memory of this experience—should I ever venture away—would offer me support my whole life long, and that is exactly how it has been (*Quand ces choses commenceront*, 190–194).

Girard's Work in Overview

In the following I will provide a general view of Girard's published works. In 1961 his first book, *Mensonge romantique et vérité romanesque* (English 1966: *Deceit, Desire and the Novel: Self and Other in Literary Structure*), was published in Paris, in which he systematically analyzes the novelistic creation of Cervantes, Flaubert, Stendhal, Proust, and Dostoyevsky. This book can be seen today as Girard's first main work. In it he argues that these authors attempt to show with their novels that human beings base their own desires on the desires of others, in contrast to the romantic lie of the autonomy of mankind. When analyzing the great novels of the European tradition, Girard characterizes the protagonists as exhibiting "mimetic desire," the imitation of the other. In connection with the increasing dissolution of medieval social differences, he shows how the relatively harmless external mediation of desire found in Cervantes transforms into the internal mediation—which threatens even intrafamilial relations—found in Dostoyevsky's novels.

In 1963, two years after *Deceit, Desire and the Novel*, Girard published a book devoted completely to analysis of Dostoyevsky—*Dostoievski: Du double à l'unité* (*Resurrection from the Underground*)—in which he further develops his mimetic theory and displays its significance for human existence. Girard addresses the connection between biography and work with particular clarity in this book. Dostoyevsky's late work is thereby understood as a critique of his earlier works, which runs parallel to Dostoyevsky's personal spiritual development. Only after the overcoming of his romantic pride was Dostoyevsky able to write his great novels, in particular *The Brothers Karamazov*. Girard's interest in the general theme of religion—especially in Christianity—is discussed in more depth in his book on Dostoyevsky than in his first work. His interpretation of the Grand Inquisitor, above all, shows that he recognizes in Christianity the only way to protect man from the consequences of mimesis.

Girard took a decisive step in expanding the mimetic theory into a universal anthropological and cultural theory with his second main work, *La violence et le sacré* (*Violence and the Sacred*), which appeared in 1972, almost a decade after his first books. Girard attempts in this work to explain the nature of the "sacred" in archaic societies prior to their development of legal and judicial systems. His analysis frequently incorporates the classical tragedies of Sophocles (e.g., *Oedipus the King*) and Euripides (e.g., *The Bacchae*). Using these ancient texts, and based on ethnological data, he demonstrates that the sacred, and with it archaic religion, is based on what he terms the *scapegoat mechanism*: the mimetic snowballing of all against one in order to resolve a crisis brought about by the social consequences of mimetic desire, which creates within the group a war of all against all. After its death, the victim is experienced by the community as good and evil at once (= sacred) because the victim is perceived as both responsible for the crisis and as that which rescues the community from being completely engulfed by it. Girard traces the central elements of all religions (myth, rituals, and taboos), as well as political power (e.g., sacred kingship), the judiciary (capital punishment), ancient practices of medicine, theater, philosophy, and anthropology, all the way back to the scapegoat mechanism. However, in the process of articulating his theory, he in no way isolates himself from the standard scientific community, but rather shows through analyses of thinkers such as Sigmund Freud and Claude Lévi-Strauss that the mimetic theory has fundamental similarities to and differences from established psychoanalytical and structuralist models of thought. Girard originally intended to delve into biblical texts in *Violence and the Sacred* and thus to incorporate the Judeo-Christian tradition into his theory; he was unable, however, after over a decade of research, to clarify systematically the similarities and differences between mythical and biblical texts, therefore deciding to publish the work without any analysis of the Bible.

Girard's book *Critique dans un souterrain* was published in Lausanne in 1976 and contains a collection of works, including his book on Dostoyevsky and essays on Camus, Dante, Victor Hugo, Gilles Deleuze, and Felix Guattari. Two years later, his first book in English appeared, *"To Double Business Bound": Essays on Literature, Mimesis, and Anthropology*. This collection includes essays—already partly published in the aforementioned French collection—that also address Friedrich Nietzsche, Richard Wagner, and Claude Lévi-Strauss, as well as the topics of myth and psychology.

Girard's third main work, *Des choses cachées depuis la fondation du monde* (*Things Hidden since the Foundation of the World*), published in 1978, represents a critical advancement of his theory. In this book, he extends his theory to biblical texts; already in the title, which quotes Matthew 13:35—"I will proclaim what has been hidden [since] the foundation of the world"—it is clear that biblical analysis stands in the foreground. The three-part text is the result of dialogue between Girard and the psychiatrists Jean-Michel Oughourlian and Guy Lefort. In the first segment, Girard presents his anthropological theory, while the core of the second part consists of analysis of the Old and New Testaments in which Girard shows that certain central texts in the Bible differ from archaic myth in that they are not the result of the scapegoat mechanism. On the contrary, he shows that these texts stand in defense of persecuted victims and function as an uncovering of veiled mythical violence. The book's third segment is devoted to psychological inquiries that focus on the topics of human sexuality, masochism, sadism, and homosexuality.

With *Le bouc émissaire* (*The Scapegoat*), published in Paris in 1982, Girard attempts to use the comparison of medieval texts of persecution and myth to expound his theory of the scapegoat mechanism. Medieval texts that refer to the murder of Jews—as punishment for the alleged poisoning of wells that led to the spread of the plague—are interpreted today by essentially all historians as texts of persecution that allude to the Jews' scapegoat role during the times of the bubonic plague. Girard shows that myths can be deciphered in a similar way to the texts of persecution. Just as these medieval texts depict an actual persecution of Jewish scapegoats from the perspective of their persecutors, he demonstrates that myths, as well, are accounts of collective violence directed at a single victim from the perspective of the mob. Real acts of violence, in other words, are what lay behind myths, which attempt to persuade that the victim was the source of the crisis and therefore justly killed by the community. Myths differ from medieval texts of persecution insofar as the religious veiling of mythical violence is more pronounced, hence the heightened complexity of their deciphering. In the later chapters of *The Scapegoat*, Girard addresses several key texts in the New Testament

(Passion of Christ, beheading of John the Baptist, Denial of Peter, Demons of Gerasa) to display how these are radically different from mythical texts. One finds the perspective of the innocent victim in the Bible, not the perspective of the persecutors.

Girard's *La route antique des hommes pervers* (*Job: The Victim of His People*), published in 1985, is completely devoted to interpretation of the Book of Job. The French title quotes Job 22:15: "Will you keep to the old way that the wicked have trod?" In contrast to traditional readings, Girard avoids the overall story in his analysis and concentrates solely on the dialogues between Job and his friends. From these, he argues that Job is the scapegoat of his community, that his friends are his persecutors, and that their God is the projection of the community's collective violence. The dialogues penetrate the pattern of mythical texts in that they convey not only the viewpoint of the persecutors, but also that of the victim, Job. In verses 16:19–21 and 19:25–27, the persecutory God is juxtaposed with a God of victims who proves to be a defender of the innocent Job. According to Girard, the overall story of the biblical book, as well as the portrayal of God's discourse—with the exception of 42:8, where in the epilogue the truth of Job's stance is recognized—represents a regression to the level of the mythical gods of persecution.

In 1991, Girard published his first English monograph, *A Theater of Envy: William Shakespeare*, which contained detailed analysis of Shakespeare's comedies and tragedies. Girard displays in this work that the essential elements of the mimetic theory are also found in the work of the English playwright; *A Midsummer Night's Dream*, *Troilus and Cressida*, *Julius Caesar*, and *A Winter's Tale* are discussed in particular depth.

Girard published *Quand ces choses commenceront* in 1994, a book containing excerpts of interviews with the French journalist Michel Treguer that were conducted over a period of ten years. The title of the book (which soon will be published in English) quotes Luke 21:28, "When these things begin to take place, stand up and raise your heads, because your redemption is drawing near," and is suggestive of Girard's apocalyptical reading of history. According to this reading, Judeo-Christian revelation forces mankind to make the ultimate choice between complete self-annihilation and a renunciation of mimetic rivalry and violence. For the first time in his published work, Girard comments at length in this book on contemporary sociopolitical issues such as democracy, nationalism, and feminism. In a longer passage (quoted in the preceding section), Girard provides an elaborate description of his conversion to Christianity.

The Girard Reader appeared in 1996 and offers a comprehensive review of all aspects of the mimetic theory. In addition to systematic explanation of the topics of mimetic desire, sacrifice, the scapegoat mechanism, myth, and the Bible, the reader also contains extensive analysis of Freud and Nietzsche. The reader is composed of excerpts from Girard's main works, as well as several essays, and an interview with Girard that is not found in any of the earlier collections.

Je vois Satan tomber comme l'éclair (*I See Satan Fall Like Lightning*) is the title of Girard's book published in 1999, which once again takes up a biblical passage, Luke 10:18, "I saw Satan fall like lightning from heaven." This book presents Girard's attempt to evolve his anthropology completely from biblical thinking. He is chiefly concerned with producing an anthropological apologetics of the Judeo-Christian tradition, that is, an intellectually comprehensible verification of the uniqueness of the Bible and Christianity. At the heart of the work, one finds a comparative analysis of religious myths and Judeo-Christian revelation. In Girard's eyes, it is precisely the difference between these two forms of religion that displays the truth of Christianity.

In the autumn of 2001, Girard's book *Celui par qui le scandale arrive* was published (English translation forthcoming). This title, as well, quotes the New Testament (Matthew 18:7), where it speaks of that person who brings scandal into the world: "Woe to the one by whom the stumbling-block comes." The book is a collection of three essays and a comprehensive interview with the political philosopher Maria Stella Barberi. One of the essays is the French original of Girard's contribution to the *Festschrift* for Raymund Schwager, "Mimetische Theorie und Theologie," which had already been published in German in 1995. The other essays address the question of the genesis of interpersonal violence and the problem of Western ethnocentrism. A diverse range of topics emerge in the interview with Barberi, among which biblical (apocalypse, Satan, scandal, katechon), anthropological (hominization, evolution), and contemporary-philosophical (Lévi-Strauss, Derrida) inquiries are discussed at great length.

Girard ventured into new territory in 2003 with a short, yet important publication on the topic of sacrifice, containing three lectures on the Indian Vedas given at the Bibliothèque nationale de France in Paris. With *Le sacrifice*

(*Sacrifice*), he presented extensive research on the religious tradition of Asia for the first time. The analysis shows that traces of mimetic rivalry and the scapegoat mechanism can be detected in ancient India as well, in particular in the Vedic reflections on sacrifice. At the end of the Vedic period, one even finds in the *Vedānta*—to which the great Hindu philosophical texts, the *Upanishads*, belong—an overcoming of ancient sacrifice that comes close to biblical revelation.

In the spring of 2004, Girard published in *Oedipus Unbound: Selected Writings on Rivalry and Desire* English translations of early essays on the Oedipus myth, most of which appeared in French in the 1960s before the publication of *Violence and the Sacred*. This collection is particularly important due to the several essays containing Girard's initial analysis of biblical revelation. He refers in his studies above all to the Jewish prophets, in particular to the Servant of Yahweh in Second Isaiah.

Les origines de la culture (*Evolution and Conversion: Dialogues on the Origins of Culture*) contains an extensive interview between Girard, Pierpaolo Antonello, and João Cezar de Castro Rocha, which was published originally in Portuguese in 2000. This book provides a comprehensive overview of Girard's life and work; one of the interview's main discussions contains a particularly enlightening description of the attempt to combine the mimetic theory with Darwin's theory of evolution.

A number of minor publications have appeared in recent years that were connected with Girard's induction into the Académie française (2007: *Le tragique et la pitié*), his reception of the Dr. Leopold Lucas Prize in Tübingen (2007: *Knowledge and the Christian Faith/Wissenschaft und christlicher Glaube*), and his dialogues with the Italian philosopher Gianni Vattimo (2010: *Christianity, Truth, and Weakening Faith*). In addition, two collections of essays on literature (2008: *Mimesis and Theory*; *La vérité de l'art*) have been published. And in 2007, the Grasset publishing house in Paris put together Girard's first four main works in one volume, entitled *De la violence à la divinité*.

In his most recent publication, *Achever Clausewitz* (*Battling to the End*), which contains conversations with Benoît Chantre and takes on the theses of the German military theorist Carl von Clausewitz, Girard once again enters new territory. He is most interested in Clausewitz's notion of war as a "duel," a "reciprocal action . . . which must lead . . . to extremes,"[17] in which Girard recognizes both the mimetic rivalry that inexorably leads to the escalation of violence, as well as the apocalyptical development of the world that followed the French Revolution. Girard sees a final stage of this dangerous escalation to extremes in the reciprocal theologization of war taking place in our contemporary world, with the United States acting as the "great Satan" juxtaposed with jihadist "forces of evil." In Girard's eyes, there is only hope if we take seriously the objective apocalyptic dangers facing our world, and, with respect to Hölderlin, Madame de Staël, or Pope Benedict XVI, succeed in bringing about a new connection between faith and reason.

CHAPTER 2

Religion and Modernity

Christianity, the great historical exorcism, seems with each coming day to be losing its footing, as the demons with their piercing, babbling screams break free from its fetters.

—Franz Werfel, "Leben heißt, sich mitteilen"

The mimetic theory is first and foremost a theory of religion. It describes the "religious" dimension of interpersonal relations—the idolatry of models or sexual partners—just as it explains the origins of archaic religions and the qualitative difference between these and the Judeo-Christian tradition. In the following chapters, these three areas will serve as the basis for extensive discussion of the mimetic theory, the scope of which finds itself between the conflicting poles of religion and modernity.

Concerning the Necessity of a Theory of Religion

The contemporary debate has seen the need for religious inquiry reemerge after being pushed aside within the humanities and social sciences for decades. This has led to radical skepticism of traditional approaches to the field of cultural theory. Until a few years ago, the modern world—especially the sciences—was dominated by theories of secularization, which said all religions—or religion as such—would disappear with the increasing modernization of the world. Religion, according to the secularists, is a phenomenon of the past. Such claims, however, have proved to be obsolete, with many questioning the tenability of such unilinear secularization. In the modern Western world, for example, there has been a marked increase in practices of the occult, including sects, magic, and the esoteric. This growing need for religious experience on the individual level has carried political consequences in Germany, Austria, and Switzerland, where social pressure has led the governments to use state aid in an attempt to control the growth and proliferation of sects.

On the geopolitical level, meanwhile, the return of the religious element has been even more apparent. For over two decades, religions—especially those giving rise to fundamentalist groups—have played an increasingly important role on the global stage. The year 1979, in particular, comes to mind, when Ayatollah Khomeini declared Iran an Islamic theocratic state. However, one must not look solely to the Islamic realm when considering the return of religion in the modern world. Countries in the secularized West, too, have seen the rise of fundamentalist movements.[1] Though relatively unknown in Europe, one must also note the spread of evangelical Protestantism—most of all, Pentecostalism—in East and South Asia, sub-Saharan Africa, and, above all, Latin America.[2]

Another example of the political significance of religion was witnessed in the ethnic conflicts that took place after the end of the Cold War in several of the former Soviet states and in the former Yugoslavia.[3] Inquiries into the conflicts, however, avoided the religious dimension, being too heavily influenced by theories of secularization. Leading contemporary sociologists have shown that the concept of religion must be taken seriously, and that it will continue to be an important factor in global political developments.[4] The Israeli military historian Martin van Creveld, for instance, has stressed the importance of religion in his analysis of violent conflicts, in particular those in connection with Islamist rebel groups willing to implement violence in support of their causes. However, van Creveld says that the militarization of Islam will not spare other religions, arguing that the Christian answer to the problem could result in the reemergence of "not the Lord of love, but of battles."[5]

The French political scientist Jean-Marie Guéhenno has argued that our globalized world will lead to what he calls a "new polytheism."[6] Religion, says Guéhenno, will be the only way for cultures to hold onto their differences in the face of the contemporary drive for universality. Benjamin Barber, an American political scientist, has made similar claims.[7] He argues that globalization will bring with it a religiously driven counter-movement resulting in mass tribalization and fundamentalist balkanization, or what he calls "Jihad versus McWorld."

Since the attacks of September 11, 2001, which showed just how much the world is branded by religiously motivated violence, sociological studies such as those mentioned above have become ever more relevant to the public debate. The question of religion is one of the most central aspects of current research examining the nature of terrorism.[8] It is no longer disputed that one must delve into the concept of religion in order to fully understand the phenomenon of modern terrorism.

However, apart from the spread of sects and the dangers of fundamentalist terrorism, there are other issues pushing the concept of religion back into the foreground of sociological debate. With the theory of secularization being increasingly held as untenable, phenomena previously subject to mere secular modes of inquiry are now being analyzed for deeper religious meaning. Just as Eric Voegelin and Denis de Rougemont saw what they called "political religions" in the twentieth-century political movements of fascism, National Socialism, or Marxism, modern-day superstructures such as capitalism or the media are also being understood as religious phenomena.[9] In 1921, when Walter Benjamin described capitalism as a form of religion, he remained an outsider to the theoretical discussion of the time.[10] Today, however, Benjamin's insight is at the core of several leading social analyses.[11] With regard to the world of modern media, one sees from the way tragedies are reported—for instance the death of Princess Diana—the extent to which our media culture uses religious or quasi-religious phenomena to determine reality. Sociological inquiries have made note of this for some time now.[12]

These various social phenomena display the need for a theory with which one can understand the role of religion in general human existence.

Moreover, a closer look at the political dimension of religion shows that such a theory must be able to explain the complex relationship of violence and religion. The following sections will attempt to show that Girard's mimetic theory can provide an essential approach to the examination of these issues.

Divergence from Traditional Secularization

From the outset, René Girard's mimetic theory was independent of the influence of traditional theories of secularization. This was due to the fact that at the beginning of his career, he was more interested in theoretical approaches that assumed a maverick role with regard to the question of religion and, in great contrast to the secularist theories dominating the humanities, did not foresee any impending end to religion. In his early work, Girard makes numerous references to the work of Alexis de Tocqueville and Denis de Rougemont, two thinkers who explicitly rejected the modern secularization thesis.[13] Tocqueville stresses in his studies of American democracy that the religious nature of man will not only survive modern democratization, but also will show its true meaning in the age of increasing egalitarianism: "Men cannot abandon their religious faith without a kind of aberration of intellect and a sort of violent distortion of their true nature; they are invincibly brought back to more pious sentiments. Unbelief is an accident, and faith is the only permanent state of mankind. If we consider religious institutions merely from a human point of view, they may be said to derive an inexhaustible element of strength from man himself, since they belong to one of the constituent principles of human nature."[14] The French sociologist Marcel Gauchet, meanwhile, argues against Tocqueville's assertion of man's inescapable religious nature. He says the process of democratization, which in his view was started and advanced by Christianity, will ultimately become a "grave for all religions."[15] The process of secularization, Gauchet claims, which has long been witnessed in Europe, is a worldwide development not to be stopped.[16] However, Gauchet's arguments for a secularized world, formulated around 1980, are now being called into question. It is not the United States, but rather Europe that has proved to be an exception with regard to the reemergence of religion.[17] From the sociological perspective, arguments for an end to religion are no longer tenable, despite efforts by sociologists like the German Ulrich Beck—who follows Gauchet with his concept of "second modernity."[18]

Girard's early support of Tocqueville's position can be seen today as trendsetting. He explains his rejection of Gauchet's position in his book *Quand ces choses commenceront*: "Christianity is not the religion that will bring the world out of its religiosity, as Marcel Gauchet believes. . . . Our exalted humanism will only last for a short time—during the interlude between two different religious forms" (*Quand ces choses commenceront*, 178).[19] In addition to Tocqueville, however, one must note the influence of Denis de Rougemont in connection with Girard's early work. The Swiss writer was one of the first to recognize National Socialism as a "political religion," and by assessing religion as one of the central problems facing mid-twentieth-century society, he had already then disassociated himself from the secularist viewpoint. While working on his book *Love in the Western World*, which influenced Girard's first major work, *Deceit, Desire and the Novel*, de Rougemont was in close contact with the "Collège de Sociologie" in Paris, where he organized a "sacral-sociology"—together with George Bataille, Roger Caillois, Pierre Klossowski, Michel Leiris, Hans Mayer, and others—in an attempt to analyze the society of 1930s France.[20]

Girard also incorporates the ideas of atheist authors in his early studies, insofar as they are open to the "religious" dilemma of human existence. In an article on Dante and the sociology of the novel published in 1963—after the release of his first major work—Girard makes reference to both the Marxist philosopher Georg Lukács and the father of psychoanalysis, Sigmund Freud. Both Lukács and Freud, according to Girard, made explicit use of religious metaphor in order to provide adequate descriptions of human reality.[21] Girard's attention was turned to Lukács after the Marxist theorist Lucien Goldmann praised Girard's first book and pointed out parallels between it and Lukács's early study *The Theory of the Novel*.[22] Girard took up Goldmann's reference and began analyzing Lukács's texts, which led to an interesting discovery concerning the issue of religion. Just as Lukács used religious metaphor in his earlier analysis—for instance his use of Goethe's "demonic" to characterize the protagonist's quest for authenticity—he also made use of religious imagery in his later Marxist period to criticize the western avant-garde movement, in particular the work of Franz Kafka.[23]

Formulations such as "ghastly," "infernal," "devilish," and "the power of the netherworld" can be found throughout Lukács's critique of the literary avant-garde (e.g., Kafka) and realist literature (e.g., Thomas Mann). With regard to Freudian psychoanalysis, Girard also points out multiple uses of the term "daemonic" in Freud's explication of repetition compulsion in *Beyond the Pleasure Principle*.[24]

European Literature and Religion

The connections between Girard's thought and theories concerning the modern question of religion, however, only explain the surface of his understanding of religion. Much more significant is his analysis of the major works of modern European literature, which were essential for the development of his theoretical positions. Literary creation, as opposed to the sciences, was free from the influence of theories of secularization, and the works of several major European novelists can be shown to contain significant examination of the religious dimension of human existence. Even in the modern era, poetry and literature, together with music and the plastic arts, show an inherent openness to religion.[25] Europe's most celebrated artists—those whose works have shaped the way we view human existence—provide the most striking insight into man's religious nature.

Fyodor Dostoyevsky

For the development of Girard's theory of religion, the works of Dostoyevsky and Proust—in addition to Cervantes, Flaubert, and Stendhal—were most significant. Dostoyevsky is widely acknowledged by critics as having had the greatest impact on the modern understanding of religion. No other novelist articulates the phenomenon of religious nationalism—one of Dostoyevsky's religious themes with particular contemporary relevance—with more precision. In his novel *Demons*, the character Shatov embodies an extreme nationalism—one of Dostoyevsky's own self-criticisms—seen in his view of the Russian people as "God's people," who are alone capable of redeeming the world. The ultimate objective of every nation, in Shatov's eyes, is to seek its own god:

God is the synthetic person of the whole nation, taken from its beginning and to its end. It has never yet happened that all or many nations have had one common God, but each has always had a separate one. It is a sign of a nation's extinction when there begin to be gods in common. When there are gods in common, they die along with the belief in them and with the nations themselves. The stronger the nation, the more particular its God.[26]

In response to Stavrogin's criticism that his nationalization of God is a debasement of religion, Shatov counters that he is attempting to raise the Russian people to divine heights: "The nation is the body of God. Any nation is a nation only as long as it has its own particular God and rules out all other gods in the world with no conciliation; as long as it believes that through its God it will be victorious and will drive all other gods from the world."[27] Shatov's "God of the people," capable of banishing all other idols, embodies his philosophy that every great nation has the duty to raise itself above all others:

If a great nation does not believe that the truth is in it alone (precisely in it alone, and that exclusively), if it does not believe that it alone is able and called to resurrect and save everyone with its truth, then it at once ceases to be a great nation, and at once turns into ethnographic material and not a great nation. A truly great nation can never be reconciled with a second-ary role in mankind, or even with a primary, but inevitably and exclusively with the first. Any that loses this faith is no longer a nation. But the truth is one, and therefore only one among the nations can have the true God, even if the other nations do have their particular and great gods.[28]

Dostoyevsky's reflections on religious nationalism—seen here in *Demons*—are developed more fundamentally in his final novel, *The Brothers Karamazov*, where he addresses man's inexorable religious nature directly. In the eyes of the Grand Inquisitor, for instance, all humans have a "need for communality in worship."[29] This will persist until the "end of the world, even when all gods have disappeared from the earth: they will still fall down before idols." The Grand Inquisitor's "fundamental secret of human nature" not only belongs to this negatively marked character, but can also be shown to be Dostoyevsky's own conviction as well. In an earlier novel, *The Adolescent*, the pilgrim Makar shares the same insight into human nature. In stark contrast to the Grand Inquisitor, however, Makar is a devoutly religious character—perhaps one of the holiest figures in Dostoyevsky's entire novelistic creation. In all his travels, Makar says he never met a godless person: "A man cannot live without worshiping something; without worshiping he cannot bear the burden of himself. And that goes for every man. So that if a man rejects God, he will have to worship an idol that may be made of wood, gold or ideas. So those who think they don't need God are really just idol worshipers, and that's what we should call them."[30] Dostoyevsky's insight into man's religious nature is due in large part to his intensive study of biblical scripture. One of the main sources for the legend of the Grand Inquisitor, for instance, is the apocalypse in the Gospel of John, as well as the temptation of Christ found in the synoptic Gospels.

Marcel Proust

Dostoyevsky is one of the great religious novelists known for exploring the religious nature of man, making it no surprise that his works challenge the modern theory of secularization. Marcel Proust, meanwhile, whose work was critical for the development of Girard's theory, also explores the issue of religion in his novels, although he was himself a known agnostic. Girard points out frequent use of religious metaphor in Proust's magnum opus, *Remembrance of Things Past*, particularly in passages where Proust describes the importance of the mediator to the desire of the individual subject.[31] Many of the characters in Proust's work adore their role models as if they were gods and approach them with corresponding religious devotion.

A significant example of this can be found in the last chapter of *Sodom and Gomorrah*, the novel's fourth volume. At the beginning of the chapter, the narrator, Marcel, is convinced that he wants to separate once and for all from his longtime girlfriend, Albertine, and he tells his mother he will never marry her. By the end of the chapter, however, the exact opposite holds true, as Marcel, once again talking to his mother, announces that his sole wish is to marry Albertine. The change in Marcel's desire is caused by his extreme jealousy, which brings about the dramatic reversal in his relationship with his girlfriend. Marcel is led—by a remark Albertine makes in passing—to believe that his girlfriend has been involved in a sexual relationship with another woman. The idea alone that Albertine could love somebody else causes Marcel to see her in a new light, and his indifference is suddenly transformed into romantic desire. Marcel is left with the sole longing to possess Albertine for eternity, which Proust describes at length in a passage that delves into other instances in Marcel's romantic life in which his desire was swayed by the pains of jealousy. Proust makes clear that objective reasoning fails to explain the quasi-religious fascinations to which Marcel is prone:

> The mistresses whom I have loved most passionately have never coincided with my love for them. That love was genuine, since I subordinated everything else to seeing them, keeping them for myself alone, and would weep aloud if, one evening, I had waited for them in vain. But it was more because they had the faculty of arousing that love, or raising it to a paroxysm, than because they were its image. When I saw them, when I heard their voices, I could find nothing in them which resembled my love and could account for it. And yet my sole joy lay in seeing them, my sole anxiety in waiting for them to come. One would have said that a virtue that had no connection with them had been artificially attached to them by nature, and that this virtue, this quasi-electric power, had the effect upon me of exciting my love, that is to say of controlling all my actions and causing my sufferings. But from this, the beauty, or the intelligence, or the kindness of these women was entirely distinct. As by an electric current that gives us a shock, I have been shaken by my loves, I have lived them, I have felt them: never have I succeeded in seeing or thinking them. Indeed I am inclined to believe that in these relationships (I leave out of account the physical pleasure which is their habitual accompaniment but is not enough in itself to constitute them), beneath the outward appearance of the woman, it is to those invisible forces with which she is incidentally accompanied that we address ourselves as to obscure deities. It is they whose good will is necessary to us, with whom we seek to establish contact without finding any positive pleasure in it. The woman herself, during our assignation with her, does little more than put us in touch with these goddesses. We have, by way of oblation, promised jewels and travels, uttered incantations which mean that we adore and, at the same time, contrary incantations that mean that we are indifferent. We have used all our power to obtain a fresh assignation, but one that is accorded to us without constraint. Would we in fact go to

so much trouble for the woman herself, if she were not complemented by these occult forces, considering that, once she has left us, we are unable to say how she was dressed and realize that we never even looked at her?[32]

Many such instances can be found throughout Proust's work where characters—like Marcel—show a reverence for others that is actually rooted in jealousy. In *The Past Recaptured*, Proust provides a general reflection on the phenomenon of interpersonal divinization, or the peculiar tendency of characters to revere those who make them suffer by hindering them in the acquisition of the objects of their desire: "Every individual who makes us suffer can be attached by us to a divinity of which he or she is a mere fragmentary reflection, the lowest step in the ascent that leads to it, a divinity or an Idea which, if we turn to contemplate it, immediately gives us joy instead of the pain which we were feeling before."[33] Proust's thoughts here on inter-character divinization are, according to Girard, at the heart of the insight he says all major novelists possess: the modern, Nietzschean proclamation that "God is dead" does not signify an end to religion, but rather merely a displacement of God.[34] In Girard's eyes, the death of God leads simply to the worship of one's neighbor. Modern man, robbed of traditional divinity and thus thrown back into the depths of his individual being, is faced with the fundamental need to find his divine self in the other. This divinization of the other, however, diverges greatly from the anthropology of Ludwig Feuerbach, whose optimistic philosophy can be summed up in the proclamation *Homo homini deus*, or "Men will become gods for one another."[35] The novelistic authors show that this interpersonal divinization is rooted in jealousy, emotional bondage, masochism, sadism, and other forms of violence. Girard argues that Proust and, to a further extent, Dostoyevsky explore the ramifications of interpersonal divinization most intensely among all modern European authors. Dostoyevsky's Underground Man, for instance, describes the fundamental plight of modern man with the words "I am alone, and they are *everybody*."[36] The Underground Man yearns for ultimate superiority over others and, for this very reason, perceives himself as insignificant as dirt and useless as a worm; the "others" become gods for him insofar as they prevent his own rise to divinity. Dostoyevsky's *Demons* contains a further, yet more extreme example of such interpersonal divinization. Shatov, who calls himself nothing but an "insect," sees in his model Stavrogin "the sun."[37] For the young Verkhovensky, meanwhile, Stavrogin is the divine idol *par excellence*: "You are my idol. . . . You are precisely what's needed. I, I need precisely such a man as you. I know no one but you. You are a leader, you are a sun, and I am your worm."[38]

Friedrich Hölderlin

Girard's literary analysis incorporates other European figures whose work contains many of the same attributes found in Dostoyevsky or Proust. Frequent reference is made to the German writers Friedrich Hölderlin and Friedrich Nietzsche, who both show in distinct fashion the tragic potential of interpersonal divinization.[39] Hölderlin's relationship to Friedrich Schiller, a contemporary, yet older and more established German poet, is a characteristic example of the dynamic described by Proust, in which the subject reveres his mediator or model to the point of obsession. Hölderlin believed he had found in Schiller a divine genius, a "poet-god" and source of terror, but also someone the young poet could not live without. One finds numerous instances in their correspondence of Hölderlin's idolization of Schiller, for instance in this letter to Schiller from June 30, 1798:

> As much as I am depressed from various sides, as much as my own unbiased judgment robs me of confidence, I still cannot distance myself from you—for fear of being criticized by the man whose singular spirit I feel so deeply, and whose power would have perhaps long taken my courage—if it were not so much pleasure, as it is pain, to know you. You see through mankind so completely. It would be senseless and useless not to be true before you. You know yourself that every great man takes away the peace of mind of those who are not great, and that balance and the freedom from compulsion [tr. *Unbefangenheit*] can exist only between human beings who share the same spirit. This is why I feel allowed to admit to you that I often find myself in a secret battle with your genius—to rescue my freedom from it—and that the fear of being ruled by you, through and through, has often prevented me from nearing you with serenity. But I can never remove myself completely from your sphere; only with the utmost difficulty could I forgive myself for such a fall. And this is how it must be; as long as I am in some form of relation with you, it is impossible for me to become a mere

ordinary human being. And even if the transition from the ordinary to excellence is worse than the ordinary itself, I will still in this case choose the worse of the two.[40]

Such descriptions—taken from Hölderlin's actual relationship to Schiller—can be found in Hölderlin's literary work as well. Girard makes reference to a significant passage in the "Thalia Fragment," the first draft of Hölderlin's only novel, *Hyperion*, in which the hero oscillates between a godlike state and one of utter nothingness.[41]

Friedrich Nietzsche

In Girard's eyes, Nietzsche's relationship to the German composer Richard Wagner contains significant parallels to that of Hölderlin to Schiller, but is yet more extreme with regard to the degree of devotion. Initially, Nietzsche openly regarded Wagner as nothing short of a divinity, dedicating his first major work, *The Birth of Tragedy*, to his worshiped "master," whom he identifies throughout with Dionysos. Soon after this first phase of their relationship, however, Nietzsche breaks all ties with Wagner as the composer's cult of followers becomes unbearable for the young philosopher. In both his published and unpublished writings, Nietzsche attempts to cast Wagner from the throne he had built for him and usurp his former model's divine stature. In one of his final works, the autobiographical *Ecce Homo*—written in 1888 at a time when Nietzsche's rejections of Wagner had reached their extreme in both frequency and vehemence—Nietzsche literally attempts to build a cult around his own being and openly expresses the desire to replace his former God, Wagner, with himself:

> A psychologist might still add that what I perceived as a young man in Wagnerian music really has nothing at all to do with Wagner, that when I described Dionysian music I described what *I* had felt—that instinctively I had to transpose and transfigure everything into the new spirit that I carried in me. The proof of that, *as strong as any proof can be*, is my essay 'Wagner in Bayreuth': in all psychologically decisive places I alone am discussed—and one need not hesitate to put down my name or the word 'Zarathustra' where the text has the word 'Wagner.'[42]

After initially identifying Wagner with Dionysos, Nietzsche now explicitly connects himself with the Greek god: He signs *Ecce Homo* with the signature "Dionysos versus the Crucified."[43] In a later letter addressed to Wagner's then widow, Cosima, Nietzsche's attempt to possess divinity for himself becomes absurdly apparent. He identifies himself not only with Wagner, but also with a host of gods and other literary and historical figures:

> Among the Hindus I was Buddha, in Greece Dionysos—Alexander and Caesar were incarnations of me, as well as Lord Bacon, the poet of Shakespeare. Most recently I was Voltaire and Napoleon, perhaps also Richard Wagner. However, I now come as victorious Dionysos, who will prepare a great festival on earth.[44]

Nietzsche's attempts to attain divinity ultimately fail, however; with himself as his lone follower, he is unable to successfully initiate a "Nietzsche-cult." He falls from self-proclaimed divine heights into the abject depths of self-victimization. One sees a clear instance of this in the above letter to Cosima Wagner—the very letter containing proclamations of Nietzsche's own greatness—which ends with the words: "I, too, hung on the cross." Nietzsche signs his final letters with either "Dionysos" or "The Crucified," two personalities that refer indirectly to the title of Nietzsche's last major work, *Ecce Homo*, or "Behold the Man," taken from the Gospel of John (19:5). It can be argued that Nietzsche's manic-depressive oscillations between his alter egos Dionysos and Jesus are what ultimately drove him to madness, a fate he incidentally shared with his literary predecessor Hölderlin.

God or Idol?—Camus and Girard

Girard's mimetic theory is based in essence on the literary insight into man's unalterable religious nature. Looked at systematically, his position can be understood as follows: Human beings have the choice between recognition of the one true God and arbitrary idolatry. The French original of his first book, *Deceit, Desire and the Novel*, is prefaced with a Max Scheler phrase that summarizes this thought succinctly: "*Man believes in either a God or in an idol. There is no third course open!*"[45] Girard connects here above all with Dostoyevsky, whose work he analyzes intensively in *Deceit, Desire and the Novel* and also in his second literary study, *Resurrection from the Underground*, which he devotes entirely to analysis of Dostoyevsky. From the beginning, thus, Girard's position is rooted in biblical thinking. In Dostoyevsky's legend of the Grand Inquisitor, the alternatives "God or idol" (tr. *Gott oder Götze*) are brought up distinctly. The backdrop for the legend is provided by Matthew's portrayal of the temptation of Christ (4:1–11)—in which Jesus invokes the First Commandment (Deuteronomy 5:9), the prohibition of idolatry, in his rejection of Satan—and Girard stresses emphatically this biblical background. In particular, Girard refers to the Gospel story of the return of the impure spirits (Matthew 12:43–45) to highlight the central idea behind Dostoyevsky's passage.[46] Just as the Grand Inquisitor sees in Jesus's allegory an overestimation of man's capacity for freedom, Jesus speaks of the dangerous potential of exorcism, proclaiming that the driving out of one evil spirit will result in the return of seven more just like it. Girard himself attaches central importance to this Gospel story. When he considers in *Quand ces choses commenceront* whether Christianity can be held responsible for the negative aspects of globalization, he refers to this passage in his argument that Christianity, though it may have enabled the rise of these phenomena, cannot be automatically blamed for their emergence. Girard argues that Christianity is akin to the overcoming of demonic possession; if we fail to use our freedom in a positive way, it can lead to an explosion of the demonic:

> Our world's reflection of Christianity distorts it from its original nature. It is just like the individual in the Gospels who is delivered from the demon but fails to use this experience to give his life a more positive meaning. The demon, in turn, profits from this and returns to his old home—but this time accompanied by seven others who are all much worse! This individual symbolizes the generations that have misunderstood the Bible's message; we must be careful not to resemble him. But we must also not blame Christianity for the seven additional spirits who assail us. (*Quand ces choses commenceront*, 105–106)[47]

The biblical passage to which Girard refers here sheds light on the present state of religion; the "death of God" has led to an explosion of religious phenomena around the world.

A comparison between Girard and another twentieth-century French thinker, Albert Camus, will prove helpful at this point to further clarify Girard's specific stance on religion. Camus took up the Dostoyevskian position on human idolatry ten years prior to Girard in his essay *The Rebel*, in which he attempts to explore how the twentieth century became an epoch of unprecedented, systematic genocide, a "space of fifty years" in which "seventy million human beings" were "uprooted, enslaved, or killed."[48] He finds the answer in what he refers to as man's "metaphysical revolt," which Dostoyevsky's Ivan personifies in *The Brothers Karamazov*. This revolt, as has been shown, is essentially man's attempt to take the place of God. Camus claims in his analysis that modern history is shaped by this metaphysical revolt and the resulting tendency of humans to worship one another. Similar to Girard, Camus sees in Feuerbach's *homo homini deus* not an indication of human progression, but rather "the birth of a terrible form of optimism."[49] Of the various philosophical and historical manifestations of human divinization that emerged in the nineteenth and twentieth centuries, Camus finds most emblematic Nietzsche's *Übermensch*, which he views as the "sordid god" at the heart of Nazi ideology; Rousseau's "new Gospel" of the *Contrat social*, which he sees as a precursor for the terror of the French Revolution; the divinization of the state in Rousseau and Hegel; and finally the socialism of Marx and Lenin, which also ends in terror.[50] Camus's rejection of Marx, "the prophet of justice without mercy, who rests, by mistake, in the unbelievers' plot at Highgate Cemetery," and of Lenin, "the deified mummy of the man of action in his glass coffin," was a radical break from the leftist French thinkers of Camus's time—most notably Sartre—who championed such human divinization.[51] Camus calls for a renunciation of all idolatry as a way out of the practice of human divinization, which in his view leads inexorably to terror: "To learn to live and to die, and in order to be a man, to refuse to be a god. . . . Each tells the other that he is not God; this is the end of romanticism."[52] Less convincing, however, is Camus's belief that so-called "Meridian" thought processes—or his "solar thought" motif that argues for a return to natural antiquity through an emphasis on moderation, symbolized by the Greek goddess Nemesis—can abolish the practice of human divinization.[53] Girard sides with Camus's critique of idolatry, but ultimately diverges from Camus insofar as he proposes that the only way for humans to free themselves from idolatry is through biblical revelation. Girard diverges

from Camus's attempt to sustain the revolt of man by the means of moderation, for he knows—with Dostoyevsky—that this revolt must be overcome,
because it ultimately fails to bring about the release that is made possible only
by the freedom found in Christ.[54]

Camus's philosophical renunciation of idolatry can also be found in his
literary works. In an essay entitled "Camus's Stranger Retried" (1964), Girard
traces Camus's intellectual development from his early work, *The Stranger*,
to the last novel published during his lifetime, *The Fall*.[55] One sees from this
progression that Camus's final novel contains a radical critique of his earlier
work; the later Camus condemns his earlier belief in man's autonomy and
authenticity as the mere attempt to become god over others—in order to
judge them.[56] In Girard's eyes, Camus converges in his version of self-criticism
on biblical revelation. The central theme in *The Fall* is a direct reference to
the Epistle to the Romans: "Therefore you have no excuse, whoever you are,
when you judge others; for in passing judgment on another you condemn
yourself, because you, the judge, are doing the very same things" (Romans
2:1).[57] Camus's tragic death only a short time after the publication of *The Fall*
leaves the question open of whether his insight into idolatry would have ultimately led him—like Girard or Dostoyevsky—to a Christian conversion.[58]
The Fall, like Dostoyevsky's *Notes from the Underground*, shows insight into
the nature of romantic idolatry—without, however, revealing a positive way
out of the problem. As a result of his early death, Camus was not able to
develop a Christian answer to the problem of idolatry, such as one finds in
Dostoyevsky's later works, especially *The Brothers Karamazov*.

The Mimetic Theory as a Universal Theory of Religion

Although Girard's theory is based on insights gathered from the major novels
of modern European literature—and therefore only indirectly on the biblical
tradition—it goes well beyond the realm of literature. Girard himself did not
write any novels or dramas, but rather attempts to use the truths contained in
literature to systematically explain human existence; his work, therefore, can
be called a scientific theory.[59]

With regard to his ensuing theory of religion, which he built upon the
insight of modern man's propensity for idolatry—following the death of

God—Girard incorporates analysis of ancient myth to explain the origins of religion. These analyses lead Girard in his later work to focus on the concepts of victimization, scapegoating, and sacrifice. According to Girard, processes of divinization can be identified in the origins of human culture. The first gods of human civilization take the form of scapegoats, which are collectively expelled by the members of those communities. The mechanism by which these victims are expelled is, in Girard's eyes, the origin of religion in human communities. Ensuing ritual sacrifice is then the controlled restaging of the original, or founding murder, which was initially carried out by the community in a state of ecstatic and blind fury.

The mimetic theory is one of the major attempts at a universal and all-encompassing theory of religion, which is centered on a hypothesis regarding the genesis and origin of human sacrifice.[60] Girard's attempt to create a universal theoretical explanation is not the first; however, it has garnered much contemporary critique. It follows up on an intellectual development—between 1860 and 1939—that saw several attempts to develop universal theories of sacrifice, including, among others, Numa Denis Fustel de Coulanges's *The Ancient City* (1864); William Robertson Smith's *Lectures on the Religion of the Semites* (1889); James G. Frazer's multivolume *The Golden Bough* (1907–1915); Emile Durkheim's study on primitive religions, *The Elementary Forms of Religious Life* (1912); Arthur Maurice Hocart's *Kings and Councillors* (1936); and Sigmund Freud's socio-anthropological studies, *Totem and Taboo* (1912–1913) and *Moses and Monotheism* (1939). With the death of Freud, such attempts to develop universal explications of religion were aborted, and by the middle of the twentieth century, these theories were mostly considered to have failed.[61] By this time, analytic philosophy, structuralism (C. Levi-Strauss), and poststructuralism (J. Derrida) dominated the theoretical discussion. These new directions of thought, however, put aside the larger universal questions in favor of the many smaller concrete inquiries; a type of scientific skepticism had taken over in most academic circles. The positivist-inclined ethnologist Edward E. Evans-Pritchard, for example, calls the search for universality "nonsensical," as he strives to display in his work not only the past failures of such theories, but also the impossibility of a successful universal theory in the future: "I think that most anthropologists would today agree that it is useless to seek for a *primordium* in religion."[62] The American theologian Bruce Chilton, together with the German ethnologist

Josef Drexler have denied—in direct critique of Girard—the feasibility of explaining the phenomenon of religious sacrifice with a universal theory.[63] In modern academia, the search for general theoretical explications of phenomena garners almost automatic suspicions of ethnocentrism.[64] The skeptical rejection of universal theories may appear at first glance to be a cautious attempt to escape the dangers of overinterpreting data; however, it also begs the question whether such minimalistic practices could mean an end to scientific inquiry. For without universal explanations, scientists are only left with the ability to collect data of observed phenomena—without being able to understand or establish connections between them.[65]

Girard's mimetic theory shows his clear stance with regard to the feasibility and necessity of universal explication. The failure of past attempts should not dissuade one from continuing the search for a universal understanding of religion; false answers of the past, in other words, do not mean that the original question can no longer be posed. Girard finds himself, therefore, directly under the microscope of contemporary critique, for he must show that his mimetic theory can classify and explain unrelated data more aptly than these previous attempts. With this in mind, one must note that Girard has learned from his predecessors not to pursue monocausal modes of thought; as we will see, the mimetic theory takes a double approach that enables it to approach and explain many diverse and "mixed" phenomena [tr. *Mischphänomene*].

At the beginning of the present chapter, the necessity of such a theory of religion was presented, with particular regard to the pressing contemporary topics of fundamentalism, terrorism, and ethno-religious nationalism. In recent years, Girard himself has focused directly on these topics, together with other proponents of the mimetic theory. In 1989, a conference devoted solely to the problem of religious fundamentalism was held in which the mimetic theory played a significant role.[66] In 1996, Stanford University organized a conference on the issues of ethnic and national conflicts, which were analyzed from the perspective of Girard's theory. The results of that conference were published among other places in *Contagion: Journal of Violence, Mimesis, and Culture*, a journal with essays focusing on the mimetic theory.[67] Following the terror attacks on September 11, 2001, Girard has used the mimetic theory to attempt to explain the issue of modern-day terrorism in a number of publications.[68]

CHAPTER 3

Mimetic Desire

If it is dangerous to make a friend acquainted with the perfections of one's beloved, because he also may find her charming and desirable, no less is the reverse danger, that he may perplex us by his dissent.

—Johann Wolfgang von Goethe

The increasing relevance of the mimetic theory is based not only on the light it sheds on religion, but also on its ability to explicate violent conflict in human society. In essence, it is a "theory of conflict," one that both elucidates the causes of interpersonal clashes and also offers solutions to them.[1]

The Mimetic Theory as a Theory of Conflict

In the German-speaking world, the mimetic theory has long been excluded from theoretic discussion. In other countries, Girard's works were quickly translated and given significant attention in academic circles, but scholars in the German realm have been hesitant to tackle Girard's works until only recently. It appears that the trauma of National Socialism—and the rapid return to prosperity in West Germany during the Cold War—hindered engagement with a theory that focuses foremost on crisis and conflict. The commitment to peace in German politics and society was something that dominated the public sphere, even if for more perceptive thinkers the ideal of peace was far from eternal; the Cold War era in postwar Germany was, in the end, dominated by an atmosphere of nuclear deterrence. When the Iron Curtain fell in 1989, the world was made aware of the enormous potential for violence that was lurking beneath the ice sheet of the Cold War. Ethnic conflicts in and around Europe—as well as violence against asylum seekers and foreigners—soon became part of our new, "peaceful" world. Throughout Europe, people began to ask themselves where this sudden surge of aggression had come from. Even in the German-speaking world, one saw an increasing willingness to address conflict and violence in an unbiased and open manner. Hans Magnus Enzensberger's essay "Civil War," written in 1993, is a lucid example of how the terrain had changed in Europe. The work initially met with vehement critique, as Enzensberger was attacked for turning his back on his leftist roots—he was part of the 1968 protests in Germany—and for supporting the cause of political and cultural reactionism. These reactive attempts to incriminate Enzensberger, however, showed the defensive stance taken by contemporary intellectuals who were ill-prepared to accept the reality of post–Cold War Europe. Two years later, Antje Vollmer, German Green Party member and vice president of the Bundestag, took a similar approach to Enzensberger in her book *Heißer Frieden* [tr. Hot Peace], which analyzes the problem of modern violence in yet more depth. From the perspective of the mimetic theory, Vollmer's book is especially important and interesting, considering that she makes reference to Girard—in addition to Hannah Arendt and Mahatma Gandhi—in her explication of the modern political atmosphere.[2]

Mimetic Rivalry

Why are human relations so prone to conflict and violence? Among living species, why is the human the most violent? A short sentence summarizes Girard's position: "The principal source of violence between human beings is mimetic rivalry, the rivalry resulting from imitation of a model who becomes a rival or of a rival who becomes a model" (*I See Satan*, 11). With this sentence, Girard diverges from Rousseau's faith in the human being's natural goodness and from all theories that branch out from Konrad Lorenz's postulation that aggression or an aggressive drive alone is the cause of all manifestations of violence.[3] In particular, one must stress Girard's distance from theories that see violence between humans as an instinctual phenomenon, as the mimetic theory has often been misunderstood in this regard—especially in the German-speaking realm.[4] Superficial readings of Girard have linked the mimetic theory with the German philologist Walter Burkert, whose work focuses on the ritualized killing of humans (*homo necans*) and is explicitly based on Lorenz.[5] Girard rejects any natural aggressive drive and argues that human beings can overcome their violent nature. In this sense, Girard holds the Sermon on the Mount—or Jesus's call for nonviolence—as a plausible, objective, yet very complex attempt to argue for an overcoming of violence. He is vehemently against any theory that sees violence as an "ineradicable trait of human nature, an instinct or fatal tendency that is fruitless to fight" (*Things Hidden*, 197).

Girard's critique of such theories of aggression does not mean, however, that he overlooks the magnitude of human instinct. An example of this can be found in his analysis of Sancho Panza in Cervantes's *Don Quixote*. Girard points out Panza's instinctual reaction to cheese and wine, or how his hunger and thirst are activated by the mere sight of the desired objects.[6] Girard argues, however, that such natural appetites ultimately fall short of explaining the essence of desire. Once basic needs and appetites are satisfied, humans remain governed by an intense yearning, which is at first uncertain about which objects to desire.[7] From a perceptive reading of the major novels of European literature, Girard postulates that human desire is not based on the spontaneity of the subject's desire, but rather the desires that surround the subject. He argues that humans do not themselves know what to desire; as a result, they imitate the desires of others. He uses several formulations to describe this phenomenon throughout his work, including *triangular desire* (*Deceit, Desire and the Novel*, 2; *De la violence à la divinité*, 36: "désir triangulaire"), *desire according to Another* (*Deceit, Desire and the Novel*, 4; *De la violence à la divinité*, 37: "désir *selon l'Autre*"), *imitated desire* (*Deceit, Desire and the Novel*, 21; *De la violence à la divinité*, 50: "désir imité"), and above all, both *mimetic desire* (*Violence and the Sacred*, 148; *De la violence à la*

divinité, 476: "désir mimétique") and *mimesis* (*Violence and the Sacred*, 146):
"Human beings influence each other, and when they are together, they tend
to desire the same objects. This is not because these objects are scarce, but
because . . . imitation . . . governs desire. Man attempts to create a being out of
himself that is essentially based on the desire of his fellow" (*Quand ces choses
commenceront*, 27).[8] Girard describes his concept of mimetic desire in the
following way: "Our neighbor is the model for our desires" (*I See Satan*, 10).

Girard's emphasis on imitation must not be understood in the superficial
sense of the term, however. His theory is not an anthropological caricature
of human beings, portraying them as a merely imitative species, but rather
a description of the fundamental—if not extreme—openness of humans to
others.[9] The mimetic theory describes man as a social being that is dependent on relations to others. No human being, in other words, is intrinsically
complete. Girard's first book argues against the romantic "illusion" of the
autonomy of mankind, which in its blasphemous pride attempts to take
the place of the divine creator.[10] This idea of autonomy is the "romantic lie"
par excellence, a kind of Promethean arrogance. Girard traces the roots of
romantic individualism back to Descartes's subjectivist "cogito ergo sum," the
anthropocentric turning point that enabled humans to break free of Augustinian individuality—anchored in the relationship to the Christian God—
and to foster ideas of man as an intrinsically self-contained being.[11] Girard
follows this intellectual development all the way to Nietzsche, who stands
for the radical individualism that ends necessarily in mental and physical
(self-)destruction. Dostoyevsky insightfully incorporates Descartes's famous
cogito phrase into Ivan's insane dialogue with the devil.[12] Descartes's dualism
represents not only the beginning of modern solipsism but also the renunciation of traditional views of mimesis.[13] Girard clearly rejects Descartes's
position and sees humans as being formed fundamentally by their mutually
mimetic relations. Mimesis, according to Girard, is a fundamental part of
man's constitution—and not merely an external addition to an essentially
autonomous being.[14]

As much as the mimetic theory emphasizes the social character of man,
it is nevertheless incongruent with Aristotle's concept of the *zoon politikon*,
or "political animal," which by nature tends toward a peaceful and harmonious coexistence with others.[15] Girard's anthropology resembles much more
that of Hobbes, who clearly differentiates humans from peaceful social

species such as ants or bees.[16] Girard's proximity to Hobbes in this regard, however, does not mean that he adopts the essential individualism that pervades Hobbes's liberalist political philosophy.[17] The mimetic theory stresses the social nature of man, but it also highlights the many conflicts that can arise as a result of cohabitation. Man's social nature often transforms into an "unsociable sociability" [*ungesellige Geselligkeit*], to borrow a phrase from Kant that aptly summarizes the potential consequences of mimesis.[18] Girard's mimetic theory finds itself between the two poles mentioned above—Aristotle's and Aquinas's optimistic *homo homini amicus*, or "man is a friend to man," and Hobbes's pessimistic *homo homini lupus*, or "man is a wolf to man"[19]—and can be characterized by its proximity to the anthropology of Augustine. In Augustine's words, "The human race is, more than any other species, social by nature and quarrelsome by perversion."[20] Augustine's insight into the consequences of Original Sin for human coexistence had a significant influence on Girard's anthropology; the Latin church father argues that, though human nature is principally directed at harmonious coexistence, after the Fall it proved greatly ridden by conflict. He interprets Original Sin as man's blasphemous attempt to usurp the divinity of God. Girard's thesis converges with Augustine insofar as he also links the cause of mimetic rivalry and interpersonal violence to man's propensity for idolatry: "The conflicts resulting from this double idolatry of self and other are the principal source of human violence. When we are devoted to adoring our neighbor, this adoration can easily turn to hatred because we seek desperately to adore ourselves, and we fall" (*I See Satan*, 11).

From the perspective of the mimetic theory, mimesis is the determining factor for social relations, and this can result in both negative and positive consequences. Violence and murder can ensue from mimetic desire—just as easily as can devotion to one's fellow man or openness to God. The difference lies in the varying ways mimesis can manifest itself in human relations, ranging from acquisitive desire and rivalry to imitation resulting in the spreading of peace.

Instincts and instinctual human behavior can be viewed as a starting point for mimesis, which then generates an overactivation, overlapping, and perhaps even an elimination of the original instinctive component.[21] Mimesis gives human desire its full shape, and this clarifies why the human being can be so much more violent and conflict-prone than other merely instinctual species. Rivalry and interpersonal violence threaten whenever two people direct their respective desires at a single object, which they are unable to both possess. That such objects of desire are strictly forbidden in many of the world's cultures is clearly a sign of the danger mimetic desire poses for society. Especially enlightening in this regard is the Tenth Commandment, which explicitly prohibits mimetic desire: "You shall not covet your neighbor's house; you shall not covet your neighbor's wife, or male or female slave, or ox, or donkey, or anything that belongs to your neighbor (Exodus 20:17)."[22] Mimesis and violence, however, are not one and the same; similarly, mimetic desire does not lead inexorably to violent conflict. In later chapters, greater attention will be paid to the complex connection between mimesis and violence, and furthermore to how humans can avoid the danger of this relationship.

It is essential to point out here another potential misunderstanding of the mimetic theory. Girard's emphasis on the mimetic nature of desire does not mean that all human actions and interpersonal relationships are governed by a rivalrous and violent mimesis. Likewise, his renunciation of the possibility of autonomous individuality must not be understood as absolute.[23] His intention is not to reduce all human phenomena to any violent drive or instinct, but simply to highlight a central dimension of human nature—mimetic desire—which can help to better explain man's propensity for crisis and conflict.[24] For Girard, there is also a life outside the rivalry resulting from mimetic desire: "I believe, for example, in the love of parents for their children and find it impossible to interpret this as mimetic. Sexual gratification, with respect to the other, is also possible, but I believe that true satisfaction is only achievable when the shadow of the rival has left the loved one's bed; this is why it is so rare!" (*Quand ces choses commenceront*, 28).

Sexuality and Violence

Although for Girard sexuality is not confined to mimetic desire, it is worth taking a closer look at the phenomenon, as it illustrates particularly well the human propensity for mimetically induced conflict and violence.[25] Sexual desire is one of the human passions that can very easily produce situations in which two people fight over an object that cannot be shared. Human sexuality, according to Girard, is much more violent than animal sexuality. Human sexuality is only determined to a certain extent by instinctual drives—in comparison to that of animals. The highly mimetic dimension of human sexuality is what differentiates it from animal sexuality, and this is also what explains its extreme proneness to altercation and violence.[26] With regard to the proximity of human sexuality and violence, Girard does not give in to any humanistic illusions:

> The connection between sexuality and violence is a heritage common to all religions and is supported by an impressive array of convergent facts. Sex and violence frequently come to grips in such direct forms as abduction, rape, defloration, and various sadistic practices, as well as in indirect actions of indefinite consequences. Sex is at the origin of various illnesses, real or imaginary; it culminates in the bloody labors of childbirth, which may entail the death of mother, child, or both together. Even within the ritual framework of marriage, when all the matrimonial vows and other interdictions have been conscientiously observed, sexuality is accompanied by violence; and as soon as one trespasses beyond the limits of matrimony to engage in illicit relationships—incest, adultery, and the like—the violence, and the impurity resulting from this violence, grows more potent and extreme. Sexuality leads to quarrels, jealous rages, mortal combats. It is a permanent source of disorder even within the most harmonious of communities. (*Violence and the Sacred*, 35)

Camille Paglia

Girard's emphasis on the connection of sexuality and violence converges on Camille Paglia's postfeminist critique of the repression of human sexuality. Paglia introduces her main work, *Sexual Personae*, with a consciously polemical chapter that looks into the modern repression of sexually motivated violence.[27] For her, this repression began with Rousseau, whose work she juxtaposes with the diametrically opposed writings of Marquis de Sade. Despite the proximity of Paglia and Girard with regard to the relationship of sexuality and violence, however, the difference between these two thinkers is important for an understanding of the mimetic theory. Paglia completely avoids the mimetic cause of violence in the sexual realm, arguing instead that the connection of the two phenomena is a natural constant. Sexuality and violence, she says, are intrinsically connected and therefore necessarily problematic.[28] Paglia's position is thus similar to theories that reduce human violence to mere aggression. Girard rejects such general conclusions and the notion that sexuality is intrinsically violent, arguing instead that it becomes violent only when motivated by mimetic desire. This difference between Girard and Paglia is of fundamental importance for any study of sexual ethics.

Jean-Jacques Rousseau

The optimistic view of sexuality found in the Rousseauian tradition must now also be looked at in comparison with the mimetic theory. Throughout his work, Girard repeatedly rejects Rousseau's high esteem of human nature, and his unchallenged belief in the goodness of man.[29] Girard diverges directly from Rousseau's optimism precisely with regard to the difference between animal and human sexuality. In the *Discourse on Inequality*, in which Rousseau first expresses his belief in the natural goodness of humanity, he also addresses the concept of sexuality. In critique of his contemporary Pufendorf—who, like Girard today, characterizes human sexuality as "more evil" than animal sexuality—Rousseau argues that sexuality leads to violence only among humans in society; the man of nature, in contrast, is characterized by a peaceful and harmonious sexuality. Rousseau believes, thus, that only the man of society is subject to the dangerous propensity for violence: "Of the passions that stir man's heart, there is one that is ardent, impetuous and makes one sex necessary to the other, a terrible passion that braves all dangers, overcomes all obstacles, and in its very frenzy seems liable to destroy Mankind which it is destined to preserve."[30] Similar to Girard, Rousseau speaks indirectly of mimesis in his explanation of why sexuality is a source of conflict for human society. He mentions the need for competitive "comparisons," of which the man of nature is unaware because "every woman suits him."[31] This need for "comparison," in other words, causes the man of society to prefer certain women over others: "A tender and sweet sentiment steals into the soul, and at the least becomes an impetuous frenzy; jealousy awakens together with love; discord triumphs, and the gentlest of all passions receives sacrifice of human blood."[32]

The essential difference between Rousseau and Girard is found in their respective interpretations of man in the state of nature. For Girard, the peace and harmony of nature is neither intrinsic nor automatic; the permanent sexuality of human beings—compared to the merely periodic excitation observed among animals—leads to an increase in the potential for conflict among humans, whether in society or nature. Rousseau, however, argues that periodic sexual excitation among animals, though lowering the overall possibility for sexual contact, gives rise to a scarcity of females, and thus a higher potential for conflict. Rousseau argues that this danger does not exist for the man of nature, seeing as how, in nature, there is a perpetual surplus of women. Only in society—by means of the competitive "comparison"—does man face a scarcity of women and the ensuing threat of conflict and violence. Rousseau's position is untenable from our contemporary perspective, however, for he fails to clarify the transition from the animal to the human world. In addition, he seems to have lost sight of humanity when he speaks of the "savage"; with regard to sexuality, he argues that the savage is confined to the merely physical realm, and that the "imagination" or the "moral aspect of love" remains foreign to him.[33] Rousseau's description seems to converge more on an animalistic than a human condition and begs the question whether he is merely attempting here to sustain his ideological conception of man's peaceful, "natural" condition.

Acquisitive Mimesis and the Western Tradition

At the heart of Girard's mimetic theory is the concept of mimetic desire. To get a sense of its substantial scope, it is necessary to see where it fits in the Western tradition of mimesis and, more importantly, how it diverges from this tradition. Girard is not the only thinker for whom mimesis plays a significant role. In general terms, mimesis in the Western philosophical tradition has come to mean external imitation or mere artistic representation. Starting with Aristotle—who remarks in the *Poetics*, "Imitation is natural to man from childhood, one of his advantages over the lower animals being this, that he is the most imitative creature in the world, and learns at first by imitation"—one finds countless examples of thinkers who attach great importance to the concept of imitation for an understanding of human life.[34]

For example, at the end of the nineteenth century, the French sociologist Gabriel Tarde, in his book *The Laws of Imitation*, argues that imitation builds the foundation for social harmony.[35] Examples from throughout the twentieth century show that interpretations of the central role of imitation are completely irrespective of ideological background. Both the Jewish Marxist philosopher Walter Benjamin and the national economist and prophet of neoliberalism Friedrich August von Hayek, for instance, stress the central role of mimesis in their respective fields. Benjamin maintains in regard to human beings that "no single one of their higher functions ... is not codetermined by the mimetic faculty."[36] For Hayek, meanwhile, the "ability to acquire skills by largely imitative learning" is part of man's most critical "genetic configuration."[37] Gunter Gebauer and Christoph Wulf offer in their book *Mimesis* an excellent and comprehensive overview of the many different meanings the term *mimesis* has taken on throughout the Western tradition. Even without the corroboration of all these authors, it is common knowledge that the human brain and basic learning—in particular linguistic acquisition—are based greatly on imitation. Paisley Livingston, a professor at Lingnan University, Hong Kong, points out that many recent empirical examinations have produced results that further display the central role of imitation in human existence.[38]

With regard to literary analysis, Girard is also not alone in his examination of mimesis. Erich Auerbach, in his book *Mimesis*, describes the concept as a central element in the European humanistic tradition. Girard hesitates to draw on Auerbach's work, however, due mainly to its being limited to the field of aesthetics and the concept of literary representation, as one can see from its subtitle: "The Representation of Reality in Western Literature."[39] Girard's usage of the term is far broader and transcends the field of aesthetics. In this regard, he accords more with the major thinkers of Classical Antiquity, such as Plato and Aristotle, for whom mimesis plays an important role in several different areas of human existence. However, one must be cautious when comparing Girard with the thinkers of the Greek tradition, for here, as well, significant differences exist. A comparative analysis of the mimetic theory and Plato's understanding of mimesis makes this readily apparent.[40]

Plato

Plato belongs to the many great Greek philosophers who recognize the significant influence of imitation on human behavior. According to Girard, Plato's work establishes an "ontology of imitation" in which every reality is imitated.[41] At the same time, however, one finds in Plato's writings a tendency to disapprove of imitation, to the degree that he classifies it as even quite dangerous. Plato seems to have a premonition of the violence that can accompany mimetic desire, even if he never addresses this in his writings in any systematic way.

One can find three distinct features of mimesis in Plato's main work, *The Republic*. On the one hand—as is typical with the Western tradition—Plato reduces the concept of mimesis merely to external gesture or facial expression. The following question found in book 3 displays Plato's reduction of mimesis to external forms of representation and performance: "Isn't [the poet's] likening of himself to someone else, either in voice or in looks, the same as imitating the man he likens himself to?"[42] Beginning with the philosophy of Aristotle, such narrowed interpretations of mimesis—which exclude its influence on acquisitive desire—have dominated the Western traditional understanding of the concept.

Also in *The Republic*, one finds traces of the central ethical dimension of mimesis—very much prevalent in contemporary society—manifested in the distinction between the imitation of positive and negative role models. The guardians in Plato's *Republic*, for instance, are encouraged to imitate only good examples: "And if they do imitate, they must imitate what's appropriate to them from childhood: men who are courageous, moderate, holy, free, and everything of the sort; and what is slavish, or anything else shameful, they must neither do nor be clever at imitating, so that they won't get a taste for the being from its imitation."[43] For the guardians, imitation of women, servants, whinnying horses, raging bulls, rushing rivers, and thundering seas is strictly forbidden. This logic—that positive role models should be imitated and negative examples avoided—is part of virtually every child's upbringing in modern human society. In academia, this insight has even become a point of origin for the study of the social sciences.[44]

These first two features of Plato's concept of mimesis are not particularly surprising. Much more interesting is a passage from book 10 of *The Republic* in which one gains a direct sense of the fear connected with the incalculable power of mimesis. Plato begins the book with a call to ban all imitative art, and provides two reasons for this: On the one hand, he says such artists are imitating merely a simulacrum of perfection and therefore distancing themselves still further from the truth of ideas. On the other hand, Plato says that imitation can only access the less worthy—or "non-reasonable"—aspects of the soul: "And as for sex, and spiritedness, too, and for all the desires, pains, and pleasures in the soul that we say follow all our action, poetic imitation produces similar results in us. For it fosters and waters them when they ought to be dried up, and sets them up as rulers in us when they ought to be ruled so that we may become better and happier instead of worse and more wretched."[45] These words allude to the dangers of mimesis when combined with desire; however, they remain unable to explain in exact terms why this combination can be so disastrous.

Nevertheless, Plato's direct treatment of mimesis allows readers to perceive other areas in his writings in which the potential dangers of acquisitive desire are taken up—without referring directly to the concept as such. According to Girard's understanding of mimesis, conflicts arise when desiring subjects fight over objects that cannot be shared or mutually possessed. With respect to archaic communities, Girard names "nourishment, territory, and women" as the three main objects that perpetually lead to rivalry (*Quand ces choses commenceront*, 29).[46] Plato's conception of the ideal republic prevents rivalry over precisely these objects.[47] For instance, the guardians are to control the fight over food by implementing the practice of mutual nourishment. To prevent territorial conflict, the guardians are forbidden from owning both land and property; simple dwellings and private food storage, as well, are prohibited. The shared possession of women and children is ultimately also a measure aimed at preventing conflict and altercation among the guardians.

Notwithstanding Plato's extensive criticism of mimesis, he remains ultimately bound to the concept, as one can gather from his praise of the imitation of the divine and eternal ideas. He excludes poetry and songs that praise good men and the gods from the arts that he otherwise vehemently criticizes.[48] Only such songs of divine praise are allowed as poetry in Plato's ideal state. This juxtaposition of a permitted imitation of the divine, on the one hand, and skepticism of imitation in the human sphere, on the other hand, converges on Augustine's understanding of mimesis, which had a significant impact on the Christian tradition that followed him. Consider the following passage from *The Republic*—Plato's famous argument in support of the "philosopher king"—which illustrates the differentiation between positive and negative forms of mimesis: "A man who has his understanding truly turned toward the things that are has no leisure to look down toward the affairs of human beings and to be filled with envy and ill will as a result of fighting with them. But, rather, because he sees and contemplates things that are set in a regular arrangement and are always in the same condition—he imitates them and, as much as possible, makes himself like them. Or do you suppose there is any way of keeping someone from imitating that which he admires?"[49] This passage illuminates Girard's interpretation of Plato's "ontology of imitation." When it comes to admiration and religious devotion, Plato argues that imitation is indispensable; it is necessary, in other words—as we will see later in our analysis of Augustinian theology—that human beings also imitate what they worship. To avoid envy and conflict, however, Plato adds that this reverence must not be directed at other human beings, but rather exclusively at divine being itself. One sees that Plato apprehends, or at least suspects, the disastrous power of mimesis, despite the absence of any systematic reflection in *The Republic* that explains these dangers in explicit terms.

In the Western tradition following Plato, this fear of mimesis essentially disappears. From Aristotle onwards, the traces of mimesis gradually vanish from philosophical discourse.[50] In the *Poetics*, apart from pointing out the human being's uncanny aptitude for imitation, Aristotle speaks of the "pleasure man feels when imitating," calling it one of the principle origins of all art.[51] He goes on to praise the imitative aspects of dramatic tragedy that he says lead to a purification of the passions of pity and fear, or the famous Aristotelian "catharsis."[52] For the Western tradition in the wake of Aristotle, mimesis is reduced to the study of external representation and the ethical insight that one must imitate "good" elements and avoid all "bad" models.

Acquisitive Mimesis

Girard's concept of mimesis—as distinguished from the examination of the concept in the Western tradition—looks into the influence of imitation on human desire. Where Plato speaks only vaguely of desire—in his reflection on the dangerous dimension of poetry—Girard focuses almost entirely on the conflict-inducing relationship of mimesis and desire. The expressions or gestures of other people are not central to the mimetic theory, but rather the *desires* of others, their acquisitive urges. According to Girard, human beings strive to possess the exact objects that others already possess or desire. He argues that mimesis is most active in acquisitive human behavior, and his term for this concept is *acquisitive mimesis* (*Things Hidden*, 26; *De la violence à la divinité*, 734: "mimésis d'appropriation").

Not every instance of mimetic behavior, however, results necessarily in conflict. As long as desire is directed at an object that can be shared—learning a language, reading a book, listening to a piece of music, etc.—mimesis poses no problems. As soon as the object of desire can no longer be shared—as with objects of sexual desire, social positions, and the like—mimetic desire generates competition, rivalry, and conflict. No thinker describes this phenomenon more precisely than the English political philosopher Thomas Hobbes. On the cusp of the modern world of competition, Hobbes was well aware of the inescapable logic of acquisitive mimesis: "If any two men desire the same thing, which nevertheless they cannot both enjoy, they become enemies; and in the way to their End, . . . endeavour to destroy, or subdue one another."[53] On account of its extreme potential for conflict, Girard also refers to acquisitive mimesis as *conflictual mimesis* (*Violence and the Sacred*, 187; *De la violence à la divinité*, 524: "mimésis conflictuelle").[54] The role model who designates to us the desirability of an object soon becomes our rival and obstacle, once we also desire the acquisition of this same object.

William Shakespeare

Girard's model of desire takes the shape of a triangle; the apex represents the mediator and the two base vertices the imitating subject and the object.[55] With this conceptual structure, Girard is able to explicate conflicts that conventional theories cannot. Let us examine, for instance, the prevalent view that one should simply imitate a model's positive aspects and avoid the negative. On the surface, there is nothing wrong with this notion; however, are there not many situations that simply cannot be fully explained by this? Consider the example of two friends who experience a sudden falling out and become hateful enemies. We are all aware of the violent vicissitudes of human relations; any such superficial theory of human relations appears insufficient when love all of a sudden transforms into hatred. There are countless examples of this in literature. Shakespeare, for one, is adept at describing the fickle nature of human emotions, for instance in his historical tragedy *Coriolanus*:

> O world, thy slippery turns! Friends now fast sworn,
> Whose double bosoms seems to wear one heart,
> Whose hours, whose bed, whose meal and exercise
> Are still together, who twin, as 'twere, in love
> Unseparable, shall within this hour,
> On a dissension of a doit, break out
> To bitterest enmity; so fellest foes,
> Whose passions and whose plots have broke their sleep
> To take the one the other, by some chance,
> Some trick not worth an egg, shall grow dear friends
> And interjoin their issues.[56]

The major works of world literature demonstrate that such conflicts are oftentimes caused by mimetic desire. In Shakespeare's early comedy *The Two Gentlemen of Verona*, Proteus and Valentine—two old friends who since childhood have shared everything with one another—suddenly and almost automatically become enemies.[57] The drama begins with their planned trip to Milan, before Proteus abruptly changes his mind and decides to stay behind in Verona because he wants to be with his beloved, Julia. However, he reassesses soon after and follows Valentine to Milan. True friendship, in the end, means to share everything with one's friend and to display excitement for the same things. When Proteus arrives in Milan, he discovers that Valentine has since fallen in love with Silvia, and he is irked by the way Valentine sings of his newly beloved. She is his "heavenly saint, . . . if not divine, yet let her be a principality, sovereign to all creatures on the earth."[58] Even Julia, Proteus's lover, is subordinate to Silvia; Valentine sings that Julia is worthy enough only to be Silvia's slave. However, in this song of love, the influence of mimesis is already apparent. For, if Valentine were so convinced of his love for Silvia, he would not need to persuade Proteus of her beauty, or compete with him over the desirability of their respective lovers. Proteus, meanwhile, in order to demonstrate his own desire, must quickly join the fight. Even the smallest hint of doubt could destroy Valentine's love. This extreme form of mimesis reminds one of the Goethe passage quoted at the top of this chapter; if our friends "dissent" from our desire, we are "perplexed" and made unsure of ourselves. Proteus finds himself faced with this precise predicament: As Valentine's friend—with whom he is to share everything—he must follow and admire Silvia; any sign of indifference could endanger their friendship. At the same time, however, if he agrees with his friend that Silvia is the most beautiful and desirable of all women, then he will become Valentine's rival and enemy, for he will seek to possess her for himself. This latter, more dangerous scenario is precisely what unfolds, as the brief sight of Silvia—together with Valentine's song of admiration—proves sufficient for Proteus to succumb to her beauty. From a romantic standpoint, this is a classic Shakespearean portrayal of "love at first sight." Closer inspection, however, reveals the clear traces of mimesis. Proteus's monologue leaves no doubt that Valentine's song of love was the deciding factor in the transformation of his desire. He admits himself that there were no objective grounds for his sudden reversal, for Julia is just as "fair" as Silvia. His friendship with Valentine, meanwhile, suffers, as rivalry and enmity ensue:

> Even as one heat another heat expels,
> Or as one nail by strength drives out another,
> So the remembrance of my former love
> Is by a newer object quite forgotten.
> Is it mine, or Valentine's praise,
> Her true perfection, or my false transgression,
> That makes me reasonless to reason thus?
> She is fair; and so is Julia that I love—
> That I did love, for now my love is thaw'd;
> Which, like a waxen image, 'gainst a fire,
> Bears no impression of the thing it was.
> Methinks my zeal to Valentine is cold,
> And that I love him not as I was wont.
> O, but I love his lady too too much,
> And that's the reason I love him so little.
> How shall I dote on her with more advice,
> That thus without advice begin to love her![59]

The dramatic climax occurs as Proteus attempts to rape Silvia. The comedic nature of this drama, however, lends the play a happy end; Valentine prevents the rape, and the enemies resolve their dispute and save their friendship. This "end," however, is of secondary importance, at least as far as any mimetic interpretation is concerned. The play could have just as easily ended in tragedy, as in Shakespeare's dramatic poem "The Rape of Lucrece."[60] Here, Collatinus's exuberant praise of Lucrece excites Tarquin's desire. Unlike Proteus, Tarquin rapes Lucrece, and she subsequently commits suicide.

These two examples—like many others in Shakespeare's works—demonstrate how humans, even the best of friends, can often fall into violent conflict with one another. In light of Girard's articulation of the conflictual dimension of mimesis, many of these types of otherwise paradoxical quarrels—involving lovers, friends, coworkers, and family members—become more easily understandable.

Mimesis and Difference

In Girard's first book, *Deceit, Desire and the Novel*, he uses the works of Cervantes, Flaubert, Stendhal, Proust, and Dostoyevsky—authors he refers to as *novelistic* (*Deceit, Desire and the Novel*, 17; *De la violence à la divinité*: "romanesque")—to develop his theory of the triangulation of desire. These novelists, in comparison to "romantic" writers, see through the notion of the autonomous self, which in a quasi-divine manner produces its own desire without the help of others. Such spontaneous and original heroes are for Girard the romantic illusion par excellence.[61] In his view, the hero's desire is always determined by the mediator or model.

Miguel de Cervantes

A first example of mimetic desire can be found in Cervantes's *Don Quixote*.[62] At the outset, Quixote's ultimate goal is to one day become a knight. To achieve this end, he imitates Amadis of Gaul, the hero of a famous novel of chivalry. He explains his desire to his servant, Sancho Panza: "Amadis was the pole star, day star, sun of valiant and devoted knights, whom all we who fight under the banner of love and chivalry are bound to imitate. This, then, being so, I consider, friend Sancho, that the knight-errant who imitates him most closely comes nearest to reaching the perfection of chivalry."[63] Don Quixote devotes himself to the imitation of Amadis in all areas of his life. Just as his hero was scorned by his wife, Oriana, Don Quixote also wants to experience the sufferings of love. He breaks his fantasized relationship with Aldonza Lorenzo—his "Dulcinea"—in order to faithfully imitate Amadis. In an inner monologue, Quixote offers the reader a sense of the extent of his imitation of Amadis: "Long live the memory of Amadis, and let him be imitated so far as is possible by Don Quixote of La Mancha, of whom it will be said, as was said of another, that if he did not achieve great things he died in attempting them. If I am not repulsed or rejected by my Dulcinea, it is enough for me, as I said, to be absent from her. And so, now to business! Come to my memory, ye deeds of Amadis, and show me how I am to begin to imitate you."[64]

Sancho Panza, too, is governed by the imitation of a model. He yearns one day to become duke of an island; this is no spontaneous desire, however, but much more a byproduct of the imitation of his master, Don Quixote, who has supplied Sancho with this idea: "You must know, friend Sancho Panza, that it was a practice very much in vogue with the knights-errant of old to make their squires governors of the islands or kingdoms they won. I am determined that there shall be no failure on my part in so liberal a custom; on the contrary, I mean to improve upon it."[65]

Gustave Flaubert

The concept of imitation is also central in the novels of Gustave Flaubert.[66] The heroine of his masterpiece, *Madame Bovary*, takes her desire from the protagonists of romantic novels, which she reads voraciously as a teenager: "They were about love, lovers, loving, martyred maidens swooning in secluded lodges, postilions slain every other mile, horses ridden to death on every page, dark forests, aching hearts, promising, sobbing, kisses and tears, little boats by moonlight, nightingales in the grove, gentlemen brave as lions, virtuous as a dream, always well-dressed, and weeping pints."[67]

Flaubert shows the influence these novels have on Emma Bovary in certain deciding aspects of her life, in particular in her desire for extramarital romance. She is bored with unhappy marriage to Charles and yearns for the passion that she thinks to have found with Rodolphe. After having succumbed to his love and courtship, she suddenly sees herself vicariously in the role of her romantic heroines:

> She kept saying to herself: 'I have a lover! A lover!,' savoring this idea just as if a second puberty had come upon her. At last, she was to know the pleasures of love, that fever of happiness which she had despaired of. She was entering something marvelous where everything would be passion, ecstasy, delirium; blue immensity was all about her; the great summits of sentiment glittered in her mind's eye, ordinary existence appeared far below in the distance, in shadow, in the gaps between those peaks. She summoned the heroines from the books she had read, and the lyric host of these unchaste women began their chorus in her memory, sister-voices, enticing her. She merged into her own imaginings, playing a real part, realizing the long dream of her youth, seeing herself as one of those great lovers she had long envied.[68]

One sees a further instance of the influence these novels exert on Emma Bovary when she finds a new lover to replace Rodolphe. Even when their relationship has essentially fallen apart, and Emma wants nothing more than to leave Rodolphe, she still writes love letters to him, addressed—from Flaubert's perspective—to a phantom figure from the parallel world of her novels: "None the less she continued to write love-letters to him, by virtue of the following notion: a woman should always write to her lover. But, as she was writing, she beheld a different man, a phantom put together from her most ardent memories, her favorite books, her most powerful longings; and by the end he became so real, so tangible, that her heart was racing with the wonder of it, though she was unable to imagine him distinctly, for he faded, like a god, into the abundance of his attributes."[69]

Stendhal

Stendhal is another "novelistic" author who incorporates intense forms of mimetic desire into his works.[70] In *The Red and the Black*, Mathilde de la Mole finds her role models within her family history. Julien Sorel, meanwhile, the main character of the novel, attempts to imitate Napoleon in all he does. Consider the passage where Julien is overcome with fascination after seeing a "solitary eagle" fly over, "cutting immense silent circles in the sky." Stendhal explains the grounds for Julien's secret admiration of the bird's solitude and strength: "Such had been the destiny of Napoleon; would it someday be his?"[71] Julien's imitation of Napoleon is not restricted to military aspirations, however; just as strong is his desire to emulate Napoleon's powers of seduction. Julien's wish to possess Madame de Rênal—the mother of his pupils—is dominated by the notion that Napoleon, too, would easily entice her. Stendhal describes the initial stages of this desire in the following way: "Certain things Napoleon says on the topic of women . . . now gave Julien for the first time certain ideas which any other young man of his age would have had years ago."[72] In complete imitation of Napoleon, Julien views his seduction of Louise de Rênal as if it were a military fight: "He looked her over like an enemy with whom he was bound to fight." And, having successfully seduced her, Julien "was intent on examining all the details of his conduct like a soldier just back from review."[73]

Marcel Proust

As we have already pointed out, imitation plays a central role in Marcel Proust's *Remembrance of Things Past*.[74] Two examples can further highlight the importance of imitation in this voluminous work. In *Swann's Way*, Proust describes the relationship between Swann and Odette, which is characterized by the traditional highs and lows of romantic love.[75] At times, Swann is so deeply in love with Odette that he yearns to kill himself—or Odette—to quiet the pains of his unrequited passion: "Sometimes he hoped she would die in an accident without suffering, she who was outside, in the streets, on the roads, from morning to night. . . . And Swann felt very close in his heart to the sultan Mohammed II . . . who, realizing that he had fallen madly in love with one of his wives, stabbed her to death in order, as his Venetian biographer ingeniously says, to recover his independence of mind. Then he would be filled with indignation that he should be thinking thus only of himself, and the sufferings he had endured would seem to him to deserve no pity since he himself had placed so low a value on Odette's life."[76] However, the objective grounds of Swann's extreme passion remain completely mysterious. Odette is not particularly beautiful and does not even correspond to Swann's taste in women. Neither her social position, nor her intelligence makes her an adequate match for Swann. After his desire for her quiets and eventually disappears, he realizes how objectively incompatible she was as his lover: "He . . . saw once again . . . Odette's pale complexion, her too thin cheeks, her drawn features, her tired eyes, everything which . . . he had ceased to notice since the earliest days of their acquaintance, days to which no doubt, while he slept, his memory had returned to search for their exact sensation. And with the intermittent coarseness that reappeared in him as soon as he was no longer unhappy and the level of his morality dropped accordingly, he exclaimed to himself: 'To think that I wasted years of my life, that I wanted to die, that I felt my deepest love, for a woman who did not appeal to me, who was not my type!'"[77] At one point, Proust seems to hint that Swann's desire for Odette is brought about by a certain piece of music, which alone transforms her into the most desirable woman he has ever seen: "He was aware that this love was something that did not correspond to anything external, anything verifiable by others beside him; he realized that Odette's qualities did not justify his attaching so much value to the time he spent with her. And often, when Swann's positive intelligence alone prevailed, he wanted to stop sacrificing so many intellectual and social interests to this imaginary pleasure. But as soon as he heard it, the little phrase had the power to open up within him the space it needed, the proportions of Swann's soul were changed by it."[78] However, the notion that a musical phrase can engender sexual desire is rather nebulous and remains unpersuasive. Proust offers a much more plausible explanation of this seemingly inexplicable passion where he elaborates on how the desires of other men affect the way Swann sees Odette. The "hell" that Swann goes through in his passion for Odette is ultimately explained by the mimetic nature of desire: "Of course Swann had often reflected that Odette was in no way a remarkable woman, and the ascendency he exerted over a creature so inferior to him was not something that ought to appear to him so flattering to see proclaimed to all the 'faithful,' but from the time he had first noticed that many men found Odette an enchanting and desirable woman, the attraction her body had for them had awoken in him a painful need to master her entirely even in the smallest parts of her heart."[79] Swann desires Odette because other men desire her, not because he is objectively attracted to her. Such instances of mimetic desire can be found throughout Proust's work. Consider the following from the closing passage of *The Captive*:

Were we better to analyze our loves, to see that women often attract us only because of the counterpoise of all the men with whom we have to compete for them, although we suffer agonies from having thus to compete; this counterpoise removed, the charm of the woman declines. We have a painful and cautionary example of this in the predilection men have for women who have strayed before they came to know them, for those women whom they feel to be sinking in perilous quicksands and whom they must spend the whole period of their love in rescuing; a posthumous example, on the other hand, and one that is not in the least tragic, is the man who, conscious of a decline in his affection for the woman he loves, spontaneously applies the rules that he has deduced, and, to make sure that he does not cease to love the woman, places her in a dangerous environment where he is obliged to protect her daily.[80]

A further example of mimetic desire is found in *Within a Budding Grove*.[81] Marcel's attraction to the actress Berma is awakened by Bergotte, a great admirer of Berma's performances. Marcel's imitation of Bergotte's admiration generates the desire to attend one of Berma's performances, but Marcel's expectations turn into disappointment once he finally sees Berma on the stage. The comparison with two actresses in the same play has devastating consequences for Marcel's desire: "She did not attain even to the heights which Oenone or Aricie would naturally have reached, she played down into a uniform chant the whole of a speech in which there were mingled together contrasts so striking that the least intelligent of actresses, even the pupils of an academy, could not have missed their effect; besides which, she delivered it so rapidly that it was only when she had come to the last line that my mind became aware of the deliberate monotony which she had imposed on it throughout."[82] Marcel's disappointment proves only transitory, however. When the audience rapturously applauds Berma's performance, Marcel joins in and changes his initial evaluation: "Then at last I felt my first impulse of admiration, which was provoked by the frenzied applause of the audience. I mingled my own with theirs, endeavoring to prolong it so that Berma, in her gratitude, should surpass herself, and I be certain of having heard her on one of her great days."[83] After the performance—and after the effect of the audience's applause wears off—Marcel seeks further confirmation that the performance was indeed extraordinary. When Monsieur de Norpois comes to visit, Marcel attempts to elicit corroboration from him of Berma's greatness. "M. de Norpois, a man a thousand times more intelligent than myself, must know that hidden truth which I had failed to extract from Berma's playing, and would reveal it to me; in answering his question I would ask him to let me know in what that truth consisted; and he would thereby justify me in the longing that I had felt to see and hear the actress."[84] De Norpois praises Berma and stresses above all her effortlessness and the truth of her art. This is crucial for Marcel in his process of overcoming his initial—and lingering—disappointment. He repeats once more to himself: "It's true! . . . what a beautiful voice, what an absence of shrillness, what simple costumes, what intelligence to have chosen *Phèdre*! No, I have not been disappointed!"[85] The deciding factor in Marcel's ultimate judgment, however, is the critical acclaim he reads later that evening in *Le Figaro*, which praises Berma's *Phèdre* as the purest and most exalted manifestation of dramatic art: "As soon as my mind had conceived this new idea of the 'purest and most exalted manifestation of dramatic art,' it, the idea, sped to join the imperfect pleasure which I had felt in the theater, adding to it a little of what it lacked, and the combination formed something so exalting that I exclaimed to myself: What a great artist!"[86] Marcel's aesthetic enjoyment is clearly dependent on external, mimetic corroboration. Marcel is convinced that he was part of a great artistic experience only after others also praise its greatness. Proust explains precisely how important the others are for one's own perception: "One discovers the touch of genius in Berma's acting either a week after one has heard from her, from a review, or else on the spot, from the thundering acclamation of the stalls."[87]

Fyodor Dostoyevsky

Dostoyevsky also belongs to the group of novelistic authors whose work is permeated with imitation.[88] Girard names Dostoyevsky's short story *The Eternal Husband* as a fundamental example.[89] After the wife of Pavel Pavlovitch Trusotsky dies, the civil servant sets off for Saint Petersburg to seek out two of her lovers with whom she deceived him. A strange mixture of love and hate characterizes the relationship that ensues between Trusotsky and his rivals. After one of them dies, he attends the funeral and displays his deepest mourning. He constantly pesters the second—Velchaninov—and even suggests that Velchaninov is the real father of his daughter. Trusotsky's revenge is manifest not only in negative outbursts, however; during a midnight visit to Velchaninov's home, he drinks to the health of his rival and forces Velchaninov to kiss him: "'Kiss me, Alexei Ivanovitch!' [Trusotsky] suggested suddenly. 'You're drunk!' Velchaninov declared, stepping back. 'Yes, but kiss me all the same, Alexei Ivanovitch. Oh kiss me! Why, I kissed your hand just now.' For some minutes Velchaninov was silent, as though stunned by a blow on the head. But suddenly he bent down to Pavel Pavlovitch, whose face was on a level with his shoulder, and kissed him on the lips, which smelt very strongly of spirits. He was not, however, perfectly certain that he had kissed him."[90]

This kiss is of particular interest for the present discussion. On the surface, it seems to confirm Freud's diagnosis of Dostoyevsky's bisexuality and thus latent homosexuality: "A strong innate bisexual disposition becomes one of the preconditions or reinforcements of neurosis. Such a disposition must certainly be assumed in Dostoyevsky, and it shows itself in a viable form (as latent homosexuality) in the important part played by male friendships in his life, in his strangely tender attitude towards rivals in love and in his remarkable understanding of situations which are explicable only by repressed homosexuality, as many examples from his novels show."[91]

However, Girard dismisses Freud's interpretation as false, and explains the "erotic deviation towards the fascinating rival" without reverting to any arguments concerning sexual predisposition.[92] Mimetic desire is directed at the mediator from the outset and can thus develop into direct erotic fantasies with the rival. Throughout his work, Dostoyevsky repeatedly illustrates this phenomenon.[93]

Velchaninov is for Trusotsky role model and rival, model and obstacle at the same time. This ambivalence is incorporated into a story he tells Velchaninov concerning Colonel Golubenko, who excites the love and hatred of Livtsov after seducing his girlfriend:

> And what do you think? This Livtsov formed a genuine friendship with Golubenko, he quite made it up with him, and, what's more—insisted on being his best man, he held the wedding crown, and when he came from under the wedding crown, he went up to kiss and congratulate Golubenko; and in the presence of the governor and all the honorable company, with

his swallow-tail coat, and his hair in curl, he sticks the bridegroom in the stomach with a knife—so that he rolled over! His own best man! What a disgrace! And, what's more, when he'd stabbed him like that, he rushed about crying: 'Ach! What have I done! Oh, what is it I've done!' with floods of tears, trembling all over.[94]

Much like Livtsov, Trusotsky's feelings for his mimetic model Velchaninov oscillate between the extremes of affection and rage. He ultimately gives in to his rage and attempts to murder Velchaninov with a razor, only to be hindered by his rival's great physical strength. Following the attempted murder, Velchaninov summarizes Trusotsky's absurdly ambivalent behavior in the following internal monologue:

> He comes here 'to embrace me and weep,' as he expressed it in the most abject way—that is, he came here to murder me and thought he came 'to embrace me and to weep.' . . . He brought Liza too. But, who knows? if I had wept with him, perhaps, really, he would have forgiven me, for he had a terrible longing to forgive me! . . . At the first shock all that was changed into drunken antics and caricature, and into loathsome, womanish whining over his wrongs. . . . He came drunk on purpose to speak out, though he was playing the fool; if he had not been drunk, even he could not have done it. . . . And how he liked playing the fool, didn't he like it! Ough! wasn't he pleased, too, when he made me kiss him! Only he didn't know then whether he would end by embracing me or murdering me. Of course, it's turned out that the best thing was to do both. A most natural solution![95]

After Trusotsky decides to remarry, he persuades his rival to help him select an engagement gift for his future bride, and even asks Velchaninov to accompany him when he presents it and asks for her hand. He needs Velchaninov in order to obtain confirmation of his own desire. Velchaninov brings this to the fore in a reflection on Trusotsky's decision to remarry. Because the eternal husband began to doubt his dream, "he needed the high sanction of Velchaninov whom he revered. He wanted Velchaninov to approve, he wanted him to reassure him that the dream was not a dream, but something real."[96] Initially, Trusotsky intended to bring his beloved a "whole set of jewels." At the shop together with Velchaninov, however, his wish falls apart. Dostoyevsky shows that the advice of Velchaninov—Trusotsky's mimetic model—retains the upper hand: "It ended . . . in his only buying a bracelet, and not the one he wanted to, but the one that Velchaninov fixed upon."[97]

On the way to the woman's house, Trusotsky's uncertainty emerges again as he argues with Velchaninov whether he should keep the black crape ribbon on his hat, which he wore during the funeral of his former wife's first lover. After a long discussion, Trusotsky decides to wear the ribbon against the opinion of his rival. Later, however, he takes off the hat, rips the crape off and flings it on the road.[98] Once again, Trusotsky is influenced completely by his model. Once the two arrive at the woman's house, Trusotsky's plans fall apart. Next to Velchaninov—whom both the woman and Trusotsky himself admire—Trusotsky comes across as ridiculous and fails in his attempt to win the woman for himself.

The conclusion to *The Eternal Husband* offers a final glimpse into the triangular structure of desire in Dostoyevsky's story. Two years after the episode described above, Velchaninov meets Trusotsky in the street, accompanied by a new, beautiful wife—and a young officer. Trusotsky is ultimately incapable of escaping the mediator's influence; he always needs the desire of a third party in order to find his women attractive. Mimesis, the imitation of a model, is a constant and persistent characteristic of the eternal husband.

From External to Internal Mediation

The novelists presented here are in accord that human beings borrow their desires from models. However, there are significant differences with regard to their respective interpretations of desire. In the case of Cervantes and Flaubert, the conflictual dimension of mimesis is almost invisible, whereas Proust and Dostoyevsky seem to concentrate directly on these consequences of mimetic desire. The reason for this difference lies in the relationship between the role model and the imitating subject. In the works of Cervantes and Flaubert, the role model remains outside the personal sphere of the protagonist. Don Quixote cannot fall into conflict with his fictive role model Amadis of Gaul, for the distance between the two is unbridgeable. Similarly, the social difference between Don Quixote and Sancho Panza—Quixote's admitted disciple—prevents any form of rivalry from occurring between the two. In short, Sancho Panza would never dare fight with Don Quixote over the same object. Girard calls this kind of mimesis *external mediation* (*Deceit, Desire and the Novel*, 9; *De la violence à la divinité*, 41: "médiation externe"). As long as social difference or any other form of differentiation is present to channel mimetic desire, its conflictual dimension remains contained.

Stendhal, meanwhile, speaks of a different kind of mimetic desire, which he connects above all with the concept of vanity. The vain subject desires an object only when he is convinced that another also desires this same object. The mediator thus becomes a rival for the desiring subject. The two find themselves on the same plane, and the subject's vanity demands that the rival be defeated. One finds similar manifestations of mimetic desire in Proust, in particular where the yet-stronger emotions of jealousy and envy emerge. The subject needs a rival in order to feel love or sexual desire. Stendhal's vanity is Proust's snobbism; the snob does not trust his own judgment, for he desires the objects that the other already possesses and is therefore a slave to the fashion of the times. In Stendhal and Proust, one can say the rival is part of the imitating subject's world. This mediation is no longer external, as was the case with Don Quixote and his hero Amadis of Gaul, but rather within the subject's sphere of influence: Girard calls this phenomenon *internal mediation* (*Deceit, Desire and the Novel*, 9; *De la violence à la divinité*, 41: "médiation interne").

Dostoyevsky, meanwhile, goes one step further. Here, there is no love without jealousy and no friendship without envy. Admiration and hatred are one and the same among Dostoyevsky's characters and lead all the way to murder. Stendhal's internal mediation is confined to the political and public sphere: Proust incorporates the private sphere, but only to a limited degree; he leaves familial relations outside the realm of rivalrous desire. Dostoyevsky transcends this last barrier and pursues the destructive potential of mimetic conflict within the family—where social differentiation has all but disappeared, and the powers of mimesis are most destructive. One need only consider the patricidal plot in Dostoyevsky's *The Brothers Karamazov*. With regard to internal mimesis, Girard therefore introduces one final differentiation; he refers to mediation in Stendhal and Proust as *exogamic* ("exogamique"), because it remains outside the realm of the family, and in Dostoyevsky as *endogamic* (*Deceit, Desire and the Novel*, 42; *De la violence à la divinité*, 67: "endogamique").

From Cervantes to Dostoyevsky, one can trace the development of an increasing proximity between the imitating subject and its role model. The difference or distance between imitating subject and role model becomes less and less important, and, simultaneously, the actual object of desire decreases in significance. The mediator, not the untouchable hero, as is the case in Cervantes's *Don Quixote*, is in the foreground of the novel. This is best illustrated by Dostoyevsky's *The Eternal Husband*. Velchaninov, who is role model, mediator, and obstacle all at once, is the point around which Trusotsky revolves like the planets around the sun.[99]

However, these subtle differences between external and internal mediation do not imply that Girard maintains such a narrow classification of all mimetic predicaments. On a more profound level, he argues for the fundamental unity of mimetic desire, notwithstanding its manifold forms: "Triangular desire is one" (*Deceit, Desire and the Novel*, 48). This is the exact insight at the foundation of his study on the novel. The uncanny similarities between the tale of "Ill-advised Curiosity" within Cervantes's *Don Quixote* and Dostoyevsky's *The Eternal Husband* led Girard to identify mimetic desire as the hermeneutic tool with which to understand all truly novelistic creation.[100] At the center of the story in Cervantes's narrative one finds Anselmo, who has just married the young and beautiful Camilla. The two were brought together by Lotario, Anselmo's longtime friend and mimetic model. A short time after the marriage, Anselmo bids his friend to attempt to seduce his wife in order to see if she is truly faithful. Lotario is at first opposed to his friend's strange request. He eventually gives in to Anselmo's insistence, however, and endeavors to seduce Camilla. The novella ends tragically, as Anselmo commits suicide after discovering his wife together with his friend. Despite the over three hundred years separating Cervantes's novella and Dostoyevsky's *The Eternal Husband*—and because Cervantes had no traceable literary influence on Dostoyevsky—the two texts converge with regard to the presence of mimetic desire. Just as Trusotsky needs a mediator in order to find women attractive, Anselmo ultimately also needs the mediation of his friend in order to desire his wife. Cervantes's novel represents one pole of mimetic desire—the ideal type of external mediation between Don Quixote and Amadis of Gaul—and Dostoyevsky's novella embodies the other end of the mimetic spectrum. However, the parallels between Cervantes's novella and

Dostoyevsky's *The Eternal Husband* point to a deeper unity, which Girard argues encompasses all novelistic authors: "The simultaneous presence of external and internal mediation in the same work seems . . . to confirm the unity of novelistic literature" (*Deceit, Desire and the Novel*, 52).

Potential Dangers of Modern Equality

Girard's insight into the potential for conflict that accompanies internal mediation can help us better understand our modern, increasingly egalitarian world. As the metaphysical distance between desiring subject and model diminishes—the key component of internal mediation—the potential for rivalry and violence increases. The more negligible this distance becomes, the more probable it is that mimesis will end in rivalry and violence. The ancient proverbial truth found in mythical texts, primitive practices, and even the Bible, that brothers or sisters are much more prone to rivalry and conflict than others, can be easily understood with the help of Girard's insight.

The development of mimetic desire from Cervantes to Dostoyevsky reflects the emergence of the modern world, one in which the spread of democracy and equality have meant the vanishing of rigid hierarchical differences. The limits on mimesis have essentially disappeared, as internal mediation increasingly takes the place of external mediation. The modern world has in turn seen a surge in competition, envy, and rivalry. In Girard's eyes, this development is described most precisely by the French sociologist Alexis de Tocqueville in his work *Democracy in America*:

> When all the privileges of birth and fortune are abolished, when all professions are accessible to all, and a man's own energies may place him at the top of any one of them, an easy and unbounded career seems open to his ambition and he will readily persuade himself that he is born to no common destinies. But this is an erroneous notion, which is corrected by daily experience. The same equality that allows every citizen to conceive these lofty hopes, renders all the citizens less able to realize them; it circumscribes their powers on every side, which it gives freer scope to their desires. . . . They have swept away the privileges of some of their fellow-creatures which stood in their way, but they have opened the door to universal competition.[101]

Tocqueville is cognizant of the dangers posed by the modern phenomenon of equality. The strength of his analysis lies merely at the political level, however, in that he avoids pursuing the deeper anthropological roots of modern egalitarianism and the dangers it poses to society. Girard's insight into the effects of mimetic desire allows one to understand why the phenomenon of equality—or the disappearance of social differences—poses these dangers. Reactionary or anti-egalitarian movements, in their attempt to maintain social differences, are aware of the conflictual potential of equality.

One gains a sense of this from the contemporary struggle between the sexes, and the phenomenon of democracy. On the one hand, the equality of the sexes and political equality enhance moral quality in human relations, but, on the other hand, they also increase the possibility of rivalry, competition, and violence. Antje Vollmer, for one, points out in her book *Heißer Frieden* [Hot Peace] that modern equality is one of the major factors responsible for this increase in social violence.[102]

The workings of mimetic desire, meanwhile, explain the problematic consequences of equality. We will see in the following sections that Girard's theory of mimetic desire only offers an initial and preliminary answer to modern social dynamics. In his eyes, social differences are not God-given or a product of nature—as Aristotle and his conservative followers contend—but rather a product of mimesis. Just as Heraclitus saw social differences as a product of war—"the father and king of all, . . . some it makes gods, others men; some slaves, and others free"—Girard also maintains that these distinctions result from the violence of mimetic rivalry.[103] The mimetic theory does not, therefore, defend the perpetuation of social differences, but rather sides with Tocqueville in maintaining that any struggle against the increasing phenomenon of equality is akin to an act against divine providence itself.[104] This, however, already touches on the relationship of Girard's theory to biblical revelation, which will receive significant attention in later parts of this book.

Civil War and Mimesis: the Narcissism of Small Differences

The modern world offers a host of examples that can demonstrate the aforementioned correlation between equality and an increasing tendency for social conflict. Among these, violent clashes that resemble civil war are particularly illustrative.

Massacre in Civil War

In his inquiry into what can be learned from excessive political violence—such as the recent massacres in Bosnia, Rwanda, Chiapas, or Algeria—Wolfgang Sofsky points out an unambiguous prevalence of violence in cultures where victims and their perpetrators are in close proximity. He argues that violence is not caused by foreignness or distance, as is often contended, but rather by proximity and equality: "It is a misapprehension to assume that human bestialities require social distance or any depersonalization and dehumanization of victims. . . . In Algeria, survivors in many cases recognized former neighbors, friends, and even relatives among their murderers. During the 'ethnic cleansing' in the former Yugoslavia, many of the incendiary murderers [tr. *Mordbrenner*] were particularly brutal with neighbors and coworkers from their villages. Proximity, not anonymity, brings about the most vicious atrocities; far from increasing the threshold of attack, it heightens the passion of violence."[105] The Bosnian civil war highlights in particular clarity one characteristic that Sofsky holds as general for all massacres. His analysis goes against Samuel Huntington's *The Clash of Civilizations and the Remaking of World Order*, which emphasizes the cultural differences in the conflict, and focuses on the negligible distance between the enemy groups. The English journalist Misha Glenny, as well, recognizes the lack of difference between the individual groups—or in other words, their equality—as one of the central causes for the extreme atrocities that occurred during the war:

> What causes this depth of hatred which has provoked atrocities and slaughter on such a wide scale over such a short period of time? . . . Obviously, the conflict has been caused by complex historical and political forces. But the hatred has a slightly different origin. To a large degree, the wars of the Yugoslav succession have been nationalist in character. They are not ethnic conflicts, as the media would often have it, as most of those doing the killing are of the same ethnos. Indeed what is striking about Bosnia-Hercegovina, in particular, is just how closely related are the Serbs, the Croats and the Moslems. Religion is the crucial factor dividing these people, although this

is not a confessional conflict. For centuries, these people have been asked to
choose between competing empires and ideologies, which have invariably
been defined by religion. . . . The Bosnian Serbs, Croats and Moslems have
been adorned with many different cultural uniforms over the centuries by
which they identify one another as the enemy when conflict breaks out.
Despite this, underneath the dress they can see themselves reflected—it is
the awful recognition that these primitive beasts on the other side of the
barricade are their brothers which has led to the violence assuming such
ghastly proportions in Bosnia. The only way that fighters can deal with
this realization is to exterminate the opposite community. How else does
one explain the tradition of facial mutilation in this region? How else can
we account for the high incidence of women and children being killed in
cold blood?[106]

How should one interpret Glenny's observation theoretically? The Canadian
historian and journalist Michael Ignatieff has suggested implementing Sigmund Freud's concept of the "narcissism of small differences" to better understand Glenny's insight and the actual causes of the atrocities in Bosnia.[107] In his
own report on the situation in the former Yugoslavia, Ignatieff summarizes his
interpretation of the conflict in the following way: "Freud once argued that
the smaller the real difference between two peoples, the larger it was bound to
loom in their imagination. He called this effect the narcissism of minor difference. Its corollary must be that enemies need each other to remind themselves
of who they really are. A Croat, thus, is someone who is not a Serb. A Serb is
someone who is not a Croat. Without hatred of the other, there would be no
clearly defined national self to worship and adore."[108]

In contrast to Ignatieff, Samuel Huntington expressly denies Freud's "narcissism of small differences" in his interpretation of the Bosnian conflict.[109]
This is no surprise, seeing as Freud's concept calls into question the main
thesis in Huntington's *Clash of Civilizations.* However, it is worth mention-
ing that Huntington's book contains several observations that pinpoint the
original roots of the conflict within the individual groups themselves. This
allows one to understand his theory as the conscious attempt to ignore these
deeper roots in his attempt to re-enable a global structure that makes civil
wars more controllable.[110] Huntington's remark that the confidence between
brothers rises when they fight together against other boys, as well as his

many observations concerning Islamic culture and how it minimizes internal antagonisms through enmity against the West, demonstrate—against the conscious intentions of the author—that the actual roots of human conflict are found in the interrelations *within* the groups themselves.

In the passages concerning war in *Things Hidden since the Foundation of the World*, Girard underlines his observation that war emerges from within the cultural group itself—and that it cannot be explained by any external cultural differences: "Primitive warfare takes places among proximate, neighboring groups, which is to say among men who cannot be distinguished objectively in terms of race, language, or cultural habits. There is no real difference between the external enemy and the internal friend" (*Things Hidden*, 85–86).[111]

The "Narcissism of Small Differences"

Freud makes frequent mention in his writings of the "narcissism of small differences," a concept according to which petty distinctions between social groups give rise to especially vicious conflict. Freud points out that "it is precisely communities with adjourning territories, and related to each other in other ways as well, who are engaged in constant feuds and in ridiculing each other—like the Spaniards and the Portuguese, for instance, the North Germans and South Germans, the English and Scotch, and so on."[112] In connection with his analysis of anti-Semitism, Freud expressly supports the seemingly paradoxical notion that "racial intolerance finds stronger expression . . . in regard to small differences than to fundamental ones."[113] At the same time, however, Freud is aware that the nomenclature of his concept remains rather ambiguous.[114] On the one hand, he is able to explain the consequences of this "narcissism," namely, that the group is able to increase its feeling of camaraderie by venting its aggression against a common enemy. On the other hand, however, Freud fails to offer an explanation of why decreasing difference between groups leads to more frequent and extreme instances of intolerance and cruelty between them.

Freud is not the first thinker to observe and articulate this concept, however. An early example can be found in the writings of Saint Thomas Aquinas, who identifies the struggle over mutual borders as one of the principal prerequisites for violent conflict. "People, who hold nothing in common, such as the Spaniards and Persians, do not seem to get into legal disputes, but, rather, those who do hold something in common. This is why there are disagreements even among brothers."[115] Hobbes uses different language to describe the same phenomenon, where he speaks of the envy that frequently emerges between "neighbor nations over one another's honour."[116] Around a century later, Adam Smith stresses that national feelings of hatred "seldom extend beyond neighboring nations."[117] At the beginning of the twentieth century, the German sociologist Georg Simmel conducted a more comprehensive study of this type of narcissism, concluding that conflicts emanating from the same source are the "most passionate and radical" of all. As an example, Simmel refers to ancient Jewish law, which permitted bigamy as such, but strictly prohibited Jewish men from marrying two sisters (Leviticus 18:18).[118] Also interesting are the examples he takes from religious history, where the minimizing of difference oftentimes led to irreconcilable conflicts. Simmel makes note of the altercations that arose among Protestant churches after the Reformation, pointing out that these quarrels were much more intense than their common opposition to the Catholic Church. Simmel also points out that in 1875 the pope permitted Mass in the Reformed Church, while the Old Catholic Church remained forbidden as a place of worship for Catholics. Simmel's example sheds light on the current situation in Ireland and Northern Ireland, where the religiopolitical dilemmas bear distinct characteristics of the "narcissism of small differences" and can effectively be interpreted using this concept.[119]

Freud's well-known phenomenon, however, remains in need of theoretical articulation. He and the other authors mentioned here have only described the connection of violence and diminishing difference; an explanation of its origins or causes is still missing. The mimetic theory offers this explanation by showing quite simply that the disappearance of difference—physical or metaphysical—results in an increase in the frequency and intensity of conflict between the groups. Conflicts between equals have the greatest risk of turning violent, because the social limitations that normally prevent or channel mimetic desire are missing. Such insight allows one to better comprehend, for instance, the unique brutality of civil and fratricidal wars.

Mimesis and Modernity: The Predominance
of Negative Imitation

One of the difficulties facing the mimetic theory in contemporary society lies in the modern rejection of imitation. We live in a world in which imitation is frowned upon, because most human beings strive to be unique and original. Any person caught imitating or following the herd almost automatically attracts our complete scorn. It is thus certainly no surprise why most reactions to Girard's mimetic theory have been negative, for it attempts to argue that all human beings are determined by imitation—a scandalous claim in our world that so highly praises originality. Girard refers throughout his work to this obsession with originality, which in his eyes is a distinctly modern phenomenon, compared to past societies in which imitation was an accepted and essential part of public life: "Instead of seeing imitation as a threat to social cohesion or as a danger to the community, we view it as a cause of conformity and gregariousness. We despise it rather than fear it. We are always 'against' imitation, though in a different way than Plato; we have excluded it from just about everything, including our aesthetics. Our psychology, psychoanalysis, and even sociology, accommodate it only grudgingly. Our art and literature take great pains to resemble nothing and no one—mimetically" (*Things Hidden*, 17).[120] However, the modern rejection of imitation does not mean that human beings escape mimesis in any way; in fact, this "rejection" is a product of already intensified mimetic desire. Since the modern world is characterized by the dominion of internal mimesis—in which imitable role models transform into obstacles worthy of hatred—imitation merely lurks in the underground, where its hegemony is even more absolute. The enemy brothers of internal mimesis adamantly reject imitation and are resolute about their difference from one another; what they miss, however, is that their need to differ only increases their identicalness, as they become more exact mirror reflections of one another. The original admired model quickly becomes an anti-model; the mimetic nature of desire, meanwhile, is retained—if not intensified.

Girard sees the concept of modern individualism as marked by this "rejection" of imitation. The discovery of the individual, in his eyes, is one of the positive effects of Christianity. However, it was not immune to degeneration. The romantic divinization of fully autonomous individuality paved the way for modern idolatry, which parades itself as "anti-mimetic voluntarism"—only to end in "reinforced mimetism" (*Quand ces choses commenceront*, 46). As mimetic desire transforms into idolatrous autonomy, it becomes more and more desperate to rid itself of its mimicry.[121] This wish, however, can never be fulfilled. Girard has already taken this up in his first book, where he describes the phenomenon of *negative imitation* (*Deceit, Desire and the Novel*, 100; *De la violence à la divinité*, 115: "imitation négative") as the principle consequence of mimetic desire: "Modern society is no longer anything but a negative imitation and the effort to leave the beaten paths forces everyone inevitably into the same ditch."[122] An analysis of two modern phenomena can show just how much our world is dominated by mimesis, despite its ostensible rejection. Both modern advertising and fashion make evident the intense "mimetism" lurking beneath our modern, anti-mimetic world.

Anti-Mimetic Mimesis of Advertising

No other phenomenon displays the workings of mimetic desire more clearly than modern advertising. In television commercials, the advertised object only rarely appears directly on the screen; most often what is shown are the people in possession of the object—or those who desire it—in order to activate the viewer's imitation. This is a clear illustration of the triangular structure of mimetic desire. Even among scientists unfamiliar with the mimetic theory, the triangular structure of advertising is nothing new. The German psychologist Rolf Haubl describes advertising as a "phenomenon of envy," thereby alluding—unknowingly—to the workings of mimesis: "The economies of developed consumer societies are not faced with the task of eliminating shortages, but rather—in a world of superabundance—of creating them. Advertising is the portal through which these shortages are communicated. One strategy of creating shortages consists of making consumers envious: they should desire the goods that the models on billboards and commercials already possess."[123]

It is thus relatively straightforward to demonstrate advertising as a mimetic phenomenon. The thrust of Girard's argument, however, lies more in his elucidation of its paradoxical nature. For advertising, as much as it presupposes mimetic desire, must in the end conform to the anti-mimetic atmosphere of the modern world. Advertising promises originality. The consumer is supposed to believe that possession of the advertised product will guarantee the exceptional uniqueness embodied by those who model it. Only after purchasing the product can human beings escape the mundane horde. However, this promise remains steeped in contradiction, for imitation and originality are mutually exclusive. Only by imitating the desire of our original models—the heroes of advertising—are we able to enjoy the pleasure of an autonomous existence. The French social philosopher Jean-Pierre Dupuy, in response to Girard, describes advertising very rightly as an intrinsic "paradox." For, Dupuy says, the "paradise of non-imitation" can only be achieved "thanks to imitation."[124]

Georg Simmel's Philosophy of Fashion

The world of fashion offers another clear instance of the anti-mimetic mimesis of modernity. Girard makes reference throughout his work to this phenomenon and emphasizes the degree to which the modern rejection of imitation has paradoxically led to an unprecedented tyranny of fashion.[125] The link between fashion and imitation is self-evident; one finds explicit connections between the two concepts already in Kant:

> The human being has a natural tendency to compare his behavior to that of a more important person (the child with adults, the lower-ranking person with those of higher rank) in order to imitate the other person's ways. A law of this imitation, which aims at not appearing lower than others, especially in cases where no regard to utility is paid, is called fashion. Fashion therefore belongs under the title of vanity, because there is no inner worth in its intention; and also of foolishness, because in fashion there is still a compulsion to let ourselves be led slavishly by the mere example that many in society give us.[126]

In 1905, the German sociologist Georg Simmel published his *Philosophy of Fashion*, in which he examines more closely the connection between imitation and fashion. Fashion, for Simmel, is the "imitation of a given pattern and thus satisfies the need for social adaptation; it leads the individual onto the path that everyone travels, it furnishes a general condition that resolves the conduct of every individual into a mere example."[127] However, is imitation really the determining factor for fashion? Can one not argue that fashion is the exact opposite—namely, the desire for differentiation and distinction? Sociologists distinguish between two disparate elements of fashion in their analyses. They examine either the initial moment of imitation or the ensuing desire for difference. Girard is skeptical of such essentialist theoretical models, for the most part because he rejects sociological categorizations that miss the deeper connection between these two sides of fashion, which he says can both be explicated by mimetic desire.[128]

On the surface, Simmel appears in his *Philosophy of Fashion* to follow other sociologists who focus merely on one of the two clearly detached dimensions of fashion. However, Simmel also seeks to unite the two. The more fashion is determined by "imitation," the more, he says, it also "satisfies the need for distinction, the tendency towards differentiation, change and individual contrast."[129] Fashion, in other words, is determined by two self-contradicting tendencies. Simmel takes his analysis a step further, however, with a more precise examination of the two components of fashion. He offers two examples of the interaction between them that can be shown to confirm Girard's mimetic theory, which argues that imitation and the need for differentiation are not at all self-contradictory, but merely intricate forms of the same phenomenon.

Simmel's first example is the "slave to fashion" [*Modenarr*], whom he describes as someone whose individuality is based on an intensified form of imitation. The slave to fashion is always one step ahead—or so he thinks—of the models he imitates:

> In slaves to fashion [*Modenarren*] the social demands of fashion appear exaggerated to such a high degree that they completely acquire a semblance of individuality and particularity. It is characteristic of the slave to fashion that he carries the tendency of a particular fashion beyond the otherwise self-contained limits. If pointed shoes are in style, then he wears shoes that resemble spear tips; if pointed collars are all the rage, he wears collars that reach up to his ears; if it is fashionable to attend scholarly lectures, then he is never seen anywhere else, and so on. Thus he represents something totally individual, which consists in the quantitative intensification of such

elements as are qualitatively common property of the given social circle. He leads the way, but all travel the same road.[130]

Simmel sees in the slave to fashion a prototype of the typical modern-day politician who is aware that "the leader" [*der Führende*] is essentially also "a follower" [*der Geführte*]:[131] "Democratic times obviously favor such a condition to a remarkable degree, so much so that even *Bismarck* and other very prominent party leaders of constitutional governments have emphasized the fact that, inasmuch as they are leaders of a group, they are bound to follow it. . . . The conceit of the slave to fashion is thus the caricature of a democratically fostered constellation of the relations between the individual and the totality."[132] Simmel's reference to modern democracy refers indirectly to Girard's notion of internal mimesis, which is especially conducive to such singular forms of imitation. The atmosphere of social equality promotes this imitation that claims to be free from all mimesis. At the same time, however, Simmel's reference also touches on what Girard refers to as the "paradox of the sovereign power" (*I See Satan*, 20), in which rulers such as Pontius Pilate or Herod, despite their social superiority, are still shown to be mimetically bound to the crowd.[133] When the people refuse to imitate their ruler, in short, the ruler himself must follow the people. Politics, like fashion, are inextricably linked to imitation.

Simmel's second example displays the anti-mimetic mimesis of fashion still more directly. He refers to the attempt to demonstrate one's non-imitative nature by means of imitation, and terms this directly a form of "negative imitation":

> Whoever consciously clothes or deports themselves in an unmodern manner does not attain the consequent sensation of individualization through any real individual qualification of his or her own, but rather through the mere negation of the social example. If modernity is the imitation of this social example, then the deliberate lack of modernity represents a similar imitation, yet under an inverted sign, but nonetheless one which offers no less a testimony of the power of the social tendency, which makes us dependent upon it in some positive or negative manner. The deliberately unmodern person accepts its forms just as much as does the slave to fashion, except that the unmodern person embodies it in another category;

in that of negation, rather than in exaggeration. Indeed, it occasionally becomes decidedly fashionable in whole circles of a large-scale society to clothe oneself in an unmodern manner. This constitutes one of the most social-psychological complications, in which the drive for individual conspicuousness primarily remains content, first, with a mere inversion of social imitation and, secondly, for its part draws its strength again from approximation to a similarly characterized narrow circle. If a club or association of club-haters were founded, then it would not be logically more impossible and psychologically more possible than the above phenomenon.[134]

Simmel's caricature of the "club of club-haters" [*Verein der Vereinsgegner*] is a depiction of an all-too-modern phenomenon. For, the most vehement critics of contemporary fashion are often those who march in concert clad in "nonconformist" uniforms.

Snobbism

Girard's precise insight into the strange paradox of anti-mimetic mimesis is based on readings of the novelists mentioned above whose knowledge he prefers to sociological classifications. Proust's treatment of the phenomenon of snobbism is one of the central influences on the mimetic theory, though Girard also attributes significance to Stendhal's exploration of vanity, and Dostoyevsky's underground universe.[135] The self-important snob—who on the surface despises imitation—attempts to differentiate from the herd, but is unable to shake off his imitative tendencies, thus producing the ridiculous façade of one attempting to use imitation to conquer one's own imitative nature. The snob is caught in the world of internal mediation where negative imitation is king. The disgust inspired by the snob in others, according to Girard, is based on the originality the snob attempts to exude, which others meanwhile perceive as rehearsed and imitated.[136] In other words, we detest the snob because he reflects too extremely our own mimetic nature; as we ourselves become more snobbish, the more clearly we detect snobbism in others and deny it in ourselves.[137] Similar to the faddist whom Simmel places in the era of democracy, Girard also argues that the modern atmosphere of equality is a necessary prerequisite for snobbism.[138] Girard underlines the mimetic structure of snobbism—moreover, the snob's utter subservience to fashion—in his recapitulation of Proust's insight.

> The triangular structure is no less obvious in social snobbism than it is in love-jealousy. The snob is also an imitator. He slavishly copies the person whose birth, fortune, or stylishness he envies. . . . The snob does not dare trust his own judgment, he desires only objects desired by others. That is why he is the slave of the fashionable. For the first time, moreover, we come across a term in current usage, "snobbism," which does not conceal the truth of triangular desire. Just to call a desire snobbish is enough to underscore its imitative character. The mediator is no longer hidden; the object is relegated to the background for the very reason that snobbism is not limited to a particular category of desires. One can be a snob in aesthetic pleasure, in intellectual life, in clothes, food etc. (*Deceit, Desire and the Novel*, 24).

Mimesis and the Lack of Being: Sartre and Girard

Although the concept of "mimetic desire" is at the heart of Girard's theory, one must note that he does not adhere to it as if it were a kind of *idée fixe*. Much more important than the way the concept is formulated is the way it is understood. In an interview published in 1996, Girard even suggests that other theoretical formulations could perhaps be used in place of "mimetic desire"—for instance, Bergson's *élan vital*, "vital force," which emphasizes the dynamic of the entire person; or Sartre's *projet*.[139] However, the use of these concepts can also lead to misunderstandings. Girard adds in the interview that any exaggerated interpretation of Sartre's influence on the mimetic theory would fail to do justice to his position.

Jean-Paul Sartre

Girard's reference to a convergence with Sartre's philosophy is worthy of further analysis, however, as it raises a significant facet of the mimetic theory.[140] Sartre's magnum opus *Being and Nothingness* is one of the few philosophical works that Girard makes use of in the development and articulation of his insights gained from the novelists previously mentioned. Apart from Camus, he remarks that Sartre—the first philosopher whose thought he ever understood—had a major influence on his early work.[141] His interest in Sartre's thought is not found in the philosophical system for which Sartre is so well known, but rather in the many observations that display a certain understanding of the mimetic nature of desire. Girard is especially impressed by Sartre's insight into man's fundamentally religious nature—convergent with that of the novelistic authors examined above—which the atheist philosopher claims is ultimately driven by a desire to be God.

Sartre differentiates fundamentally between two forms of being: *en-soi* (in-itself), or the objects of consciousness that possess no consciousness themselves, and *pour-soi* (for-itself), which enables self-perception, consciousness, and human freedom. While being *en-soi* is in itself being— i.e., is exactly what it is—man is characterized by a fundamental "lack of being" (*manque d'être*).[142] In other words, humanness is not being in the same way glass is glass, but rather is an essence that transcends its own facticity. Sartre argues that man is determined by perceptions, possibilities, and imagination; desire confirms his view that man is directed at a being that is not necessarily its own. Human reality, or being for-itself, is thus a "being which is what it is not and which is not what it is."[143] By means of a project (*projet*), each human being thus sets for itself the goal of its desire. The ultimate objective of any being *pour-soi* is to become being *en-soi*, or to achieve the transcendence of being in-and-for-itself.[144] Sartre does not, however, imply transcendence in the traditional, religious sense of the term—this would represent mutual exclusivity; once being *pour-soi* becomes completely *en-soi*, it automatically loses consciousness. With that being said, however, Sartre adheres to the "religious" dimension of being in order to explain what he calls the "final objective" of human desire: "To be man means to reach toward being God. Or, if you prefer, man fundamentally is the desire to be God."[145]

A concrete example of Sartre's position, which Girard incidentally praises, is the café waiter whom Sartre uses to illustrate his concept of *mauvaise foi*, or "bad faith":[146]

> Let us consider this waiter in the café. His movement is quick and forward,
> a little too precise, a little too rapid. He comes toward the patrons with a
> step a little too quick. He bends forward a little too eagerly; his voice, his

eyes express an interest a little too solicitous for the order of the customer. Finally there he returns, trying to imitate in his walk the inflexible stiffness of some kind of automaton while carrying his tray with the recklessness of a tight-rope-walker by putting it in a perpetually unstable, perpetually broken equilibrium which he portrays by a light movement of the arm and hand. All his behavior seems to us a game. He applies himself to chaining his movements as if they were mechanisms, the one regulating the other; his gestures and even his voice seem to be mechanisms; he gives himself the quickness and pitiless rapidity of things. He is playing, he is amusing himself. But what is he playing? We need not watch long before we can explain it: he is playing at *being* a waiter in the café.[147]

What, however, is the exact nature of the waiter's "bad faith"? His effort to appear as a waiter is proof enough that he is no waiter *en-soi*, but rather that he is merely following his external plan, his *projet*, to become a waiter. The waiter is thus a being that he himself is not. One sees here a clear instance of what Sartre refers to as the desire for tangible being "in itself"—embodied in the automatic and self-generating "being" of the waiter.

Sartre's work contains many such examples of the yearning for tangible being. Consider his essay "Faces" from 1939, where he describes a fictive "society of statues" inhabited by phlegmatic, disinterested people who on account of their inactivity live without "fear or anger" because there is no competition present to disrupt social harmony.[148] One finds a remark in his notes from December 1939 that refers to man as a "being who flees from himself into the future" in order to "found himself."[149] However, Sartre shows that such attempts at self-creation only end in disappointment, or with the discovery of one's own groundlessness, "gratuitous to the marrow." He uses this example of the never-ending search for being to illustrate two forms of reification. Man as creator seeks in the "created object" human reality "founded upon itself," and as a desiring subject, he seeks in the possessed object human reality "in possession of itself."

In a later essay, "Anti-Semite and Jew," Sartre uses the yearning for being "in-itself" to explain the personality type of the anti-Semite. The typical anti-Semite, in Sartre's eyes, is unable to bear the freedom of the individual— represented by the groundlessness of human existence—and decides instead in favor of an existence that will guarantee the physical tangibility of a thing (tr. *Beständigkeit eines Dinges*), for instance, of "stone." By creating—and exterminating—an eternal enemy for himself, the anti-Semite attempts to create an indubitable sense of identity:

> [The anti-Semite] is a man who is afraid. Not of the Jews, to be sure, but of himself, of his own consciousness, of his liberty, of his instincts, of his responsibilities, of solitariness, of change, of society, and of the world—of everything except the Jews. . . . In espousing anti-Semitism, he does not simply adopt an opinion, he chooses himself as a person. He chooses the permanence and impenetrability of stone, the total irresponsibility of the warrior who obeys his leaders. . . . The Jew only serves him as a pretext; elsewhere his counterpart will make use of the Negro or the man of yellow skin. The existence of the Jew merely permits the anti-Semite to stifle his anxieties at their inception by persuading himself that his place in the world has been marked out in advance, that it awaits him, and that tradition gives him the right to occupy it. Anti-Semitism, in short, is fear of the human condition. The anti-Semite is a man who wishes to be pitiless stone, a furious torrent, a devastating thunderbolt, anything except a man.[150]

Sartre shows that even the "inauthentic Jews"—those who choose Judaism as part of an attempt to assimilate and not out of revolt—desire to become "stone." These Jews flee to the reality offered by Judaism, a "lifeless thing," because they are perpetually cast back to their religion by the anti-Semites.[151] They allow themselves to be constituted by the anti-Semites, "like a stone is a stone," in order to seek the "repose and passivity of a thing."

René Girard

Girard examines several concepts found in Sartre's philosophy and incorporates them into his thought by placing them in a different context, thus altering them in certain key areas. The two thinkers are in agreement with regard to the fundamental lack of being, which Girard articulates with his concept of mimetic desire. In Girard's eyes, however, this lack is not ultimately directed at a tangible being in-itself, as Sartre argues, but rather at the being of a role model—chosen directly by the desiring subject. "Once his basic needs are satisfied . . . , man is subject to intense desires, though he may not know precisely for what. The reason is that he desires *being*, something he himself lacks and which some other person seems to possess. The subject thus looks to that other person to inform him of what he should desire in order to acquire that being. If the model, who is apparently already endowed with superior being, desires some object, that object must surely be capable of conferring an even greater plentitude of being" (*Violence and the Sacred*, 146).[152]

Goethe's epistolary novel *The Sorrows of Young Werther* illustrates clearly the lack of being and the model's primacy in determining the subject's desire. Werther describes in one of his letters how the inexorable need to compare oneself with others is linked to perceptions of one's own "imperfection" (tr. *Unvollkommenheit*):

> Since we are so made that we compare everything with ourselves and ourselves with everything, happiness or misery lies in the objects we associate ourselves with. . . . The power of our imagination, driven by nature to elevate itself, nourished by the fantastic images of literature, raises up a series of beings of whom we are the lowest and everything outside ourselves seems more glorious, every other person more perfect. And that happens quite naturally. We feel so often that we are lacking so much, and just what we lack another person often seems to possess, to which we also add everything that *we* possess, and project a certain ideal contentment on top of it. And thus the other person is made happy, complete, and perfect, a creature of our own making.[153]

While Sartre believes he has located the fundamental dilemma of human existence in the difference between being in- and for-itself, Girard emphasizes much more the importance of the other. However, there are direct convergences between the two thinkers' positions, as one can see from Sartre's third ontological form, "being-for-others," which enables him to make a number of interesting observations regarding the concepts of shame, pride, affection, and sadomasochism that show distinct parallels to the mimetic theory.[154] In a central chapter of *Being and Nothingness*, Sartre examines the glance of the Other and thereby converges on Girard's arguments for the mimetic constitution of human relations. In Sartre's terms, "in order for me to be what I am, it suffices merely that the Other look at me."[155] Thus, through the Other, the human becomes a being "in-itself." Sartre uses this insight to describe the grounds for human affection as well, arguing that "the joy of love" is based on the other's justification of our own existence.[156] Sartre is not trying to say here, however, that the human subject's relation to others is necessary for the constitution of its individual being; for the subject can only exist "in-itself" for the others and never in-itself on its own. There exists an unbridgeable gap between the self and others. Sartre remains caught in the individualism of Cartesian ontology; he shows a fundamental unwilling-ness—and incapability—to overcome Descartes's philosophy.[157] He speaks, on the one hand, of an expanded Cartesian *cogito*, which reveals the existence of others for the subject; on the other hand, however, he fails to clarify any fundamental difference between being "for-itself" and "for-others."[158] There is no reciprocal constitution, no ontological connection between the two; one is left with Sartre's claim that the two merely coincide. Autonomy is so unbridled in Sartre's philosophy that Peter Bürger—in reference to Sartre's remark "The first value and first object of will is: to be its own foundation"— speaks of a masculine "phantasm of self-creation" in which "mankind is no longer born of a mother," but rather of self-consciousness that finds itself as a mere facticity that must seek its own reason for being.[159] Girard's critique of Sartre targets this dependence on Cartesian individualism, in particular Sartre's understanding of human desire as the unbridled striving for being "for-itself" in which the other has only a peripheral significance. In contrast to contemporary novelists—Girard names Virginia Woolf's *The Waves* as a prime example—Sartre is unable to see that "the subject is torn between Self and Other" (*Quand ces choses commenceront*, 163).

Using the lens of the mimetic theory, one can gain deeper insight into Sartre's being for-itself, in particular its ultimate desire for being in-itself. The human yearning for tangible being in-itself, in Girard's eyes, is no original human desire per se, but rather *the consequence* of intensified mimetic desire. The lack of being leads man on the search for the perfect role model, a being that radiates complete inner tranquility and an overcoming of desire. The more self-assured the model appears to be, the more the desiring subject assumes that the model possesses this perfect being. This search is therefore directed at a transcendent form of being; only models that radiate indiffer-ence are able to excite human fascination, making those that appear inac-cessible increasingly desirable.[160] The idolization of "coolness" that pervades our world is a clear expression of this tendency. The attractive power of all things cold and indifferent has lent even subhuman being—due to its inaccessibility—an otherwise inexplicable attraction. This explains how even certain instances of stupidity—attributed, for instance, to women in "typical blonde" jokes—can awaken strong forms of male sexual desire. In a similar way, cats have taken on a particular interest, and it is certainly no accident that felines have become a universal symbol of sexual attraction. In the end, according to Girard, true being seems to have hidden itself behind the mechanical and the automatic, behind even nature itself: "The Other is more fascinating the less accessible he is; and the more despiritualized he is, the more he tends toward an instinctive automatism, the more inaccessible he is. And the absurd project of self-divinization ends up by going beyond the animal to the automatic and even the mechanical. The individual becomes increasingly bewildered and unbalanced by a desire which nothing can satisfy and finally seeks the divine essence in that which radically denies his own existence: the inanimate" (*Deceit, Desire and the Novel*, 286). Because we continually experience indifference as being so attractive, we use indifference—consciously or not—as a strategic means to enhance our own attractiveness in the eyes of the other. Insofar as we ourselves appear self-assured, others assume to see in us that which can fill their lack of being. All forms of coquetry can be deduced from this logic, which is completely determined by the mimetic nature of desire.

The Yearning for Being In-Itself in Dostoyevsky, Proust, and Kleist

Literature is full of examples of the yearning for simplified, lower forms of being—extending to the tangible—and these examples portray all philosophies that attempt to raise this yearning to ontological heights as mere products of mimetic despair. In Dostoyevsky's *The Brothers Karamazov*, the hyper-mimetic Satan—a mimetic double of the intellectual, Ivan—yearns "to be incarnated in the soul of a two-hundred-and-fifty-pound merchant's wife and light candles to God" in order to be delivered from spiritual agony.[161] Later in the novel, Dostoyevsky also provides an example of the human fascination with felines, which function as symbol for the attractiveness of human indifference. Dmitri refers to Grushenka, the object of his desire, as a "cat," a "tiger," and an "infernal woman" who deserves "the scaffold" because she never returns his affections.[162] A similar, yet even more extreme example is found in Proust's *Remembrance of Things Past*. In *Swann's Way*, Swann insults the object of his desire, Odette, whom he calls "that creature which ranks lowest in mentality," "not even a person," a "formless stream of water," a "fish without memory or reflection" and finally "lower than all other things."[163] Odette avoids Swann's insults—clear evidence of her, and by extension, Proust's insight into the essence of coquetry—for she is aware that further indifference will only reinforce Swann's desire for her.

A final, yet significant example is found in Heinrich von Kleist's essay "On the Marionette Theater," which in many ways can be read as a precursor to Sartre's existentialist philosophy.[164] One finds several instances in the essay suggesting the superiority of animal instinct over human consciousness, illustrated best by Kleist's example of a bear whose ability to catch trout trumps any fisherman's tactics. Kleist also describes the dancing marionettes as more graceful than human dancers, at least with regard to the attractive force they exert on humans. Only the marionettes are able to emanate self-assurance and inner balance, which is normally reserved only for God, whom Kleist describes as the paradigm of tranquility. Throughout the text, one finds several references to the problems arising from mimetic desire. Grace, the essay's central issue, is shown to be based on the impression evoked only in others. This is displayed in Kleist's text through the story of the young man and the "Boy with Thorn" (*Dornauszieher*), which carries direct parallels to the Narcissus myth. In the story, two young men view the well-known ancient sculpture of the "Boy with Thorn" during a visit to Paris. One of the young men, whose physique bears a striking resemblance to that of the sculpture, points out this resemblance as he and his friend stand in front of a mirror. The young man's envious friend, however, strongly rejects the resemblance, although, in secret, he shares the observation and admires his friend's beauty. This rejection causes the graceful young man to doubt his beauty and casts him into ruminations of despair. The conclusion to Kleist's essay touches on the interconnectedness of human consciousness, the tangible being of marionettes, and God, thereby recalling distinctly Sartre's differentiation between being *en-soi* and *pour-soi*: "We see that in the organic world, as reflection grows darker and weaker, grace emerges more brilliantly and commandingly. But just as the section drawn through two lines suddenly appears on the other side of a point after passing through infinity, or just as the image in a concave mirror turns up before us again after having moved off into the end-less distance, so too grace itself returns when knowledge has gone through an infinity. Grace appears purest in that human form which has either no consciousness or an infinite one, that is, in a puppet or in a god."[165]

Modern Philosophy and the Yearning for Death

The mimetic despair articulated in the great novels of European literature has all too often been incorporated into philosophical articulation in the modern world. Rousseau's ideal natural condition (in which all human beings require no reflective powers and live "an almost automaton life" like "Swiss Mountaineers,")[166] or Hegel's "End of History" (where people simply vegetate as "automata")[167] are products of mimetic desire, just as are Nietzsche's "amor fati"—the love of the necessity of fate, tangibility, "fatu-ity," "stone," and nature—and Freud's theory of narcissism that ultimately leads to his formulation of the death drive.[168] Claude Levi-Strauss's structur-alism, which incidentally bears many similarities to Rousseauian naturalism, shows similar effects of mimetic despair, as it features the proclamation of a "twilight of man," the entropic death of the earth, and a song of praise for the beauty of "minerals," the "scent that can be smelt at the heart of a lily," and the "cheerful exchange with a cat."[169] The low point of this philosophi-cal development can be seen in the thought of the contemporary German philosopher Ulrich Horstmann. His treatise *Das Untier* calls for a return to the inorganic by the means of modern weapons of mass destruction. In Horstmann's eyes, "universal salvation" will only be complete when the "dust of organic life" remains but frosted on the earth's naked stones. His philosophy is about the descending of lunar lifelessness onto the animate earth [tr. *Vermondung der belebten Erde*]: "For not until the sickle of the moon reflects itself here on earth in a thousand craters, not until the image before and after—moon and world—have become indistinguishable and quartz crystals blink at each other across the abyss under starlight, not until the final oasis dries up, the last sigh drowns out, and the last seed withers will Eden return to the earth."[170]

A cursory analysis of Freud's theory of narcissism can help shed light on the mimetic component of this yearning. Though Freud does not make explicit reference to any yearning for the inorganic—as seen in his later death drive—he clearly displays the human desire for lower, intellectually reduced forms of being. Where Freud speaks of the narcissistic, self-centered tendencies of women, he does not fail to mention their simultaneous attractiveness. He also speaks of the attractiveness of children, which is based on "narcissism, self-assuredness, and inaccessibility"; the appeal of certain animals, like cats and large beasts of prey, who "seem to pay no attention to their owners"; and also literary representations of criminals and humorists.[171] What Freud fails to understand, however, in great contrast to novelists like Dostoyevsky and Proust, is that narcissism as such is illusory; it is simply a strategy utilized by the coquetry described above, a form of pseudonarcissism, a concept we will examine in more depth in the seventh chapter of this book. Particular attention will be given to the metaphors Freud implements in his description of the "narcissistic woman." In Girard's eyes, these desires are directed at subhuman forms of being, or purely tangible being, and thus anticipate Freud's later death drive, a concept which he places at the center of his theory of narcissism. In a critical analysis of Freud's death drive, Girard stresses its mimetic roots: "For me, the death drive exists, but it is absolutely connected with mimetic rivalry. Mimetism turns us into rivals of our models: We fight over objects that they themselves showed us we should desire. This situation reinforces desire and raises the value of the obstacle. The supreme obstacle, of course, is death, or that which can kill. The death drive is the logical end of this vicious circle. But Freud was not able to connect the paradoxically narcissistic desire for a return to the biological, to lifelessness, with this other phase of desire" (*Quand ces choses commenceront*, 159).

Apart from Rousseau, Hegel/Kojève, Nietzsche, Freud, Levi-Strauss, or Horstmann, one must mention above all the philosophy of Sartre, which, with its yearning for lifeless being "in-itself," contains unequivocal traces of the kind of mimetic desire that leads to reverence for the inorganic. This mimetic background sheds light on significant aspects of Sartre's existentialist thought—for instance, the underlying bad faith in the desire for being in-itself, embodied by the café waiter. This bad faith is not so much the result of the waiter not "being" a waiter as it is a mere expression of coquetry, which the waiter himself uses in an attempt to enhance his own attractiveness. It is no coincidence that Sartre—in a passage directly preceding that of the waiter—names the phenomenon of coquetry as a further example of bad faith.[172] For, in the end, it is the mechanical, almost automatic movements of the waiter that make him so appealing. Much like Kleist's "mechanical puppet," the waiter radiates complete self-assuredness, which fascinates those around him who suffer from the lack of being.[173] In the end, the waiter more than achieves his goal; he is successful in getting the attention of not only the guests in his café, but also Sartre himself, making him easily the most renowned servant in modern philosophy.

This mimetic interpretation of Sartre's waiter allows insight into how Girard uses Sartre's concept of "bad faith" to develop his own theory. Girard uses the concept chiefly to describe the duplicity produced by mimetic desire, all the while avoiding Sartre's philosophical usage of the term.[174]

Girard and Sartre also display parallels and differences with regard to their respective interpretations of man's religious nature. Girard expressly praises Sartre's insistence on man's "insurmountable" religious nature, in the wake of Nietzsche's proclamation of the death of God.[175] However, while Sartre interprets man's attempt to fuse the two forms of being (for-itself and in-itself) as the desire to become God, Girard sees it as a mere divinization of the role model, who, in the eyes of the desiring subject, remains unaffected by the lack of being. It is not the relationship between tangible being and consciousness that is central, but rather the relationship between human beings. Girard argues that the novelistic authors recognize this and describe the essence of man's predicament more precisely than Sartre.[176]

Here, as well, Girard's explicit use of Sartre's vocabulary displays where the two thinkers diverge. With regard to Stavrogin's character in Dostoyevsky's *Demons*, Girard comments: "Stavrogin is neither god *in himself* nor even *for himself*. . . . Stavrogin is god *for the Others*" (*Resurrection from the Underground*, 90). Of particular importance is the difference between the way Girard and Sartre view man's possible way out of modern idolatry. Whereas Sartre, a known atheist, propounds a kind of promethean humanism, seeing in Christianity an obstacle to man's complete self-assertion, Girard—much like Dostoyevsky and the church fathers—sees the imitation of a positive role model as the only way out of the "metaphysical underground."[177]

Kierkegaard, not Sartre, Elucidates Girard's Concept of Being

The differences between Sartre's and Girard's respective interpretations of man's religious nature point to a much more fundamental issue, which we must examine systematically in order to prevent any misunderstanding of the mimetic theory. Insofar as Girard takes up Sartre's concept of the lack of being to explicate the deeper roots of mimetic desire, he risks the danger of confirming all critics who accuse the mimetic theory of representing an ontology of violence.[178] Sartre's philosophy shows traces of such an ontologization of violence, and we saw with Kleist's essay "On the Marionette Theater" how the inextricable presence of violence in the Sartrean philosophical system can be interpreted mimetically. The autonomous individual, who is in perpetual denial of his dependence on others, is besieged by conflict in his search for a way out of his predicament. In *Being and Nothingness*, Sartre is unambiguous with regard to his claim that human relations are defined by this conflict: "Everything which may be said of me in my relations with the Other applies to him as well. While I attempt to free myself from the hold of the Other, the Other is trying to free himself from mine; while I seek to enslave the Other, the Other seeks to enslave me. . . . Conflict is the original meaning of being-for-others."[179]

One also finds in many of Sartre's other writings instances of his stance regarding the primacy of conflict in human relations. Consider the close of his famous drama, *No Exit*, where Garcin concludes: "Hell is—other people!"[180] Sartre is yet more direct in his analysis of anti-Semitism, concluding: "Violence . . . is necessary in human relations."[181] This ontologization of violence relativizes his thoughts on the anti-Semitic personality. In "Anti-Semite and Jew," he seems to argue that anti-Semitism is merely the consequence of a divided class society, which can be overcome by means of a revolution resulting in an abandonment of the classes. This thesis, however, backed by Sartre's own political beliefs, proves naive in the face of his earlier philosophy. Why should the negation of private property liberate human society from conflict, the cause of which is not found in the fight for tangible objects, but rather much deeper in the relations between individual human beings? Sartre's thought, viewed from the perspective of the mimetic theory, produces an image of humanity radically formed by the competition for being in which there is no possible way to overcome violence. Sartre himself makes note of this; his interesting remark that the majority of anti-Semites are "nonproducers," that is, in occupations in which their fate is dependent on others, suggests a link between anti-Semitism and competition, which alludes to a major issue facing contemporary society.[182] The more humans are forced to compete with one another, the more intensely they will seek flight into such intellectually reduced forms of being [tr. *Versteinerungen*]. Anti-Semitism or general xenophobia, as well as the flight into the commodification of mass consumerism, are all examples of such forms. Here and there one finds such references in Sartre's work; however, he decides not to provide any systematic explanation of their position within his philosophy.

The question remains whether Girard's claim—that man's lack of being leads to mimetic rivalry—represents just as much an ontology of violence as Sartre's arguments examined above. If the lack of being is an intrinsic part of human experience, with every human being thus forced into mimetic rivalry, it appears that violent conflict is a necessary and unavoidable consequence of humanness. Such an interpretation is certainly plausible, if one fails to consider the subtle differences between Girard and Sartre in a larger, more systematic context. Girard himself has only hinted at these differences in recent passing remarks, which point to the Christian basis of his thought.

With regard to the issue of the lack of being, the American theologian Charles K. Bellinger provides a significant advancement in the understanding of the mimetic theory. Bellinger, not distracted by the more superficial connection between Girard and Sartre, argues that the Danish philosopher Søren Kierkegaard can better elucidate Girard's concept.[183] In Kierkegaard's work, one incidentally finds numerous insights into the mimetic nature of human desire; Bellinger is so impressed by the Danish poet and thinker that he places him in the company of the major novelistic authors.[184] Let us now take a look at one of the many examples in Kierkegaard's work in which he reveals mimetic desire: the story of the "worried lily," taken from his *Upbuilding Discourses in Various Spirits*.[185]

Kierkegaard tells the story of a fair lily that lived in happiness on a field near a small brook together with other small flowers. A little bird comes to visit one day with stories of the world, in particular of a special place where there are many beautiful crown imperial lilies. The lily is filled with sadness and distress, for "the little bird had told it that of all the lilies the Crown Imperial was regarded as the most beautiful and was the envy of all other lilies." The small lily asks the bird to free it from the ground by the little creek in order to be planted by the other, more beautiful crown lilies. After having its roots pulled from the soil, however, the small lily withers on the way to the destination of its desire. Kierkegaard's interpretation of the story focuses on the mimetic causes for the lily's state of distress, in which he refers to the oftentimes tragic human tendency to measure oneself against others: "The lily is the human being. The naughty little bird is the restless mentality of comparison, which roams far and wide, fitfully and capriciously, and gleans the morbid knowledge of diversity; and just as the bird did not put itself in the lily's place, comparison does the same thing by either putting the human being in someone else's place or putting someone else in his place."[186] The moral of Kierkegaard's story is that human beings should come to the realization that they are created by God, in order to avoid the fate of the small lily that is ruined by envious comparison.

Kierkegaard's notion of human creatureliness leads to the question regarding the significance of the lack of being in his thought. According to Bellinger, Kierkegaard's concept for Sartre's lack of being is "anxiety," which finds its deeper roots in man's "creatureliness," the state of being created.[187] For Kierkegaard, anxiety is the consequence of man's dependence on his creator and the inability to escape his createdness. He argues that man is created with a free spirit, providing the perpetual potential to fall from God, thus condemning man to a life in fear and anxiety. As God's creation, humans are characterized by a fundamental, yet positive lack, which is directed toward God and finds consummation in divine love. In an exegesis of James 1:17–22, Kierkegaard remarks, for instance, that "to need the good and perfect gift from God is a perfection."[188] Where humans turn away from God through the Fall of Man, the lack of being—with its roots in man's creatureliness—leads to the worldly attempt to fill itself through the imitation of another's desire. This attempt, however, must end in despair and violence, as no worldly good or human being can negate the lack that only God himself can replenish.

Kierkegaard's supposition of man's positive lack of being, which he argues is an intrinsic part of human creaturality, represents a central Christian doctrine.[189] The best-known example for this is found in the writings of Saint Augustine, who at the beginning of his *Confessions* writes of an inner disquietude that has its roots in man's search for his creator. Augustine, addressing God, refers to man as a "piece of Your creation," after which he alludes to the human lack of being, which only God can replenish: "You prompt us yourself to find satisfaction in appraising you, since you made us tilted toward you, and our heart is unstable until stabilized in you."[190] In a similar way to Augustine and Kierkegaard, the Catholic philosopher Josef

Pieper also describes man, on account of his creatureliness, as "by nature a needful being; he is himself one vast need."[191]

Where Girard speaks of man's fundamental lack of being, he means this fundamentally positive lack granted by God in the process of creation. However, his arguments for the problematic nature of the lack of being, with regard to the role it plays in causing interpersonal strife, imply the state of man after the Fall, in which salvation is needed to overcome rivalry and violence. From the perspective of the mimetic theory, humans after the Fall must refocus their desire on God in order to avoid worldly seduction and to escape their violent nature.[192] Insofar as Girard holds this as a plausible way out of violence, his mimetic theory represents a fundamental shift from other modes of thought, which prevent human beings from directing their desire at a transcendental God and therefore remain necessarily and eternally plagued by violence. Sartre diverges directly from Girard's notion that man is incapable of overcoming interpersonal violence without the help of the biblical God. He radically rejects the notion of a creator-God and the idea of man being "created," equating it with the "total enslavement" of humanity.[193] For Sartre, "being-created-by-God" is analogous to alienation: it is akin to one "outside" teaching those "inside" what and how to be, or, in Sartrean terms, it implies that "being-an-object-for-God" is more real than being "for-itself."[194]

Kierkegaard and Girard consciously place their work in the context of the Christian tradition. For both thinkers, the biblical account of the Fall of Man takes on central significance, whereas Sartre rejects this framework. He offers his own version of the Fall, but this account inverts the very meaning of the biblical story. From the perspective of the Bible, the Fall stands for man's proud rejection of his own createdness, and the accompanying desire to usurp God's place as creator. After the Fall, Adam and Eve were genuinely ashamed of their own behavior. For Sartre, the Fall of Man does not result from misbehavior, but rather from the mere contact with the Other: "My original fall is the existence of the Other."[195] Human beings, through the eyes of others, become "defenseless objects," "things," that evoke the original shame of Adam and Eve: "Shame is the feeling of an original fall, not because of the fact that I may have committed this or that particular fault but simply that I have 'fallen' into the world in the midst of things and that I need the mediation of the Other in order to be what I am."[196] Where the Bible contends that pride led to the Fall of Man, Sartre describes the cause as an "authentic attitude . . . by which I apprehend myself as the free object by which the Other gets his being-other."[197] Sartre's espousal of man's radical autonomy breaks with the biblical tradition and leads ultimately to the ontology of violence that characterizes his concept of the lack of being. Girard's mimetic theory differs fundamentally from this position.

Mimetic Passions of Competition: Vanity, Pride, and Envy

In order to position Girard's theory within the scope of occidental thought, one must take into account more than just the concept of mimesis. For as mimesis has been essentially avoided in the Western tradition when it comes to the study of human desire, analysis of the concept neither shows any predecessors to Girard, nor is it sufficient for a proper demonstration of the specific profile of the mimetic theory. One must explore the full scope of what Girard refers to as mimetic desire, in order to approach an understanding of the concept. As a first step, let us here turn to a discussion of passions such as pride, vanity, and envy, which have long received significant attention in the course of occidental thought. These passions are at the core of the more extreme manifestations of mimetic desire; moreover, theoretical observations of these passions, which span the entire occidental tradition, can provide a more specific context of the mimetic theory than any mere historical analysis of the concept of mimesis. Where discussions of vanity, envy, or other passions connected with competition emerge, in other words, one is certain to find interesting insights into the mimetic nature of desire.

Augustine

A first great predecessor to Girard's mimetic theory is the Latin church father Augustine of Hippo.

Girard was already conscious of Augustine's influence while working on his first book, *Deceit, Desire and the Novel*, a central part of which contains reference to Augustine's knowledge of self-destructive pride.[198] However, in the rest of the book, Girard's spiritual proximity to the church father remains merely implicit. In an essay published two years thereafter, Girard first mentions Augustine's *Confessions* as an archetype of the conversion found in the novelistic works that led to the discovery of mimetic desire.[199] It comes as no surprise, therefore, that Girard concedes in *Quand ces choses commenceront* that "three-fourths of that which I have said is already found in St. Augustine" (196).[200]

Indeed, the *Confessions* are formed in large part by Augustine's understanding that human desire is based on the imitation of role models.[201] The most telling example of this is perhaps found in the story of Augustine's friend Alypius, who denounces the gladiator battles, the most popular form of entertainment in fifth-century Rome. Alypius accompanies Augustine and friends to the Colosseum and says he will keep his eyes closed during the most gruesome of the battles, in order to "stand above them and the show." Inside, however, he is unable to withstand the mimetic contagion; he is quickly drawn in by the power of the crowd and becomes an excited mediator of its bloodthirsty passion:

> For when the fight took a dramatic turn, a huge roar from the crowd crashed over him. Yielding to curiosity—though determined to scorn and reject what he saw, no matter its nature—he opened his eyes. The wound given to the gladiator he now wished to see was nothing to the wound inflicted on his soul. His fall was sadder than the fighter's, at which the crowd was cheering. That shout, entering his ears, made his eyes fly open. The mind thus buffeted and overthrown was more rash than steady, and all the weaker for reliance on itself rather than on you. The minute he saw blood, he was sipping animality, and turned no more away. With eyes glued to the spectacle, he absentmindedly gulped down frenzies. He took a complicit joy in the fighting, and was drunk with delight at the cruelty. No longer the person he was when he entered, he was now entered into the crowd, at one with those who forced him there. More—he stared, he shouted, he burned, he took away the madness he had found there and followed it back again, not only with those who had first drawn him, but dragging them and others on his own.[202]

Examples of mimetic desire appear in Augustine's text primarily in connection with passions such as vanity, pride, and envy. He contends that already among infants, envy is an important component of desire. It is not the scarcity of material goods that awakens jealous rivalry, but rather the sight of the other: "With my own eyes I was a present witness at what we have all observed, a tiny thing's fierce competitiveness—how, though he could not speak, he made himself clear by his sudden pallor and the sour contortion of his features at a rival for the nipple. Mothers and nurses claim they can check the tantrum by some trick of their trade, treating as harmless a baby's effort to deprive another of the food it depends on, though the milk flows abundantly for both."[203] Envy remains throughout childhood and manifests itself in rivalry between adolescents. Its presence is just as strong, however, among the adults and teachers who discipline them: "Who, in these terms, was worse—my teacher, who writhed with bitter envy when caught in a solecism by a fellow pedant, or I, when I resented losing my ball game to a fellow player?"[204]

At the heart of the *Confessions* is Augustine's discovery of his own mimetic nature. His observations of Alypius describe likewise the core of his own being. Augustine comes to the realization that from the beginning, he was always intrigued by the crowd; moreover, that he was driven by mere pride and vanity.[205] A famous example of this is found in the stealing of the pears, which he committed purely out of peer pressure and the excitement of following his friends.[206] From age nineteen to twenty-eight—during his Manichean period—Augustine describes himself as being seduced by the crowd, full of "arrogance" and empty vanity, and in pursuit of "the bauble fame, applause in the arena for poetry contests, for crownings with a flimsy garland and the puerilities of the stage."[207] He later becomes fascinated by the Roman orator Hierius, whose allure, Augustine admits, is not only based on his impressive speeches: "Actually, I was more taken by what others thought of him, by the way they lavished praise on him."[208] "Enthusiasm," he writes further, "kindles enthusiasm, and praise can cause admiration when the praise is believed to be heartfelt."[209] Augustine admires Hierius "as I would be admired myself, giddy pride leading me astray to be 'buffeted by every wind.'"[210] Augustine runs through a series of different role models until he finally converts to Christianity, a process that is incidentally also influenced by the example of others.

Augustine's theological system is largely determined by his insight into the fundamental necessity of mediation for human desire. Just as Girard argues that human beings are ultimately faced with the choice between following divine and human role models, Augustine also classifies the human race into "two branches," namely, those "who live by human standards" and those "who live according to God's will."[211] These two different models entail two different types of love.[212] Where human beings are taken as role models, Augustine speaks of the love of "oneself," or *amor sui*, which seeks fame "from other human beings" and is connected with "hubris" or "pride." Divine love, or *amor Dei*, by contrast, finds its "highest glory in God" and is rooted in humility. Original Sin is for Augustine man's denial of God and, moreover, the proud attempt to take God's place. Augustine describes this sin as a "perverse imitation" of God, or *perversa imitatio Dei*, a form of vain madness identical to the essence of the devil.[213]

Next to the biblical tradition, Augustine's theological system is based most substantially on the philosophy of Plato. Augustine shares Plato's ontology of imitation in his recognition of man's tendency to "model oneself on the object of one's worship" as the "core of all religion."[214] He also praises Plato's ethics, which in his view is ultimately directed at divine imitation.[215] Under the influence of Plato's ethical system, Augustine develops his comparative differentiation of human desire, which has shaped the entire Christian tradition—and which gains a new plausibility in the context of Girard's mimetic theory. Augustine separates desire according to its temporal or eternal goods. Only eternal goods, Augustine contends, are worthy of human aspiration, for this desire is humanity's ultimate aim. Earthly goods should be utilized only to achieve the joy of eternal happiness.[216] This differentiation with regard to the potential aim of human desire—in Augustine's words, between eternal pleasure, *frui*, and earthly utility, *uti*—allows one to separate life-enhancing forms of mimesis from destructive forms. On the one hand, Augustine shows that worldly desire results in the disastrous consequences of mimetic desire, as it divides humans in rivalry over goods that cannot be shared. On the other hand, however, Augustine fashions a way out of this vicious cycle; the more humans direct their desire at eternal goods—such as the desire of God (*fruitio Dei*)—the more fulfilling this desire becomes. Throughout his work, Augustine provides insightful examples for both the rivalrous desire that pervades the earthly city, and the overcoming of this desire in the heavenly city.

The earthly city, according to Augustine, is branded by self-love, which results in the inverted imitation of God discussed above and an atmosphere of desire that can lead only to conflict: "The earthly city . . . has its good in this world, and rejoices to participate in it with such gladness as can be derived from things of such a kind. And since this is not the kind of good that causes no frustrations to those enamored of it, the earthly city is generally divided against itself by litigation, by wars, by battles, by the pursuit of victories that bring death with them or at best are doomed to death."[217] Augustine names the scarcity of objects as a deeper cause for the ubiquity of violence in the earthly city, alluding to one of the central consequences of mimetic desire where he says that an "unhappy poverty" prevails when the warring sections contend for objects that they cannot "both possess at the same time."[218] He cites the example of the twin brothers Romulus and Remus, whose relationship ends in murder over their fight for exclusive rule of the Roman Empire: "Both sought the glory of establishing the Roman state, but a joint foundation would not bring to each the glory that a single founder would enjoy."[219] Augustine argues that the violence pervading humanity is rooted in the mimetic passions of pride and envy. Both are entirely worldly desires, directed inexorably at objects that cannot be shared, and by their nature lead to enmity among humans. In *On True Religion*, Augustine calls envy a "terrible vice, by which you are bound to be tormented and defeated, if you are unwilling to be conquered and surpassed in temporal matters."[220]

The heavenly city, by contrast, is characterized by the humble imitation of God, which is free of the violence connected with mimetic rivalry. In God's love, human beings desire an object that does not divide, but rather brings them together in harmony; the more humans pursue the imitation of God, the more they are bound in reciprocal love. Augustine names Abel as an archetypal citizen of the heavenly city who rejects the worldly desire for dominion in favor of God's love: "A man's possession of goodness is in no way diminished by the arrival, or the continuance, of a sharer in it; indeed, goodness is a possession enjoyed more widely by the united affection of partners in that possession in proportion to the harmony that exists among them. In fact, anyone who refuses to enjoy this possession in partnership will not enjoy it at all; and he will find that he possesses it in ampler measure in proportion to his ability to love his partner in it."[221] Augustine sees in the imitation of God's love the only possible way to avoid envy, which is perhaps the principle divisive consequence of mimetic desire: "So, if you only love what cannot be snatched out of its lover's hand, you undoubtedly remain unbeaten and are not tormented in any way by jealousy. You are loving something, after all, for which all the more abundant gratitude is felt, the greater the number of those who come to love and obtain it."[222]

The mimetic theory makes Augustine's differentiation between eternal and temporal goods plausible. By its very nature, mimetic desire directs human beings towards the same objects, giving the nature of the object itself control over whether desire ends in violent conflict—as in the Hobbesian war of all against all—or in the mutual enrichment of humanity on its way towards its eternal aim.

Christian Order of Goods [tr. Christliche Güterlehre]

Augustine's differentiation between eternal and temporal goods is a cornerstone of the Christian ethical system, which provides central guidance for avoiding the mimetic passion of envy. One can find parallels to Augustine's differentiation in the work of several important Christian thinkers—for instance, Thomas Aquinas. In his treatise on envy, Aquinas examines the ways in which emulation and envy relate to one another, a question which today is still very relevant. Aquinas's answer refers initially to Aristotle and consists of the differentiation between positive emulation and negative envy. He goes beyond Aristotle, however, in his exploration of zealous imitation. Aquinas follows Augustine in his argument that the essential difference between emulation and envy lies in the question of temporal and eternal desires: "If zeal is about virtuous goods it is laudable. Scripture (I Corinthians 14:1) says, *Be zealous for spiritual gifts.* If zeal is about temporal goods it may or may not be sinful."[223] Aquinas draws on the differentiation between temporal and eternal goods in his arguments for a way out of the dangers posed by mimetic rivalry, which can very easily plague relations between people living in close contact—such as brothers—whose desires are directed at the same objects. In the case of friars living together, however, Aquinas argues that such conflicts are not to be expected, because servants of God tend to disregard such divisive earthly desires.[224]

Dante's *Divine Comedy* offers the most striking literary example of the Christian order of goods and its connection to the consequences of mimetic desire. In reference to Augustine's insight into the necessary disunity caused by desire of earthly goods—and the contrary consequences of desire of eternal goods—Dante also distinguishes clearly between envy and God's love:

Because you make things of this world your goal,
which are diminished as each shares in them,
Envy pumps hard the bellows for your sighs.

But if your love were for the lofty sphere,
your cravings would aspire for the heights.
And fear of loss would not oppress your heart;

the more there are up there who speak of 'ours,'
the more each one possesses and the more
Charity burns intensely in that realm.[225]

At the outset of modernity, one finds Blaise Pascal's insight concerning the Christian order of goods as an answer to the problem of envy. Pascal insists that humanity must recognize that the "true good" is found in God alone, that which "all can possess at once, without diminution and without envy."[226]

The German philosopher Max Scheler, at the beginning of the twentieth century, incorporates the Christian order of goods in his hierarchical system of values. From the perspective of the mimetic theory, Scheler's remark concerning the way a value's worth is affected by its divisibility is of particular importance: "There is . . . no question that values are 'higher' *the less they are divisible*, that is, the *less* they must be divided in *participation by several*."[227] Scheler argues that material values, on account of their divisibility, are subordinate to "divine" values that unite human beings instead of dividing them: "Nothing unites beings more immediately and intimately . . . than the common worship and adoration of the 'holy,' which by its nature excludes a 'material' bearer, though not a symbolic one. . . . No matter how men have been divided by what came to be considered holy in history (e.g., wars of religion, denominational quarrels), it lies in the essence of the intention toward the holy to unite and join together. All possible divisions are based solely on symbols and techniques, not on the holy itself."[228] Scheler's reference to the history of religious wars, however, makes it clear that concentration on the essence of values alone is insufficient for an explanation of human conflict. The desire for material as well as nonmaterial objects, as long as they remain worldly, can be equally conflictual.[229] As we will see in more depth further on, Girard criticizes Scheler's overly exclusive focus on the desirability of objects,

arguing that this prevents the philosopher from discovering the more fundamental mimetic processes governing desire.

Girard himself does not offer any explicit analysis of the Christian order
of goods in his work, though his references to Augustine and Dante make
it clear that his theory is greatly influenced by the Christian tradition. In
his early essay on the adulterous couple Paolo and Francesca—who inhabit
the fifth circle in Dante's *Inferno*—Girard criticizes those who adore Dante's
portrayal for its praise of romantic passion, arguing that this reading misses
Dante's insight into the mimetic origins of Paolo and Francesca's love. Girard
points out that the two did not fall in love spontaneously—as the romantic
reading suggests—but rather simply imitated the desires of Lancelot and
Guinevere, the two main characters of the book the two were reading during
the process of courtship. For Girard, Paolo and Francesca are in hell because
they chose the fictive desires of an arbitrary book over the Word of God.
"The Word of man becomes the Word of the devil if it usurps the place of
the divine Word in our souls" (*To Double Business Bound*, 2). Girard's arguments here are an indirect reference to the Christian ethical tradition, which
adheres to the necessity of human desire being directed towards an eternal,
transcendent end.

"Reflection" or "Revelation" of Mimetic Desire

While Girard argues that Augustine and the great European novelists
pave the way for the revelation of mimetic desire, he is critical of modern
philosophy and argues that the former is vastly superior when it comes to
an understanding of desire. At first glance, Girard's general criticism seems
rather exaggerated, and one can perhaps attribute it to his lack of exposure
to the modern philosophical tradition.[230] A number of philosophers writing
at the dawn of the modern world of competition—such as Hobbes, Spinoza,
Rousseau, and Kant, to name only the most well-known—describe the
consequences of mimetic desire where they speak of emotions such as pride,
vanity, jealousy, and envy. Similar to Augustine, who was able to study the
mimetic passions during the crisis-ridden period of the fall of the Roman
Empire, these philosophers were able to observe the reemergence of these
passions at the outbreak of modernity. Girard's objection to modern philosophy is not due solely to his overlooking of these philosophical analyses of

mimesis, but rather more to his general suspicion that this mode of analysis is unable to uncover the roots of mimetic desire. With regard to literature, he distinguishes systematically between novelists whose work merely *reflects* mimetic desire, and those who fully *reveal* its roots.[231] As we will see from analysis of Hobbes and Rousseau, Girard places modern philosophy in the former category: In order to attain the depth of Augustine or Dostoyevsky, who expose the roots of mimetic passion, Girard argues that philosophers such as Hobbes or Rousseau must first address and overcome their own pride. On a deeper level, the difference between reflection and revelation of mimetic desire is connected to a necessary openness to transcendence. If this openness is lacking, there is no possibility for any authentic conversion, with any analysis of mimetic desire made from this perspective remaining a mere reflection of the phenomenon.

Thomas Hobbes

A first example of the modern analysis of mimetic passion is offered by the English political philosopher Thomas Hobbes, whose thought is situated on the threshold of modernity.[232] At the time Hobbes began writing, the class-based society of eighteenth-century England was already dissolving, and social equality was beginning to spread throughout the population, giving rise to competition and rivalry that posed a growing threat to social relations. Hobbes compares life in this world of competition to a "race" in which there is "no other goal . . . but being foremost."[233] Hobbes's view of life as a race converges on key examples found in literature. Goethe's Werther is likewise aware that the constant need to compare oneself with one's peers can produce true self-worth when "one keeps up with others or even gets ahead of them."[234] In a similar way, Dostoyevsky's Underground Man is assailed by the perpetual desire to be foremost.[235] By comparing life—or rather the individual emotions connected with human striving—to a race, Hobbes characterizes these emotions as mimetic passions that are fueled by competitive desire:

> To endeavour is appetite.
> To be remiss is sensuality.
> To consider them behind is glory.
> To be holden, hatred.

To turn back, repentance.

To be in breath, hope.

To be weary, despair.

To endeavour to overtake the next, emulation.

To supplant or overthrow, envy.

To resolve to break through a stop foreseen courage.

To break through a sudden stop anger.

To break through with ease, magnanimity.

To lose ground by little hindrances, pusillanimity.

To fall on the sudden is disposition to weep.

To see another fall disposition to laugh.

To see one out-gone whom we would not is pity.

To see one out-go we would not, is indignation.

To hold fast by another is to love.

To carry him on that so holdeth, is charity.

To hurt one's-self for haste is shame.

Continually to be out-gone is misery.

Continually to out-go the next before is felicity.

And to forsake the course is to die.[236]

These mimetic passions play a significant role in Hobbes's political philosophy. In his study of Hobbes, Leo Strauss subsumes all the emotions that emerge in Hobbesian discourse under the concept of vanity, the exact concept Stendhal uses for his interpretation of mimetic desire.[237] Hobbes himself uses the term "vainglory," which he also identifies directly with ostentation and pride.[238] He calls the "imitation of others" a clear sign of vanity, and disdains the "futile practice" of young people to imitate role models from romance novels—a clear, albeit indirect, reference to quixotic ambition.[239] Vanity enters the foreground of Hobbes's inquiry through his analysis of the difference between the world of social species—such as bees and ants—and the human world, which he finds pervaded by the "competition for honour and dignity," and consequently "Envy and Hatred, and finally Warre."[240] One sees from the title of his masterpiece, *Leviathan* (King of the Proud), how much importance Hobbes attributes to the concepts of pride and envy, which are incidentally also passions that Girard links with mimetic desire.[241] "Hitherto I have set forth the nature of Man, (whose Pride and other Passions have compelled him to submit himself to Government;) together with the great power of his Governour, whom I compared to Leviathan, taking that comparison out of the two last verses of the one-and-fortieth of *Job*; where God, having set forth the great power of *Leviathan*, calleth him King of the Proud."[242]

Hobbes places imitation at the heart of his interpretation of mankind. In *Behemoth*, his historical analysis of the English Civil War, the characters are so branded by their mimetic tendencies—as well as by the passions of ambition and envy—that the political philosopher Stephen Holmes refers to man in this atmosphere as the "imitative being," or *L'homme copie*.[243]

For Hobbes, interpersonal relations are determined by competition, which he interprets as the perpetual need to compare oneself to others. With regard to the passions addressed above in his comparison of life to a "race," Hobbes sees "all joy and grief of mind consisting . . . in a contention for precedence to them with whom they compare themselves."[244] Power, honor, and prestige are no longer viewed by humans as absolutely great, but rather as only achievable by means of competition. Hobbes thus defines "Naturall Power" in *Leviathan* as "the eminence of the Faculties of Body, or Mind."[245] Honor, according to Hobbes, is a further manifestation of power, which also possesses no absolute value. Much like the way prices of goods fluctuate in markets, honor is dependent on the evaluation of other people, or in other words, on the concept of comparison: "The manifestation of the Value we set on one another, is that which is commonly called Honouring and Dishonouring. To Value a man at a high rate, is to *Honour* him; at a low rate, is to *Dishonour* him. But high, and low, in this case, is to be understood by comparison to the rate that each man setteth on himselfe."[246] However, with power depending completely on the perception of the other, the desire for it becomes boundless in the human world. This idea is at the base of Hobbes's famous remark in *Leviathan* concerning "humanity's general inclination of . . . a perpetual and restless desire of Power after power, that ceaseth only in death."[247] One finds a similar passage in an earlier work that confirms Hobbes's connection between the limitless striving for power and the mimetic comparison with other people. For as soon as humans "come to the outmost degree of one kind of power, they pursue some other, as long as in any kind they think themselves behind any other."[248]

Hobbes's realistic view of modern society clarifies his ability to describe—as we saw above—the consequences of competition in the modern world. He recognizes that the constitution of desire brings humans into the constant situation of mutually desiring the same objects. When these objects cannot be shared, the result is rivalry, violence, and war.

Hobbes proposes that the absolute state can prevent civil war and other internal conflict by transforming internal rivalries into competition between the individual states. This by no means solves the problem of pride, however, but merely displaces it. Hobbes is unable to overcome mimetic desire at its roots and therefore belongs to the list of authors who merely reflect its consequences. On the surface, Girard's theory appears identical to Hobbes's philosophy; one could say that both represent an ontology of violence in which rivalry and conflict between humans remain unavoidable. However, this argument fails to take into account the fundamental difference between the mimetic theory and Hobbes's philosophy.

While Girard's theory argues expressly for openness to transcendence and, together with Augustine and the Christian tradition, sees in God the only way to overcome the violence of an intrinsically competitive mimesis, Hobbes expressly rules out any possible way of escaping man's violent nature. Eric Voegelin's comparative analysis of Augustine and Hobbes emphasizes Hobbes's exclusion of transcendence as one of the aspects that differentiates the two. Voegelin claims that Hobbesian pride corresponds to Augustine's archetypal *amor sui*, or proud self-love.[249] The central difference between Augustine and Hobbes is found in Hobbes's insistence that this "disoriented type" is man's intrinsic nature, whereas Augustine contrasts proud beings with those who pursue *amor Dei*, or the love of God.[250] Voegelin argues that Hobbes's anthropology is characterized by the reduction of human existence to *amor sui*, which corresponds to the immanence of his philosophy. For Hobbes, there is no *fruitio Dei*, or indulgence in God, which for Augustine and the Christian tradition is the ultimate goal of all human aspiration.[251] All that remains in Hobbes's universe is the fear of death, or *summum malum*, and the struggle for worldly precedence. It follows logically that this idea of man results in Hobbes's arguments for the absolute state. The "King of the Proud"—Hobbes's Leviathan—"must break the *amor sui* that cannot be relieved by the *amor Dei*."[252]

Benedict de Spinoza

Hobbes is not the only philosopher at the dawn of the modern world to recognize the significance of competition for human desire.[253] The Dutch philosopher Benedict de Spinoza—in his *Tractatus Theologico-Politicus*—also uses the metaphor of a race to describe the negative consequences of competition: "And so it comes to pass, that, as all are equally eager to be first, they fall to strife, and do their utmost mutually to oppress one another."[254] Spinoza systematizes his conception of desire in his anthropological magnum opus, *The Ethics*. The point of origin for these reflections is established by Spinoza's proposition of the link between imitation and emotion:

> PROP.: *By the very fact that we conceive a thing, which is like ourselves, and which we have not regarded with any emotion, to be affected with any emotion, we are ourselves affected with a like emotion* (affectus).
>
> Note I.—*This imitation of emotions, when it is referred to pain, is called compassion; when it is referred to desire, it is called emulation, which is nothing else but the desire of anything, engendered in us by the fact that we conceive that others have the like desire.*[255]

Human desire for material objects, Spinoza proposes further, is either reinforced or impaired by imitation:

> PROP.: *If we conceive that anyone loves, desires, or hates anything which we ourselves love, desire, or hate, we shall thereupon regard the thing in question with more steadfast love, etc. On the contrary, if we think that anyone shrinks from something that we love, we shall undergo vacillations of soul.*
>
> Corollary.—From the foregoing . . . it follows that everyone endeavors, as far as possible, to cause others to love what he himself loves, and to hate what he himself hates: as the poet says: "As lovers let us share every hope and every fear: iron-hearted were he who should love what the other leaves."[256]

Spinoza explains that the striving for mimetic confirmation of desire can lead quickly to reciprocal hatred, as one can see in his commentary of the above proposition:

Note.—This endeavor to bring it about, that our own likes and dislikes should meet with universal approval, is really ambition . . . ; wherefore we see that everyone by nature desires (*appetere*), that the rest of mankind should live according to his own individual disposition: when such a desire is equally present in all, everyone stands in everyone else's way, and in wishing to be loved or praised by all, all become mutually hateful.[257]

The hatred-inducing desire for all to follow one's own example is connected inextricably to envy, as Spinoza demonstrates in the following proposition:

PROP.: *If we conceive that anyone takes delight in something, which only one person can possess, we shall endeavor to bring it about that the man in question shall not gain possession thereof.*[258]

Spinoza refers in his commentary to the close relation of envy and pity, which he describes explicitly as two imitative emotions:

Note.—We thus see that man's nature is generally so constituted, that he takes pity on those who fare ill, and envies those who fare well with an amount of hatred proportioned to his own love for the goods in their possession. Further, we see that from the same property of human nature, whence it follows that men are merciful, it follows also that they are envious and ambitious. Lastly, if we make appeal to Experience, we shall find that she entirely confirms what we have said; more especially if we turn our attention to the first years of our life. We find that children, whose body is continually, as it were, in equilibrium, laugh or cry simply because they see others laughing or crying; moreover, they desire forthwith to imitate whatever they see others doing, and to possess themselves of whatever they conceive as delighting others.[259]

Let us now turn to literature to conclude this brief summary of Spinoza's position. Spinoza himself refers to many literary examples—e.g., Ovid's love poem *Amores*—in order to illustrate his conception of mimetic desire. From a literary perspective, however, the influence of Spinoza's philosophy on Goethe is most worthy of mention. Goethe refers to his many readings of *The Ethics* as a significant contribution to an understanding of his own "whimsical existence." The "all-composing calmness" of Spinoza's philosophy engendered in Goethe the first instances of tranquillity from his "all-disturbing activity."[260] For Goethe, Spinoza's thoughts on the necessity of the other for confirmation of one's own desire was corroboration of a peculiar experience he encountered while working on *The Sorrows of Young Werther.* The impetus for the novel was Goethe's own infatuation with Charlotte Buff; a closer look, however, shows that he was just as obsessed with his rival, Johann Heinrich Merck, from whom he was seeking confirmation of his own desire. Merck's indifference to Charlotte Buff provided Goethe with first-hand experience of Spinoza's remarks concerning the fickleness of human desire: "I could scarcely wait any time, till I had introduced him to Charlotte; but his presence in this circle did me no good: for . . . so did he, by his indifference toward that beloved person, cause me no joy, even if he did not make me waver."[261] These experiences with Merck allowed Goethe to gain the insights into desire found in the quotation at the top of this chapter regarding the "dangers" of introducing a friend to one's romantic partner. Goethe's knowledge, gained from experience, converges with that found in Spinoza's philosophical discourse outlining the connection between imitation and emotion.

Jean-Jacques Rousseau

In addition to Hobbes and Spinoza, one must name Rousseau as a thinker who also recognizes the mimetic passions of vanity, pride, and envy as phenomena that shape the modern world. Rousseau uses the central concept of *amour-propre*, a type of competitive self-love, to describe the world of mimetic desire, which he juxtaposes with the self-assured love, *amour de soi*, of the naive man of nature.[262] Whereas *amour de soi* is based on the self in healthy egocentricity, Rousseau describes *amour-propre* as based completely on the comparison with others: "Self-love, which regards only ourselves, is contented when our true needs are satisfied. But *amour-propre*, which makes comparisons, is never content and never could be, because this sentiment, preferring ourselves to others, also demands others to prefer us to themselves, which is impossible. This is how the gentle and affectionate passions are born of self-love, and how the hateful and irascible passions are born of *amour-propre.*"[263] Rousseau's *amour-propre* is later adapted by Proust in his novelistic creation and is thus connected with Girard's mimetic desire. Just as Rousseau describes *amour-propre* as formed by the comparison with others, Proust likewise stresses the self-alienation that accompanies this "spirit of imitation."[264] The mimetic passions of vanity, pride, and envy are in Rousseau's eyes an immediate product of the amour-propre that manifests itself first in society:

> Everyone began to look at everyone else and to wish to be looked at himself, and public esteem acquired a price. The one who sang or danced best, the handsomest, the strongest, the most skillful or the most eloquent came to be the most highly regarded; and this was the first step at once toward inequality and vice: from these first preferences arose vanity and contempt on the one hand, and shame and envy on the other; and the fermentation caused by these new leavens eventually produced compounds fatal to happiness and innocence.[265]

Rousseau's link between *amour-propre* that shapes society and outward comparison is so pronounced that in some places he even refers to it as *amour comparative*, or "comparative love."[266] We have already noted above the significance of comparative love for Rousseau's conception of human sexuality in society. This phenomenon, however, is of great import for Rousseau in all areas of human life; he sees both the positive and the far more numerous negative achievements of humanity as a product of competitive self-love. Like Hobbes, Rousseau uses the metaphor of the race to describe the destructive potential of perpetual comparison:

> I would show how much this universal desire for reputation, honors, and preferment which consumes us all exercises and compares talents and strengths, how much it excites and multiplies the passions and, in making all men competitors, rivals, or rather enemies, how many reverses, how many successes, how many catastrophes of every kind it daily causes by leading so many Contenders to enter the same lists: I would show that it is to this ardor to be talked about, to this frenzy to achieve distinction which almost always keeps us outside ourselves, that we owe what is best and what is worst among men, our virtues and our vices, our Sciences and our errors,

our Conquerors and our Philosophers; that is to say a multitude of bad
things for a small number of good things.[267]

Like Hobbes, Rousseau represents a break from the Christian tradition,
which in itself is significant for a study of the mimetic theory. In contrast
to Hobbes, Rousseau sees the human being confronted with competitive
amour-propre only in society; the peaceful man of nature finds himself not
in a war of all against all, but rather in a condition of tranquillity in which
human beings coexist in natural harmony. At first glance, this appears to converge on the philosophy of Pascal or Malebranche, thinkers who argue—in
accordance with the Christian teachings of Original Sin—for a differentiation between the evil self-love that emerged after the Fall of Man and the
peaceful love that existed before in the Garden of Eden.[268] This impression
proves deceptive, however, as Rousseau's anthropology stands in distinct
contrast to the biblical tradition. While Augustine identifies solipsistic self-
love (*amor sui*) with pride, thus contrasting it to the love of God (*amor Dei*),
Rousseau characterizes the asocial, or natural condition of man as unequivocally positive. For Augustine—and the Christian tradition influenced by
him—the only positive form of self-love is that which is directed at God's
love; autonomous self-love is the sheer embodiment of the Fall of Man that
leads inexorably to the negative aspects that Rousseau himself observes in the
amour-propre of man in society. Rousseau interprets the autonomous man of
nature by contrast as a completely innocent and peaceful being. The essential
characteristic and precondition of Rousseau's peaceful man of nature is his
lack of sociability (*fehlende Geselligkeit*).[269] He lives in absolute self-assurance
and in isolation from all other human beings, and embodies the ideal of the
"truly happy being," which, like God, must remain "solitary."[270] Man's actual
need for society, Rousseau argues, is in the final analysis merely a concession
of his "weakness."[271] It is thus no surprise that Rousseau recommends Daniel
Defoe's novel *Robinson Crusoe* as the first book in the "natural education" of
his protégé, Émile.[272]

From the perspective of the mimetic theory, Rousseau's idea of the asocial man of nature is merely a product of the romantic striving for individual
autonomy, which leads inevitably to the abyss of mimetic desire that Rousseau himself so aptly describes in his critical analysis of human society.[273] In
his autobiographical *Reveries of the Solitary Walker*, it becomes clear that the

positive self-love of man in nature corresponds to Rousseau's own yearning for quasi-divine self-sufficiency.[274] As much as Girard's description of mimetic rivalry coincides with Rousseau's insight into the essence of competitive *amour-propre*, the two diverge just as much with regard to the deeper causes of man's destructive competitive disposition. Girard's stance is similar to that of Augustine or Pascal in that he sees the actual cause for the self-destructive tendencies of mankind in the striving for individual autonomy, rooted in Original Sin, which Rousseau praises in his romantic anthropology. Girard uses a comparative analysis of Rousseau and Dostoyevsky to highlight the difference—discussed above—between the romantic reflection and the novelistic revelation of mimetic desire.[275] Dostoyevsky's early work, which was clearly influenced by eighteenth-century Romanticism, shows many similarities to Rousseau's romance novel *Julie, or the New Heloise.* One finds numerous reflections of mimetic desire in this novel, without, however, any deeper explanation of the phenomenon. While Dostoyevsky's later works transcend mere reflection of the mimetic nature of desire and delve into his own personal romantic entanglements, Rousseau is unable to offer any equivalent study. Both are located on the precipice of romantic self-divinization; only Dostoyevsky, however, is able to overcome the seduction of autonomy in his portrayal of mimetic desire as a (self)-destructive phenomenon. Rousseau, on account of his unwillingness to abandon his romantic individuality, was ultimately struck by madness, a fate Dostoyevsky incidentally describes as the only alternative to authentic conversion.[276] Similar to Ivan Karamazov, whose mental breakdown in *The Brothers Karamazov* results in hallucinations of his double-self, Rousseau himself encounters symptoms of paranoid schizophrenia that are manifest in discourse between his two selves in his late work *Rousseau: Judge of Jean-Jacques.* Like Nietzsche, Rousseau also belongs to the radical defenders of the romantic ideal who in the end were forced to pay the full price for their position.

However, putting aside Rousseau's critical stance towards human sociality, he also argues that the peaceful man of nature is not fully free of mimetic tendencies and can thus be seen as an important precursor for Girard. Just as many thinkers before and after him, Rousseau recognizes that imitation is an integral human trait that represents man's essential difference from animals. Human beings in the state of nature, according to Rousseau, compensate for lacking instincts by means of imitation. Men "would observe and imitate their industry, and thus attain even to the instinct of the beasts, with the advantage that, whereas every species of brutes was confined to one particular instinct, man who perhaps has not any one peculiar to himself, would appropriate them all."[277] This distinct reference to man's imitative nature is reinforced by Rousseau's view that "natural pity," which he interprets primarily as the capacity for "identification," is necessary for peaceful harmony in nature.[278] This natural compassion—which drives man to identification with all other living beings, thus mitigating and modifying self-love—represents for Rousseau the epitome of "natural goodness." He argues that compassion is based on a trait accessible to all living beings that he equates with natural "sentience."[279] This capacity, meanwhile, which Rousseau perceives as the "faculty of attaching our affections to beings who are foreign to us," can easily be demonstrated as a basic form of mimesis.[280] For Rousseau, this is the source of all passion, accounting for both the negative manifestations of vanity, pride, and envy, as well as positive compassion. In the latter case, in which sentience springs immediately from nature, i.e., from noncompetitive self-love, it manifests itself in gentle passion that unifies humans. In the negative case, sentience is deformed by the conscious awareness of one's own *amour-propre* and is thus transformed into cruel passion that divides humans. With these arguments for the double nature of sentience, Rousseau touches on the ambivalence of human desire, which, as Girard also demonstrates, can lead to both positive and negative consequences.

Even on this basic level, however, there is a grave problem with Rousseau's anthropology that further underscores its divergence from the mimetic theory. Although Rousseau hints at the mimetic nature of desire with his arguments for natural sentience, he only refers here to the possibility of positive manifestations of mimesis in nature. It is only gentle and unifying compassion that arise in nature, and not the malevolent passions of vanity, pride, or envy. He argues that this can be confirmed by humans who grow up in natural simplicity and, as a result, remain free of destructive passions, knowing only compassion.[281] Rousseau even claims that he himself is proof of the innocence of man's natural state. In the *Confessions*, he provides only a very short list of "naughty habits" he acquired as a young boy. His first sinister emotions, he writes, came from unfortunate interactions with his teacher: "My whims were so little encouraged and so little opposed that it never occurred to me to have any. I am ready to swear that, until I was myself

subjected to the rule of a master, I never even knew what a caprice was."[282]
Rousseau soon experienced a kind of fall after being unjustly punished for
breaking a comb. For the young Rousseau—who, until this point, claims he
had yet to encounter the "notion of injustice"—the world of happy childhood collapsed as he was forced to experience the "violence" and "injustice"
felt by the "first man" who was banished from "paradise."[283] Where the Bible
speaks of Adam and Eve having rightfully deserved their banishment from
Eden, Rousseau holds only the others accountable for his being banished
from the innocent paradise of childhood. In *Rousseau: Judge of Jean-Jacques*,
he expands on his innocent childhood to create a self-portrait that is characterized—despite a strong capacity for perception—by an exclusively positive
natural sentience that remains undefiled by passions such as pride and vanity.[284] This demonstrates clearly the degree to which Rousseau diverges from
Augustine and the Christian doctrine of Original Sin.[285] In his *Confessions*,
Augustine not only refers to the possibility of envy among small children, but
much more importantly speaks of his own fallen nature. While Augustine,
starting with his theft of the pears, accepts the guilt of his own mimetically
induced tendencies, Rousseau ultimately seeks acquittal, for it is not he, but
the others who are afflicted with vice.

Similar to Girard, Rousseau is aware that human existence is determined
by the ability to sense deeper emotions—a kind of emotional imitation—
which antecedes any conscious reflection and is present even in animals.
However, while Rousseau holds that this mimetic sense is fundamentally
positive and poses no risks to humans in their natural state, Girard argues—
together with Augustine and the Christian tradition—that mimesis is
acquisitive by nature and therefore can lead to rivalry and violence. Rousseau's attempt to keep compassion and competitive *amour-propre* completely
separate overlooks their overarching structural identity and is rooted in the
romantic endeavor to liberate man from his distorted nature without the
help of divine grace.

Immanuel Kant

With regard to the passion of envy, Immanuel Kant, whose anthropology
shows the distinct influence of Rousseau, offers interesting insights for the
mimetic theory. Kant belongs to the list of great philosophers who recognize

the significance of envy, and is notable for his particularly harsh critique of this passion:

> Envy (livor) is a propensity to view the well-being of others with distress, even though it does not detract from one's own. When it breaks forth into action (to diminish well being) it is called envy proper; otherwise it is merely jealousy (invidentia). Yet envy is only an indirectly malevolent disposition, namely a reluctance to see our own well-being overshadowed by another's because the standard we use to see how well off we are is not the intrinsic worth of our own well-being but how it compares with that of others.[286]

Kant's reference to the "comparative" nature of envy exhibits his awareness of its mimetic roots. His assessment is not only negative, however. Although he does refer to envy as a "vice leading to human hatred," a closer look at Kant's analysis shows that he does not completely condemn envious comparison, but rather views it as part of human nature, only "indirectly malignant" and in some cases even positive. As long as envy does not lead to negative actions against others, it represents for Kant no malevolent passion. His careful classification of envy is linked to his interpretation of the phenomenon as a form of healthy emulation, which in itself represents an irreplaceable component of human coexistence. Similar to Hobbes, Spinoza, or Rousseau, Kant also attributes great importance to emulation for human relations, referring to the "self-love that involves comparison," a typical human characteristic that is positive in principle but can also easily lead to "jealousy and rivalry" and other vices springing from envy.[287] Kant argues that human nature is *intrinsically* problematic, and compares human beings to trees that grow necessarily "stunted, crooked and awry."[288] He illustrates the paradoxical nature of human society further with his description of man's *ungesellige Geselligkeit*, or "unsociable sociability."[289] While human beings strive for a convivial coexistence with others, they also attempt to establish their own individuality, which triggers direct resistance from others. Kant goes on to argue, however, that "vices of culture" such as reciprocal emulation are absolutely necessary for the survival and development of human civilization.[290] In an interesting essay entitled "Idea for a Universal History with a Cosmopolitan Purpose," Kant reflects on the cultural importance of emulation and the antagonism it engenders between humans. Without this antagonism, he argues, humans

would remain arrested in laziness [tr. *in Faulheit verharren*], ruling out the
possibility of any cultural advancement:

> Without these qualities of unsociability from which the resistance arises,
> which are not at all amiable in themselves, qualities that each of us must
> necessarily encounter in his selfish pretensions, all talents would, in an arca-
> dian pastoral life of perfect concord, contentment and mutual love, remain
> eternally hidden in their germs; human beings, as good-natured as the sheep
> they tended, would give their existence hardly any greater worth than that
> of their domesticated beasts; they would not fill the void in creation in
> regard to their end as rational nature. Thanks be to nature, therefore, for the
> incompatibility, for the spiteful competitive vanity, for the insatiable desire
> to possess or even to dominate! The human being wills concord; but nature
> knows better what is good for his species: it wills discord.[291]

From the Christian perspective, as one might expect, Kant's ode to cultural discord gives rise to certain reservations. It reminds one of Goethe's
Faust, where Mephistopheles, the devil, refers to himself as "part of that
force which, always willing evil, always produces good."[292] Is Kant's praise
of "begrudging and competitive vanity" not a glorification of the envy that
Augustine and the Christian tradition identify as the devil's essence? Kant
himself appears to have considered this; he ignores his doubts, however, with
his justification of interpersonal antagonism as belonging to the divine order
of creation—and his rejection of antagonism as an "envious" manifestation
of an "evil spirit."[293] The mimetic theory sides more with Goethe here than
with Kant: for although Girard accepts man's mimetic nature, he also argues
that man must ultimately overcome the rivalry connected with acquisitive
mimesis in order to remain part of the divine order of creation.

Max Scheler

Of all the modern thinkers who offer reflections on the mimetic passions of
vanity, pride, and envy, Girard focuses most extensively on Max Scheler.[294]
He praises Scheler for his insightful analyses of the mimetic nature of envy,
and for his emphasis on the significance of the comparison in human relations. Two passages from Scheler's *Ressentiment* demonstrate his position:

> "Envy," as the term is understood in everyday usage, is due to a feeling of impotence which we experience when another person owns a good we covet. . . . If we are merely displeased that another person owns a good, this can be an incentive for acquiring it through work, purchase, violence, or robbery. *Envy* occurs when we fail in doing so and feel powerless.[295]
>
> Each of us—noble or common, good or evil—continually compares his own value with that of others. If I choose a model, a "hero," I am somehow tied to such a comparison. All jealousy, all ambition, and even an ideal like the "imitation of Christ" is full of such comparisons.[296]

Although Scheler does point out the mimetic roots of ressentiment, Girard also criticizes him for doing this only sporadically. He argues that this leads to Scheler's insistence on the significance of the object for human desire. In this respect, Girard sees the masters of novelistic literature as distinctly superior to Scheler, for whom the presence of the mediator, or rival, is central.

Scheler's thought, meanwhile, did not escape the influence of literature. In his analysis of "existential envy," in which he very nearly approaches Girard's mimetic conception of desire, Scheler makes the following remark in reference to Goethe's *Torquato Tasso*: "*Existential envy*, which is directed against the other person's very *nature*, is the strongest source of *ressentiment*. It is as if it whispers continually: 'I can forgive everything, but not that you are—that you are what you are—that I am not what you are—indeed that I am not you.'"[297] Scheler concludes, however, that the yearning for the other's being only emerges under "exceptional" circumstances—and only among great humans—thus greatly constricting his insight into the mimetic nature of desire. Even Goethe himself shows that this ontological longing is found in "normal" individuals as well, which is immediately apparent from *The Sorrows of Young Werther*.

Mimesis and the Desire for Recognition

As one of the central points in the present discussion of mimetic desire, we have been able to establish that the decreasing distance between subject and object increases the potential for conflict. In plain terms: Brothers, sisters, or next-door neighbors are far more likely to become enemies than unrelated strangers. This important insight is found not only in Girard's writings, how-ever, but also in those of many other thinkers who have focused on the nature of human antagonism.

Hans Magnus Enzensberger

A current example is found in the work of the German author Hans Magnus Enzensberger, whose essay "Civil War" portrays the contemporary world as a macrocosmic civil war. Enzensberger refers in his work not only to Bosnia, Georgia, or Somalia—areas rife with civil war when his essay was published in 1993—but also to the perpetual strife in cities such as Los Angeles, Paris, Lon-don, or Hamburg. He mentions violence against asylum seekers in Germany as modern examples of civil war just as much as violent attacks by Islamist fundamentalists. From a systematic perspective, Enzensberger's essay is impor-tant because it sees in contemporary civil war no merely passing phenomenon, but rather an original and perpetual form of human conflict: "Our current situation enables us to recognize that civil war is not merely an old custom, but the primary form of all collective conflict."[298] According to Enzensberger, "it is generally the rule, rather than the exception, that man destroys what he most hates, and that is usually the rival on his own territory. There is an unexplained linkage between hating one's neighbor and hating a stranger. The original tar-get of our hatred was probably always our neighbor; only with the formation of larger communities was the stranger on the other side of the border declared an enemy."[299] Similar to Girard, who refers to man's "centripetal tendency" (*Things Hidden*, 86) for violence, Enzensberger argues that violence within the group precedes any violence that manifests itself outwardly. He describes "cultivated war waged between nations and against external enemies" as an explicitly "recent development."[300] Enzensberger also attempts in his essay to identify the anthropological roots of man's propensity for civil war, thereby dismissing Freud's theory of the death drive, as well as other, more contempo-rary biological hypotheses.[301] He rejects likewise all optimistic theories of non-simultaneity that assess "negative phenomena" as merely short-term relapses in the face of general and constant human progress.[302] Enzensberger claims to find a more plausible explanation in Hegel's assumption that society's original state is a mutual struggle for recognition: "You don't have to be a Hegelian to see that the longing for recognition is a fundamental anthropological fact."[303]

Carl Schmitt

Enzensberger's essay displays strong parallels to the German political philosopher Carl Schmitt, whose provocative theses continue to hold sway—
despite his support of Hitler following the *Machtergreifung* in 1933—in the
contemporary political debate.[304] Similar to Enzensberger, Schmitt argues
that civil war is a particularly gruesome form of war and one that precedes
wars between individual states, thus agreeing with Hobbes that the state
stands for the permanent prevention of civil war.[305] Moreover, international
wars, in Schmitt's eyes, are merely a humanized and rationalized form of civil
war.[306] His insight that civil war is a primary form of collective conflict leads
him—like Enzensberger—to the realization that the origin of human conflict
is located within the community or group. Schmitt is best known for *The
Concept of the Political*, a text in which he portrays the friend/enemy distinction as a determinant criterion of global politics.[307] Enzensberger's insight,
however, that rivalry is most prevalent between groups in close proximity is
absent from Schmitt's famous text. Here, the enemy is simply "the other, the
stranger,"[308] and thus finds a contemporary parallel in Huntington's *Clash of
Civilizations*. In Schmitt's morally unconvincing book *Ex Captivitate Salus*,
in which he attempts to justify his controversial stance during the Second
World War, he arrives at an understanding of enmity comparable to that of
Enzensberger. Schmitt's inquiry into the nature of enemies focuses explicitly
on the concept of brotherhood:

> Who is my enemy? . . . Theologians tend to define the enemy as someone
> who has to be annihilated. But I am a jurist not a theologian. Whom can
> I recognize as my enemy at all? Apparently only the one who can question
> me. By recognizing him as an enemy I accept that he can question me. And
> who can really question me? Only I myself. Or my brother. That's it. The
> other is my brother. The other turns out to be my brother and the brother
> turns out to be my enemy. Adam and Eve had two sons, Cain and Abel. That
> is the beginning of humanity. That is what the father of all things looks like.
> That is the dialectical tension that keeps world history moving, and world
> history has not yet come to its end. . . . Remember the great sentences of
> the philosopher: The relation of the other to oneself is true eternity. The
> negation of the negation, says the philosopher, is not a neutralization, but

true eternity depends on it. Of course, true eternity is the basic concept of his philosophy. The enemy is the gestalt of our self-questioning.[309]

This quotation contains a number of ideas present throughout Girard's work: the brother as enemy; the fratricide of Abel, which represents the first death in the Bible; and Heraclitus's famous description of war as the "father and king of all things." For the purposes of the present study, Schmitt's analysis of Hegel is most important, as it is most certainly Hegel to whom Schmitt refers as "the philosopher" in the above quotation. In his inquiry into the causes of enmity, Schmitt, like Enzensberger, arrives ultimately at Hegel and the issue of recognition. Both are in accord—together with Girard—that the "neighbor" or "brother" is the actual potential enemy, an insight directly linked to Hegel's analysis of the human need for recognition. Let us therefore now take a closer look at how Girard's concept relates to Hegel, in order to gain a better understanding of how mimetic desire functions as a source of human conflict.

Georg Wilhelm Friedrich Hegel and Alexandre Kojève

In the *Phenomenology of Spirit*, Hegel handles the concept of recognition in a way that has strong parallels to Girard's mimetic desire. In the following analysis, I will not refer directly to Hegel's text, but rather to Alexandre Kojève's interpretation—in France, above all, the definitive reading of the *Phenomenology*—which sees the key element to Hegel's philosophical system in the master-slave dialectic.[310] Several influential twentieth-century intellectuals were shaped by Kojève's Hegel lectures in Paris (1933–1939), including Hannah Arendt, Raymond Aron, Georges Bataille, André Breton, Roger Caillois, Henry Corbin, Pater Gaston Fessard SJ, Pierre Klossowski, Jacques Lacan, Robert Marjolin, Maurice Merleau-Ponty, Raymond Polin, Raymond Queneau, and Eric Weil.[311] Kojève's reading of Hegel was significant for Girard as well, in particular for his early formulations of mimetic desire found in *Deceit, Desire and the Novel*.[312]

Kojève interprets Hegel's point of origin in the *Phenomenology* as the following: "Man is Self-Consciousness."[313] Hegel summarizes here the fundamental difference between man and lower animals, which, in his eyes, are granted a mere "feeling of self." This raises the question, however: what

exactly constitutes human consciousness? Descartes's conception of consciousness, or contemplation (*cogito ergo sum*), is insufficient for Hegel, for to
concentrate exclusively on cognition would be to negate the significance of
the ego [tr. *das Ich*]. He argues that one can say "I," that is, attain consciousness of one's self, only after experiencing the desire for an object. However,
if this desire remains directed at natural, tangible, or merely living objects,
it resides on the level of animal instinct: Natural objects of desire, Hegel
argues, cannot induce self-consciousness, but rather only the "feeling" of self
conferred by animal desire. To attain self-consciousness, on the other hand,
desire must be directed at an "unnatural" object: the desire of another. For
humans to transcend their mere "feeling of humanness"—as with animals
and their desire for merely natural objects—Kojève writes, "Desire must be
directed toward another Desire."[314]

> Human Desire, or better still, anthropogenetic Desire, produces a free
> and historical individual, conscious of his individuality, his freedom, his
> history, and finally, his historicity. . . . Anthropogenetic Desire is differ-
> ent from animal Desire (which produces a natural being, merely living
> and having only a sentiment of its life) in that it is directed, not toward a
> real, "positive" given object, but toward another Desire. Likewise, Desire
> directed toward a natural object is human only to the extent that it is
> "mediated" by the Desire of another directed toward the same object: it is
> human to desire what others desire, because they desire it. Thus, an object
> perfectly useless from the biological point of view (such as a medal, or the
> enemy's flag) can be desired because it is the object of other desires. Such
> a Desire can only be a human Desire, and human reality, as distinguished
> from animal reality, is created only by the action that satisfies Desires:
> human history is the history of desired Desires.[315]

To desire another's desire means to become the object of that other's desire:
It is the desire *to be recognized* by the other. Self-consciousness is thus for
Hegel a function of the desire for recognition.

Kojève argues that Hegel sees the essence of desire in negation; in order
to pacify the longing for an object, in other words, that object must be
negated or annihilated: "For Desire is *absence* of Being, (to be hungry is to
be deprived of food); it is a Nothingness that *nihilates* in Being, and not a

Being that *is*."[316] Negation and annihilation are integral to desire; both forms of desire, animal and human, strive for pacification through the negation of objects.[317] In the case of human desire, e.g., that of recognition, this negation implies the assertion of man's exclusive right to satisfaction, his right to certain objects, and, ultimately, his superiority and dominion over others.

Hegel argues that to attain self-consciousness, multiple desires must be present, for only this way can another's desire become the object of desire. Like Girard, Hegel sees man as a social entity that attains being exclusively by forging relations with others. The social act, however, is no harmonious or peaceful occurrence, but rather resembles the Hobbesian warlike state; multiple human desires directed simultaneously at general recognition lead necessarily to violent struggle. According to Hegel, all humans strive to subject others to their dominance.

Humanness implies transcendence of one's purely animal condition. For animals, there is no higher aspiration than survival. This is something that man must overcome in order to fully differentiate himself from animals. To attain humanness, man must negate his animal self; in other words, he must risk his life. Hegel claims that the desire for recognition is not just a struggle to subsist, as it appears among animals, but rather, and necessarily, a "life and death fight":

> If ... there is a *multiplicity* of these Desires for universal Recognition, it is obvious that the Action that is born of these Desires can ... be nothing but a life and death *Fight* (*Kampf auf Leben und Tod*). A *Fight*, since each will want to subjugate the other, *all* the others, by a negating, destroying *action*. A life and *death* Fight because Desire that is directed toward a Desire *goes beyond* the biological given, so that Action carried out for the sake of this Desire is not limited by this given. In other words, Man will risk his biological *life* to satisfy his *nonbiological* Desire.[318]

Hegel states that the origin of self-consciousness is found in the life-and-death struggle for recognition. It is in this fight for prestige that humans attain their humanness. This primal conflict ends in Hegel's master-slave dialectic, a protracted process that drives history forward and ultimately brings about its ideological end. The master is the victor in the struggle of life and death, because he is the one who risks his life and chooses death over subordination.

The slave is the vanquished, because his fear of death leads to the recognition of the master's dominion over him, that is, his own bondage. The outcome of this struggle, however, does not result in an eternal division of humans into masters and slaves, as Aristotle suggests, but rather starts Hegel's peculiar dialectic that ultimately leads to his concept of the "end of history." The master's dominion is recognized, but only from the menial self-consciousness of the slave, which for the master is insignificant. The master remains confined to a life of pleasure and is unable to contribute to the development of history. The slave, by contrast, is bound to a life of labor, but it is precisely this labor that enables him to develop over time a self-contained form of consciousness. As a master of nature, and by means of his labor, the slave alters the world and history. At the same time, the slave makes use of ideological means to reconcile his servitude with his growing self-consciousness in a bid to bring the two into harmony. Hegel distinguishes between three different stages of the slave's ideological development, referring to them as stoicism, skepticism, and "unhappy consciousness," the latter of which Hegel links to pre-Reformation Christianity. The Christian idea of universal equality before God forges a path toward political emancipation and leads to the slave's yearning to overcome his alienation and to force the master to recognize his liberty. According to Hegel, this final stage manifested itself historically in the French Revolution. He claims that Napoleon's empire was akin to the forging of a universal, homogenous constitutional state in which masters and slaves experience *mutual* recognition, the consummation of the *Ende der Geschichte*, or the "End of History." Kojève, writing over a century later, accepted Hegel's general assumption, but attempted to revise it with regard to the actual "end" of history. In the 1930s—during his famous Hegel lectures in Paris—Kojève replaced Hegel's Napoleon with Stalin.[319] After the Second World War, he changed his position again, arguing this time that the United States, modern Japan, and the European Union represented the ultimate embodiment of universal recognition.[320]

Francis Fukuyama

With the end of the Cold War, Kojève's interpretation of Hegel took on a new significance in leading political and philosophical discourse. Francis Fukuyama, the American philosopher and former deputy director for European political-military affairs at the U.S. Department of State, incorporates Kojève's thesis in *The End of History and the Last Man*, which received massive attention after its first publication in 1992. The book does not concern any absolute end to human history, in the sense of a future in which events no longer take place, but rather ponders the end of man's ideological development. Fukuyama focuses his inquiry on whether liberal democracy—which in the last decades has spread throughout the world—is the final and ultimate form of government. His answer, a careful yes, is based on the observation that the political and economic liberalism that emerged in the late twentieth century—in other words democracy and free market capitalism—has experienced a universal triumph around the world. He cites as examples both developing countries and former Soviet nations. An interesting aspect of Fukuyama's thesis is his remark that economic grounds alone fail to justify this progression towards political democracy. He shows that market-oriented authoritarian states like Franco's Spain, or military regimes such as those in South Korea or Argentina, can achieve the same economic results as liberal democracies. Most human beings, meanwhile, reject such systems, for Fukuyama argues that these forms of government are incapable of satisfying man's need for recognition. Liberal democracy, in the end, is the only political structure capable of enabling universal recognition. Fukuyama sees the question of recognition as the deciding factor—apart from economic issues—in the revolutions of the former communist Soviet states.[321] Hegel's concept of the desire for recognition plays a central role in Fukuyama's book,[322] which can help us establish a link between the present section on Hegelian recognition and the previous section dealing with those philosophers who described the mimetic passions at the dawn of the modern era: In his book, Fukuyama equates Hobbes's vainglory and Rousseau's *amour propre* with Hegel's description of the "desire for another's desire." In their own way, these disparate conceptions of desire all lead to Kant's depiction of man's "asocially social" condition.[323]

Fukuyama's thesis regarding the end of history, however, remains more than questionable, with the years following the end of the Cold War having robbed his arguments of any persuasiveness. Enzensberger, for instance, who himself sees human conflict based on the struggle for recognition, strictly rejects the plausibility of Hegel's *Ende der Geschichte*—or any revisions made to it by Hegel's followers. He argues against the notion that any form of government can fully satisfy the desire for recognition, be it the constitutional state with its guarantee of equality before the law, or the welfare state with its social promises. Enzensberger argues that, if anything, the need for recognition has only expanded in contemporary democracies: "But the desire for recognition, first in the cities and then across the whole world, has gathered a momentum that a certain philosopher in 1806 could never have dreamed of. Every community, even the richest and most peaceful, continually creates inequalities, slights, injustices, unreasonable demands and frustrations of all kinds. The more freedom and equality people gain, the more they expect. If these expectations are not fulfilled, then almost anyone can feel humiliated. The longing for recognition is never satisfied. Newspaper editors know the story well enough: the ghetto kid who wants a pair of designer training shoes enough to kill for them; the office worker who fails in his ambition to become a pop star and robs a bank or shoots into the crowd of people to get his own back for the humiliation he has suffered."[324]

Interestingly, Fukuyama acknowledges such arguments in reference to Nietzsche's warning of the "last man" in the final chapter of *The End of History*.[325] From the perspective of the mimetic theory, Fukuyama's counterarguments are much stronger than his main thesis. He poses the question whether the worldwide spread of democracy can really solve man's need for universal recognition. With respect to the people who fought for human rights in Eastern Europe, he expresses very justified concerns about whether the mere granting of these rights represents any solution to the original problem: "But it is another matter again whether they are humanly *satisfied* by the mere act of being granted rights. One is reminded of Groucho Marx's joke that he would never want to be a member of a club that would admit him as a member: what is the value of recognition that comes to everyone merely by virtue of being a human being?"[326]

René Girard

Already in his first book, Girard criticizes Hegel's—or any of his Marxist successors'—proclamation of the end of history. Girard argues that humans, even without directly physical violence, will find ways to transform their vanity and snobbism, that is, their mimetic desire, into new possibilities for conflict.[327] In his book *Quand ces choses commenceront*, Girard confirms this position and distances himself explicitly from Fukuyama's thesis.[328]

Much like Enzensberger, Girard sees no end of history as Kojève and Fukuyama interpret it from Hegel's philosophy. With that being said, however, the mimetic theory does show clear parallels to several concepts connected with the Hegelian dialectic, including the fascination with the other's desire and the violent origins of history. It must be noted, though, that these parallels can be misleading, for they are ultimately merely superficial. Girard's concept of mimesis diverges fundamentally from Hegel's conception,[329] for Girard stresses the importance of mimetism already in prehuman stages and during the process of hominization; Hegel's analysis of recognition, meanwhile, focuses solely on human behavior beyond the threshold of hominization.[330] Girard also questions the Hegelian notion that human conflict stems from the contemplation of another's desire, arguing rather that interpersonal conflict can be shown to originate much more spontaneously and to precede consciousness. What's more, Hegel's definition states that desire is *necessarily* linked with violence, negation, and annihilation, whereas Girard's system allows for the overcoming of these consequences: "Hegel's concept of the 'desire for another's desire' implies, indeed, something different than my notion of mimetic striving. . . . It is crucial, in my opinion, to see that Hegel sacralizes violence. For Hegel, violence is positively sacred; it is at the very center of his thought."[331] Negation and annihilation are for Hegel and Kojève—and for Schmitt, who continues this line of thought—a constitutive aspect of humanness.[332] Such a position is faced with the same problem as Konrad Lorenz's arguments concerning man's instinctually violent nature, for it nullifies the human endeavor to overcome violence. Hegel's assumption of the master-slave dialectic at the advent of human history is likewise ultimately unpersuasive. He appears here to have incorporated the concept of animal struggle—which results in stable group hierarchies by means of a preventive killing mechanism—into his philosophy of man.

Girard's concept of mimesis avoids such problematic arguments and provides a logical development of human desire that ultimately even converges with Hegel's observations. The systematic difference between Hegel and Girard is found in their respective definitions of desire: Hegel speaks of the desire for the other's desire (recognition), while Girard argues for a desire *according* to that of another (mimetic desire).[333] In the Hegelian conception, the object of desire is absent as the subject concentrates on being recognized by the other. In the Girardian conception, the other's desire is at first no object of one's desire, but rather the model that designates the desirability of all objects. Girard's theory produces a triangular structure of desire; Hegel's concept of recognition remains bipolar. This fundamental difference enables Girard to account for the forms of desire that do not end necessarily in violent struggle.

The difference between Kojève's reading of Hegel and Girard's mimetic theory must be outlined on a deeper level, however, with particular regard to their respective positions on the Christian religion. Kojève follows Feuerbach and Marx in his ultimately radical atheist interpretation of Hegel's philosophy, which he refers to as a "secularized Christian theology."[334] Where Hegel claims that "all statements of Christian theology" are "absolutely true," Kojève argues that these claims must not be applied to a transcendental or imaginary God, but rather to man, who is alive in the world. Hegel's passage concerning the "revealed God" at the end of chapter 6 of the *Phenomenology*—in which he concludes his reflections on the entirely self-conscious Absolute Spirit—is, according to Kojève, the "God-Man" that manifests itself in the "dyad Napoleon-Hegel."[335] All references to Christ in the *Phenomenology*, according to Kojève, are to be interpreted as directed at either Napoleon, that is, "the man completing historical evolution through a bloody battle," or Hegel himself, that is, "the man revealing through his discourse the meaning of this evolution"—and not at the Jesus of the New Testament.[336] Kojève takes Hegel's description of pre-Reformation Christianity as "unhappy consciousness," a "deficient form of occidental religion," to mean all forms of Christianity, which he goes on to characterize as the "last stage of the slave's alienation" or "absolute bondage to a divine master" that must be overcome by wisdom gained at the end of history through contemplation of man's own mortality.[337] Kojève grants philosophers, on account of this contemplative wisdom, the right to attest the achievement of this final state.[338]

One can gain a better understanding of the way Girard's theory relates to Kojève's reading of Hegel by turning to the novels of Dostoyevsky, as they serve as a unique frame of reference for the two. Kojève, who grew up in Russia before emigrating to Germany and then France, was very familiar with Dostoyevsky's works. He formulated his atheist philosophy in conscious rejection of Dostoyevsky's religious vision, as one can read in an essay Kojève wrote in 1931 just prior to writing his lectures on Hegel's *Phenomenology*.[339] Kojève's interpretation of Hegel, as well, is proof of his distance from Dostoyevsky. He sympathizes with those of Dostoyevsky's characters that champion the radically atheist freedom of man, and he decidedly rejects the characters that stand for faith in the resurrection of Christ and the immortality of the soul. He places his ideological hopes much more in the human god represented by Kirilov in *Demons*, or Ivan Karamazov in *The Brothers Karamazov*.[340] Humans, Kojève argues, can only overcome their servitude and attain absolute freedom by becoming God. Whereas Dostoyevsky recognizes envy and atheist pride as passions that lead to violent conflict and (self-)destruction, Kojève's philosophy stands for the satisfaction of man's "infinite pride," which he finds in death or consciousness of his finite nature—that is, in the liberation from God's authority and all other forms of predestination.[341] The tragic figure Kirilov—who strives with his attempt at suicide to affirm his "self-will" and liberate humanity from God and the faith in immortality—is for Kojève a positive example because his autonomous deed represents an overcoming of God's "omnipotence" and "divinity."[342] With that being said, however, Kojève's assessment of Kirilov is not strictly positive. Though he does see in Kirilov's suicide attempt an expression of man's radical freedom before God, he characterizes the act of destroying oneself at the same time as an embodiment of mere nihilistic skepticism and no viable realization of human freedom.[343] This is perhaps the reason why Kojève secretly adopts Ivan Karamazov—Kirilov's spiritual brother, who likewise represents human autonomy and pride—as the role model for his thought. While Kirilov tries to redeem humanity by attempting to commit suicide, Ivan manifests his plan for peace on earth in the intellectual creation of the Grand Inquisitor. Ivan's plan concerns the universal organization of mankind into a "common, concordant, and incontestable anthill" that will create a "kingdom of peace and happiness."[344] Kojève's vision of the universal and homogenous world at the end of history harmonizes with Ivan's plan to complete the construction of the Tower of Babel.[345]

Girard rejects Kojève's position in support of Dostoyevsky and recognizes in Kirilov and Ivan Karamazov the (self-)destructive potential of man's proud attempt to assert his autonomy before God. In Stavrogin, the "divine" center of *Demons*, Girard identifies parallels to Kojève's Napoleon, or the "revealed God" of Hegel's *Phenomenology*.[346] Girard also devotes extensive analysis to Kirilov—just one of Stavrogin's idolizers—whose failed suicide attempt, he argues, far from "redeeming humanity," demonstrates the futility of the striving for autonomy.[347] As we have seen, Kojève grants Dostoyevsky's damning depiction of Kirilov's suicide attempt as an impossible and destructive endeavor; however, this "theistic objection" remains insufficient to dissuade him fully. Kirilov's shameful failure at killing himself remains for Kojève a "free act" that "limits infinity or God." His espousal of Kirilov's atheist pride—at the cost of violence, suicide, and the transformation of man into herd animals—displays clearly the difference to Girard's position, which identifies this pride as the true cause of interpersonal violence and all forms of self-destruction. From the perspective of the mimetic theory, Kirilov, and also indirectly Kojève's reading of Hegel represent an instance of Augustine's definition of Original Sin: *perversa imitatio Dei*. Kirilov and Kojève replace the humble imitation of Christ with the proud imitation of Satan. For Girard, Hegel's "unhappy consciousness" belongs not to Christians, but rather to those who succumb to the seduction of pride, and thus murderous forms of mimetic desire.[348]

From Primary Mimetism to the Mimesis of the Antagonist

The mimetic theory is capable of tracing the development of human desire from acquisitive mimesis through to the Hegelian desire for recognition.[349] Girard contends that desire is a dynamic phenomenon, which traverses different stages of development. In the following section, we will take a look at these stages individually, beginning with the period prior to the process of hominization. According to Girard, mimetic behavior can also be observed among animals, and this allows his conception of desire to be placed in the greater context of a theory of evolution.

Mimesis in the Animal Kingdom

Girard argues that among humans and the more highly developed mammals, desire is borrowed from the desire of others: "Mimesis appears to be present in all forms of life, but in the so-called higher mammals and particularly in man's nearest relatives, the anthropoid apes, it manifests itself in some quite spectacular forms. In certain species the propensity to imitate and what we would call a quarrelsome, bickering mood are one and the same thing; it is a question of acquisitive mimesis" (*Things Hidden*, 90).[350]

These observations—formulated over two decades ago and based on the ethological texts available at the time—are finding increasing corroboration in contemporary behavioral-science research. According to the Dutch ethologist Frans de Waal, the capacity for imitation among animals relates directly to their capacity for empathy.[351] Among primates, the capacity for imitation is so pronounced that "aping" is synonymous with the term. De Waal argues that, with regard to imitation, anthropoid apes possess the most similar traits to humans. A surprising aspect of de Waal's findings, however, concerns the central importance of imitation among species that possess only marginal capacities for empathy and display less apparent similarities to humans. Consider the following two examples in which de Waal refers to experiments with aquarium fish and octopi:

> A female guppy courted by two males ends up associating with one of them while another female follows the entire process from an adjacent tank. When this guppy "voyeuse" is introduced to the same males to see which one she likes better, she follows her predecessor's choice. Lee Dugatkin, an American ethologist who conducted these experiments, speculates that female guppies rely on each other's assessments of potential mates. The I-want-what-she-wants principle that Dugatkin found had the power of reversing a female's independent preferences known from earlier tests.
>
> Similarly, two Italian scientists, Graziano Fiorito and Pietro Scotto, trained an octopus to attack either a red or a white ball. After the training another octopus was allowed to watch four demonstrations from an adjoining tank. The spectator closely monitored the actions of the demonstrator with head and eye movements. When the same balls were dropped in the spectator's tank, he attacked the ball of the same color as the first octopus.[352]

Everything begins for Girard with rivalry over a single object. The terminology used in connection with this phenomenon is *primary mimetism*, which he argues precedes all consciousness, representations, language, or other systems of symbols (*Things Hidden*, 290; *De la violence à la divinité*, 1046: "mimétisme primaire").[353] With this supposition, Girard breaks from traditional philosophical conceptions branching from Plato and Hegel that view consciousness as preceding any human acquisitive behavior.[354] At this elementary stage, however, Girard does not yet speak of "desire" as such. Conflict emerges here simply from the imitation of a demeanor or gesture that merely suggests desire for possession of an object. At this stage of primary mimetism, mimesis is an unconscious act. There is thus no conscious imitation, for the mimesis is virtually automatic.[355] In Girard's words, this form of mimesis takes place in a "quasi-osmotic immediacy."[356]

Metaphysical Desire

Such spontaneous or automatic imitation is sufficient for generating conflict. The role model that provides the original impetus for the subject's desire of the object attempts simultaneously to prevent the subject from acquiring it. This resistance on the part of the original role model increases the value of the object in the eyes of the imitating subject; the subject desires the object that is most difficult to obtain, for it perceives a direct relationship between the model's resistance and the object's actual value. Goethe's *Sorrows of Young Werther* provides a particularly illustrative example of this. Werther finds himself ensnared in a love triangle after falling hopelessly in love with an already betrothed Lotte. As Werther's yearning increases in virulence, Lotte begs him to stop visiting her, in a plea that exposes the mimetic nature of his desire: "Don't you feel that you are deceiving yourself, deliberately destroying yourself? Why me, Werther, why precisely me, the property of another? Precisely that? I fear, I fear it is only the impossibility of possessing me that makes this wish so attractive to you."[357]

The increasing desirability of the object leads to intensified efforts on the part of the subject to possess it. Consequently, the model's resistance intensifies, and the perceived value of the object is reinforced. The value of the physical object becomes more and more "imagined" until all connection to its original value is lost. At this stage of desire, Girard speaks of the metamorphosis into a "hyper-real" or "metaphysical" object. Cervantes's *Don Quixote* contains a famous example of this phenomenon where mimetic rivalry turns a simple copper soap bowl into the coveted golden helmet of Mambrino.[358] Stendhal, as well, illustrates the metamorphosis of objects with his concept of "crystallization," which he portrays, however, not in the context of mimetic rivalry, but rather mere romantic passion: "In the salt mines of Salzburg a bough stripped of its leaves by winter is thrown into the depths of the disused workings; two or three months later it is pulled out again, covered with brilliant crystals: even the tiniest twigs, no bigger than a tomtit's claw, are spangled with a vast number of shimmering, glittering diamonds, so that the original bough is no longer recognizable."[359] Girard argues that this metamorphosis of the original object of desire into a metaphysical object signals the moment in which one can speak of desire as such.[360] From this stage of the mimetic process onwards, he applies the expression *metaphysical desire* (*Deceit, Desire and the Novel*, 81; *De la violence à la divinité*, 99: "désir métaphysique").[361]

Marx offers a very interesting example of the metaphysical transformation of objects in *Das Kapital*, where he describes the "fetishism of the commodity" as a typical characteristic of capitalist society. Marx says that to describe the "mystical character of the commodity" he must flee into the "nebulous regions of religion," a world "abounding in metaphysical subtleties and theological niceties." He argues that at first glance there is nothing extraordinary about commodities; a more precise analysis, however, reveals their "strange" character: "So far as it is a use value, there is nothing mysterious about it. . . . It is absolutely clear that, by his activity, man changes the forms of the materials of nature in such a way as to make them useful to him. The form of wood, for instance, is altered if a table is made out of it. Nevertheless the table continues to be wood, an ordinary, sensuous thing. But as soon as it emerges as a commodity, it changes into a thing which transcends sensuousness. It not only stands with its feet on the ground, but, in relation to all other commodities, it stands on its head, and evolves out of its wooden brain grotesque ideas, far more wonderful than if it were to begin dancing of its own free will."[362] Whereas Marx argues that the fetishism of commodities is the result of capitalist society—and can be easily eluded by altering the relations of possession—Girard shows that the metaphysical transformation of objects is a much more fundamental issue concerning human coexistence.[363] Desire is capable of metamorphosing all possible objects into fetishes, which form the basis for competition and rivalry.

The best example to illustrate Girard's position is found in the rivalry over prestige or honor—as in sports competitions, duels, etc.—in which there is no longer any physical object present. The Latin word for prestige, *praestigiae*, is suggestive of this void, for it signifies an "illusion" or "mirage."[364] The fact, however, that rivalry over honor and prestige can be more virulent than that over real objects shows that it concerns metaphysical objects that result from mimetic rivalry. In this regard, Girard's theory converges on Kojève's anthropology, which, as we saw in his reading of Hegel, emphasizes the central importance of the human struggle for recognition—or prestige— in which seemingly insignificant objects, such as accolades or the flag of an enemy nation, can become the focus of a life and death struggle. Thomas Hobbes, likewise, mentions the struggle for prestige as one of the three main causes of human conflict. In Hobbes's words, the "desire for glory can lead to violence for trifles, as a word, a smile, a different opinion, and any other signe of undervalue, either direct in their Persons or by reflection in their Kindred, their Friends, their Nation, their Profession, or their Name."[365] The fight for empty glory, thus, is a fight over *nothing*: There is no longer any real object present.

William Shakespeare

Shakespeare is particularly adept at illustrating the nothingness at the heart of conflict, a phenomenon referred to directly in the title of his comedy *Much Ado About Nothing*. Several of Shakespeare's tragic conflicts feature episodes that examine the desire for honor and prestige.[366] Consider Hamlet's reaction to the news of Fortinbras's plans to attack a part of Poland, a "little patch of ground that hath in it no profit but the name."[367] Hamlet says that, although neither Denmark nor Norway would pay five ducats for the land itself, "two thousand souls and twenty thousand ducats will not debate the question of this straw." The young Dane's words display in total clarity that the endeavor is the mere consequence of the desire for glory and honor, "for a fantasy and trick of fame":

> Witness this army of such mass and charge,
> Led by a delicate and tender prince,
> Whose spirit, with divine ambition puff'd,
> Makes mouths at the invisible event,
> Exposing what is mortal unsure
> To all that fortune, death and danger dare,
> Even for an eggshell. Rightly to be great
> Is not to stir without great argument,

But greatly to find quarrel in a straw
When honour's at the stake.[368]

Shakespeare's insight into the nothingness at the heart of ambition—which can lead to the bloodiest of wars—is by no means far from reality. The modern world is pervaded by examples of bloody conflict and war that, even afterwards, remain inexplicable. With insight into the workings of metaphysical desire, however, one can begin to comprehend such conflicts of honor—for instance, the Falklands War or the ongoing ethnic divisions in the former Yugoslavia and other former Soviet states.[369]

Hamlet's soliloquy—when one takes into account its remaining verses—can well be read as a compact summary of the Hegelian dialectic outlined above. When the Danish prince is forced to watch Fortinbras's army march past, he is once again made aware of his "problem," the inability to avenge the murder of his father. He is left pondering the fundamental difference between man and animal—the capacity for thought, or "godlike reason"—which he feels should spur him to act. Fortinbras is for Hamlet the exemplary human being, someone who goes to war merely for the sake of empty prestige. Hamlet's reflections culminate in a vow of "bloody" revenge:

What is a man,
If his chief good and market of his time
Be but to sleep and feed? A beast, no more.
Sure, he that made us with such large discourse,
Looking before and after, gave us not
That capability and godlike reason
To fust in us unused. . . .

How stand I then,
That have a father kill'd, a mother stain'd,
Excitements of my reason and my blood,
And let all sleep, while to my shame I see
The imminent death of twenty thousand men
That for a fantasy and trick of fame
Go to their graves like beds, fight for a plot
Whereon the numbers cannot try the cause,

Which is not tomb enough and continent
To hide the slain? O, from this time forth,
My thoughts be bloody, or be nothing worth!

Hamlet's soliloquy—similar to Kojève's reading of Hegel—identifies the fundamental difference between man and animal in man's ability to fight to the death over prestige and honor. While Hegel and Kojève believe they find in this insight the highpoint of philosophical thought, Shakespeare clearly expresses the deadly nonsense contained therein.

The Model-Obstacle

Primary mimetism leads from an automatic imitation of appropriation to rivalry based purely on prestige, in which the rivals are no longer conscious of the object of their original desire. The two opponents are now faced off in a fight over nonexistent objects. However, this "nothingness" is only apparent as such from an outside perspective. For the rivals themselves, the struggle on its own means everything. Their original desire is now metaphysical desire, which is based on rivalry and violence to which the rivals are reciprocally impelled. Girard describes this as a "self-perpetuating process, constantly increasing in simplicity and fervor. Whenever the disciple borrows from his model what he believes to be the 'true' object, he tries to possess that truth by desiring precisely what this model desires. Whenever he sees himself closest to the supreme goal, he comes into violent conflict with a rival. By a mental shortcut that is both eminently logical and self-defeating, he convinces himself that the violence itself is the most distinctive attribute of this supreme goal!" (*Violence and the Sacred*, 148).[370]

To gain a more immediate sense of the process by which violence consumes the rival subjects, we must first consider two particularly critical properties of mimetic desire. Firstly, desire is characterized by an inner dynamic that is rooted in self-reflexivity. In Girard's words, "*desire is always reflection on desire*," in that it builds on previous experiences and thus perpetuates itself (*Things Hidden*, 328; *De la violence à la divinité*, 1091).[371] Secondly, mimetic desire is easily intensified by the resistance of the original model, who attempts to prevent the subject from acquiring the desired object after initial interest has been displayed. The model's resistance quickly becomes the starting point for new desire on the part of the original subject. In the eyes of the subject, this increased resistance to the acquisition of the object increases its value; in the span of this process, the subject's perception of the value of the desired object is altered to the extent that, ultimately, it is resistance itself that is pursued. The model, in other words, now reinforces the subject's original desire by desiring it himself. The model's resistance makes the original object—over which the struggle began—all but meaningless, as the conflict is now centered on the model's violence; the subject's fascination with the model's resistance prompts Girard to speak here of a "fetishism of violence."[372]

Girard portrays this fetishism as central to the phenomena of sadism and masochism. He emphatically rejects any essentialist interpretation of these concepts and traces their origins back to the mimetic structure of desire. According to Girard, masochism does not even exist on its own—that is, there is no independent desire directed naturally at pain, defeat, or violence; rather, he argues, it is a mere form of (pseudo-)masochism, which arises once the craving for the model's resistance has replaced the desire for the original object. Girard argues that metaphysical desire tends toward this form of (pseudo-)masochism, which, in a conscious challenge to the accepted understanding of the phenomenon, he says is logically superordinate to sadism. (Pseudo-)masochism is simply the subject's imitation of the violence—directed at itself—witnessed in the model's resistance to its original desire.

The relationship between the subject and model, as well, goes through a process of transformation as the conflict between the two intensifies. As with the nature of the object, Girard observes a "metaphysical transformation" in the magnitude of the model. The increasing attraction of the model is based on the possession of the object that becomes more "valuable" as rivalry and violence increase. Eventually, the object and the model that possesses it become one; at this conclusive point in the mimetic process, Girard argues that the subject's fascination ultimately extends beyond the model's desire; it is now much more the model's being—fundamentally ambivalent and full of violence—that the subject desires.[373]

At this stage in the mimetic process, the model becomes an idol, a god, for the desiring subject. At the same time, however, the model remains the essential obstacle for the subject by blocking access to the divinity of the desired object. The subject's worshipped idol, in other words, becomes its absolute enemy at the same time. The original model—and now obstacle—takes on both a divine and a diabolical function for the subject; it is worthy of the subject's simultaneous adoration and hatred. Girard calls this ambivalent form of mimetic desire the *model-obstacle* (*Violence and the Sacred*, 165; *De la violence à la divinité*, 497: "modèle-obstacle").[374] To illustrate his concept, Girard recalls Kafka's parable *Before the Law*, in which the gatekeeper shows the man from the country the way to paradise while simultaneously denying him entry.[375] The model-obstacle is for Girard the key to understanding Freud's concept of "ambivalence" and is also essentially identical to Gregory Bateson's "double bind," if one ignores Bateson's exclusive focus on pathological cases.[376]

Double Mediation

The present discussion has thus far excluded one key element: the mimetic nature of the model's desire. In the advanced stages of mimetic desire, that is, the realm of metaphysical desire, imitation is extremely contagious.[377] It propagates unchecked in the form of what Girard refers to as an *ontological sickness* (*Deceit, Desire and the Novel*, 97; *De la violence à la divinité*, 112: "maladie ontologique"). The more the subject and model converge on each other—a prerequisite for metaphysical desire—the more probable it becomes that the model will begin to imitate the desire of the original subject. Girard describes this phenomenon as *double imitation* or *double mediation* (*Deceit, Desire and the Novel*, 101; *De la violence à la divinité*, 116: "médiation double").

Goethe refers to this double imitation in *The Sorrows of Young Werther*, where Werther—who, as we have seen, is involved in mimetic rivalry with Albert over his fiancée, Lotte—writes in a letter that his love of Lotte has reinforced Albert's own love for her: "My devotion to Lotte, my keen joy at everything she does, increases his triumph, and he loves her the more for it."[378] An even more illustrative example can also be found in Stendhal's novel *The Red and the Black*.[379] The mayor of Verrières, Monsieur de Rênal, is involved in a mimetic relationship with the director of the town's poorhouse, Monsieur Valenod. Rênal decides together with his wife to hire Julien Sorel as a tutor for their children. The decision, however, as one can see from the following dialogue between Rênal and his wife, is not a spontaneous wish, but rather a mere product of Rênal's rivalry with Valenod:

"I've really decided to take on young Sorel, the carpenter's son," said M. de Rênal; "he will look after the children, who are starting to be too much for us." . . . "This arrangement works out in several different ways," M. de Rênal went on, glancing at his wife with the air of a diplomat; "that fellow Valenod is proud of the two Norman horses he's just bought for his carriage. But he doesn't have a tutor for his children."

"He might very well get this one away from us."

"Then you approve of my plans?" said M. de Rênal, thanking his wife for the excellent insight she had just had.[380]

Rênal negotiates afterwards with Sorel how much his son should earn for his tutoring services. Julien's father, a clever farmer, reacts to Rênal's initial offer with conscious reluctance. Rênal's interpretation of this reluctance is immediately influenced by his rivalry with Valenod, and he says to himself: "Since Sorel is not overwhelmed with joy at my proposal, as he ought to be, it's clear that he has been receiving offers from some other quarter; and where could they come from, if not from Valenod?"[381] Julien's father has an intuitive understanding of the situation. In further negotiations over the salary, he lies to Rênal: *"We can do better elsewhere."*[382] Rênal, in fear of losing Julien to his rival Valenod, raises his offer by a quarter. The value of Julien, the metaphysical "object" between Renal and Valenod, is clearly determined by the mimetic rivalry between the two. Rênal's behavior is particularly interesting in this case, for his desire to hire Julien as a tutor in the first place was not based on any real model desire, but rather purely imagined. At no point did Valenod ever show interest in Julien. Later, however, Rênal's originally imagined desire becomes reality. Valenod seeks Julien's services in his home as well, which is nothing other than an imitation of Rênal's desire. This is a clear instance of Girard's concept of double mediation, the stage in the relationship between subject and model at which imitative desire is generated most readily.[383]

Looked at systematically, this form of desire is even more fundamental than Girard's original triangular structure, for it incorporates the model's desire as well as that of the subject. Insofar as the mimetic theory excludes the possibility of the model's genuine and autonomous desire, the model must direct its desire either at an outside, third party or—as in the case of double mediation—at the desire of the original imitating subject. Girard uses this

central observation—with significant collaboration with the French psy-
chiatrist Jean-Michel Oughourlian—to develop the concept of *interdividual
psychology*, which rejects any interpretations of social relations as constituted
by inter-individual relations (*Things Hidden*, 368; *De la violence à la divinité*,
1132: "psychologie interdividuelle").[384] In contrast to the romantic ideal of
individual autonomy, Girard and Oughourlian argue that human beings are
constituted first and foremost by their relations to others.

Mimesis of the Antagonist

Everything we said about the subject's relationship to the model in the realm
of metaphysical desire is valid for the model's relationship to the subject in
the realm of double mediation. Both subject and model perceive one another
as worthy of both worship and hatred, as we saw in Girard's concept of the
model-obstacle. As mimesis intensifies, the object over which the rivals
wrestle moves further and further into the background until it has completely disappeared.[385] At this stage, the rivals are completely fixated on each
other; desire is consumed by reciprocal violence.[386] A strike from the one is
met with a counterstrike from the other as the two now imitate each other's
resistance. From an outside perspective, the two rivals resemble one another
more and more. They become mirror images of one another or, in Girard's
words, "mimetic doubles." The acquisitive mimesis of prior stages thus gives
way to the *mimesis of the antagonist* (*Things Hidden*, 26; *De la violence à la
divinité*, 734: "mimésis de l'antagoniste").[387]

A particularly illustrative example of the disappearance of the object in
the mimesis of the antagonist can be found in Baudelaire's prose-poem *Cake*,
which is told from the perspective of two hungry boys who resemble twin
brothers in their fight over a piece of bread, conjured up as a piece of cake.
After the fight, the two realize in their exhaustion that the "cake" has been
reduced to nothing but crumbs:

> Together they rolled on the ground, disputing the precious acquisition,
> neither one willing, obviously, to sacrifice a half to his brother. The first,
> exasperated, grabbed the other by his hair; who in turn clamped his teeth
> on the first one's ear, spitting out a bloody bit of it along with a superb
> dialect oath. The rightful possessor of the cake then tried to dig his nails

into the usurper's eyes while the other put all he had into strangling his opponent with one hand while, with the other, slipping the contested article into his pocket. But revived by desperation, the conquered made a comeback and brought his conqueror down by ramming his head into the other's stomach. . . . The cake traveled hand to hand and changed pocket to pocket moment by moment; but, alas, changed also in volume; and when finally, exhausted, panting, bloody, they stopped because they could fight no more, there was no longer, actually, anything to fight about; the bread had disappeared, scattered in crumbs like the grains of sand it fell among.[388]

The mimetic doubling of the rivals in this stage is a phenomenon that can only be observed from an outside perspective. Each rival sees in the other its absolute opposite.[389] The more they attempt to establish this difference, however, the more identical they appear. Girard refers to Proust's *Within a Budding Grove* to demonstrate this. The walk taken by the vacationers at the seaside resort in Balbec displays how reciprocal disdain can bring humans "together" against their will:

All these people who paced up and down the esplanade, . . . pretending not to see, so as to let it be thought that they were not interested in them, but covertly eyeing, for fear of running into them, the people who were walking beside or coming towards them, did in fact bump into them, became entangled with them, because each was mutually the object of the same secret attention veiled beneath the same apparent disdain.[390]

With the topic of enemy brothers who, like mirror images, seek each other's destruction, we arrive again in the realm of Hegel, Kojève, and Fukuyama. The struggle of life and death over prestige and recognition, however, represents merely a special case—when viewed from the perspective of the mimetic theory.[391] Negation, annihilation, and violence are not a necessary consequence of human nature, as Hobbes, Hegel, Schmitt, and also Sartre argue, but rather one possible consequence of mimetic desire. Only in the realm of the mimesis of the antagonist do negation, violence, and the struggle of life and death appear to be manifestations of man's true nature.[392] In contrast to Hegel, Girard is capable of explicating the development of the mimetic process without having to rely on such speculative and dubious suppositions.[393]

In Dostoyevsky's *The Brothers Karamazov*, one finds an indirect, yet radical critique of Hegelian philosophy with its fixation on negation. In the midst of hallucination, Ivan meets his own *doppelgänger*, who appears as the devil. This devil—a slight modification of Mephistopheles from Goethe's *Faust*—describes himself as an entity bent on perpetual denial and negation. He is the "necessary minus" without which all occurrences on earth would cease and history would come to an end.[394] This connection between negation and the end of history, one of the central aspects of Hegel's philosophy of recognition, is portrayed directly as the logic of the devil. Furthermore, Dostoyevsky places this satanic logic in the context of the mimetic double, a realm in which, according to Girard, Hegel's philosophy itself belongs.

CHAPTER 4

The Scapegoat Mechanism as Origin of Culture

Brute force is overcome by union; the allied might of scattered units makes good its right against the isolated giant. Thus we may define "right" (i.e., law) as the might of a community. Yet it, too, is nothing else than violence, quick to attack whatever individual stands in its path, and it employs the selfsame methods, follows like ends, with but one difference: it is the communal, not individual, violence that has its way.

—Sigmund Freud, *Why War?*

Girard's work on mimetic desire leads to the second large step of his theory in the direction of an all-encompassing theory of culture. The core of this second part is formed by his thesis of the scapegoat mechanism, which posits that human culture emanated from a founding murder. Girard claims that the first forms of human civilization were engendered by the collective deterrence of violence in archaic situations of crisis.

Mimetic Crisis and the Monstrous Double

Up to this point, our analysis of mimetic desire has focused merely on its manifestations in relations between individual human beings. The next stage of Girard's theory pursues the effects of mimesis on larger groups, and its role in the workings of society.

The Mimetic Crisis

As we saw in the preceding section, mimesis in the more intensified stages of desire (metaphysical desire) carries with it an extreme potential for contagious proliferation. The spatial, social, and above all mental proximity of humans to one another in situations of internal mediation transforms mimetic rivalry into a sickness that can spread through the community like a plague.[1] One finds the recurring symbol of the plague in many archaic myths and literary texts, as it symbolizes the threat of social collapse brought about by the violent proliferation of mimesis.[2] The plague, like imitation, is fundamentally contagious; both threaten social order in similar ways. The direct consequence of social crises is the outbreak of reciprocal violence that can lead to the self-annihilation of the community. It is no surprise, therefore, that natural and social catastrophes are habitually linked in the primitive psyche. In myths, for instance, natural disasters often function as metaphors for socially induced crises.

For an understanding of social crisis, it is of no great import whether the outbreak is caused by a natural disaster, an epidemic, an external military threat, or internal rivalries. In each of these cases, the decisive factor is the way the conflict is dealt with inside the community. The conflict is ultimately always internal, as it threatens the relations between the individual members of the community.[3] One must emphasize this point when considering Gunnar Heinsohn's theory of religion, which maintains that the blood rituals at the beginning of the Bronze Age were caused by a cosmic catastrophe.[4] Even if Heinsohn's data are viable, his theory lacks a persuasive social-psychological explanation. Such a theory can only be achieved by means of a fundamental understanding of archaic examples of crisis, which Girard attempts to provide with his mimetic theory.

Girard uses an array of concepts to describe the crisis-ridden dissolution of social order. With reference to instances of disorder caused primarily by the consequences of violent mimesis, he speaks of a *mimetic crisis* (*Things Hidden*, 78; *De la violence à la divinité*, 795: "crise mimétique").[5] He uses the term *sacrificial crisis* to describe the disorder caused by the failure or disappearance of sacrificial rituals (*Violence and the Sacred*, 49; *De la violence à la divinité*, 355: "crise sacrificielle").[6] The concrete and visible consequences of this cultural breakdown lead finally to what Girard describes as a *crisis of distinctions* (*Violence and the Sacred*, 49; *De la violence à la divinité*, 355: "crise des différénces").[7] The following examples, taken from a range of mythical and literary texts, will help to illustrate how the symbol of the plague is used as a metaphor for these social crises.

Oedipus the King (Sophocles)

Sophocles's tragedy *Oedipus the King* begins with a description of an epidemic plague that threatens to destroy the entire city of Thebes. An aged priest tells Oedipus of the misery that has descended upon the city:

> Our city—look around you, see with your own eyes—cannot lift her head from the depths, the red waves of death. . . . Thebes is dying. A blight on the fresh crops and the rich pastures, cattle sicken and die, and the women die in labor, children stillborn, and the plague, the fiery god of fever hurls down on the city, his lightning slashing through us—raging plague in all its vengeance, devastating the house of Cadmus! And black Death luxuriates in the raw, wailing miseries of Thebes.[8]

At first glance, these verses seem to describe an epidemic plague, which upon closer inspection, however, emerges as a social crisis.[9] Sophocles mentions not only the deaths of those affected by the plague, but also the collapse of cultural order in Thebes in which women and animals are unable to reproduce, and even the earth no longer yields fruit. Only a society wrought with conflict and interpersonal violence could precipitate such a condition. The advice of the Delphic Oracle, who is called upon to resolve the plague in Thebes, reinforces this understanding of the social nature of the crisis: "Banish the man, or pay back blood with blood. Murder sets the plague-storm on the city."[10] A comparison of these verses with Hobbes's portrayal of man's bellicose nature shows how much they converge on a description of social crisis. Both accounts culminate in complete social sterility, which, in Hobbes's view, renders all of man's social pursuits unattainable: "In such condition, there is no place for Industry, because the fruit thereof is uncertain: and consequently no Culture of the Earth; no Navigation, nor use of the commodities that may be imported by Sea; no commodious Building; no Instruments of moving, and removing such things as require much force; no Knowledge of the face of the Earth; no account of Time; no Arts; no Letters; no Society; and which is worst of all, continuall feare, and danger of violent death."[11]

"The Earthquake in Chile" (Heinrich von Kleist)

We find a particularly enlightening description of a mimetic crisis in Heinrich von Kleist's short story "The Earthquake in Chile."[12] Jeronimo Rugera, imprisoned on account of his forbidden romance with Donna Josephe, is in the act of hanging himself in his cell,

> when there came a mighty crash, as though the heavens were falling, and the entire city seemed to fall apart, burying almost every living creature under the ruins. . . . The ground shuddered beneath his feet, the walls around him were cracked from top to bottom and the whole prison threatened to topple over into the street; only the collapse of the building opposite, which fell towards the prison and formed a kind of supporting arch, prevented it from crashing to the ground.[13]

Jeronimo climbs his way to freedom just as a second earthquake destroys the entire street. Fleeing for his life, Jeronimo heads in the direction of the city gate,

> where suddenly another house collapsed, scattering dust and debris in all directions and driving him into a side street; tongues of flame were shooting up through billowing clouds of smoke and flashing out of the houses, forcing him, terrified, into another street. Here the raging River Mapocho, which had overflowed its banks, swept him into a third street, thick with the corpses of those who had been crushed to death; an occasional groan

came from beneath the ruins, people were screaming from the burning roofs, men and beasts fought against the torrent.

Kleist includes just about every conceivable instance of natural violence in his description of the earthquake. Together with the collapse of the entire structure of nature, however, the social relations of the community are also affected. Social differences—like the order of nature—seem to dissolve in the aftermath of the earthquake: "Men and women of all classes were scattered across the fields as far as the eye could see—grandees and beggars, dames and peasant women, officials and laborers, monks and nuns."[14] Social chaos, plundering, and other crimes follow the catastrophe:

> Tales were told of how after the first powerful tremors the city had been crowded with women who had given birth in full view of their menfolk, of how a sentry, ordered by the Viceroy to evacuate one of the churches, had replied that Chile no longer had a Viceroy, how the Viceroy had put an end to the looting, and how an innocent man who had managed to escape through the back door of a burning house was apprehended by the owner of the house and immediately strung up on the nearest gallows.[15]

Kleist's description displays the natural violence of the earthquake as inseparable from the collapse of social order; as is typical for the primitive consciousness, manifestations of natural and social catastrophe are linked here inextricably.

Crime and Punishment (Fyodor Dostoyevsky)

Raskolnikov's dream at the close of Dostoyevsky's *Crime and Punishment* contains a vision of a plague that spreads throughout the world via microbes, threatening to transform mankind into a vicious struggle of all against all. The more the plague spreads, the more human relations are engulfed by mutually imitated violence:

> He dreamt that the whole world was condemned to fall victim to a terrible, unknown pestilence which was moving on Europe out of the depths of Asia. . . . There had appeared a new strain of trichinae, microscopic

creatures parasitic in men's bodies. But these creatures were endowed with intelligence and will. People who were infected immediately became like men possessed and out of their minds. But never, never, had any men thought themselves so wise and so unshakable in the truth as those who were attacked. Never had they considered their judgments, their scientific deductions, or their moral convictions and creeds more infallible. Whole communities, whole cities and nations, were infected and went mad. All were full of anxiety, and none could understand any other; each thought he was the sole repository of truth and was tormented when he looked at the others, beat his breast, wrung his hands, and wept. They did not know how or whom to judge and could not agree what was evil and what good. They did not know whom to condemn or whom to acquit. Men killed one another in senseless rage. They banded together against one another's great armies, but when the armies were already on the march they began to fight among themselves, the ranks disintegrated, the soldiers fell on their neighbors, they thrust and cut, they killed and ate one another. In the towns, the tocsin sounded all day long, and called out all the people, but who had summoned them and why nobody knew, and everybody was filled with alarm. The most ordinary callings were abandoned, because every man put forward his own ideas, his own improvements, and there was no agreement; the laborers forsook the land. In places men congregated in groups, agreed on some action, swore not to disband—and immediately began to do something quite different from what they themselves had proposed, accused one another, fought and killed each other. Conflagrations were started, famine set in. All things and all men were perishing. The plague grew and spread wider and wider.[16]

The Dykemaster (Theodor Storm)

Theodor Storm's novella *The Dykemaster* also contains a description of a plague that precedes both a natural catastrophe (severe storm) and the sacrificial death of the story's protagonist, the dykemaster Hauke Haien. At the height of summer, and before the arrival of the storm, a strange form of vermin falls from the sky. A village maid reports that "horrible red-headed caterpillars" covered the fields of the next town over, which have "eaten up corn and flower and bread . . . and even fire couldn't destroy them." The plague is composed not only of insects, however, but also of blood, which "falls from the sky like rain."[17] However, as much as nature functions as a source of danger for the people in the novella, Storm describes the actual conflict as taking place not between man and nature, but rather between the villagers themselves, who at the end of the story stage the murder of the dykemaster—whom they hold responsible for the crisis.

Troilus and Cressida (Shakespeare)

The collapse of social differences is a prerequisite for the infectious spread of violent mimesis. The predominance of internal mediation must first be present within the community before mimesis can exert its contagious force. A stabile social hierarchy, by contrast, prevents the spread of conflict and violence by restricting desire to external mediation. On the surface, this appears to go against the modern understanding of social violence. Our spontaneous intuition tells us that social differences (e.g., rigid hierarchies) are the very source of violence.[18] Girard refers to literary examples in his first book to demonstrate that the opposite is true. Perhaps the most distinct of these is found in Shakespeare's grotesque tragedy *Troilus and Cressida*. Within the military camp of the Greeks—who have besieged Troy—a dangerous crisis has broken out among the soldiers. Achilles, the hero of the Greek army, challenges the commander Agamemnon openly. The conflict quickly spreads beyond the two warriors and threatens to destroy the entire hierarchical order of the Greek camp—and with it the prospect of their military success. Ulysses is cognizant of the roots of the crisis and brings this insight into focus as he addresses his infected camp:

> O, when degree is shaked,
> Which is the ladder to all high designs,
> Then enterprise is sick! How could communities,
> Degrees in schools and brotherhoods in cities,
> Peaceful commerce from dividable shores,
> The primogenitive and due of birth,
> Prerogative of age, crowns, sceptres, laurels,
> But by degree, stand in authentic place?
> Take but degree away, untune that string,

And, hark, what discord follows! each thing meets
In mere oppugnancy: the bounded waters
Should lift their bosoms higher than the shores
And make a sop of all this solid globe:
Strength should be lord of imbecility,
And the rude son should strike his father dead:
Force should be right; or rather, right and wrong,
Between whose endless jar justice resides,
Should lose their names, and so should justice too.
Then every thing includes itself in power,
Power into will, will into appetite;
And appetite, an universal wolf,
So doubly seconded with will and power,
Must make perforce an universal prey,
And last eat up himself. Great Agamemnon,
This chaos, when degree is suffocate,
Follows the choking.
And this neglection of degree it is
That by a pace goes backward, with a purpose
It hath to climb. The general's disdain'd
By him one step below, he by the next,
That next by him beneath; so every step,
Exampled by the first pace that is sick
Of his superior, grows to an envious fever
Of pale and bloodless emulation.[19]

Ulysses's speech sheds light on the danger of eradicating social differences, and also singles out imitation as the principal cause of the collapse of the Greek camp. The last two verses, in particular, refer directly to the consequences of mimetic desire, describing the "envious fever"—one of the main mimetic passions examined in the previous section—resulting from "emulation." Moreover, this emulation is "pale and bloodless," a clear signal that Shakespeare aims to describe that form of rivalry over nothingness that is typical of the more advanced stages of desire.

Another interesting element of this Shakespearean text concerns the proliferation of the crisis into the order of nature itself; here, too, one finds the symbol of the plague. This natural spectacle, however, is but a prelude to the core of Shakespeare's description of a mimetically induced crisis, which ultimately reaches cosmic dimensions:

The heavens themselves, the planets and this centre
Observe degree, priority and place,
Insisture, course, proportion, season, form,
Office and custom, in all line of order;
And therefore is the glorious planet Sol
In noble eminence enthroned and sphered
Amidst the other; whose medicinable eye
Corrects the ill aspects of planets evil,
And posts, like the commandment of a king,
Sans cheque to good and bad: but when the planets
In evil mixture to disorder wander,
What plagues and what portents! what mutiny!
What raging of the sea! shaking of earth!
Commotion in the winds! frights, changes, horrors,
Divert and crack, rend and deracinate
The unity and married calm of states
Quite from their fixure![20]

The equality and nondifferentiation that fostered the initial outbreak of the plague-like crisis continue to proliferate via more intensified forms of mimesis. As we saw above, the intensification of mimetic conflicts produces rivals faced off against each other as enemy brothers. For the primitive psyche, this connection between violent crisis and the nondifferentiation of the rivaling doubles manifests itself in a phobia of twins, which has been well documented in many archaic cultures.[21] In these communities, it was common practice for twins to be either murdered at birth or—in a paradoxical reversal of the same principle—worshipped as particularly sacred members of the community. Only an understanding of culture that is aware of the relationship between nondifferentiation and violence can explain this widespread and otherwise inexplicable phenomenon.

Ancient Tragedy (Aeschylus, Sophocles, Euripides)

The metamorphosis of rivals into violent twins can be observed particularly well in ancient tragedy. In *Violence and the Sacred*, Girard stresses—with reference to Hölderlin—that the tragedians' insight into the identical nature of rivals forms the essence of their works: "If the art of tragedy is to be defined in a single phrase, we might do worse than call attention to one of its most characteristic traits: the opposition of symmetrical elements. There is no aspect of the plot, form or language of a tragedy in which this symmetrical pattern does not recur.... The symmetry of the tragic dialogue is perfectly mirrored by the stichomythia, in which the two protagonists address one another in alternating lines" (*Violence and the Sacred*, 44).[22] Furthermore, the tragedies of Aeschylus, Sophocles, and Euripides blur the divisions between "good" and "evil" among opposing characters to such an extent that their relations are ultimately marked by symmetrical reciprocity. The crisis in the drama is composed precisely of the lack of difference between the protagonists. Their identity is not always immediately perceivable within the drama, however. This can only be observed from an external vantage point, i.e., by viewing the sequence of the plot in its entirety; an examination of merely individual scenes, by contrast, produces a one-sided understanding of the drama. From the latter perspective, only one of the characters is shown attacking or inculpating the other; one of the two rivals is always the victor or the vanquished. Each scene, taken individually, also always shows an apparently stabile relationship between the two protagonists. One dominates the other like a violent god, while the other plays the role of the defeated imitator. In the next instance, a complete reversal can take place in which the imitator strikes back and with his violence usurps the dominant position. Violence itself—which in the crisis increasingly takes center stage—makes this constant reciprocity possible; it becomes the actual object of desire in the escalating melee and bequeaths godlike attractiveness upon him who implements it most fully.

This insight into the identical nature of the rivaling protagonists emerges from the drama's entire development. It is the insight into the mimetic crisis, the interplay between enemy brothers, in which no instance of violence goes unanswered. Each strike gives rise to a counterstrike as the relationship between the rivals becomes one of inescapable repetition. The victor in the first scene is vanquished in the next, as the rivals exchange positions ever more rapidly. This relationship is the quintessence of classical tragedy and, for Girard, that which demonstrates the fundamental equality of all mimetic opponents: "The reciprocal relationship between the characters is real, but it is the sum of nonreciprocal moments. The antagonists never occupy the same positions at the same time, . . . but they occupy these positions in succession" (*Violence and the Sacred*, 158).

The Emergence of Monsters

The more the mimetic crisis intensifies, the quicker violence is exchanged between the rivals. The rhythm of vengeance is thus one of pure acceleration. From an outside perspective, the high frequency of violence makes it clear that the rivals are faced off in reciprocal confrontation, i.e., that of enemy brothers; between the rivals themselves, however, a completely different picture arises. On account of the rapidity with which violence is exchanged, and with which the rivals reciprocally occupy the positions of triumph and defeat, they are no longer able to distinguish between the two. The disparate, conflicting moments swiftly blur into one single image: "The differences that seem to separate the antagonists shift ever faster and more abruptly as the crisis grows in intensity. Beyond a certain point, the nonreciprocal moments succeed each other with such speed that their actual passage becomes blurred. They seem to overlap, forming a composite image in which all the previous 'highs' and 'lows,' the extremes that had previously stood out in bold relief, now seem to intersect and mingle. Where formerly he had seen his antagonist and himself as incarnations of unique and separate moments in the temporal scheme of things, the subject now perceives two simultaneous projections of the entire time span—an effect that is almost cinematographic" (*Violence and the Sacred*, 159–160). The rapid sequence of reciprocation results in a "hallucinatory state that is not a synthesis of elements, but a formless and grotesque mixture of things that are normally separate" (*Violence and the Sacred*, 160). In short, from their own perspective, the rivals confront each another as monsters.

*A Midsummer Night's Dream (*Shakespeare*)*

To help clarify this nebulous process, we can refer to the emergence of monsters in *A Midsummer Night's Dream.*[23] Four lovers in Shakespeare's comedy, in the course of one night, live through a mimetic crisis. At the outset of the drama, we encounter Lysander and Hermia, a functioning couple, and Demetrius and Helena, of which the opposite is true. Helena loves Demetrius, but he wants nothing to do with her, for he is in love with Lysander's Hermia. Thus, Helena finds herself in a defeated position as she looks up to her exalted role model, Hermia, and the object of her desire, Demetrius. In accordance with the insights of the mimetic theory, Helena divinizes her model and, with it, the object of her desire. On account of this idolization, she sees herself as relegated to the animal level; the divinization of others brings with it extreme forms of self-deprecation.

Let us first examine Helena's relationship to her model, Hermia. Although we hear in the opening scene that Helena's beauty compares to that of Hermia—"Through Athens I am thought as fair as she"—Helena praises the divine beauty of her model and finds herself as "ugly as a bear":

> No, no, I am as ugly as a bear;
> For beasts that meet me run away for fear:
> Therefore no marvel though Demetrius
> Do, as a monster fly my presence thus.
> What wicked and dissembling glass of mine
> Made me compare with Hermia's sphery eyne?[24]

We find a similar scenario upon observance of the relationship between Helena and the object of her desire, Demetrius. Once again, we see divinization of the object accompanied by extreme self-degradation:

> I am your spaniel; and, Demetrius,
> The more you beat me, I will fawn on you:
> Use me but as your spaniel, spurn me, strike me,
> Neglect me, lose me; only give me leave,
> Unworthy as I am, to follow you.
> What worser place can I beg in your love,—

> And yet a place of high respect with me,—
> Than to be used as you use your dog?[25]

Mimesis, however, soon disrupts the relationship between Helena and Demetrius. All of a sudden, the entire constellation of the four young lovers is toppled. Apparently influenced by Puck's love potion, but in reality caught in the throes of the mimetic crisis, which accelerates increasingly and makes any stability in relations impossible, Lysander and Demetrius suddenly lose interest in Hermia and both begin to desire Helena.

Although Shakespeare provides no direct reference to a mimetic cause of the sudden transformation, there are two instances that make this interpretation very plausible. Firstly, the crisis in the drama directs attention away from the actual objects of rivalry insofar as they disappear increasingly from the vantage point of the rival characters. The attraction of any single character can be won—and lost—simply due to the rivalry between other characters; any one of the characters at any point can seemingly become the focus of the others' desire. Secondly, one sees that reciprocal violence and aggression increasingly take the place of the object of desire. Every act of violence that appears attractive in the moment it is committed can tip the fragile balance of desire in the drama's mesh of unstable relationships.

Another sudden change of roles occurs as Hermia, once the object of Helena's adoration, is regarded as the animal and Helena the goddess. From one scene to the next, Helena is no longer Demetrius's bear or spaniel, but rather "goddess, nymph, perfect, divine!"[26] Prior to the transformation, when Helena was still in pursuit of Demetrius, she anticipated this complete reversal with her own words:

> Run when you will, the story shall be changed:
> Apollo flies, and Daphne holds the chase;
> The dove pursues the griffin; the mild hind
> Makes speed to catch the tiger.[27]

One finds a distinct mixture of divine and animal imagery in these words, as Shakespeare offers us an abbreviated portrayal of the mimetic crisis. Despite its brevity, all elements of the crisis are visible, as the characters exchange positions with each other in rapid succession. Metaphors for divinity and animal metaphors reciprocate likewise throughout the drama. If we conjure the image of an extreme acceleration of this process, we arrive at that which the four characters themselves perceive: a blurred mixture of gods, humans, and animals. This accords exactly to the definition of monsters, which are formed by the random combination of divine, animal, and human attributes. In Greek mythology, for example, we find the famous Sphinx in the Oedipus cycle, a lion's body with a human head; or the centaur, a fantastical creature composed of the head, arms, and trunk of a man and the body of a horse. Shakespeare's midsummer melee, as well, produces such monsters. One sees elves with their king, Oberon, and queen, Titania. The monstrous climax of the drama is achieved when the elf queen falls in love with Bottom, a man who in the course of the night has transformed into a centaur-like creature with a donkey's head and human body. In short, Shakespeare illustrates with his drama how the intensification of the mimetic process leads to the emergence of monsters.

Let us return once more to Girard's systematic portrayal of this emergence. The outside perspective perceives the identical nature of the enemy brothers—or the doubles—whereas the inside perspective produces the image of monsters. The rival characters are distracted by their own hallucination of monsters and are thus unable to perceive their own reciprocal, double nature. However, the double nature of the rivals does, at times, penetrate their monstrous hallucination. Analysis of mythical and literary texts shows that all monsters have a propensity for doubling, and that in turn, all doubles—at least under the surface—possess monstrous qualities.[28] In *A Midsummer Night's Dream*, one sees the tendency for doubling where the elf queen Titania wants to elope with the monster Bottom.[29] It also rings in the words of the characters themselves—after they awake from the trance of their summer night and reflect on the events with "double vision":

> HERMIA: Methinks I see these things with parted eye,
> When every thing seems double.
> HELENA: So methinks:
> And I have found Demetrius like a jewel,
> Mine own, and not mine own.[30]

Girard refers systematically in his work to the phenomenon of the *monstrous double*, which he describes as comprising "all the hallucinatory phenomena provoked at the height of the crisis by unrecognized reciprocity" (*Violence and the Sacred*, 164; *De la violence à la divinité*, 496: "double monstrueux").

Obsession and Masks

With the help of Girard's concept of the "monstrous double," one can explain a number of interesting phenomena that belong to the nebulous and otherwise inexplicable areas of human culture. As a first instance, Girard names the concept of *obsession*.[31] When the mimetic crisis reaches the stage of the monstrous double, the subject experiences itself and its rival as a monster. The subject attempts to explain this extreme self-perception by interpreting it as originating from completely outside itself. The subject understands its own monstrosity, in other words, as a product of having been possessed by another being. In a quasi-hysterical mimesis, the subject, as puppet, obeys the commands it hears emanating from outside itself.

The second phenomenon that can be elucidated by means of the monstrous double is the use of *masks* in many archaic cultures that are geographically separated and otherwise bear no similarities to one another.[32] Just as with monsters, the mask unifies gods, man, and the inanimate object; it mixes together elements that are normally kept strictly apart. For Girard, the mask and the monstrous double are ultimately one and the same. The rites in which masks are worn tend to recreate the situations that the society experienced at the height of the mimetic crisis—during the original emergence of the monstrous double. The wearing of masks in Greek tragedy finds here an immediate explanation.

Crisis and Natural State

Girard's conception of the mimetic crisis describes how the collapse of cultural order transforms the entire society into a violent struggle of all against all. One gains insight into this process from texts written during times of such crisis—for instance, the Greek tragedies or the books of the Old Testament. According to Girard, one can draw hypotheses from these crises regarding the origins of human civilization. Since mimetic desire can turn all members of a society against each other in violent conflict—if violence is not held in check by institutions of cultural order—he postulates that there must have been such violent chaos, i.e., mimetic crises, before institutions of cultural order were established. This shows the convergence of Girard's theory with that of Thomas Hobbes, who argues explicitly for the violent nature of man's natural state.[33] Hobbes, like Girard, is unable to provide direct evidence for his arguments, but he concludes from his observations of the English Revolution—itself a great mimetic crisis—that the natural state of human society is characterized by inexorable violence, or the warlike struggle of all against all. In Hobbes's view, humans are to have behaved like wolves towards one another: *homo homini lupus.*

The extent to which Hobbes really believed in a violent origin of human civilization, however, remains unclear. Girard, on the other hand, goes a decisive step further: He claims that at the outset of civilization, there were actual mimetic crises that led to a universal chaos of violence.

The Scapegoat Mechanism

At the climax of the mimetic crisis, the violence of all against all pervades the community, with its members faced off against each other as monstrous doubles. In Girard's words, a *mimetic snowballing* (*I See Satan,* 22; *Je vois Satan,* 45: "emballement mimétique") takes control of the community, and a situation of mass delirium akin to Durkheim's concept of "collective effervescence" takes over.[34] According to Girard, many archaic cultures and societies that encountered such warlike states were unable to move beyond this stage, thus perishing in self-obliteration.

Reconciliatory Mimesis

Mythical texts and archaic rituals show us, however, that aside from reciprocal annihilation there is another way of overcoming social crisis, and that here, as well, mimesis plays the decisive role. There is no divine intervention at work here, or any other external influence that brings about an end to the chaos. Mimesis, in and of itself, carries the potential to resolve the crisis; while acquisitive mimesis polarizes the society into groups divided against each other, antagonistic mimesis can overcome this conflict and reunite the conflicting factions.[35] The latter form of mimesis is characterized by the

disappearance of the concrete objects of desire, which are replaced by reciprocal rivalry and violence. Whereas possession of the original objects led to
conflict—because these could not be shared—the possibility of mutuality [tr.
Gemeinsamkeit] arises once again at this stage. Any act of violence within the
group can be imitated by the other members without giving rise to any new
rivalry. Imitation of this violence can even engender a form of reconciliation;
if a strike or any hint of suspicion against one of the community's members
is imitated by several others, this can lead to a snowballing of imitated violence that affects the entire community: "Each member's hostility, caused
by clashing against others, becomes converted from an individual feeling
to a communal force unanimously directed against a single individual. The
slightest hint, the most groundless accusation, can circulate with vertiginous
speed and is transformed into irrefutable proof. The corporate sense of conviction snowballs, each member taking confidence from his neighbor by a
rapid process of mimesis" (*Violence and the Sacred*, 79). The initial acquisitive
mimesis gives way to what Girard refers to as *reconciliatory mimesis* (*Things
Hidden*, 29, 35; *De la violence à la divinité*, 745: "mimésis réconciliatrice"):
"Order in human culture certainly does arise from an extreme of disorder,
for such disorder is the disappearance of any and all contested objects in the
midst of conflict, and it is at such a point that acquisitive mimesis is transformed into [mimesis of the antagonist] and tends toward the unification
of conflict against an adversary" (*Things Hidden*, 29). The chaotic violence
of all against all snowballs into the violence of all against one; the victim
is killed by the collective or banished from the community, which in most
cases results likewise in his or her death. Since virtually any form of violence
in this atmosphere of collective possession is capable of bringing about the
snowballing of all against one, essentially any member of the community can
become the victim of this mechanism.

The Scapegoat Mechanism

Insofar as mimesis unites all members of the community against a single
enemy, a feeling of collective reconciliation is engendered throughout the
mob. All violence, all hatred that was previously interspersed throughout
the community in the form of individual rivalries is now directed at a single
victim. In the eyes of the mob, the victim is responsible for the emergence of

the crisis and is thus the incarnation of all evil. The monstrosity of the preceding crisis is now manifested in one single monster; we are dealing with one victim, which has become the scapegoat for the entire community. Girard refers to this phenomenon as the *mechanism of the surrogate victim* (*Violence and the Sacred*, 82; *De la violence à la divinité*, 397: "mécanisme de la victime émissaire"), the *victimage mechanism* (*Things Hidden*, 95; *De la violence à la divinité*, 814: "mécanisme victimaire"), or the *scapegoat mechanism* (*The Scapegoat*, 120; *De la violence à la divinité*, 1376: "mécanisme du bouc émissaire").

To better understand this concept, we must examine Girard's usage of the term "scapegoat" more closely. The term first appears in the book of Leviticus (16) and describes a rite in which the high priest symbolically laid the sins of the community on the back of a goat, which was then cast into the wilderness to the demon Azazel. Girard does not use the concept in this ritual sense, but rather more in accordance with its use in contemporary language.[36] The modern understanding of a scapegoat is someone who—as a result of a spontaneous psychological mechanism—is blamed for the mistakes or sins of others. While the transfer of sin found in the Leviticus ritual takes place in a completely conscious and controlled manner, modern scapegoating remains an unconscious—or at most partially conscious—psychological phenomenon. Girard uses the term "scapegoat mechanism" to highlight the unconscious nature of this solution to social crisis.[37] The *delusion* (*Violence and the Sacred*, 103–104; *De la violence à la divinité*, 422: "méconnaissance") on the part of the group of the actual happening is a necessary condition of the mechanism.[38] Only when the members of the group are unaware that they are transferring their own guilt and responsibility onto the victim can the crisis truly be overcome. Girard also uses the terms "ignorance" and "unconscious" to describe the state of the persecutors (*I See Satan*, 126; *Je vois Satan*, 198: "ignorance"; "inconscience"). It is important to note, however, that although Girard makes use of concepts here that are central to psychoanalysis, his insistence on the unconscious nature of the victimage mechanism is not a concession to any psychology of "the unconscious."[39] He strictly rejects any notion that unconscious incestuous or patricidal drives influence human behavior, as well as the conception of any self-contained—individual or collective—unconscious. The unconscious processes to which Girard refers concern, on the individual or interdividual level, the misapprehension of the mimetic nature of desire and, on the collective level, the religious disguising of these interpersonal processes. His concepts of misapprehension, ignorance, and unconsciousness must therefore not be understood in connection with psychoanalysis; they find their earliest expression in the New Testament, where Jesus asks that his persecutors be forgiven, "for they know not what they do" (Luke 23:24).[40]

Origin of Religion

In the process of the scapegoat mechanism, the persecutory group unloads its negative energy, that is, the entire responsibility for the crisis, onto the victim. Vestiges of this process can be observed even today. In the case of the original founding murders, however—which Girard assumes took place at the beginning of civilization, and the traces of which we find in archaic myth—not only negative elements were transferred onto the victims. On account of the reconciliation engendered among the members of the violent mob, the scapegoat is also associated with the positive effects of the scapegoat mechanism. Girard refers therefore to a *double transference* (*Things Hidden*, 37; *De la violence à la divinité*, 746: "le double transfert") that results in the scapegoat embodying both negative aggression and positive reconciliation.[41]

As we saw in connection with the more intensified stages of the mimetic crisis, those within the group are unable to perceive the actual nature of the mechanism as it unfolds. For them, everything is blurred by the hallucinatory effect described by Girard's concept of the monstrous double. This misperception continues in the scapegoat mechanism, in the form of the double transference. The agitators fail to see that they themselves are responsible for both the origin of the crisis and its murderous resolution. They attribute both these characteristics to the victim alone; in the eyes of the mob, the scapegoat is absolute "good" and absolute "evil" at the same time. That which during the crisis was observed in the monstrous double is now completely conferred upon the victim alone.[42]

This monstrosity—embodied in a single person who is perceived by the community as simultaneously good and evil—corresponds to the essence of the archaic sacred. The persecutors observe in their victim a divine entity; out of the mimetic chaos a god is born. The *homo homini lupus* that marked the original crisis transforms into the *homo homini Deus* of a community pacified by the divinized victim. All archaic gods are marked by the monstrous combination of concurrent forms of good and evil. The German ethnologist Adolf Ellegard Jensen displays this in his analysis of Dema deities in ancient planter cultures, which, beyond good and evil, simultaneously encompass both benevolent and malevolent aspects of reality.[43]

The metamorphosis of the scapegoat into a sacred being, which bestows both destruction and salvation on the community, is for Girard the creation of the "supernatural," a "transcendental force of violent unanimity" (*Violence and the Sacred*, 87), or also of "social transcendence" (*Job*, 70): "If this victim can extend his benefits beyond death to those who have killed him, he must either be resuscitated or was not truly dead. The causality of the scapegoat is imposed with such force that even death cannot prevent it. In order not to renounce the victim's causality, he is brought back to life and immortalized, temporarily, and what we call the transcendent and supernatural are invented for that purpose" (*The Scapegoat*, 44).[44] This divinization of the victim shows that the persecutors experience the scapegoat mechanism as a religious experience. The archaic sacred corresponds exactly to the perceptions that emerge in the course of the scapegoat mechanism. The Latin root *sacer*, which can be construed as "holy" and "cursed," points to the double meaning—both positive and negative—of the phenomenon of the sacred (*Violence and the Sacred*, 257).[45] This can also be observed in the ambiguous expressions for the sacred in other languages (e.g., the *mana* of the Melanesians). In his famous work *The Idea of the Holy*, the German theologian Rudolf Otto describes the ambivalent nature of the sacred as "fascinating and terrifying" (*fascinosum* and *tremendum*).[46]

To recapitulate, Girard argues that all archaic religions find their origin in the scapegoat mechanism. This enables him to explain all essential elements of the primary religions: myth, ritual, and taboos are all rooted in the founding murder.

- *Myths* depict the violence of the scapegoat mechanism from the perspective of the persecutors and represent the viewpoint of the mob.
- *Rites* are the community's controlled repetition of the scapegoat mechanism and can be defined as a "mimesis of an initial collective founding murder" (*Violence and the Sacred*, 97).[47] Peace and unity in the community are thereby continually restored.
- Taboos or prohibitions have the function of preventing any new outbreak of the social crisis. The crimes for which the sacrificial victim was

held solely accountable during the original crisis are now absolutely forbidden within the community.

Archaic religions emanate from an innerworldly misinterpretation of the victimage mechanism and remain therefore strictly divergent from the transcendental God of the Bible. The lynch mob believes that it is under the control of an external, transcendent power. In reality, however, the mob is possessed by the hysteria of collective violence, as it attempts to reconcile itself through the persecution of an arbitrary victim. This interpretation of religion as a mere human projection suggests an initial convergence between the mimetic theory and Feuerbach's critique of religion.[48] As we will see later, however, the mimetic theory must not be reduced to such a reading, for Girard sees in biblical revelation much more than mere human projection. He sees in the Bible the truth that can be used to penetrate the mechanisms that led to the foundation of archaic religions. Between Girard and Feuerbach, in other words, there remains a significant disagreement.[49]

The following examples will help to show how Girard discovered the scapegoat mechanism in ancient texts. In the above analysis of the mimetic crisis, we saw a number of mythical and literary texts in which the symbol of the plague signified the presence of a mimetic crisis. We find in these examples traces of the scapegoat mechanism, as well.

Oedipus the King (Sophocles)

Let us begin with Sophocles's tragedy *Oedipus the King*, which describes how a deadly plague threatens the city of Thebes, and leads to a search for the person responsible.[50] Oedipus, Creon, and Tiresias fall victim to mimetic rivalry in their search, as each attempts to place the blame for the murder of Laius—the apparent cause of the plague and crisis—on the others. Oedipus initially accuses the blind prophet Tiresias of involvement in the crime:

> Oh I'll let loose, I have such fury in me—
> now I see it all. You helped hatch the plot,
> you did the work, yes, short of killing him with your own hands—and given eyes I'd say
> you did the killing single-handed![51]

Tiresias immediately reciprocates Oedipus's accusation and claims that
Oedipus was responsible for the crisis:

> Is that so! I charge you, then, submit to that decree
> you just laid down: from this day onward
> speak to no one, not these citizens, not myself.
> *You* are the curse, the corruption of the land![52]

A quarrel breaks out between Creon and Oedipus, too, as the former accuses
the latter of being an unjust ruler.[53] The crisis comes to an end when all unite
against Oedipus, who is held responsible for the plague in Thebes for committing patricide, regicide, and having had incestuous relations with his
mother, Jocaste. According to Girard's interpretation, however, Oedipus is
nothing more than a scapegoat who blindly accepts his condemnation and
subsequently vacates the city:

> Quickly,
> for the love of god, hide me somewhere,
> kill me, hurl me into the sea
> where you can never look on me again.[54]

One sees that Oedipus is made into a scapegoat from Sophocles's characterization of him in the second drama of the cycle *Oedipus at Colonus*. After the
banishment, Sophocles portrays his hero as no longer merely evil and responsible for the social crisis, but also as a savior of the city whose future corpse
Thebes and Athens fight over while Oedipus is still alive. Girard remarks
further that the rivals in *Oedipus the King*—as with many other tragedies of
classical antiquity—resemble the enemy brothers of mimetic doubling. Oedipus, Creon, and Tiresias share the same responsibility for the mimetic crisis
in Thebes. It appears to be mere coincidence that Oedipus is forced to bear
the entire blame for the situation. The unequivocal allocation of responsibility remains unclear from the action in the drama and belongs to its mythical
core, which depicts the perspective of the victors in a tragic conflict that took
place long before Sophocles wrote his text. Sophocles was forced to respect
the roots of the Oedipus myth and to not go beyond its scope, of which
his audience was well aware. It is Sophocles's adaptation of the traditional

material, however, that makes a critical reading such as Girard's possible. In his adaptation, the sole witness of the murder of Laius testifies that the king was murdered by a group—and not by a single person. This statement, which is not contradicted in the drama, should be sufficient for Oedipus's release, as he was tried and convicted of murdering Laius on his own. Sophocles thus leaves the question of who actually killed Laius completely unresolved.[55]

These references alone, however, are not enough to portray Oedipus as an indisputably innocent scapegoat. If this were the case, it would also be a complete mystery as to how the traditional mythical interpretation of Sophocles's text could remain predominant up to the present day. As we will see later, a greater methodological effort is required to wrest the truth from myth. This requires a theory of myth—illuminated by the light of biblical revelation—that is capable of bringing about a vindication of innocent victims.

The Earthquake in Chile

We find similar moments of crisis in Kleist's "Earthquake in Chile" in which clear traces of both mimetic elements and the scapegoat mechanism can be discovered. Immediately after the earthquake, for instance, we see how an innocent man—after having rescued himself from a burning house—is grabbed by the owner of the house and immediately hanged in the street.[56] Since the scapegoat is not only the cursed one, but also the savior, Kleist's story contains traces of the scapegoat in reverse form, namely, as the sole redeemer. In the course of the story, Donna Josephe makes a last-second escape from execution, as well as from certain death in the earthquake.

Girard finds examples in several myths in which the story of a miraculous rescue—as witnessed in Kleist's "Earthquake in Chile"—is ultimately the mere reversal of the story of a murder. He refers explicitly to a myth of the Bororo people in Brazil passed on by Lévi-Strauss, as well as to the Bible story of Noah.[57] It fits with this interpretive pattern that Josephe, after being rescued by the earthquake in Kleist's story, suddenly functions as the community's quasi-divine founding mother, who is at the center of an ephemeral familial ideal, symbolizing a rebirth of culture. She offers her breast to a foreign child, thereby symbolizing her function as the source of life and nourishment for the community.[58] Many myths would stop at this point and bury the deeper truth under this apparent paradise. Kleist's story, however, belongs to the kind of literature that reveals the mechanisms at work in mythical thinking. In the concluding scene—during a church service devoted to the prevention of future earthquakes—Jeronimo, Josephe, and their followers are lynched, after being accused of causing the original earthquake. Kleist ends his story with a haunting description of how Jeronimo, Josephe, and another woman and her infant are murdered by the vicious mob, thereby bringing to light the violence that is present throughout—though shrouded in myth and by the reversal in the narrative.[59] Kleist's description of persecutory justice uncovers the logic of scapegoating that underlies both the death sentence against the protagonists at the beginning of the story, as well as the earthquake's profound effect on the survivors, who see themselves after the catastrophe as founders of a new culture.

Crime and Punishment

In Raskolnikov's dream at the close of Dostoyevsky's *Crime and Punishment*, we also find elements of the scapegoat mechanism within the description of the plague that drives the entire world into the violence of all against all: "In the whole world only a few could save themselves, a chosen handful of the pure, who were destined to found a new race of men and a new life, and to renew and cleanse the earth."[60] Once again, the scapegoat mechanism is portrayed in the form of a reversal. Here too, the framework of all against one, or in this case all against a few, is clearly visible. The foundation of a new human race symbolizes the new life that is bestowed upon the community by means of the victimage mechanism.

The Dykemaster

In Storm's *Dykemaster*, elements evocative of the scapegoat mechanism also follow the plague.[61] The dykemaster Hauke Haien is made responsible for a flood that threatens to inundate and destroy the village. As a result of his inability to cope with the collective accusation, Hauke Haien commits suicide. With the words "Take me, Lord God; but have mercy on the others!" he throws himself into the floods and, like Oedipus, accepts the guilt of the entire community.[62] After the catastrophe, Haien becomes a haunted spirit who can be seen riding his horse along the dyke whenever the sea threatens to break through. One finds here elements of the positive transformation of the scapegoat, albeit in less pronounced form. After his death, Haien turns into a protector of the villagers; Storm's scapegoat falls short of becoming a redemptive god, as is the case in archaic myth.

Romulus

Roman and Greek antiquity offer especially illustrative examples of the scapegoat mechanism. The sudden disappearance of Romulus, the founder of Rome, is one such instance. According to the mythical account, Romulus mysteriously vanishes in a storm or whirlwind—a symbol for the mimetic crisis—during a public sacrifice on Quirinal Hill. It follows that Romulus ascended directly to heaven, where he became the god Quirinus and ruled over his city. One finds elements in the historical accounts of Livy and Plutarch, however, which suggest that the Roman king disappeared in connection with an act of collective violence, thereby making Romulus's sudden transformation into a Roman god understandable using Girard's theory of the scapegoat mechanism. The following is Livy's account: "There were some . . . who secretly asserted that the king had been rent in pieces by the hands of the senators, for this rumor, too, got abroad, but in very obscure terms; the other version obtained currency, owing to men's admiration for the hero and the intensity of their panic."[63] Plutarch's account speaks likewise of murder: "Romulus disappeared suddenly, and no portion of his body or fragment of his clothing remained to be seen. But some conjectured that the senators, convened in the temple of Vulcan, fell upon him and slew him, then cut his body in pieces, put each a portion into the folds of his robe, and so carried it away."[64]

Apollonius of Tyana

An illuminating example of the workings of the scapegoat mechanism can be found in Philostratus's biographical account of Apollonius of Tyana, a first-century neopythagorean philosopher and miracle worker who even today is often—yet falsely, as the following example will show—compared to Jesus of Nazareth. The following chapter of Philostratus's *Life of Apollonius of Tyana* is a text that Girard examines extensively in his later works:[65]

In Ephesus . . . the plague had arrived and nothing proved effective against it, and so they sent an embassy to Apollonius, hoping to make him the physician of their misfortunes. Thinking he should not delay the journey, and merely saying, "Let us go," he was in Ephesus, imitating, I suppose, Pythagoras's famous act of being in Thurii and in Metapontum simultaneously. After calling the Ephesians together, he said, "Take heart, since I will end the plague today." So saying, he led them all, young and old, towards the theater where the statue of the Averter stands. There it seemed that an old man was begging, craftily blinking his eyes. He carried a bag and a lump of bread in it, and had ragged clothing and a grizzled face. Apollonius made the Ephesians encircle the man, and said, "Stone this accursed wretch, but first collect as many stones as possible." The Ephesians were puzzled by his meaning and shocked at the thought of killing someone who was a visitor and so destitute, and who was pleading with them, and saying such pitiable things. But Apollonius was relentless, urging the Ephesians to crush him without pity. Some of them had begun to lob stones at him when, after seeming to blink, he suddenly glared and showed his eyes full of fire. The Ephesians realized it was a demon and stoned it so thoroughly as to raise a pile of stones on it. After a while Apollonius told them to remove the stones and to see what animal they had killed. When the supposed target of their stones was uncovered, he had vanished, and instead there appeared a dog, like some Molossian hound in shape but the size of the largest lion, crushed by the stones and spewing foam as maniacs do. The statue of the Averter, who is Heracles, stands near the spot were the phantom was stoned.[66]

Here, too, as in all the preceding examples, one finds a social crisis at the outset of the scapegoat mechanism. The plague that lingers in Ephesus fills the members of the community with the longing for an end to the epidemic. The solution proposed by the miracle worker Apollonius is shaped completely by the archaic logic of the scapegoat mechanism. He demands that the Ephesians stone an old beggar. The attributes of the chosen victim make it clear that we are dealing with a scapegoat; the beggar is old, dirty, apparently blinking and blind, and such a "manifestly miserable" stranger that the Ephesians are at first opposed to the notion of stoning him. Only after the mob sees that he is not blind, but rather that his "eyes were full of fire," evoking those of a "demon," the Ephesians stone the beggar to death. The stoning itself—which was so thorough that the "stones were heaped into a great cairn" on top of the beggar—is a typical form of collective execution.[67] It enables and encourages a unity on the part of the mob, while simultaneously keeping an ample distance between the mob and its victim. As a result, the responsibility for the death of the victim is shared by the group homogenously, so much so that no single member can be identified as an executioner. All are involved in a communal killing, without any single member committing murder.

We also see traces of the Ephesians' reverence of their victim if we consider that afterwards, the stoning site becomes a memorial to the gods. There is no real divinization of the victim here, however, as only a small demon, in the place of a new god, emerges from the stoning. Philostratus provides thus a mere "pale form of myth" (*I See Satan*, 67), but, due to the realistic nature of the account, Girard is able to draw conclusions about the origination of those proper myths that, on account of their complete divinization of the victim, are shrouded by a virtually impenetrable religious veil.

The Lord of the Flies (William Golding)

An example from contemporary literature can shed more light on the inner social-psychological processes at work in the scapegoat mechanism. William Golding's novel *Lord of the Flies* describes how a group of English schoolboys stranded on a desert island attempts to govern itself without the help of adults. Almost immediately, fierce rivalries emerge within the group, which are consistently resolved—at least ephemerally—by scapegoating practices. Consider as a first example the scene at the outset of the novel in which the children exchange names. Jack—who functions as an antagonist to Ralph, the group's designated leader—suddenly attacks a corpulent boy who attempts to assume an air of importance during the exchanging of names. Jack calls the boy "Fatty," a vicious attack that Ralph immediately imitates in the attempt to trump Jack. He reveals the nickname the corpulent boy had at his former school, a sensitive matter the boy had confided to Ralph:

> "He's not Fatty," cried Ralph, "his real name's Piggy!" "Piggy!" "Piggy!"
> "Oh Piggy!" A storm of laughter arose and even the tiniest child joined in. For the moment the boys were a close circuit of sympathy with Piggy outside: he went very pink, bowed his head and cleaned his glasses again.[68]

What Golding characterizes as the "closed circuit of sympathy" is the exact effect Girard describes in the scapegoat mechanism in which tension is relieved within the group at the expense of a single victim. A very similar scene takes place later on in the novel, well after the group of children has already split into subgroups. Jack is leader of the "hunters," a group that more and more of the boys choose to join. One day, Ralph and Piggy approach the hunters' camp and wait just outside on a patch of grass, as suddenly the hunters at the fire

> hauled off a great chunk of meat and ran with it toward the grass. They bumped Piggy, who was burnt, and yelled and danced. Immediately, Ralph and the crowd of boys were united and relieved by a storm of laughter. Piggy once more was the centre of social derision so that everyone felt cheerful and normal.[69]

Although Ralph, together with Piggy, belongs to the few opponents of Jack's hunter group, Jack decides to reconcile spontaneously with his enemy. Piggy is the scapegoat that unites Jack's camp, which, prior to the incident, had been besieged by inner rivalries. The novel's climax essentially follows this scene. A heavy storm breaks out in which thunder and lightning once again function as signifiers of the mimetic crisis. Jack's hunter group decides to perform one of the dances the boys had been rehearsing, and the mimetic attraction of the group drives Ralph and Piggy to join in the group's dance:

> A circling movement developed and a chant. While Roger mimed the terror of the pig, the littluns ran and jumped on the outside of the circle. Piggy and Ralph, under the threat of the sky, found themselves eager to take a place in this demented but partly secure society. They were glad to touch the brown backs of the fence that hemmed in the terror and made it governable. . . . The movement became regular while the chant lost its first superficial excitement and began to beat like a steady pulse.[70]

The boys dance and scream: *"Kill the beast! Cut his throat! Spill his blood!"* Simon, who was absent when the dance began, returns from the forest to tell the group of a discovery he made while away. The dancing group, however, deep in its collective delirium, mistakes Simon for a dangerous animal as he crawls out from the forest. Together—and resembling a wild monster—the group lets loose on Simon and kills him: "The sticks fell and the mouth of the new circle crunched and screamed."[71] Golding's description of the collective processes governing the group finds broad correspondence with Girard's theory of the scapegoat.[72]

Sigmund Freud

Girard's arguments for a violent origin to human civilization do not, however, make him unique among social theorists. His stance displays unavoidable parallels to Sigmund Freud—as one can see from the passage quoted at the top of this chapter—in particular to Freud's arguments for the original patricide [tr. *Vatermord*] by the brother horde.[73] Freud first posited his theory in the seminal work *Totem and Taboo*, and later developed it in his analyses of Judaism. In *Moses and Monotheism*, for instance, he hypothesizes that Moses was murdered by the Israelites. Girard praises Freud expressly for these insights.[74] In contrast to orthodox psychoanalysis, which views these two works skeptically, Girard believes that Freud offers therein an essential contribution to the interpretation of religion.

Nevertheless, Girard diverges from the founder of psychoanalysis on certain central points. Firstly, he argues that the original victim does not have to be the father, thereby rejecting Freud's fixation on sexuality and the family constellation. For Girard, any member of the community is capable of becoming the victim. The mimetic crisis describes a scenario in which all members are essentially identical, making each a possible candidate to be "victimized." The second point of divergence concerns Freud's hypothesis of a single founding murder; Girard contends that the scapegoat mechanism took place time and again over an extended period in the community, that is, that it is fundamentally repeatable and capable of being ritualized. In addition, he argues that Freud situates the murder falsely by placing it at the outset of the ritual sequence. According to Girard, the mimetic crisis must precede the collective murder, for it is through the sacrifice that the crisis is resolved. He also rejects Freud's supposition that the ritualized victim commemorates the collective guilt [tr. *Schuldgefühl*] connected with the prehistoric founding murder. Ritual, for Girard, is no product of any sense of guilt, but rather a controlled repetition of the original victimage mechanism that restored peace in the original community.[75]

Freud is unable to provide explicit proof for his theory and is forced, like Girard, to base it on interpreted evidence. The mimetic theory has the major advantage, however, that it is able to explicate phenomena that appear otherwise very disparate and even paradoxical. Furthermore, its interpretive capacity has increasingly come to light through confrontation with the results of contemporary ethnological research.

Adolf Ellegard Jensen

The German ethnologist Adolf Ellegard Jensen, whose research focuses above all on the rituals of archaic agricultural societies—the ancient planter cultures [tr. *altertümliche Pflanzervölker*]—discovered among these a central idea, which he describes as follows: "In the great cult festivals, despite the great differences regarding the individual occasions, the focus was always on the repetition of the mythical primordial processes. This distinctly shows that sacrificial victims (both human and animal), ripeness and fertility cults, and a host of other ceremonies and ritual customs are not random elements of any individual culture, but rather that they derive from a central idea, namely, that of the "murdered divinity," which, by means of its death, determines the order of being in the contemporary world."[76] Jensen goes on to interpret his idea of the "murdered divinity" in more depth: "Death and propagation among humans, animals, and plants formed the central idea of this view of the world. The first death on earth was a murder and the divine being that was forced to suffer this fate and which was ubiquitously identified with this murder in turn bestowed the gift of propagation on humans and plants. . . . It is completely central for these processes that the victim—human, animal, or any other symbol—was experienced as a divinity."[77]

Jensen offers no explanation as to why a divinity was killed at the beginning of the culture or community in question. He is likewise unable to explain why this "central idea" stood at the center of all planter cultures, or why the slaughtered being—human or animal—had to be recognized as identical to the "murdered divinity." These cultures remain a mystery for the German ethnologist. From the perspective of the mimetic theory, however, a direct explanation emerges immediately. The divine being is the scapegoat, which, in the founding moments of the community, was collectively murdered and subsequently sacralized. Cultic sacrifice is the strictly controlled repetition of this primeval event, which explains why the victimized must be perceived as the original "murdered divinity."

Arthur Maurice Hocart

Also enlightening are the works of the English anthropologist Arthur Maurice Hocart, whose expansive field research relates to two central insights regarding the "unity of all rituals" and the ritual origin of political institutions.[78] Hocart's theses are all the more interesting considering that they do not correspond in the least to his view of the world; namely, Hocart was unable to produce a genetic explanation for the development of political order. His thesis regarding the confluence of ritual and political institutions is based simply on his observations that the two are unequivocally correlated. Initially, Hocart displayed the inclination to attribute central importance to the ritual of "holy matrimony," the *hieros gamos* in connection with sacred kingship. His ethnological findings instructed him otherwise, however, and led to his understanding of sacrifice as the unifying essence of ritual. Hocart was compelled to propose his two central theses without himself being able to offer any further explanation of them. Lucien Scubla, a French anthropologist, has since showed how one can use Girard's theory to directly understand Hocart's observations, and moreover, how the mimetic theory can help demonstrate the full and lasting meaning of these findings.[79]

Walter Burkert

The greatest proximity to Girard's scapegoat theory is found in the work of the German philologist Walter Burkert, who focuses primarily on ancient Greek history.[80] He describes the experience of the sacred in Greek antiquity as directly connected to sacrificial killing: "The worshipper experiences the god most powerfully not just in pious conduct or in prayer, song, and dance, but in the deadly blow of the axe, the gush of blood and the burning of thigh-pieces. The realm of the gods is sacred, but the 'sacred' act done at the 'sacred' place by the 'consecrating' actor consists of slaughtering sacrificial animals. .

. . Sacrificial killing is the basic experience of the 'sacred.' *Homo religious* acts and attains self-awareness as *homo necans*."[81] Burkert's detailed description of the "normal" Greek sacrifices to the gods of Olympus—which he reconstructed from manifold data—explains more closely the central religious experience of *homo necans*, or "man the killer":

> At the start, a procession, even if still a small one, is formed. The festival participants depart from the everyday world, moving to a single rhythm and singing. The sacrificial animal is led along with them, likewise decorated and transformed—bound with fillets, its horns covered with gold. Generally it is hoped that the animal will follow the procession compliantly or even willingly. . . . The final goal is the sacrificial stone, the altar "set up" long ago, which is to be sprinkled with blood. Usually a fire is already ablaze on top of it. Often a censer is used to impregnate the atmosphere with the scent of the extraordinary, and there is music, usually that of the flute. A virgin leads the way, "carrying her blanket," that is, an untouched girl holding a covered container. A water jug must be there as well. . . . After arriving at the sacred place, the participants mark off a circle; the sacrificial basket and water jug are carried around the assembly, thus marking off the sacred realm from the profane. The first communal act is washing one's hands as the beginning of that which is to take place. The animal is also sprinkled with water. "Shake yourself," says Trygaios in Aristophanes, for the animal's movements is taken to signify a "willing nod," a "yes" to the sacrificial act. The bull is watered again, so that he will bow his head. The animal thus becomes the center of attention. The participants now take unground barley grains, the most ancient agricultural product, from the basket. These, however, are not meant for grinding or to be made into food: after a brief silence, the solemn "euphemein," followed by a prayer out loud—the participants fling the barley grains away onto the sacrificial animal, the altar and the earth. They are after another kind of food. The act of throwing simultaneously as a group is an aggressive gesture, like beginning a fight, even if the most harmless projectiles are chosen. Indeed, in some ancient rituals stones were used. Hidden beneath the grains in the basket was the knife, which now lies uncovered. The leader in this incipient drama steps toward the sacrificial animal, carrying the knife still covered so that the animal cannot see it. A swift cut, and a few hairs from the brow are shorn and thrown into the fire.

This is another, though more serious, act of beginning (archestai), just as the water and the barley grains were a beginning. Blood has not yet been spilled and no pain whatsoever has been inflicted, but the inviolability of the sacrificial animal has been abolished irreversibly. Now comes the death blow. The women raise a piercing scream: whether in fear or triumph or both at once, the "Greek custom of the sacrificial scream" marks the emotional climax of the event, drowning out the death-rattle. The blood flowing out is treated with special care. It may not spill on the ground; rather, it must hit the altar, the hearth, or the sacrificial pit.[82]

The group's "aggressive sprinkling of barley grains" onto the victim and the simultaneous "piercing scream" of the women—triumphant and terrifying at once—make it clear how, at the climax of the ritual process, the unloading of collective aggression runs parallel to the experience of the sacred, which corresponds completely to Girard's hypothesis of the scapegoat mechanism.

Mircea Eliade

The strength of Burkert's observations can be reenforced by the insights of the French religious scholar Mircea Eliade, who argues that religious rituals are not to be understood merely from an examination of the present in which they occurred, but rather that they have the objective of returning humans to the primeval moment in which the transition was made from chaos to order. He stresses that "every feast of its very nature involves something of an orgy."[83] For Eliade, the term *orgy* implies the creation of a new order resulting from the chaos of the dissolution of preexisting order and social difference:

At the cosmological level, the "orgy" represents chaos or the ultimate disappearance of limits and, as time goes, the inauguration of the Great Time, of the "eternal moment," of non-duration. The presence of the orgy among the ceremonials marking the periodic divisions of time shows the *will to abolish the past totally by abolishing all creation*. The "merging together of forms" is illustrated by overthrowing social conditions (during the Saturnalia, the slave was master, the master obeyed his slaves; in Mesopotamia the king was dethroned and humiliated); by combining opposites (matrons were treated as courtesans, and so on); and by the suspension of all norms.

License is let loose, all commands are violated, all contraries are brought together, and all this is simply to effect the dissolution of the world—of which the community is a copy—and restore the primeval *illud tempus* which is obviously the mythical moment of the *beginning* (chaos) and the end (flood or *ekpyrosis*, apocalypse).[84]

Eliade's "merging together of forms" corresponds to Girard's description of the sacrificial crisis. However, Eliade is unable to provide a clear explanation for why rituals must continually restage the original crisis. Parallels between Eliade and Girard can also be seen where the former speaks of the "creative murders" that he argues are documented in several founding myths.[85] Here as well, however, Eliade fails to offer a universal explanation of his findings.[86]

The mimetic theory, on the other hand, offers a clear and persuasive interpretation of data collected by diverse anthropologists whose work remains otherwise puzzling. The interpretive power of Girard's theory can be seen in connection with a further topic of inquiry—already addressed by Hocart—namely, the confluence of sacrificial order and the emergence of political structures.

Critique of the Social Contract

No idea is more incongruous with Girard's theory than the modern notion that societal institutions emanate from a social contract, that is, an act of will [tr. *Willensakt*] governed solely by reason.[87] Girard has clarified his stance here on numerous occasions, as in the following, where he addresses Hobbes and Freud directly:

All thinkers see the origin of society in a voluntary decision, which, despite everything else, they see as subject to a kind of compulsion, namely, the need to agree on certain things. This is ultimately the case with Hobbes, who, on account of his lack of knowledge of the scapegoat mechanism, is forced to conclude: "Violence threatens to break out, thus humans are forced to cooperate." This even goes for Freud in *Totem and Taboo*: First comes the patricide, then the brother horde falls into reciprocal violence and one day decides to reconcile. In other words, they just sit down together at the table of peace! I am against this idea of any rational origin of culture. (*Quand ces choses commenceront*, 46–47)

At the height of the mimetic crisis—the violent chaos on which human civilization is based—it is inconceivable that human reason suddenly interferes to restore peace among the members of the violent community. Together with Durkheim, the great exception among modern thinkers, Girard emphasizes much more the religious origins of the Social [tr. *des Sozialen*].[88]

Girard's critique of the social contract corresponds to the general historical rejection of this philosophical idea. From a historical perspective, there are no indications that the state finds its origins in a social contract. Indeed, the modern representatives of this idea do not even base their claims on any historical contract; they merely use the idea as a logical construct with which to explain the functioning of the state. Girard's critique finds certain parallels in Jacob Burckhardt's historical assessment of the idea of the social contract, without, however, adopting Burckhardt's deterministic form of pessimism. The state, according to Burckhardt, finds its origins in a religious resolution of crisis in which a violent crime played the central role: "Violence is always the prius."[89] Burckhardt therefore dismisses the idea of society reunifying itself by means of a contract as nonsensical: "The hypothesis of the State as founded upon an antecedent contract is absurd. Rousseau makes use of it only as an ideal, an expedient. His purpose is not to show what happened, but what, according to him, should happen. No State has ever yet been created by a genuine contract, i.e. a contract freely entered into by all parties. . . . Hence no State will come into being in that way in the future. And if ever one did, it would be a feeble thing, since men could quibble for ever over its principles."[90]

As much as the mimetic theory diverges from the modern conception of the social contract, however, one can nevertheless observe traces of the scapegoat mechanism in the classical formulations of the concept. Regardless of the great effort on the part of these philosophers to construct a rational origin of human society, they were steered by historical data and logical reasoning in the direction of the founding murder. We find these traces in the work of both Hobbes and Rousseau.[91]

Thomas Hobbes

Girard's argument against the thesis that the mimetic crisis could be solved by means of human reason finds indirect parallels in the work of Hobbes, who argues that all contracts are fragile and unstable on account of man's war-like nature, where there is no central governing power. In Hobbes's universe, all contracts agreed upon without the sword are reduced to empty words. How, in such a situation of crisis, can a binding agreement be reached to establish the authority that will render all future contracts stable? Hobbes's answer to this question is enlightening. He invokes the fear of God, which he sees as the only feasible form of stability for humans in their natural state: "Before the time of Civill Society, or in the interruption there of by Warre, there is nothing can strengthen a Covenant of Peace agreed on, against the temptations of Avarice, Ambition, Lust, or other strong desire, but the feare of that Invisible Power, which they every one Worship as God; and Feare as a Revenger of their perfidy."[92] Hobbes refers concretely to the swearing of religious oaths in which the fear of God was historically implemented to enforce the potency of contracts and the commonwealth: "All therefore that can be done between two men not subject to Civill Power, is to put one another to swear by the God he feareth: Which *Swearing,* or OATH, is a *Forme of Speech, added to a Promise, by which he that promiseth signifieth, that unless he performe, he renounceth the mercy of his God, or calleth to him for vengeance on himselfe.*"[93] As an example of such an oath, Hobbes takes up the vow between the Romans and Alba Longa, which the Romans repeated during animal sacrifice and which was described by the Roman historian Livy as the oldest known contract: "Hear, Jupiter; . . . the Romans will not be the first to depart. If it shall first depart from them, . . . then on that day do thou, great Diespiter, so smite the Roman People as I shall here smite this pig."[94] Clear traces of the scapegoat mechanism are found in this rite, the first of which can be observed in the sacrificial victim around which the oath revolves. The slaughtered pig plays the central role in this self-execratory oath, as it stands for the penalty that future transgressors of the contract will be forced to pay. The connection between the contract and the sacrifice is so pronounced that Livy uses the same verb for the forging of the union and the slaughtering of the pig. *Ferire* means not only to reach agreement, or enter a contract, but also to punch, hit, kill, slaughter, slay, or stab. These additional meanings of the Latin verb clearly suggest that the roots of the Roman contract can be found in the violence of the scapegoat mechanism. This is not unique to the Roman world, however, but can also be seen in practically every culture, as Walter Burkert points out: "Whether in Israel, Greece, or Rome, no agreement, no contract, no alliance can be made without sacrifice. And, in the language of the oath, the object of aggression that is to be 'struck' and 'cut' becomes virtually identical with the covenant itself."[95] If one pursues still further Hobbes's understanding of the deeper roots of the social contract, one encounters the "sacred oath," which Durkheim—the antipode of modern social-contract theories—likewise recognizes as the origin of this tradition.[96]

A further element of Hobbesian political philosophy that harkens back to the scapegoat mechanism can be found in the basic structure of the contract. Hobbes speaks of a contract in which all members of society form reciprocal agreements with one another in order to confer their individual rights upon the sovereign. The sovereign itself, meanwhile, remains explicitly outside these agreements. As we saw in the scapegoat mechanism, where all members of the community unite against one single member, Hobbes's portrayal of mankind's transition to a civic state also assumes the structure of a "unity minus one." In the sixth chapter of this book, we will examine these parallels between the excluded scapegoat and the empowered sovereign in more depth; they concern not only a significant part of Hobbes's political philosophy, but also a structural principle of sacred kingship in general.

Jean-Jacques Rousseau

One finds similar traces of the founding murder in Rousseau's analysis of the social contract. Like Hobbes, Rousseau is unable to establish a purely rational origin of human society. At the heart of Rousseauian theory, one finds the concept of the general will (*volonté générale*), which takes on a quasi-religious character. We can gather an initial linguistic sense of this from Rousseau's description of sovereign power as "sacred."[97] Systematically, we see it in his arguments for the necessary combination of religion and politics with regard to the origin of nations. Rousseau spends an entire chapter of his *Contrat Social* calling for the institution of a civil religion that promotes the "social sentiments."[98] While Hobbes refers only indirectly to the ancient practice of religious oaths, these find a more central importance in Rousseau's system. In his political treatise *Plan for a Constitution for Corsica*, he establishes his own formula for a religious oath, which he claims should be sworn during the conclusion of any social contract.[99] Rousseau's reflections on the religious reinforcement of political unity find parallels in Durkheim's emphasis of the connection between religion and society.[100]

Aside from a general religious underpinning of the social contract, one finds a more obvious link to scapegoat logic in Rousseau's thoughts on the nature of society as a whole. The general will, as with the collective will (*volonté de tous*), is not merely the summation of the individual wills of the society, but rather takes on an added magnitude that transcends all private desires. He explains this differentiation with a quotation from Marquis d'Argenson, who states: "Agreement of two particular interests is formed by opposition to a third." This is an indirect reference to scapegoat logic, which demonstrates that the community can be most easily unified by the mutual hatred of a single enemy.[101] In the following quotation, Hannah Arendt remarks that the modern state has pursued this strategy of exclusion to its bitter end. It comes as no surprise, therefore, that Carl Schmitt—the modern representative of the "friend/enemy" distinction—was a great admirer of Rousseau's work. According to Arendt, Rousseau's arguments for how to best bind the "multitude into a unity"

> relied on a deceptively simple and plausible example. He took his cue from the common experience that two conflicting interests will bind themselves together when they are confronted by a third that equally opposes them both. Politically speaking, he presupposed the existence and relied upon the unifying power of the common national enemy. Only in the presence of the enemy can such a thing as *la nation une et indivisible,* the ideal of French and all other nationalism, come to pass. Hence, national unity can assert itself only in foreign affairs, under circumstances of, at least, potential hostility. This conclusion has been the seldom-admitted stock-in-trade of national politics in the nineteenth and twentieth centuries; it is so obviously a consequence of the general-will theory.[102]

The Origin of Culture: Space, Time, and Social Difference

Together with religion, thus, culture also finds its origins in the scapegoat mechanism, from which all fundamental social differences emerge.[103] This can be utilized to help explicate the crucial differentiation between the "profane and sacred" in archaic religion, as well as that between space and time. God is the sacrificial victim and therefore sacred; the religious community is profane. The victimage mechanism divides time into a "before" (a time of crisis) and an "after" (a time of social peace). Archaic space, meanwhile, is created by the division of an "outside" and an "inside," which are represented by the victim and the community, respectively.

The Old Testament account of Cain's murder of Abel signifies this violent origin of cultural differences.[104] The murderer, Cain, is given a sign that differentiates him from the others (Genesis 4:15); he becomes the first founder of a city, and his descendants adopt the first forms of the division of labor: "Adah bore Jabal; he was the ancestor of those who live in tents and have livestock. His brother's name was Jubal; he was the ancestor of all those who play the lyre and pipe. Zillah bore Tubal-cain, who made all kinds of bronze and iron tools" (Genesis 4:20–22).

Similarly, fundamental differences in many other cultures emerge from the founding murder. In the Vedic Purusha myth, for instance, the sacrifice of the "primeval giant" [tr. des Urwesens] Purusha brings about all essential social differences.[105] Worldly and natural order, spatial orientation, as well as the order of the four castes (1. priests, 2. warriors, 3. traders and craftsmen, 4. slaves and workers) all originate from the "Cosmic Sacrifice" of Purusha:

> From that Cosmic Sacrifice, in which everything has been offered as oblations, the Rks (verses), and the Samans (songs) were born. The Chandas (meters) of the Atharva and the Yajuh are also born from that Sacrifice. From that Cosmic Sacrifice horses are born, and all other cattle having two rows of teeth. Cows are born out of it and so are goats and sheep. The Man from the sacrificed Purusha they create, in what portions do they figurize it? What is His mouth? Which the two arms, which the two thighs and which are said to be His feet? The Brahmana is His mouth, the Rajanya is made his two arms; what is the Vaisya is His two thighs and Sudra is born

of His two feet. The moon is created from His mind and the sun is born from His eyes. The wind and the life-breath are born from His ear and the fire from His mouth. The mid-space is created from His navel, and the sky from His head; the earth from His feet; various quarters from his ear, and in this way, all these worlds are formed.[106]

What was self-evident for ancient religions finds expression in ancient philosophy as well. Heraclitus's renowned description of war speaks of a violence that forms the basis of all culture: "War is father of all, and king of all. He renders some gods, others men; he makes some slaves, others free."[107]

The capacity of the scapegoat mechanism to establish cultural order is best illustrated by the example of archaic ideas of space. With reference to Durkheim, Girard summarizes the connection between spatial structure and the founding murder in the following way:

There is good reason to think that the [surrogate victim] has imposed its image on the very structures of some communities, at those special locations forming the center of the community, sites generally dedicated to the spirit of collective unity. . . . In Greece these sites include the tombs of heroes, the omphalos, the stone of the agora and, finally, that perfect symbol of the polis, Hestia, the common hearth. Louis Gernet's essay on these sites leaves this reader at least with the overwhelming conviction that these are places where the surrogate victim met his death or where he was believed to have died. The traditions attached to these localities and the ritualistic functions associated with them lend credence to the theory that sacred mob violence formed the origin of the polis. There is reason to believe that these symbolic sites of unification gave birth to all religious forms; it was there that various cults were established, spatial relationships fixed, the clock of history set in motion, and the beginnings of a social life plotted. (*Violence and the Sacred*, 307)[108]

With regard to the science of religion, Girard's thesis can best be buttressed by Mircea Eliade's works on "sacred space."[109] Eliade points out throughout his work that archaic conceptions of space were always interconnected with religious experience, arguing that the figurative demarcation between sacred and profane space is what enabled the primeval cultures to establish a sense of orientation. Eliade alludes to sacrifice as well, which he argues is brought about by this initial spatial differentiation. He analyzes the institution of building sacrifice in particular depth, which he interprets in connection with certain myths of the creation of the world.[110] These cosmogonies tell of a world that came into existence with the sacrifice of a primeval being [tr. *eines ursprünglichen Wesens*]; building sacrifice, thus, is the ritual imitation of this "original sacrifice."

The issue of space has reemerged as an important question in the contemporary political debate. In the face of the dangers of globalization, thinkers as ideologically opposed as Carl Schmitt and Hannah Arendt, for instance, are calling for a new understanding of the significance of space for political order.[111] Schmitt attempts to contrast globalization with his new "nomos of the earth" that reconnects to ancient space and accentuates the return of the interweaving of "order and orientation."[112] A more precise analysis of Schmitt's work reveals numerous instances of the founding violence inscribed in traditional archaic space.[113] His conception of the original *nomos*, for instance, is directly connected with the violence of the mythical harbinger of peace, Heracles; furthermore, his remark that "the enclosing ring—the fence formed by men's bodies, the manring—is a primeval form of ritual, legal, and political cohabitation" recalls the lynch mob as it encircles its victim.[114] In a similar way to Schmitt, Arendt accentuates the spatial dimension of the Greek *nomos* and is therefore not as far from the latter's political philosophy as one would otherwise assume.[115] Arendt writes: "The word *polis* originally connoted something like a 'ring-wall,' and it seems the Latin *urbs* also expressed the notion of a 'circle' and was derived from the same root as *orbis*. We find the same connection in our word 'town,' which originally, like the German *Zaun*, meant a surrounding fence."[116] Arendt also incorporates traces of the founding murder into her work, though admittedly in a more concealed manner than Schmitt.[117] She sees the construction of the city wall—in her eyes both pre-political and often connected with violence—as a necessary precondition for a city politics free of violence.

Building Sacrifice

Let us now take a closer look at the concept of building sacrifice to gain a better sense of the meaning of ritual from the perspective of the mimetic theory. This form of sacrifice is based on the belief that construction projects such as houses, bridges, or dams will only last if their foundations rest on a single sacrificial victim or multiple ones.[118] For the mimetic theory, this represents a clear instance of the controlled repetition of the founding murder. Just as the killing of a scapegoat brought unity and peace to the community, all building projects should likewise receive lasting stability through corresponding sacrifice. One must keep in mind that the first human constructions were initially grave sites for scapegoats. The first pyramids, for example, arose from graves for stoned victims: "Culture always develops as a *tomb*. The tomb is nothing but the first human monument to be raised over the surrogate victim, the first most elemental and fundamental matrix of meaning. There is no culture without a tomb and no tomb without a culture; in the end the tomb is the first and only cultural symbol" (*Things Hidden*, 83).[119] Just as the tomb builds the foundation of culture, ritual sacrifice at the ceremonial beginning of construction can be seen as a repetition of the founding murder.

Building sacrifice belongs to the world's truly universal phenomena; instances can be found in essentially every culture, on all continents and throughout history. A prime example is taken from an old Indian legend in connection with a dangerous dam rupture in the Ganges. As Kurt Klusemann writes, a woman is said to have appeared among the horrified people immediately following the disaster and cried out: "'I am Ganga Bhavani. If you make a sacrifice to me, I will fix this rupture!' A farmer's child is said to have voluntarily offered himself for the sacrifice. Clothed in a bridal gown, the child is said to have walked into the ruptured dam after repeating these words as if they were a divine command. The people then filled the crack with earth and stones until the wall was once again made solid."[120]

Ancient literature, as well, contains instances of building sacrifice. An example from Roman literature concerns the murder of Remus by Romulus. The murder is seen simultaneously as the historical founding of Rome.[121] Examples of building sacrifice can just as easily be found in the Bible. A certain parallel to the founding of Rome can be observed in Cain's murder of Abel—as we saw above—and his founding of the first human city. We also encounter Joshua's curse on that person who dares to rebuild the city of Jericho (Joshua 6:26); Kings I (16:34) shows how this curse came to fruition during the reign of King Achab, and how Hiel of Bethel rebuilt Jericho: "He laid its foundation at the cost of Abiram his firstborn, and set up its gates at the cost of his youngest son Segub, according to the word of the Lord, which he spoke by Joshua son of Nun."

There are similar instances of building sacrifice in the European tradition. A North German legend, for example, tells of how children were thrown into the openings of dam ruptures.[122] This form of sacrifice, however, is by no means limited to the past and can be observed in our contemporary global society. The Austrian ethnologist Heinrich Harrer, for instance, reports of a dam sacrifice in India that took place in the autumn of 1968. In this case, a twelve-year-old boy, Khuman Singh, was sacrificed during the erection of a small dam that cost 8,000 euros.[123] The American journalist Patrick Tierney describes an example he encountered in Peru. On the Ilave River near Lake Titicaca, Tierney discovered a new steel bridge that had been severely damaged during winter floods and, directly next to it, an old stone bridge that was not damaged. For the farmers of the region, it was clear why the new bridge would not last long: "'Everyone knows that a child was sacrificed and buried in each one of the pillars of the old bridge,' commented Pablo Paredes, an engineer we'd picked up along the way. 'These people think that sacrificing and burying a child inside makes the bridge strong, so the river won't carry it away. When the new bridge was built, the people said they needed those sacrifices of the children to sustain it, and when the sacrifices weren't made and the bridge later collapsed, they blamed the absence of child sacrifices for the problem.'"[124]

A final, contemporary example can be found in the Austrian daily *Tiroler Tageszeitung* from the autumn of 1987.[125] The report describes how a ten-year-old child in West India was killed in order to rejuvenate the flow of a dried-up well.

The Dykemaster

Building sacrifice can likewise be found in modern literature. Two examples from German literature—Theodor Storm's *The Dykemaster* and Thomas

Mann's *Joseph and His Brothers*—are of particular relevance here.[126] In Storm's story, two religious world views [tr. *religiöse Weltbilder*] stand directly opposed to one other, embodied by the modern, rationalistic figure of Hauke Haien and the simple community with its archaic religiosity. A conflict breaks out between the two during the construction of one of Hauke's dams. In accordance with an old tradition, the workers throw a living dog into the ditch that is to be closed by the dyke. Hauke Haien, however, saves the dog and angrily confronts the workers, condemning this religious custom of the Wadden Sea community—which actually even calls for the sacrifice of a child—as an outrageous pagan practice:

> "Who was it?" he demanded. "Who threw this animal down there?" For a moment no one spoke, the dykemaster's gaunt face flared with anger, and they were gripped by a superstitious fear of him. Then from one of the carts a bull-necked fellow strode up in front of him. "It wasn't me, dykemaster," he said, biting the end off a small piece of chewing tobacco and putting it calmly into his mouth; "but whoever did it, did right; if your dyke's going to hold, something live's got to go into it!" "Something live? What catechism did you learn that from?" "None, sir!" replied the fellow with an impudent laugh; "even our grandfathers knew that and they were every bit as good Christians as you are! A child's best of all; when there's none to be had, a dog will do!"[127]

The central importance of this moment is foreshadowed by Hauke Haien's wife, who warns her husband that the community will demand the killing of a living victim—for instance a gypsy child, as was common in the past—during the process of the dam's construction.[128] When the actual disaster arrives and the dam breaks, even Hauke Haien is unable to maintain his rationalistic view. He throws himself into the floods as a sacrifice to appease the wrathful god and rescue his dyke and the village. In the end, though Haien was able to prevent the workers' sacrifice of the dog, he ultimately gives his own life to ensure the lasting stability of the dyke. The narrator of Storm's story, an aged and enlightened schoolmaster, compares Hauke Haien's scapegoat role to that of Socrates or Jesus—the best-known of all scapegoats in Western history.[129]

Joseph and His Brothers (Thomas Mann)

A second literary example of building sacrifice is found in Thomas Mann's novel *Joseph and His Brothers*. Mann attempts in his tetralogy to reconstruct ancient mythical thinking, and includes a reference to human sacrifice, which serves as the foundation of one of the narrative's central households. It is Laban and his wife Adina who are said to have made such a sacrifice. The novel is situated, however, in a time period in which such rituals have already become counterproductive:

> Adina, Laban's wife, ... had no sons, a fact that perhaps went far to explain Laban's gloom. Jacob later learned that they had had a son early in their married life, and sacrificed him when the house was built, burying him alive in an earthen jar, with lamps and basins, in the foundation of the building, by way of invoking the blessings of prosperity upon the house and farm. But the sacrifice had brought no particular benefit, and thereafter Adina had not proved capable of bearing sons.[130]

Mann alludes with this portrayal of the failure of building sacrifice to a development of biblical thinking that led to the overcoming of archaic religiosity.[131] We will address this biblical dissolution of myth—i.e., the Bible's uncovering of the scapegoat mechanism—in more detail further on.

This wealth of information regarding building sacrifice is of systematic importance. Since the examples come from such disparate time periods and are found on all continents, the necessity of an all-encompassing theory that can explain such a global phenomenon is of pressing importance. The mimetic theory is able to meet this challenge and proves superior to those theoretical approaches that reject any universal explanation of sacrifice and are therefore incapable of offering any essential contribution to the discussion at hand.

Myth

Girard's interpretation of myth is inextricably connected with his theory of the scapegoat mechanism. From the perspective of the mimetic theory, myths are oral accounts or written texts that portray the founding murder from the persecutors' perspective. They tell—in distorted form—of an actual happening and are derived from the collective violence directed at an actual victim: "All myths . . . have their roots in real acts of violence against real victims" (*The Scapegoat*, 25). The scapegoat mechanism, thus, is a "mechanism that produces myths" (*The Scapegoat*, 50).[132] Girard's argument that there is a historical core to mythical accounts sets him apart from many modern scholars of mythology who see in myths merely illusory products of human imagination or superstition.[133] Of all academic methods, Girard's interpretation of ancient artifacts is most comparable to that of historical analysis. His understanding of myth corresponds to Jacob Burckhardt's concept of "veiled history," which Peter von Matt explains in a way that also illuminates Girard's position.[134] In opposition to the critical "demy-thologization" predominant in the second half of the past century, which reduces the concept of myth to mere "blue mist," von Matt argues that there is significant truth behind myth. For, as he argues, "Myth is not just lies, but truth in the guise of lies. Yet more precise: It is an unbearable truth in the guise of an enthusiastic lie."[135]

Claude Lévi-Strauss's Structuralist Interpretation of Myth

The modern understanding of myth is characterized by two fundamental tendencies. On the one hand, there is the positivist school—viewed increasingly as outdated—that robs myth of all meaning [tr. *jeden Aussage-Sinn*]. For the positivists, rational thought is sufficient to clarify the errors of mythical thinking and for humans to overcome this primitive consciousness. In opposition to this devaluation of myth, one does see in the contemporary debate increasing reference to the intrinsic meaning [tr. *Eigenbedeutung*] of myth. This tendency finds most distinct expression in Lévi-Strauss's structuralism, which argues that the "savage mind" of myth possesses a quality that surpasses any scientific thought.[136] This rehabilitation of myth, however, does not imply that structuralism attributes any historical reality to mythical accounts. In his book *Totemism*, Lévi-Strauss compares two myths—originating from very disparate cultures—that speak of how the expulsion of a god establishes cultural order.[137] The first account, concerning the Ojibwa Indians to the north of the Great Lakes of northern America, tells how the

origins of this totemic culture can be found in the forcing of a divine being
back into the waters of the Great Lakes:

> A myth explains that these five "original" clans are descended from six
> anthropomorphic supernatural beings who emerged from the ocean to
> mingle with human beings. One of them had his eyes covered and dared
> not look at the Indians, though he showed the greatest anxiety to do so.
> At last he could no longer restrain his curiosity, and on one occasion he
> partially lifted his veil, and his eye fell on the form of a human being, who
> instantly fell dead "as if struck by one of the thunderers." Though the inten-
> tions of this dread being were friendly to men, yet the glance of his eye was
> too strong, and it inflicted certain death. His fellows therefore caused him
> to return to the bosom of the great water. The five others remained among
> the Indians, and "became a blessing to them." From them originate the five
> great clans or totems: catfish, crane, loon, bear, and marten.[138]

Lévi-Strauss points out distinct structural parallels between this account and
a myth from the Polynesian island of Tikopia. Once again, the expulsion of
a god builds the foundation of culture:

> A long time ago the gods were no different from mortals, and the gods
> were the direct representatives of the clans in the land. It came about that
> a god from foreign parts, Tikaru, paid a visit to Tikopia, and the gods of
> the land prepared a splendid feast for him, but first they organized trials of
> strength or speed, to see whether their guest or they would win. During a
> race, the stranger slipped and declared that he was injured. Suddenly, how-
> ever, while he was pretending to limp, he made a dash for the provisions for
> the feast, grabbed up the heap, and fled for the hills. The family of gods set
> off in pursuit; Tikaru slipped and fell again, so that the clan gods were able
> to retrieve some of the provisions, one a coconut, another a taro, another
> a bread-fruit, and others a yam. Tikaru succeeded in reaching the sky with
> most of the foodstuffs for the feast, but these four vegetable foods had been
> saved for men.[139]

Lévi-Strauss emphasizes the similarities between these myths and argues
that the individual elements must be radically *"separated"* from another in

order to bring about any system of difference and cultural order.[140] A sense of differentiated order arises from the elimination of one single part in this atmosphere of nondifferentiation.

Girard expressly praises Lévi-Strauss's insights into the logic of this exclusion and removal. He sees in structuralism a progressive theory and also applies it in his own work. However, while the structuralist emphasis of the "radical elimination" does corroborate Girard's arguments for the historical origin of myth in the scapegoat mechanism, Lévi-Strauss ultimately fails to establish any actual connection between myth and reality. For the structuralists, these two "myths concerning the origin of metaphor" are merely reflections on the abstract origin of human thought and are thus disconnected from any real event.[141] The expulsion of the god described here corresponds merely to certain logical-linguistic operations. The structuralists argue that the differences necessary for rational thought are brought about via the expulsion of an element from a continuum. From Girard's critical perspective, the collective murder hinted at in these myths is for Lévi-Strauss a mere "fictive metaphor for an intellectual operation that is alone real" (*Things Hidden*, 120). We see this disconnection of historical reality also in Lévi-Strauss's critical judgment of ritual, which he radically separates from myth and interprets as "unusable" for human thought. Ritual, for Lévi-Strauss, in direct opposition to mythical thought, represents the mere attempt to win back an undifferentiated immediacy: "On the whole, the opposition between rite and myth is the same as that between living and thinking, and ritual represents a bastardization of thought, brought about by the constraints of life."[142] In opposition to the structuralists, Girard stresses the parallels and similarities between ritual and myth, which he argues cannot be held apart from one another with regard to the categories of nondifferentiation and differentiation.[143] Both are rooted in the same mechanism and are products of the same event, for the founding violence is the "matrix of all ritual and mythological significations" (*Violence and the Sacred*, 113). According to Girard, rites can even provide essential insight for uncovering the origin of myths, for ritualized violence offers a clearer presentation of collective murder than can be found in myths, which are distorted by the religious misperceptions of the double transference.[144] Lucien Scubla offers in a recent study of Lévi-Strauss a comprehensive analysis in which he points out that the existing contradictions found in his thought can best be resolved by implementing Girard's mimetic theory.[145]

An example of the way structuralism has influenced the interpretation of myth is offered by the German ethnologist Peter Hassler, who attempts to argue that the Aztecs did not practice human sacrifice.[146] Hassler devotes the first part of his work *Menschenopfer bei den Azteken?* [tr. Human sacrifice among the Aztecs?] to a critical analysis of the historical sources suggestive of the practice, none of which, in his opinion, are dependable. He concludes that cannibalism, barbarism, and human sacrifice were not typical aspects of Aztec culture, but rather a mere projection of European conquerors. While we can safely assume that the depictions of Spanish conquistadors were enormously exaggerated, and that the widespread allegations of cannibalism were used to justify the atrocities they themselves committed, it remains completely absurd to deny that the Aztecs practiced any form of human sacrifice.[147] Hassler himself is aware of the violent and savage images in Aztec art and the myths that speak of the violent deaths of Aztec deities. The way in which he blatantly avoids the issue, however, is revealing. He writes that "figurative representations of . . . killings deliver no proof whatsoever that humans were actually sacrificed."[148] On the contrary, it remains a mystery for Hassler "how images of self-decapitations . . . or other pictorial narratives, which clearly lack any physical realism, could have ever been interpreted as evidence of human sacrifice." He goes on to argue that such depictions are to be understood in a symbolic or metaphorical sense; at the same time, how-ever, he contends that metaphors, symbols, allegories, and figurative speech have no origin in reality: "Representations, as realistic and bloodthirsty as they may appear, can very well be based on allegorical or symbolic meanings that, in and of themselves, are not immediately understandable."[149]

Hassler's arguments concerning Aztec myths are much the same. One of these accounts—regarding the Aztec vision of the creation of the world—describes how the gods Nanauatzin and Tecuciztecatl sacrificed themselves in fire to become the sun and moon, respectively. However, according to Hassler, this myth has nothing to do with sacrifice: "The gods who cast themselves into the fire are not carrying out . . . any sacrificial action, but rather are metamorphosing, which is why the term transformation would be more precise here."[150] Hassler attempts—in distinct accordance with Lévi-Strauss—to use intricate differentiations to keep myth strictly separate from ritual sacrifice: "Myth, as sacred *word*, must be kept separate from ritual, as sacred *act*, even if the two might relate to one another. For, not every myth corresponds to a ritual, and not every ritual is a sacrifice; not every sacrifice entails a killing, and not every 'killing' is physically real."[151] Hassler views the literal understanding of metaphor, symbol, and figurative expression as the greatest possible error in mythical interpretation.[152] Bloody myths are thus understood falsely as references to human sacrifice. It remains difficult to understand how Hassler can be satisfied with this explanation. Can we not assume that metaphor and figurative speech are ultimately based on reality? By the same token, is it not absurd to deny that sacrifice accounted for the origins of these "bloody" metaphors?[153] Hassler's interpretation of myth diverges fundamentally from that of the mimetic theory, which we will see at the close of this section through a Girardian reading of the Aztec creation myth mentioned above.[154] Hassler is not alone in his mode of interpretation, however, and can be seen as a typical example of the predominant trend in contemporary ethnology. This is an atmosphere in which Girard's theory has met with great skepticism, despite recent discoveries of the unequivocal remains of human sacrifice at numerous locations in the Andes.[155]

René Girard's Interpretation of Myth

In order to make his interpretation of myth more persuasive and intelligible, Girard reverts to the methodological instrument of historical analysis, which, in opposition to ethnology, does not object to the connection between texts and historical reality.[156] He makes use of the medieval *texts of persecution* (*The Scapegoat*, 7; *De la violence à la divinité*, 1234: "textes de persécution"), which include instances of collective violence against Jews, witches, foreigners, lepers, and the sick. These acts of violence occurred for the most part in connection with situations of crisis, most notably the plague. There is hardly any historical material—or none at all—that provides any objective or unbiased account of these persecutions. The accounts that we do possess are more or less distorted, as they are all told from the perspective of the persecutors. Girard assumes, together with the contemporary historical stance, that these texts of persecution are indeed based on actual acts of violence. Even the critical historians of today have no problem accepting the reality behind these distorted descriptions, not being worried at all that the Christians are thereby portrayed in a negative light.

Girard provides a detailed analysis of Guillaume de Machaut's *Judgment of the King of Navarre*, in which the Black Death in northern France, ca. 1349–1350, plays a central role:

> After that came a false, treacherous and contemptible swine: this was shameful Israel, the wicked and disloyal who hated good and loved evil, who gave so much gold and silver and promises to Christians, who then poisoned several rivers and fountains that had been clear and pure so that many lost their lives; for whosoever used them died suddenly. Certainly ten times one hundred thousand died from it, in country and in city. Then finally this mortal calamity was noticed.
>
> He who sits on high and sees far, who governs and provides for everything, did not want this treachery to remain hidden; he revealed it and made it so generally known that they lost their lives and possessions. Then every Jew was destroyed, some hanged, others burned, some were drowned, others beheaded with an ax or sword. And many Christians died together with them in this shame.[157]

There is no doubt as to how one should interpret such a text today. We are immediately able to distinguish the actual from the false elements, or, in other words, the truth from lies. From a methodological perspective, Girard singles out four elements in such texts—the *stereotypes of persecution* (*The Scapegoat*, 11; *De la violence à la divinité*, 1238: "stéréotypes de la persécution")—and interprets these in their textual interplay.

To begin with, he refers to the *stereotype of crisis*. The natural order or social structure of the community finds itself in a state of dissolution. Regardless of the concrete reason for the outbreak of the crisis, it invariably leads to a collapse of cultural order. The crucial differences within the society dissolve, and a "lack of cultural differentiation" (*The Scapegoat*, 13) ensues. In Machaut's text, the stereotype of crisis takes the form of a sign from the heavens as people are stoned to death by hail that rains down from above. Entire cities are destroyed by lightning storms. The plague rages.

Girard speaks secondly of the *stereotype of accusation*. The persecutors trace the crisis of nondifferentiation back to crimes that abolish differences within the community. The blame for the crisis is attributed to acts of violence (regicide, patricide), sexual crimes (rape, incest, bestiality), and various forms of sacrilege (host desecration, ritual murder). Accusations in connection with medieval persecutions of Jews display several of these archetypal crimes. In Machaut's text, the only stereotype of accusation is found in the Jews' alleged poisoning of wells. A potential reason for this can be found in the declining belief in occult powers during the later stage of the medieval period, which resulted in the persecutors using more "rational" accusations—such as that of poisoning.

The third stereotype concerns the *selection of victims* or the *sign of victims.*[158] In the course of history, certain groups of people or certain persons have been persecuted more frequently than others. There are certain characteristics that seem to predestine these people to their role as scapegoat. Girard calls these the "symbols of victimization," which he claims represent a difference outside the cultural system that relativizes difference within the community and engenders fear among its members. Typical characteristics of victims can come in the form of religious or cultural distinctions (ethnic or religious minorities, foreigners), physical attributes (handicaps, various deviations from the norm), gender (women), lack of protection (children), and prominent social positions (king, royalty, other forms of power). The anti-Semitism in Machaut's text represents perhaps the most typical characteristic of victims in our Christian culture.

The fourth and final element of persecution texts is the *stereotype of violence.* This is the most elementary and readily understandable of the four stereotypes. At the climax of the social crisis, the members of the community commit acts of violence against the victims they view as responsible for its outbreak. Machaut thereby describes in his text the desire to exterminate the Jews.

Girard summarizes the currently accepted interpretation of such texts of persecution in the following way: "The juxtaposition of more than one stereotype within a single document indicates persecution. Not all the stereotypes must be present: three are enough and often even two. Their existence convinces us that (1) the acts of violence are real; (2) the crisis is real; (3) the victims are chosen not for the crimes they are accused of but for the victim's signs that they bear, for everything that suggests their guilty relationship with the crisis; and (4) the import of the operation is to lay the responsibility for the crisis on the victims and to exert an influence on it by destroying these victims or at least by banishing them from the community they 'pollute'" (*The Scapegoat*, 24).

Using Girard's interpretive model, we can draw the following conclusions from Machaut's text:

1. The violence against the Jews is real.
2. The crisis, the plague, is real.
3. The Jews—as outsiders in occidental-Christian society—are falsely accused of poisoning the wells and causing the outbreak of the plague.
4. The banishment or murder of the Jews is aimed at ending the plague.

The Oedipus Myth

This method of interpretation, as mentioned above, is generally accepted by contemporary modes of study. Girard's originality consists solely in his implementation of this method to analyze myth, as well as texts of persecution. In short, he simply broadens the method's field of application, as we will see in the following Girardian analysis of the Oedipus myth.[159] This will help to provide a more precise depiction of the methodology only hinted at in our treatment of the Oedipus myth above:

1. The raging plague in the city of Thebes forms the *stereotype of crisis.*
2. The *stereotype of accusation* is found in the allegations hurled against Oedipus. He is faced with charges of regicide, patricide, and incest.
3. Oedipus is characterized by a number of *victim signs.* The orphan-turned-king walks with a limp and is a stranger to the city of Thebes, originally having come from Corinth.
4. The *stereotype of violence* is visible in the banishment and blinding of Oedipus. The application of Girard's interpretive method to the Oedipus myth displays that—as with the texts of persecution—real violence against a victim falsely accused of causing a real crisis forms the foundation of the myth.

According to Girard, this method can be used to analyze essentially all myths. The presence of at least two of the stereotypes is normally sufficient to establish the actual events on which the myth is based. However, while this method is generally accepted for the interpretation of texts of persecution, Girard's application of the same methods to myth has met with great skepticism from contemporary ethnologists. Myths cannot be deciphered so easily, it appears. In response to such criticism, Girard provides in *The Scapegoat* a version of the Oedipus myth—rewritten as a text of persecution—in order to show that simply resetting the myth in a familiar historical context can facilitate understanding of its persecutory core:

> Harvests are bad, the cows give birth to dead calves; no one is on good terms with anyone else. It is as if a spell had been cast on the village. Clearly, it is the cripple who is the cause. He arrived one fine morning, no one knows from where, and made himself at home. He even took the liberty of marrying the most obvious heiress in the village and had two children by her. All sorts of things seemed to take place in their house. The stranger was suspected of having killed his wife's former husband, a sort of local potentate, who disappeared under mysterious circumstances and was rather too quickly replaced by the newcomer. One day the fellows in the village had had enough; they took their pitchforks and forced the disturbing character to clear out. (*The Scapegoat*, 29)

As a text of persecution, the Oedipus myth is readily understandable; there are hardly any difficulties preventing one from deciphering its elements. What, however, is the deeper reason for the difficulty of interpreting myths with this method?

The Mythological Crystallization

Girard claims that one must first address the "history" or "evolution of mythology" (*The Scapegoat*, 74, 76) when tackling this issue.[160] Myths display the tendency to hide their violent elements, which prompts Girard—in reference to Freud and Derrida—to speak of the "effacement of traces" (*Things Hidden*, 65).[161] The first element to disappear is almost always the actual collective violence, which is replaced by individual violence; in the final analysis, even the traces of the latter form are lost. This effacement of traces is rooted in that religious misunderstanding which is already present at the origin of the myth. The application of Girardian method becomes increasingly complex with the development of myth, in particular in very late forms of mythology (e.g., Gnosticism).

In addition, there is a further reason—likewise connected with religious misperceptions at the heart of mythical narration—that can explain the greater difficulty facing the interpretation of myths. The religious veiling of the sacred is far more pronounced here than in texts of persecution. Mythical narrative is based on what Girard calls the *mythological crystallization* (*Things Hidden*, 247; *Des choses cachées*, 353: "cristallisation mythologique"), which makes any uncovering of the actual event virtually impossible.[162] One can work out the central difference between myths and the texts of persecution by means of an analysis of the two stages of the scapegoat mechanism, embodied in Girard's concept of the double transference examined above. Let us first compare myths with texts of persecution with regard to the negative transference, that is, the collective aggression against the single victim. In myth, this aspect is much more pronounced; physical and moral monstrosity is intrinsic to the portrayal of the scapegoat. The accused is essentially one with the crime(s) committed. The guilt belongs to the victim as a quasi-ontological attribute, and the victim's presence in the community is sufficient to bring about a spread of the crisis (e.g., plague). In the texts of persecution, meanwhile, the identification of the accused groups with their crimes is not as absolute. The persecution of Jews and witches, for instance, was often accompanied by legal proceedings that sought to determine the guilt of the accused. The accusation of poisoning in Machaut's text also exhibits the attempt to establish a rational connection between the crime and the accused. This looser connection between the accused and their crimes made it significantly easier to interpret historical texts of persecution. In his analysis of medieval witch trials, for instance, Friedrich von Spee (1591–1635) was able to demonstrate the unequivocal injustice of witch hunts.

With regard to the subsequent positive transference, as well, there are differences between myth and texts of persecution. In myth, one finds a complete conferral of the positive or benevolent influence [tr. *des positiven Aspektes*] upon the scapegoat. Though the victim is still held responsible for the crisis, it is simultaneously venerated as the harbinger of order and founder of the community. The scapegoat is not only a demonic and evil deity, but also a benevolent god. In the texts of persecution, by contrast, the positive transference—that is, the sacred—is virtually no longer present. Jews and witches, for instance, remain evil and are only capable of inspiring hatred. Only very residual traces of the positive transference can be found, which can be seen perhaps in the high esteem of Jewish medicine or the fascination with black magic or witchcraft. The absence of the positive transference, meanwhile, makes it easier to see through the texts of persecution. The scapegoats are portrayed directly as such, whereas the sacred elements in myth make any uncovering of the actual violence much more complex. If we apply the accepted method of interpreting persecution texts to myth, however, we gain insight into the truth of the latter and the essence of the sacred—which is inextricably connected to myth.

Teotihuacan: An Aztec Creation Myth

At the beginning of this section, we referred to Hassler's interpretation of an Aztec creation myth in which he rejects any presence of sacrifice, arguing rather for a mere "transmutation" of the gods. Consider the following account of the Teotihuacan myth, paraphrased by Georges Bataille, which Girard uses in his interpretation in *The Scapegoat* (57–58):[163]

> They say that before there was day in the world, the gods came together in that place which is named Teotihuacan. They said to one another: "O gods, who will have the burden of lighting the world?" Then to these words answered a god named Tecuciztecatl, and he said: "I shall take the burden of lighting the world." Then once more the gods spoke, and they said: "Who will be another?" Then they looked at one another, and deliberated on who the other should be. And none of them dared offer himself for that office. All were afraid and declined. One of the gods, to whom no one was paying any attention, and who was covered with pustules, did not speak but listened to what the other gods were saying. And the others spoke to him and said to him: "You be the one who is to give light, little pustule-covered one." And right willingly he obeyed what they commanded, and he answered: "Thankfully I accept what you have commanded me to do. Let it be as you say." And then both began to perform penances for four days. . . .
>
> And midnight having come, all the gods placed themselves about the hearth, called *teotexcalli*. In this place the fire blazed four days. The aforementioned gods arranged themselves in two rows, some at one side of the fire, some at the other side. And then the two gods above mentioned placed themselves before the fire, between the two rows of gods, all of

whom were standing. And then the gods spoke, and said to Tecuciztecatl: "How now, Tecuciztecatl! Go into the fire!" And then he braced himself to cast himself into the fire.

And since the fire was large and blazed high, as he felt the great heat of the fire, he became frightened and dared not cast himself into the fire. He turned back. Once more he turned to throw himself into the fire. But, feeling the great heat, he held back and dared not cast himself into it. Four times he tried, but never let himself go. Since he had tried four times, the gods then spoke to Nanauatzin, and said to him: "How now, Nanauatzin! You try!" And when the gods had addressed him, he exerted himself and with closed eyes undertook the ordeal and cast himself into the flames. And then he began to crackle and pop like one who is roasted.

And when Tecuciztecatl saw that Nanauatzin had cast himself into the flames, and was burning, he gathered himself and threw himself into the fire. And it is said that an eagle entered the blaze and also burned itself; and for that reason it has dark brown or black feathers. Finally a tiger entered; it did not burn itself, but singed itself; and for that reason remained stained black and white. . . .

And they say that after this the gods knelt down to wait to see where Nanauatzin, become sun, would rise. . . . And when the sun came to rise, he looked very red. He appeared to waddle from one side to the other. No one could look at him, because he snatched sight from the eyes. He shone and cast rays of light from him in grand style. His light and his rays he poured forth in all directions. And thereafter the moon rose on the horizon. Having hesitated, Tecuciztecatl was less brilliant. . . . Later the gods all had to die. The wind Kwetzacoatl killed them all; it tore out their hearts and gave life to the newborn stars.

The four stereotypes of persecution can be observed in the Teotihuacan myth, as well:

1. The *stereotype of crisis* is formed by the absence of day and night, which prompts the gods to endeavor to create the sun and moon: "They say that before there was day in the world, the gods came together in that place which is named Teotihuacan."
2. The *stereotype of accusation* is found initially in the hubris of Tecuciztecatl,

who immediately—and overzealously—accepts the task of creating the sun: "Then to these words answered a god named Tecuciztecatl, and he said: 'I shall take the burden of lighting the world.'" Tecuciztecatl's transgression is almost automatically connected with its according punishment: "Pride precedes the Fall" is the proverb that speaks of the ancient connection between this traditional crime of nondifferentiation and its penalty. Hubris, incidentally a typical trait of Greek tragic heroes, serves to lessen or abolish difference, as it destroys the social hierarchy.[164] Those who fall victim to it attempt to set themselves above social norms and inspire others to disregard social differences. Another stereotype of accusation, meanwhile, can be seen in the behavior of the second god, Nanauatzin. His crime is not hubris, but rather a pronounced passivity: "One of the gods [Nanauatzin] did not speak but listened to what the other gods were saying."

3. Nanauatzin is the god who bears the typical *sign of a victim*. The other gods refer to him as "little pustule-covered one," which refers to his shortness and sickness, branding him as a leper and a plague-stricken individual. Nanauatzin later transforms into the sun, thereby hinting at the prevalent mythological confluence of the plague and the sun god, which incidentally also applies to the Greek Apollo.

4. The *stereotype of violence* in this myth can only be detected in indirect forms. On the surface, the two "self-sacrifices" on which the myth is based could corroborate Hassler's theory that rejects any connection to collective human sacrifice. The two gods—first Nanauatzin and then Tecuciztecatl—cast themselves voluntarily into the fire and rise from the flames as sun and moon in order to solve the crisis of the absence of day and night. A more precise analysis, however, gives rise to misgivings with regard to the voluntary nature of these sacrifices. It is not Tecuciztecatl—the more vocal and active god—who sacrifices himself first, but rather Nanauatzin, the passive god whose actual desire is to escape the entire affair. The other gods call him out of his passivity with an unequivocal command: "You be the one who is to give light, little pustule-covered one." This coercion—albeit in mild form—can also be seen in the concrete execution of the sacrifice itself. Before Nanauatzin casts himself into the fire, the other gods prevent any possibility of escape by placing a circle of flames around him. The emphasis on the voluntary

nature of sacrifice is one of the most prevalent motives in mythology and is a primary element of what Girard refers to as the "effacement of traces."[165] The collective persecutors are relieved of all responsibility for the sacrificial violence, as the victim takes it on himself. The "voluntary" intention of the victim thus distracts the observer from associating any blame with the mob. Oedipus himself provides an example for this mimetic agreement with the crowd's violence. We see the same element in Storm's *Dykemaster* where Hauke Haien throws himself into the floods. The unanimity of the mob is so crucial that the victim itself must be included. This mimetic collaboration with the collective is—as Girard shows—a typical element even of the historical texts of persecution. During the medieval witch hunts, women often voluntarily accepted the community's guilt, and, in the twentieth century, similar examples can be found in the Stalinist trials in Soviet Russia. The above myth displays this clearly in the behavior of the other god, Tecuciztecatl. He is the first to announce his readiness, but fails in each of his four attempts to cast himself into the fire; only after the sacrificial death of Nanauatzin is he able to summon the strength and follow his fellow god into the flames.

Girard uses the stereotypes of persecution to support his interpretation of this Aztec myth as being based on a real founding murder: "The sacrifice of the two victims is in essence presented to us as an act of free will, a self-sacrifice, but in both cases a subtle element of constraint eats away at that freedom on two different occasions. This element of constraint is decisive. It provides yet another detail in this text to suggest the phenomenon of persecution, mythologized by the perspective of the persecutors. Three of the four stereotypes are present, and the fourth is strongly suggested as much by the victim's death as by the general configuration of the scene" (*The Scapegoat*, 62). As with many other myths, the Teotihuacan account shows that fundamental cultural differences arise from the victimage mechanism. Other creatures apart from the sun and moon also cast themselves into the fire—e.g., eagles and tigers—who receive their different colors due to the varying temperatures of the flames. All the other gods must die in the end as well, and here the violence of the process is displayed in utter openness: Kwetzacoatl, the god of wind, kills them all—tearing out their hearts—and they ascend to become the "newborn stars."

Biblical Revelation and Christianity

The original and only actual sacrifice was human sacrifice. At what moment did this practice become horrible and insane? It is in Genesis, this moment, in the image of the denied sacrifice of Isaac, the substitution of the animal. Man, advanced in God, frees himself from his stagnant ritual, from that beyond which God wants to take us—and already has.

—Thomas Mann, *Deutschland*

The third stage of the mimetic theory is formed by Girard's analysis of the writings of biblical revelation.[1] Using the same interpretive lens he used to analyze myths, Girard encountered texts in his examination of the Bible that showed a radical difference from the mythical perspective. These texts no longer took the perspective of the lynch mob, as was the case with myth, but that of scapegoats victimized by mob persecution.

Nietzsche: Dionysos versus the "Crucified"

In our analysis of texts thus far, we have yet to address the Bible in any systematic way. This corresponds also to Girard's academic path, as he turned to the Bible only in a third decisive stage of his career—after the discovery of mimetic desire and the development of his theory of the scapegoat mechanism. He was faced with the question of whether Judaism and Christianity were also religions that are rooted in the scapegoat mechanism. In truth, there are many parallels between religions, in general, and the Judeo-Christian tradition. Many religious scholars in the modern era, particularly, have argued that there is no real difference between Christianity and all other religions, thereby dismissing the texts of each as mere human projection.[2]

James G. Frazer

One of the most influential proponents of such parallels is the Scottish anthropologist James G. Frazer, whose work features comparative analysis of scapegoat rituals based on evidence discovered and collected around the world at the end of the nineteenth century. In a debate with the German philologist and biblical scholar Paul Wendland, who emphasized a distinct comparison between the Roman soldiers' mockery of Jesus and the treatment of the Roman Saturnalia kings, Frazer argued that a more striking similarity could be observed between the mock king of the Sacaea—an ancient nomadic people from eastern Iran—and the biblical account of the persecution of Jesus:[3]

> But closely as the Passion of Christ resembles the treatment of the mock king of the Saturnalia, it resembles still more closely the treatment of the mock king of the Sacaea. The description of the mockery by St Matthew is the fullest. It runs thus: "Then released he Barabbas unto them: and when he had scourged Jesus, he delivered him to be crucified. Then the soldiers of the governor took Jesus into the common hall, and gathered unto him the whole band of soldiers. And they stripped him, and put on him a scarlet robe. And when they had platted a crown of thorns, they put it on his head, and a reed in his right hand: and they bowed the knee before him, and mocked him, saying Hail, King of the Jews! And they spit upon him, and took the reed, and smote him on the head. And after that they had mocked him, they took the robe off from him" [Matthew 27:26–31]. Compare with this the treatment of the mock king of the Sacaea, as it is described by Dio Chrysostom: "They take one of the prisoners condemned to death and

scat him upon the king's throne, and give him the king's treatment, and let him lord it and drink and run riot and use the king's concubines during these days, and no man prevents him from doing just what he likes. But afterwards they strip and scourge and crucify him."[4]

Girard does not deny the many parallels between biblical texts and archaic myth and ritual. However, he rejects Frazer's approach to analysis of the Bible, arguing that the positivist viewpoint misses the actual uniqueness of the texts contained therein.

What, however, is this fundamental difference between biblical revelation and archaic religion? Girard's attempt to answer this question spans a long period of his thought. Originally, he planned to include a comparative analysis of the two in *Violence and the Sacred*, but decided instead to publish the book without any analysis of the Bible. After over ten years of grappling with the question, he remained incapable of producing a satisfactory systematic explanation of the difference between biblical and mythical texts.[5]

Friedrich Nietzsche

Girard found an essential contribution to solving this systematic problem in one of Nietzsche's unpublished aphorisms, a passage Girard has described as the "single greatest theological text of the nineteenth century" (*Quand ces choses commenceront*, 198).[6] The aphorism, part of a fragment written in 1888, alludes to both the parallels and differences between Christianity and myth:

The two types: *Dionysos* and the Crucified. . . .

Dionysos versus the "Crucified": there you have the antithesis. It is not a difference in regard to their martyrdom—it is a difference in the meaning of it. Life itself, its eternal fruitfulness and recurrence, creates torment, destruction, the will to annihilation. . . .

In the other case, suffering—the "Crucified as the innocent one"— counts as an objection to this life, as a formula for its condemnation.

One will see that the problem is that of the meaning of suffering: whether a Christian meaning or a tragic meaning. . . . In the former case, it is supposed to be the path to a holy existence: in the latter case, being is counted as *holy enough* to justify even a monstrous amount of suffering.

The tragic man affirms even the harshest suffering: he is sufficiently strong, rich, and capable of deifying to do so.

The Christian denies even the happiest lot on earth: he is sufficiently weak, poor, disinherited to suffer from life in whatever form he meets it....

The "god on the cross" is a curse on life, a signpost to seek redemption from life; Dionysos cut to pieces is a *promise* of life: It will be eternally reborn and return again from destruction.[7]

Nietzsche is aware that both mythical and biblical texts deal with the concept of martyrdom, and that both speak of the collective violence against a single victim. However, he diverges fundamentally from scholars such as Frazer in that he looks beyond these parallels and focuses on the central difference between the Gospels and myth: Myth justifies sacrifice, in Nietzsche's eyes, while the Gospel texts stress the innocence of the victim and attack the injustice of collective violence. Girard praises these insights of Nietzsche and incorporates them into his own explanation of the difference between the Bible and myth. On the other hand, however, he does not identify completely with Nietzsche's position, even referring to himself as "a kind of contra- or anti-Nietzsche."[8] The difference between the two thinkers is found in the position each takes with regard to the Bible. While Girard clearly backs the position of the Gospels, Nietzsche accuses the Bible and Christianity of bringing about the destruction of all culture. In his arguments, Nietzsche makes explicit reference to the importance of sacrifice for human existence. The "real *historical* effect" of Christianity, he argues, remains

the enchantment of egoism, of the egoism of the individual, to an extreme (—to the extreme of individual immortality). Through Christianity, the individual was made so important, so absolute, that he could no longer be *sacrificed*: but the species endures only through human sacrifice.... Genuine charity demands sacrifice for the good of the species—it is hard, it is full of self-overcoming, because it needs human sacrifice. And this pseudo-humanism called Christianity wants it established that *no one should be sacrificed*.[9]

According to Girard, Nietzsche's greatness is based on his unparalleled recognition of the truth at the heart of Christianity. At the same time, however,

Nietzsche remains a tragic figure, for he radically rejects Christianity in favor of Dionysos, which, in Girard's opinion, is what led to his madness and also anticipated—albeit on a merely individual level—the acts of political insanity [tr. *politische Wahnsinnstaten*] that followed in the twentieth century: "The wise and the scholarly are misled, but the small children are not. The latter are not afraid of Jesus, but they are afraid of Dionysos—and this has its reason. Scholars like Nietzsche wouldn't have ended the way they did, had they feared Dionysos a little more" (*Quand ces choses commenceront*, 145).[10] In Girard's eyes, the catastrophes of the Holocaust and Nietzsche's rejection of the biblical concern for victims are unmistakably connected: "By insanely condemning the real greatness of our world, not only did Nietzsche destroy himself, but he suggested the terrible destruction that was later done by National Socialism" (*I See Satan*, 175).

Max Weber

In Nietzsche's wake, Max Weber was one of the first thinkers to recognize and expressly praise the singularity of the biblical tradition, in particular its partisanship with victims. In his major study of the sociology of religion, *Ancient Judaism*, Weber poses the question whether the biblical God is identical to the pagan vegetation gods who attain dominion only by means of their own death.[11] In accordance with modern religious scholars, Weber recognizes parallels between the pagan gods and the martyrdom of both the Old Testament Servant of Yahweh—based on the account of the Second Isaiah—and the crucifixion of Jesus. These superficial parallels, however, fail to obstruct Weber's perception of the far more significant difference between the pagan religions and the biblical tradition. Weber stresses in the face of these same similarities the "fundamental change of meaning" effectuated by the Bible.[12] With reference to Second Isaiah, he points out that the Bible speaks of "the guiltless martyrdom of the Servant of God," moreover of his "unmerited suffering."[13] The biblical teachings of salvation are accompanied in Weber's eyes by an "ethical turn" [tr. *ethische Wendung*] foreign to all "known mythologies of the dying and resurrected vegetation gods or other deities and heroes."[14] The ethical singularity of the Bible is found in its partisanship with the victims of oppression and discrimination. Weber stresses in this regard that the Jews were a "pariah people," and sees in Second Isaiah the "apotheosis of suffering, misery, poverty, humiliation, and ugliness."[15] Girard praises Weber's recognition of the biblical identification with victims, but he criticizes Weber's Nietzschean stance that this revelation is based on the ressentiment stemming from the political defeats suffered by the Jewish people over centuries.[16]

To recapitulate, Girard sees myths as accounts of collective murder told from the perspective of the persecutors. In other words, the truth of the actual event—the mob's expulsion or killing of an innocent or arbitrary victim—remains radically excluded from the text. The modern world is pervaded by theories that argue that the biblical tradition represents no great difference from other religious traditions. Like Nietzsche and Weber, Girard's answer expresses the exact opposite: The Bible differentiates fundamentally from myth because it sides with the victims of persecution. We will take a closer look at this answer in the following sections.

The Old Testament

With regard to the Old Testament, one must first note that it contains many texts, or at least textual elements, that display no fundamental difference from archaic myths. The examples that follow will help to illustrate this mythical side of the Bible.

The Fall of Man as Mythical Account

At the beginning of the Old Testament, already in the Genesis stories of the Garden of Eden and the Fall of Man (Genesis 2–3), distinct traces of archaic myth can be observed. We are first confronted with God's forbiddance to eat from the tree of knowledge of good and evil (Genesis 2:16–17).[17] This God, who places a stumbling block in the middle of paradise—an expression of the model-obstacle dynamic of human relations examined above—appears to be more interested in the collapse of his plan, thus contradicting the biblical God who stands above human rivalries (cf. Matthew 5:45; Luke 12:14). The text projects the threat of violence directly into God's nature. The text gives the impression that a law was already in force prior to any original transgression. Such a priori laws and prohibitions, however, remain paradoxical.

There are numerous examples in archaic myths of criminals who, after being punished for their "crime" by the mob, become the guardians of the law retroactively put in place to prohibit the exact crime committed.[18] Our most original laws were sacralized by scapegoats who were murdered by the mob spontaneously—i.e., under the legitimacy of no law—for crimes that became law only after the fact, due solely to the religious authority bestowed upon them by the collective murder. From the perspective of myth, the victim is shown to have broken a law that, in reality, is only established by the victim's violent fate. In the mythological veiling, which attempts to erase the traces of the crisis and its violent resolution, the events are portrayed in reverse form. The mythical account focuses on the newly established order represented by the law, depicting any disorder as a mere deviance from the law. Any original disorder is thus excluded, and the law appears as God's eternal arrangement.

The prohibition that leads to the Fall of Man in Genesis contains characteristics of this mythical paradox. It has the function of prohibiting the knowledge of good and evil, but, by its very placement, the possibility for this transgression is called into being.[19] In other words, this law serves to justify the later punishment of Adam and Eve. The mythological process of veiling is too advanced for us to recognize in the text any evidence of collective violence or of the social disorder that preceded it. Nevertheless, we do encounter traces that hint at this original disorder. On the very first pages of the Old Testament, one finds the chaos (Genesis 1:2) that we can assume preceded God's forbiddance.[20] The creation of the world out of chaos is a similar theme in many other archaic portrayals of creation and differentiates from the traditional biblical understanding (2 Maccabees 7:23, 28–29; Job 26:7; Daniel 12:2; John 1:1–3; 1 Corinthians 8:6; Colossians 1:15–17; Hebrews 1:1–3), which holds that God created the world out of nothing, thus showing a gradual detachment from the mythical perspective rooted in the violence of the founding murder.[21]

Traces of violent conflict in the biblical paradise are also apparent in the two trees located in the middle of the Garden of Eden (Genesis 2:9).[22] Just as mythical sacrifice embodies both "curse and blessing" [tr. *Fluch und Segen*], the accursed "tree of knowledge" stands right next to the "tree of life," which is a source of blessing. The two remind one of the scapegoats in many myths who transform into trees and continue existing in these abstract forms.[23] A myth of the Yahuna tribe in western Brazil tells of a boy, Milomaki, who was burned at the stake and whose ashes provided the seed for the first paxiuba palm tree. Moreover, the doubling of the trees in the Garden of Eden is an example of the moral dualism that also serves to veil the original collective violence.[24]

A further mythical element in this biblical text can be found in the symbol of the serpent (Genesis 3:1–5, 14–15), which emphasizes the negative side of this nebulous dualism even more strongly than the tree of knowledge.[25] It is the serpent, in the end, that is forced to bear the full responsibility for the Fall of Man. God himself, meanwhile, the positive opponent of the serpent, is also portrayed as carrying mythical characteristics. What we saw above in the paradoxical forbiddance of the knowledge of good and evil is even more apparent at the end of the Genesis account, where God curses the serpent, pitting it in enmity against Eve (Genesis 3:14–15), and finally expels the humans from the Garden of Eden altogether (Genesis 3:23–24). These passages are examples of archaic myths in which murder or expulsion committed by human groups is masked as divine violence.[26] Behind the biblical account of the Fall of Man, in other words, there are traces of older traditions that point to an origin in the scapegoat mechanism. Consider here the parallel account found in Ezekiel (28:12–19), which tells the story of how the gods ganged up on a proud evildoer in the Garden of Eden in order to destroy him.[27]

The Mythical Account of Cain and Abel

Mythical traces can also be observed in the story of Cain and Abel (Genesis 4), which is directly connected to the Fall of Man. God's acceptance of Abel's animal sacrifice is of particular importance here, especially in contrast to his disregard for Cain's offering of agricultural produce (Genesis 4:4–5). In accordance with the logic of the scapegoat mechanism, Girard argues that the bloody sacrifice—directly associated with original human sacrifice—is more valuable than the bloodless offering:

> Violence is not to be denied, but it can be diverted to another object, something it can sink its teeth into. Such, perhaps, is one of the meanings of the story of Cain and Abel. The Bible offers us no background on the two brothers except the bare fact that Cain is a tiller of the soil who gives the fruits of his labor to God, whereas Abel is a shepherd who

regularly sacrifices the first-born of his herds. One of the two brothers kills the other, and the murderer is the one who does not have the violence-outlet of animal sacrifice at his disposal. This difference between sacrificial and non-sacrificial cults determines, in effect, God's judgment in favor of Abel. To say that God accedes to Abel's sacrificial offerings but rejects the offerings of Cain is simply another way of saying—from the viewpoint of divinity—that Cain is a murderer, whereas his brother is not (*Violence and the Sacred*, 4).[28]

The Violent Fate of Korah and His Followers

An enlightening example of the mythical side of the Old Testament is found in the Book of Numbers (16–17).[29] Korah, Dathan, Abiram, and 250 chieftains of the Israelite community have stood up in rebellion against Moses and Aaron, accusing the two of denying the general holiness of the community—and of placing too much importance on themselves: "You have gone too far! All the congregation are holy, every one of them, and the Lord is among them. So why then do you exalt yourselves above the assembly of the Lord?" (Numbers 16:3). Moses, meanwhile, returns the accusation to the rebels: "You Levites have gone too far!" (Numbers 16:7). We are dealing here with an instance of mimetic rivalry over leadership of the Israelite community. The situation, however, is ultimately one in which humans have no influence. God appears and condemns Korah and his followers to be swallowed up by the earth. The 250 chieftains, who had taken fire pans to make an offering of incense for this divine judgment, are subsequently burned in God's fire. From the perspective of the mimetic theory, this violent God is disconnected from the true biblical God and is a purely human projection. From the standpoint of the victors—here, Moses and Aaron—the cruelty connected with the resolution of the struggle appears as divine intervention. This projection of human violence into the essence of God is a typical element of mythical texts. Just as we saw in the scapegoat mechanism, this biblical story also shows that the sacred emerges from collective murder. The fire pans (censers) used in the sacrifice of the 250 chieftains considered holy after the killing are to be added to the altar: "The censers of these sinners have become holy at the cost of their lives. Make them into hammered plates as a covering for the altar, for they presented them before the Lord and they became holy" (Numbers 17:3).

The veiled account of Numbers 16 and 17, however, is not as undecipherable as archaic myth. The text shows too openly—in a similar manner to Greek tragedy—that the conflict is rooted in mimetic rivalry, as Moses and his opponents hurl seemingly identical accusations at one another. Moreover, it is not the murdered victims themselves who are ultimately sacralized—which would correspond to the general mythical pattern—but rather the fire pans merely used in the sacrifice. One even finds a hint at the truth of the events in a passage that follows. Numbers 17:6 alludes to the human—not divine—annihilation of Korah and his followers: "On the next day, however, the whole congregation of the Israelites rebelled against Moses and against Aaron, saying, 'You have killed the people of the Lord.'" However, these divergent elements from the typical mythological pattern do not allow one to recognize any radical difference between this biblical passage and archaic myth. The perspective of the victim remains lacking.

The Binding of Isaac

We could continue with further examples of mythical texts and textual elements in the Old Testament. However, exclusive focus on these elements makes only one side of the Old Testament visible, for there are also texts that clearly differentiate from myth and portray the perspective of the persecuted victim. This second side of the biblical text developed as part of a very slow and gradual process, however. It shows with increasing clarity a religion that detaches itself from the archaic practices that find their roots in the scapegoat mechanism. A fundamental moment in this process of detachment is the Genesis account of the "Sacrifice of Abraham," more appropriately referred to as the "Binding of Isaac."[30] The archaic tradition demanded human sacrifice, and Abraham was consequently forced to offer his son as a sacrifice to God. But this tradition is replaced with a religion in which, instead of humans, only animals are allowed as sacrificial victims: "Do not lay your hand on the boy or do anything to him!" (Genesis 22:12). God prohibits the sacrifice of Isaac, and Abraham decides instead to sacrifice a ram discovered in bushes nearby. This renunciation of human sacrifices—observed so perceptively by Thomas Mann in the passage heading this chapter—signifies a development that led to the creation of a religion that differentiates fundamentally from archaic myth.

The Fall of Man as Revelatory Text

This completely different side of the biblical message can also be seen in the two Genesis stories discussed above, which we first examined only for their mythical characteristics. Despite the parallels between the biblical account of the Fall of Man and archaic myth, we must add that the biblical story also sheds light on essential aspects of the complexity of human coexistence. The fact alone that the topic of God's expulsion of man is even broached shows an initial difference between the biblical text and myth.[31] Also—as with the story of Korah and his followers found in Numbers—the Genesis texts make it clear that mimetic desire is the primary cause of the "sin" committed in the Garden of Eden.[32] If we disregard the importance of the serpent, and, like Saint Paul and Kierkegaard, understand Original Sin as free from external influence, we see that the inner mimetic passions are the real cause of man's fall from God.[33] Pride and envy, in other words, are what lead to the break with God. As Augustine and Thomas Aquinas rightly point out, both are perverted forms of the imitation of God.[34] While God bestows his likeness upon man by inviting him to imitate it (Genesis 1:26–27), pride and envy—precisely that which is embodied in the symbol of the serpent—inspire man to desire the acquisition of God's divinity for himself. The humans who refuse to follow God, in other words, choose to use their own powers to be "like God" (Genesis 3:5) and inevitably fall victim to that metaphysical desire that ends in reciprocal violence and death. The murder of Abel (Genesis 4:8), the first death in the Bible, displays the direct consequence of man's rejection of God.[35] One finds in the Old Testament Book of Wisdom a concise summation of this mimetic dimension of the Fall: "God created us for incorruption, and made us in the image of his own eternity, but through the devil's envy death entered the world, and those who belong to his company experience it" (Wisdom 2:23–24).

Just as the Genesis account shows that mimetic desire is the actual cause of the Fall, it also sheds light on the human propensity to incriminate others in moments of crisis, which precipitates the hunt for scapegoats.[36] When God asks Adam to explain why he ate from the tree of knowledge, he first accuses Eve—and indirectly God himself: "The woman whom you gave to be with me, she gave me fruit from the tree, and I ate" (Genesis 3:12). Eve, in turn, accuses the serpent: "The serpent tricked me, and I ate" (Genesis 3:13). This chain of accusations is what enables us to see through any external source of guilt, which is often interpreted as being the serpent of the Genesis story. The serpent is nothing other than the embodiment of the human endeavor to escape all guilt and responsibility. While in archaic myth such symbols—such as monstrous dragons—are identical with evil, the Old Testament serpent emerges as a scapegoat. From the perspective of the Genesis account, all attempts to interpret the serpent as any extra-human evil power—which relieves man of all responsibility—remain untenable. Rüdiger Safranski, a contemporary German philosopher and self-professed agnostic, defends this position convincingly in his book *Das Böse oder Das Drama der Freiheit*.[37]

The Biblical Account of Cain and Abel

The continuation of the Fall of Man—the story of Cain and Abel (Genesis 4:1–24)—is not reduced to the mythical elements interspersed therein.[38] The singularity of this text comes forth when one compares it with other myths. We have a very similar account in Roman mythology that focuses on two brothers and the foundation of Rome. In this case, Romulus kills his brother Remus and becomes both the founder of the city and the first ruler of the Roman Empire. Cain resembles Romulus here completely. He, too, founds a city and becomes one of the forefathers of human civilization (Genesis 4:17–22). However, the radical difference between these texts is found in their diverging perspectives. While the Roman myth takes the side of Romulus and depicts the killing of Remus as a justified act, the biblical text identifies with Abel and takes the side of the innocent victim. Girard is not alone in his emphasis on the rewarding insight offered by the comparison of the Cain/Abel and Romulus/Remus accounts. This difference is also a central element of Augustine's theology of history.[39] He claims that Cain and Romulus are representatives of the earthly state rooted in murder, while Abel stands for the divine state that seeks to preserve the memory of all victims.

Joseph and His Brothers

Girard often refers to the Genesis account of Joseph and his brothers to illustrate the difference between the biblical and mythical perspective (Genesis 37–50).[40] The Oedipus myth provides an enlightening contrast here, as the two texts also show numerous points of convergence. From childhood onwards, Joseph and Oedipus are both branded as scapegoats. Oedipus is abandoned by his parents, while Joseph is sold into slavery by his brothers. Once again, however, the differences between these two texts outweigh the similarities. While Oedipus is made responsible for the plague in Thebes on account of his incestuous relationship with his mother, the biblical text is free of any comparable accusations against Joseph. It is not he who raped the wife of his paternal protector, Potiphar, but rather she who attempted to seduce him. The Bible is unequivocally on the side of the victim Joseph, as it shows no solidarity with Joseph's envious brothers or with his accusers. Also, whereas Oedipus is exalted to quasi-divine heights after his expulsion from Thebes, Joseph expressly rejects similar attempts by his brothers who had persecuted him: "Then his brothers also wept, fell down before him, and said, 'We are here as your slaves.' But Joseph said to them, 'Do not be afraid! Am I in the place of God?'" (Genesis 50:18–19). Girard points out this renunciation of idolatry as an essential aspect of the Bible's divergence from archaic myth: "The ten brothers resist the temptation to idolatry. They are Israelites, and so they don't deify human beings. Mythic heroes typically have something rigid and stylized about them. They are first demonized, then deified. Joseph is humanized. The narrator bathes him in a warm luminosity that would be unthinkable in mythology. But this is not basically due to 'literary talent,' for the genius of the text is its renunciation of idolatry" (*I See Satan*, 119).[41]

The Book of Job

Girard's most extensive analysis of the Old Testament is found in his book *Job: The Victim of his People*, in which he uses the mimetic theory to interpret the fate of Job.[42] While the contextual background blames God for Job's suffering, Girard claims that the community itself is responsible (cf. Job 16:7–10, 18; 19:13–19; 30:1–12): Job, in other words, is the scapegoat of his community.[43] His friends, who are initially described as his consolers, threaten him with harsh and violent words (cf. Job 15:20–23; 20:22–29). These are not Job's friends, but rather his persecutors.[44] One sees in their dialogues a resemblance of the "all against one" structure, which matches Job's role as the victim of universal persecution. His friends speak of divine

armies mobilized by God in order to destroy his enemies. According to
Girard, these religious and mythological metaphors are no mere product of
his friends' imaginations, but rather the expression of unconscious and collective violence against Job, which they and the other persecutors perceive as
divine violence. The God to which Job's friends refer is the projection of the
collective violence of the community. In Girard's eyes, this God is "nothing
but the fever of persecution that possesses the human group and is transmit-
ted mimetically from one to another" (*Job*, 130). If one considers Job's fate
merely from the perspective of his friends, one is faced with a myth just like
that of Oedipus.[45] The truth is just as far from Job's friends as it is from the
people of Thebes. The biblical book contains an essential element, however,
which differentiates it from all myths: It also depicts the perspective of the
victim Job. Myth requires absolute unanimity in order to function. The
persecutors must be unanimously convinced of the victim's guilt. As we saw
above, even the confession of the victim—justified or not—is required to
make the myth impenetrable to doubt. In contrast to Oedipus's immediate
self-incrimination, Job goes against the desperate attempts of his friends to
persuade him of his guilt. He insists on his innocence and thus brings about
the downfall of myth. At the same time, Girard points out that Job is unable
to fully liberate himself from the point of view of his persecutors, which one
can see in the passages where Job doubts his own innocence (*Job*, 159–174; cf.
Job 9:20–22, 27–29). In addition, just as his friends see Job as God's enemy
and persecuted by divine powers, there are parts in the dialogues in which
Job also views himself as persecuted by God (Job 16:11–14; 19:2–7). Since Job
refuses to concede any guilt in the end, however, he becomes a rebel against
this "God" whose human origins Job himself is often unable to see through
(Job 9:24, 32–35; 10:1–3; 13:7–8). Although Job's God does not differentiate
greatly from that of his friends, Girard argues that there are two central texts
that ultimately break the bond between Job and his friends:[46]

> Even now, in fact, my witness is in heaven, and he that vouches for me is on
> high. My friends scorn me; my eye pours out tears to God, that he would
> maintain the right of a mortal with God, as one does for a neighbor (Job
> 16:19–21).
>
> For I know that my Redeemer lives, and that at the last he will stand
> upon the earth; and after my skin has been thus destroyed, then in my flesh

I shall see God, whom I shall see on my side, and my eyes shall behold, and not another. My heart faints within me! (Job 19:25–27)

We see a God in both of these passages that stands in defense of the victim Job and rejects the perspective of the persecutors. These texts, according to Girard, form the climax of the dialogues. The first text juxtaposes the God of persecutors with a God that stands on the side of victims. The second text goes one step further and shows that the true God is the God of victims, one who recognizes Job for his innocence after his death. In contrast to all myths, Girard argues that the God revealed here is no longer a projection of the mob's persecutory violence, but rather the true God who stands unequivocally on the side of all innocent victims.

The Servant of Yahweh

One sees instances of the biblical defense of persecuted victims throughout the entire Old Testament. Apart from the examples already mentioned, one must emphasize in particular the psalms of lament and the texts of the prophets. The psalms of lament tell of a persecuted victim who, after being encircled by a murderous collective, screams his desperation into the air: "For I hear the whispering of many—terror all around! / as they scheme together against me, as they plot to take my life" (Psalm 31:14).[47] In this atmosphere of ubiquitous danger, the victims call to their God in hope of revenge for the violence they were made to suffer: "Do not let me be put to shame, O Lord, for I call on you; let the wicked be put to shame; let them go dumbfounded to Sheol" (Psalm 31:18). While the emphasis on the victims' plight stands for the new perspective of biblical revelation, their hope for the support of a vengeful God shows distinct traces of myth.

We can view Second Isaiah's songs of lamentation as a climax in the Old Testament (Isaiah 42:1–9; 49:1–6; 50:4–11; 52:13; 53:12).[48] They portray the fate of the Servant of Yahweh—a paradigmatic scapegoat—who is scorned, beaten, and condemned by his fellow man:

He had no form or majesty
that we should look at him,
nothing in his appearance

that we should desire him.
He was despised and rejected by others;
a man of suffering
and acquainted with infirmity;
and as one from whom others hide their faces
he was despised, and we held him of no account. (Isaiah 53:2–3)

By a perversion of justice he was taken away.
Who could have imagined his future?
For he was cut off from the land of the living,
stricken for the transgression of my people.
They made his grave with the wicked
and his tomb with the rich. (Isaiah 53:8–9)

The decisive passages are those that defend the Servant of Yahweh and stress his innocence. The end of the passage just quoted shows that the persecution took place:

Although he had done no violence,
and there was no deceit in his mouth. (Isaiah 53:9)

The text also rejects any instance of divine punishment—so typical for mythical accounts—and reveals once again the presence of the scapegoat mechanism:

Surely he has borne our infirmities
and carried our diseases;
yet we accounted him stricken,
struck down by God, and afflicted.
But he was wounded for our transgressions,
crushed for our iniquities;
upon him was the punishment that made us whole,
and by his bruises we are healed. (Isaiah 53:4–5)

It is not God, thus, who is responsible for the Servant's suffering, but rather the people who initially persecute him and then retrospectively recognize his innocence. This realization and self-incrimination on the part of the persecutors—to which the author of the text belongs—display a central difference to the perspective of mythical narrative. There are certainly myths that speak of innocent victims, or at least in which the victim is not blamed explicitly; however, we are aware of no mythical accounts comparable to this biblical text in which the persecutors simultaneously accept the blame for the violence in the text.[49] The mob is always portrayed as innocent in myth and completely free of flaws. By contrast, the mob's conversion is a critical element of this biblical text. The group of persecutors, as described in the songs above, becomes aware of its own guilt and describes this process of realization in a retrospective account that brings to light the function of the scapegoat mechanism.

Despite these fundamental differences, meanwhile, Girard interprets the songs of the Servant of God as still partly under the influence of mythical thinking.[50] In Isaiah 53:10 ("Yet it was the will of the Lord to crush him with pain"), we are suddenly faced with a God portrayed as the main instigator of persecution. Girard follows here the translation of the Jerusalem Bible. This translation, however, and with it Girard's interpretation of this passage, is not obligatory, and other scholars have rendered differing readings since. Consider the interpretation of Ernst Haag, as just one example, which sees in Isaiah 53:10(a) an additional verse that does not belong to the original text of the Servant of Yahweh.[51] According to James Williams, Isaiah 53:10 represents the point of view of the persecutors.[52] He argues that the confusion is based on a false interpretation by the original author of the verses. Meanwhile, this problem does not exist for the standard German translation of the Bible, the *Einheitsübersetzung*, which renders Isaiah 53:10 as follows and confirms the arguments above for the text's overcoming of the mythical perspective:[53]

Doch der Herr fand Gefallen an seinem zerschlagenen (Knecht).
Yet the Lord found favor in his beaten (Servant).

Notwithstanding Girard's interpretation of Isaiah 53:10, however, it is important to take note of his general remarks regarding the Old Testament. He refers to a God in these texts whose role is consistently ambiguous. Though this God is increasingly free of the elements of mythical violence, Girard argues that the Old Testament interpretation of God does not arrive fully at a conception of God devoid of all violence. In connection with these arguments, Raymund Schwager refers to the Old Testament as a "mixed text" that contains accounts "in which, on the one hand, archaic visions of the veiled world of the (violent) sacred are still prevalent and, on the other hand, which are penetrated by a completely new impulse of the revelation of the true God."[54]

We can conclude from these observations that the Old Testament offers both mythical texts, and passages that shed light on the scapegoat mechanism and convey the perspective of innocent victims. We see the beginnings of a work of revelation that has not yet reached its end. Girard argues that this consummation is found in the New Testament, which he sees—in accordance with the traditional Christian figural viewpoint—as the hermeneutic key to understanding the Old Testament: "We should not wonder that the New Testament is dependent on the Old Testament and relies on it. Both are participating in the same enterprise. The initiative comes from the Old Testament, but is brought to fruition by the New Testament where it is accomplished decisively and definitively" (*The Scapegoat*, 103).[55]

The New Testament

According to Girard, biblical revelation finds its consummation in the New Testament. In addition to the Sermon on the Mount, Girard's examination of New Testament scripture focuses above all on the Gospel accounts of the Passion.

The Passion of Jesus Christ

On the surface, one could almost read the story of the Passion as a myth, for we are dealing here, as well, with the collective murder of a single victim. According to Girard, the snowballing unanimity against Jesus is most apparent in the Acts of the Apostles, which are entirely connected to the Gospel texts: "For in this city, in fact, both Herod and Pontius Pilate, with the Gentiles and the peoples of Israel, gathered together against your holy servant Jesus, whom you anointed, to do whatever your hand and your plan had predestined to take place" (Acts 4:27).[56] Even the friends of Jesus join in on the persecution, at least indirectly. They betray, abandon, and deny him (Mark 14:10–11, 50, 66–72).[57] The texts, however, are not written from the point of view of the persecutors, but rather identify entirely with the persecuted victim: The Gospels portray Jesus as completely innocent. One of the key passages here for Girard is John 15:25, which brings to light the arbitrariness of the persecution: "They hated me without a cause" (cf. Psalms 35:19; 69:5).[58] In short, the New Testament recognizes in Jesus a falsely accused scapegoat. Though the word "scapegoat" does not emerge explicitly, the expression "lamb of God" is used to illustrate this identification with victims: "Here is the Lamb of God who takes away the sin of the world!" (John 1:29; cf. 1 John 3:5; Acts 8:32).[59]

Just as we saw in Second Isaiah, the authors who eventually wrote these texts—that uncover the scapegoat mechanism—gained their perspective in large part through the experience of conversion.[60] Only after Jesus's followers realize that they, too, were involved in their master's persecution are they capable of producing a text that brings to light the mechanism acting against the single victim. Of course, the disciples—with the exception of Judas—did not openly or fully betray Jesus.[61] They did, however, abandon him in disloyalty at certain critical moments (Mark 14:50).

The Denial of Peter

The denial of Simon Peter takes on a particular importance here in the Passion account, for Peter himself—who later becomes a leading figure of the Church—is forced to go through the necessary conversion central for any uncovering of the scapegoat mechanism.[62] Initially, Peter is confident that he can withstand the mimetic snowballing against Jesus and therefore follows his captive master into the temple of the High Priests (Mark 14:54). Not long thereafter, however, Peter gives in to the mimetic attraction of the mob and denies Jesus on three consecutive occasions (Mark 14:66–72). That the Gospel authors depict Peter's failure in such painstaking detail with the intention of preserving it for posterity belongs to one of the more outstanding aspects of biblical revelation. In stark contrast to the mythical perspective, we have a text here that does not place the blame on others, but rather focuses in on man's own weakness and inexorable entanglement in conflict. A similarly important example for the Catholic tradition can be found in Acts (9:1–22) and the letters of St. Paul (1 Corinthians 15:9; Galatians 1:13–16) where Saulus, a persecutor of the early Christian community, converts to Christianity and becomes the apostle Paul.[63] Paul himself also gains his insight into the workings of the scapegoat mechanism via conversion.

The "First Stone"

This close connection between conversion and the overcoming of persecutory mentality can be found in yet another New Testament passage (John 8:1–11), which is also an essential text for the understanding of the mimetic dynamics of the scapegoat mechanism. We encounter in John's account of the adulterous woman a mob of persecutors that has encircled a woman in order to stone her.[64] Jesus's challenge to the mob, that whoever is free of sin should "cast the first stone," functions as a creative interruption of the collective snowballing occurring around the woman. One by one, with each conscious of his own guilt, the members of the crowd leave the site of the would-be stoning without further bothering or attacking the woman. In Girard's words, Jesus puts a stop to the spreading of the mimetic contagion with his own "nonviolent contagion" (*I See Satan*, 57), which causes the members of the crowd—who now follow Jesus's example—to lay down their stones and renounce their bloody pursuit.

The Consummation of Biblical Revelation in the New Testament

The reference to the "lamb of God," the emphasis on Jesus's innocence, and the insight of the disciples into their own shortcomings all show distinct parallels between the fate of Jesus and that of the Old Testament Servant of Yahweh (Isaiah 53). As was portrayed in Isaiah, the Gospel accounts depict Jesus as falsely "numbered with the transgressors" (Isaiah 53:12; cf. Luke 22:38; Mark 15:28).[65] We can thus see in Jesus a confirmation of those Old Testament texts that stand in defense of persecuted victims and help to reveal the workings of the scapegoat mechanism.

Meanwhile, the other line of development in the Old Testament—namely, that which displays a proximity to mythical narrative—is criticized and overcome in the New Testament. We referred above to the Genesis account of the Fall of Man as a primary example of mythical narrative in the Bible. This account proved to be a "mixed text," that is, one interspersed with elements of myth and biblical revelation. In the New Testament reinterpretation of this text, these mythical remains are overcome.[66] We found traces of archaic religion in God's law, which prohibits eating from the tree of the knowledge of good and evil. This legislative ambivalence is exposed in the New Testament and replaced by faith in the figure of Jesus, which is made most apparent in Paul's letters (Romans 7:1–6; 10:4; Galatians 3:10–14, 19–25).[67] We also referred to God's expulsion of man from paradise as a further mythical element. This issue is raised in the prologue to the Gospel of John. Here, too, the idea of expulsion plays a central role in the relationship between God and man; while in the Old Testament it was God who banished man from paradise, the New Testament depicts man as responsible for the expulsion and murder of God. The Prologue to John sheds light on the actual violence of this human endeavor:

> In him [the Word] was life,
> and the life was the light of all people.
> The light shines in the darkness,
> and the darkness did not overcome it. . . .
>
> He was in the world,
> and the world came into being through him;
> yet the world did not know him.
> He came to what was his own,
> and his own people did not accept him. (John 1:4–5, 10–11)

According to Girard, this New Testament text offers the first example of an authentic overcoming of the myth that pervades God's expulsion of man from paradise: "*In the story of Adam and Eve, God manipulates and expels mankind* to secure the foundations of culture, whilst *in the Prologue to John it is mankind who expels God*" (*Things Hidden*, 275).[68]

The Nonviolent God and the Love of One's Enemy

The uncovering of the scapegoat mechanism in the Gospels necessitates the repudiation of all sacrificial theologies on which this mechanism is based.[69] According to Girard, the Gospels contain no comparative reference of Jesus's death on the cross to any form of sacrifice. On the contrary, he argues that Jesus fully accepts the words of the prophet Hosea, who claimed that God preferred "mercy over sacrifice" (Hosea 6:6; Matthew 9:13; 12:7). This renunciation of sacrificial theology—which any violent divinity ultimately requires—emanates from the image of the New Testament God. In the sermons about the Kingdom of God and above all in the Sermon on the Mount—which Girard considers central to the New Testament texts—Jesus rejects all forms of interpersonal violence. The challenge to love one's enemy found in Matthew 5:43–45 is based on the desire of a God to whom revenge is entirely foreign, one who "makes his sun rise on the evil and on the good, and sends rain on the righteous and on the unrighteous."[70] According to Girard, even the apocalyptic texts in the synoptic Gospels (Matthew 24:1–25, 46; Mark 13; Luke 17:22–37; 21:5–33) have nothing to do with a violent God.[71] The violence expressed in these texts, he argues, is brought about by the humans themselves who refuse the message of the Kingdom of God.

The Transcendence of Love

Jesus's radical nonviolence, which he lived in accordance with his own teachings, is ultimately, and not surprisingly, what makes him a scapegoat. In a culture rooted in violence, the absolutely nonviolent person is an almost inexorable target for collective persecution. It was precisely this nonviolence, however, that enabled the exposure of the scapegoat mechanism. Jesus is the innocent victim par excellence, because he is not bound to violence and owes nothing to it. It was thus necessary for Jesus to be completely independent of the world in order to uncover the mechanism of violence at work in human culture. It was also necessary for him to possess the truth about the world of violence in order to himself become a victim of this violence. Jesus's insight into the logic of violence, in other words, had to come from a source outside the human realm. Girard refers to this as the "transcendence of love" (*Things Hidden*, 233), which differentiates entirely from the false transcendence that emanates from the scapegoat mechanism.[72] The transcendence of love is a "form of transcendence that never acts by means of violence, is never responsible for any violence and remains radically opposed to violence" (*Things Hidden*, 214). Together with the Christian tradition, Girard assumes that Jesus is the Son of God and is therefore free of violence from the beginning and committed to love.[73] The divinity of Jesus, which is symbolized in the cross, is the opposite of the sacred that derives from the scapegoat mechanism: "Christ is God not because he was crucified, but because he is God born from God from all eternity" (*Things Hidden*, 219).

While religious scholars up until the present day—Gunnar Heinsohn is a contemporary example[74]—continue to identify Jesus's divinity with corresponding examples from archaic myth, the New Testament clearly differentiates between the sacred gods that originate from human sacrifice and a divine being that does not owe its existence to human violence.[75] The Gospel of Mark, for instance, reveals the extent to which King Herod, the murderer of John the Baptist, believes in the resurrection of sacrificial victims. Consider the following, where Herod is told of the public actions of Jesus:

> King Herod heard of it, for Jesus' name had become known. Some were saying, 'John the baptizer has been raised from the dead; and for this reason these powers are at work in him.' But others said, 'It is Elijah.' And others said, 'It is a prophet, like one of the prophets of old.' But when Herod heard of it, he said, 'John, whom I beheaded, has been raised' (Mark 6:14–16).

Herod's statements reflect the general understanding of the sacred among the people of Jesus's time. Many people recognized in Jesus just another resurrected prophet. It was clear for the people—just as it was for Herod—that the murdered prophets would be resurrected from their deaths. The disciples of Jesus, however, reject these apotheoses of violence and contrast them with the divinity of the Son of God:

> When Jesus came into the district of Caesarea Philippi, he asked his disciples, 'Who do people say that the Son of Man is?' And they said, 'Some say John the Baptist, but others Elijah, and still others Jeremiah or one of the prophets.' He said to them, 'But who do you say that I am?' Simon Peter answered, 'You are the Messiah, the Son of the living God.' And Jesus

answered him, 'Blessed are you, Simon son of Jonah! For flesh and blood has not revealed this to you, but my Father in heaven'. (Matthew 16:13–17; cf. Luke 9:18–21)

The Virgin Conception as an Expression of Jesus's Nonviolence

The divinity of Jesus—and with it his *a priori* nonviolence—is also central for Girard's interpretation of the virgin conception.[76] Jesus's birth implies that he is not dependent on the world of violence in which human beings are trapped. One finds numerous examples for virgin births throughout the entire ancient world, for instance in Egypt and Greece, but also Persia, India, and South America. Many mythical texts speak as well of great heroes and personalities who are the offspring of gods and human women. If we compare these myths with the virgin conception of Jesus, we see at first that all erotic and sexual moments are absent from the New Testament account, which are of essential importance for the mythical texts. This absence of the sexual, however, must not be interpreted from the vantage point of a Christianity that is hostile to bodily contact, although this position has been frequently espoused in the history of the Church. The crux of the virgin conception is not found in its demonization or devaluation of human sexuality, but rather much more in its critique of violence, which may very much be a part of human sexuality. The mythical narratives of the mating between gods and human women are stamped by deceit and violence. Divine conception itself is oftentimes even comparable to rape. Consider as an example the birth of Dionysos, which the English scholar of myth Robert Graves summarizes as follows:

> Zeus, disguised as a mortal, had a secret love affair with Semele . . . , and jealous Hera, disguising herself as an old neighbor, advised Semele, then already six months with child, to make her mysterious love a request: that he would no longer deceive her, but reveal himself in his true nature and form. How, otherwise, could she know that he was not a monster? Semele followed this advice and, when Zeus refused her plea, denied him further access to her bed. Then, in anger, he appeared as thunder and lightning, and she was consumed. But Hermes saved her six-month-old son; sewed him up inside Zeus' thigh . . . and, in due course of time, delivered him.[77]

It is in this atmosphere of duplicity and brutality that Dionysos arises. These elements are completely absent from the biblical account of Jesus's birth; neither violence nor any form of deceit is present between Mary, the Angel Gabriel, and God. These findings are buttressed by a comparison between the New Testament formulation "the power of the Most High will over-shadow you" (Luke 1:35), and the Old Testament parallel stories in which women such as Deborah (Judges 4–5), Judith, or Esther (2:7–9, 32) summon likewise the "power of the Most High" in order to legitimate their own acts of violence.[78] The nonviolence emphasized in the narrative of the virgin conception also provides a more precise description of what is meant by the term "Son of God." Jesus originates entirely from a God of love and nonviolence. He has nothing to do with the world of violence, in which human beings all too often deceive, kill, torture, and rape one another.

Positive Mimesis

For Girard, the only real and nonviolent means to overcoming mimetic rivalry is found in the New Testament. As we saw in the previous chapter, the scape-goat mechanism offers a possible way of resolving the mimetic crisis. This "solution" is based on the collective violence against a single victim. The New Testament shows us another way. We are not speaking here of a renunciation of imitation—or any romantic glorification of spontaneity—but rather of a positive form of mimesis. Girard refers to this concept as "nonviolent imita-tion" (*Things Hidden*, 430; *De la violence à la divinité*, 1202: "imitation non violente"),[79] which he understands, above all, as the imitation of Christ (cf. 1 John 2:6: "Whoever says, 'I abide in him,' ought to walk just as he walked"). German theologians refer to this concept as *Nachfolge* (discipleship)—which translates literally as "following after"—in order to prevent any superficial understanding of the sense of imitation implied here.[80] According to Girard, Jesus is the only role model who does not instigate violent struggle among those who imitate him; since he knows no "conflictual" desire, it is impossible to fall into rivalry with him over any object. Jesus leads us to God, whom he teaches us to imitate just as he does: "The Son can do nothing on his own, but only what he sees the Father doing; for whatever the Father does, the Son does likewise" (John 5:19; cf. 8:28–29). Girard stresses the necessity of the imitation of Jesus's imitation in his explanations of the positive nature of the Gospel message: "In the Gospels, everything consists of imitation, for it is Christ's Will to be both imitative and imitated. In contrast to our modern gurus, who claim to imitate nobody . . . but at the same time want everybody to imitate them, Christ says: 'Imitate me, as I imitate the Father'" (*Quand ces choses commenceront*, 76). Girard attempts to show that by imitating Jesus we can gain an attitude of *renunciation* (*Things Hidden*, 197; *De la violence à la divinité*, 947: "renoncement") that enables us to free ourselves from the deadly grip of mimetic rivalry.

Creative Renunciation

Already in *Deceit, Desire and the Novel*, Girard makes note of the importance of renunciation with regard to the overcoming of mimetic rivalry. He claims that the great novelists gained their insight into the workings of desire only after renouncing the "deceptive divinity of pride," a feat Girard also describes as their "creative renunciation" (*Deceit, Desire and the Novel*, 307).[81] In his later works, Girard labors to portray the renunciation of revenge, violence, and all other forms of rivalrous desire as the intrinsic principle of the Kingdom of God.[82] The principal commandment of this kingdom is formed by God's call in the Sermon on the Mount for humans to overcome mimetic rivalry by "turning the other cheek" (Matthew 5:38–42):

> *If you want to put an end to mimetic rivalry, you must surrender everything to your rival.* This will suffocate rivalry at its core. This is not a matter of political strategy; it is much easier and more fundamental. If the other places outrageous demands on you—because he is already under the spell of mimetic rivalry—he expects that you play along and attempt to outdo him. The only way to take the wind out of his sails is to do the exact opposite: Instead of outbidding him, yield to him doubly as much. If he demands that you run a mile, run two. If he strikes you on the left cheek, turn to him your right cheek. The kingdom of God means nothing else; but that does not mean it is easy to reach. (*Quand ces choses commenceront*, 76)

At first glance, Girard's emphasis on renunciation—especially those formulations pertaining to mimetic desire—seems to suggest a proximity to

Buddhism, which sees in the extinguishing of desire the ultimate overcoming of human suffering.[83] Girard's praise of Stendhal's "passion which keeps silent" could be seen here as corroborating evidence, for Girard evaluates Stendhalian passion—which he also describes as "hardly desire"—as an opposing force to "vanity."[84] With that being said, however, Girard's paradoxical formulation of *creative renunciation* (*Deceit, Desire and the Novel*, 307; *De la violence à la divinité*, 286: "renoncement créateur") shows that he sees the solution to mimetic rivalry not in a renunciation of life, as such, but rather of the death resulting from man's arrogant attempt at self-empowerment, which obstructs the way to the biblical God and creator. Girard distances himself in later writings explicitly from interpretations of renunciation as any kind of oriental escapism, in order to make clear that a Christian existence does not denote an extinguishing of desire, but rather a redirecting of desire towards an end free of violence and rivalry.[85] He converges here on the Christian ethical juxtaposition of finite and eternal goods examined at length above [tr. *christliche Güterlehre*], which sees in God himself the ultimate and highest aim of human desire. For Christians, renunciation—in accordance with the emulation of Jesus—implies the readiness to bear the cross in situations of conflict that call for such radical action. This readiness for the cross does not imply any overcoming of mankind, in the sense of a complete denial of desire, but rather is carried by a desire based on the imitation of Christ, who acts in accordance with the God of life: "Let us run with perseverance the race that is set before us, looking to Jesus the pioneer and perfecter of our faith, who for the sake of the joy that was set before him endured the cross, disregarding its shame, and has taken his seat at the right hand of the throne of God" (Hebrew 12:1–2).[86]

Although human beings are constantly imitating an array of different models, Girard's interpretation of the New Testament shows that these boil down to the alternatives of Christ and Satan, or God and the devil. Either we imitate God together with Jesus in the spirit of innocent obedience, or we fall into the perverted imitation of God through Satan, who acts out of the spirit of rivalry.[87] We see here, once again, distinct parallels to the theology of Saint Augustine.

Augustine

Just like Girard, the Latin church father also differentiates clearly between the humble imitation of God, or Jesus, and the perverse imitation of Satan.[88] Though Augustine does reject that mere superficial or outward imitation of Jesus can save man from sin—as represented, e.g., by Pelagianism—this does not mean that he denies the concept any ethical significance.[89] For Augustine, complete self-empowerment is not possible on one's own; he argues expressly that there must be an external impetus—the gift of grace—to bring about positive mimesis. The *Confessions*, above all, exhibit the central importance of imitation for the Christian conversion.[90] Augustine, who describes his childhood as one dominated by an array of diverse role models, refers also to the influence of imitation on his personal journey to Christ. One of his first role models in this regard is Simplician, who tells Augustine of the conversion of the Roman rhetorician Victorinus. Similar to Augustine, Victorinus was a follower of his friends, who "blushed at the evil rites of the devils' haughtiness, himself haughty as he mimicked them, shameless toward hollow things, ashamed of hollow things."[91] Even after having become a Christian, Victorinus was unable to profess his beliefs openly, for fear of falling out of favor with his friends. He ultimately summoned the courage, however, and confessed his new faith. It is Victorinus's example that also fills Augustine with the desire to convert: "No sooner had I heard Simplician's tale of Victorinus than I was on fire to do as he did."[92] A second important impetus comes from Pontician, who tells Augustine and his friend Alypius about two acquaintances who, after discovering and reading the biography of the Egyptian monk Antonius, are inspired to convert to Christianity. These role models exert an undeniable influence on Augustine on his path to conversion: "The more I loved these men who, for spiritual health, surrendered themselves entirely into your healing hands, the more disgust I felt for myself, because of the contrast with them."[93] Augustine describes the decisive moments of his conversion as an inner wrestling between his "entrenched lusts" and "Lady Self-Control." The latter, conveyed by numerous role models, is what ultimately invites him to change: "To welcome and to hug me she reached her holy arms out, and in them were throngs of persons setting me their example, innocent boys and girls, young men and women—all ages, including chaste widows and women

... in old age. She teased me with a smiling insistence: Can you not do what all these have?"[94] The final step of Augustine's conversion is complete when suddenly he hears a voice, which, similar to Antonius, summons him to read the Bible. The opened passage, Romans 13:13–14, inspires him to devote himself entirely to following Jesus's example.[95] In a similar way, Augustine's friend Alypius also ultimately finds the path to Christianity. For him, Augustine's example was particularly meaningful.[96]

Original Sin and Grace

Girard's convergence with Augustine is not limited merely to the concept of positive mimesis. His spiritual relation with the Latin church father is much deeper.[97] Emphasis of this connection is above all significant in order to prevent any rash interpretation of Girard's theory of culture as an ontologization of violence, and also to show the extent to which it is embedded in the framework of the Christian teachings of Original Sin and grace.

Ontologization of Violence?

Girard's mimetic theory has met with widespread criticism among German theologians, in particular, who argue that it represents an ontology of violence. On the surface, these arguments can appear justified: Girard's distancing from Rousseau's ideology of the natural goodness of man and his emphasis on the prevalence of evil in human relations make him out to be an apologist for man's violent nature. Throughout Girard's work, one does find formulations—taken out of context and perhaps too carelessly worded—that have contributed to this suspicion against the mimetic theory—for instance in *Things Hidden since the Foundation of the World*, where he speaks of the "principle of violence" that dominates "humanity."[98] Nevertheless, these interpretations can and must be rejected.[99] Raymund Schwager emphasized almost two decades ago that Girard's theory can only be truly understood against the backdrop of the Christian teachings of Original Sin.[100] The suspicion that Girard's theory represents an ontology of violence, Schwager argues, can only be sustained where this context is ignored.

Original Sin

In several of his later writings, Girard makes explicit reference to the concept of Original Sin in an attempt to prevent false interpretations of his theory.[101] These references, however, are no mere passing remarks found only on the fringe of Girard's main work, but rather can also be seen in rudimentary form in his early studies of desire. In *Deceit, Desire and the Novel*, he describes imitation based on pride as taking on a "promethean" or "satanic" character, which he differentiates—together with Augustine—from the genuine forms of Christian imitation.[102] This critique of "promethean" pride is a direct extension of Augustine's identification of pride with Original Sin.

In *Things Hidden since the Foundation of the World*, the same book containing the "principle of violence" quoted above, Girard refers in other arguments so unambiguously to Original Sin that any attempts to interpret these words as representing an ontology of violence are essentially eliminated.[103] In his analysis, he compares Jesus with Adam and emphasizes that both had been originally innocent before being confronted with their respective predicaments. Whereas Adam was unable to withstand the temptation of violence, Jesus was able to resist and therefore redeem humanity. With that being said—and in a similar way to Kierkegaard—Girard simultaneously rejects all interpretations of Original Sin that portray Adam as a mere scapegoat of man: "If Christ alone is innocent, then Adam is not the only one to be guilty. All men share in this archetypal state of blame, but only to the extent that the chance of becoming free has been offered to them and they have let it slip away. We can say that this sin is indeed *original* but only becomes actual when knowledge about violence is placed at humanity's disposition" (*Things Hidden*, 223).[104] One finds similar rejections elsewhere in Girard's writings of other false interpretations of Original Sin, which have frequently been put forth by leading Christian figures. Particularly noteworthy is Girard's rejection of all interpretations that blame the Fall of Man on Eve—and, by extension, the female sex—which fits with his reading of Original Sin as a message of liberation that helps human beings come to terms with their own guilt.[105] Where false pride persuades humans to believe they are consummate and free of flaw, their inevitable fall leads to overwhelming self-accusations that most often must be shifted onto others.

Furthermore, Girard's interpretation also frees him of the danger—faced by Augustine and many of his successors—of combining Original Sin with the concept of predestination and thus turning the liberating universalism of the former into a theological buttress for the friend/enemy distinction. According to Girard, Original Sin implies that all human beings are susceptible to mimetic rivalry and the ensuing propensity to ostracize scapegoats.[106] This understanding does not result in a necessary division of humans into "righteous" and "condemned," as is the case with the coupling of Original Sin and the concept of predestination. A counterexample is offered by the German law scholar Carl Schmitt, who interlinks the two concepts in an effort to underpin the friend/enemy distinction from a theological perspective: "The fundamental theological dogma of the evilness of the world and man leads, just as does the distinction of friend and enemy, to a categorization of men and makes impossible the undifferentiated optimism of a universal conception of man."[107] From the perspective of the mimetic theory, the concept of predestination—as crucial as it is for Schmitt—represents a relapse to mythical thinking.[108] A God of differences, one that decides arbitrarily between humans and serves to create friend/enemy antipodes, differs radically from the biblical God who "causes his sun to rise on the evil and the good, and sends rain on the righteous and the unrighteous" (Matthew 5:45). Such a God of differences is rooted in the scapegoat mechanism and is differentiated from the nonviolent God that Girard claims is at the heart of the biblical message.

Insofar as Girard positions the mimetic theory within the teachings of Original Sin, it is clear that he argues for the intrinsically nonviolent nature of the order of creation. Girard's thesis regarding the creation of order out of an original chaos does not refer to the act of divine creation, but rather the origins of human culture. Where Luke and Matthew speak of the blood of sacrifice, which has flowed "since the foundation of the world" (Luke 11:50–51; Matthew 13:35; 23:34–36), this corresponds in Girard's eyes to the origins of culture in the scapegoat mechanism, just as when John refers to the devil as a "murderer from the beginning" (John 8:44).[109] In contrast to Hobbes, Girard does not espouse man's violent nature; the chaos he speaks of at the beginning of human culture stands for man's fallen condition, that is, for the world after the Fall of Man. He claims that human civilization is a product of Cainian culture and is therefore strictly divergent from God's creation of the world out of nothing. Girard's theory thus represents much more an ontology of peace, placing him among a group of thinkers headed by Augustine that constitutes the Christian tradition.[110] A small detail can show the importance Girard attributes to preventing any misunderstandings here. In his comparison of mythical and biblical narrative in *Things Hidden since the Foundation of the World*, Girard mentions that many of these mythical texts, on account of their being rooted in the scapegoat mechanism, speak of a return to social order that is established only at the conclusion of the myth. The "story of the creation of the world," however, is explicitly excluded from this list; in Girard's eyes, it is not a product of the scapegoat mechanism and is thus free of violent sacrifice (*Things Hidden*, 143; *De la violence à la divinité*, 886).[111]

The Scapegoat Mechanism as Hominization Threshold

Girard's work draws most closely to the tendency of an ontologization of violence where he attempts to combine his theory of culture with Darwin's theory of evolution. In *Things Hidden since the Foundation of the World*, Girard postulates that the collective murder of the scapegoat mechanism forms the threshold of hominization, or the transition from animal species to mankind.[112] He argues that the "dominance patterns" in animal communities that had held the outbreak of destructive conflict in check are no longer able to deal with the violence caused by the influx of mimetic desire. This outbreak of violence ultimately leads to the spontaneous formation of the scapegoat mechanism and, with it, the advent of human culture:

> Beyond a certain threshold of mimetic power, animal societies become impossible. This threshold corresponds to the appearance of the victimage mechanism and would thus be the threshold of hominization. . . . Between what can be strictly termed animal nature on the one hand and developing humanity on the other there is a true rupture, which is collective murder, and it alone is capable of providing for kinds of organization, no matter how embryonic, based on prohibition and ritual. It is therefore possible to inscribe the genesis of human culture in nature and to relate it to a natural mechanism without depriving culture of what is specifically, exclusively, human. (*Things Hidden*, 95–96)[113]

Following the publication of *Things Hidden since the Foundation of the World*, the Canadian philosopher Paul Dumouchel pointed out central ambiguities in Girard's thesis regarding hominization. Dumouchel claims that on the one hand, Girard invokes the freedom of human desire and calls for humans to turn away from violence and convert to Christianity; on the other hand, however, violence is portrayed as a necessary product of mimesis, which Girard claims is a biological attribute of the human species.[114] Raymund Schwager's systematic response to Dumouchel's critique provided a significant contribution to resolving this issue. Although Schwager did acknowledge that there were certain ambiguities in *Things Hidden since the Foundation of the World*, the Swiss theologian was still able to demonstrate how Girard's anthropological thesis can be understood in the context of the Christian teachings of Original Sin.[115] In his response, Schwager distinguishes between three distinct stages within the process of hominization. In the first stage, Schwager argues that, with regard to mimesis, there is continuity between man and animal, as he points out that mimetic behavior can be observed in both. Of particular importance for Schwager, however, is the second stage. Where animal communities are no longer possible due to the proliferation of mimesis, a break appears that enables an opening to the Absolute:

> Animal societies are no longer possible where metaphysical desire or the yearning for self-divinization emerges and breaks open all "dominance patterns." Considered from the biblical perspective, this rupture represents the opening to God—where the question of freedom poses itself. Thus, between the end of animal societies and the emergence of the actual scapegoat mechanism, we find the events that are described in the story of the Fall of Man; these events accompany and even underlie the entire course of history, influenced by the scapegoat mechanism.[116]

In the third stage, however, Schwager again proposes continuity between animal and man. From the beginning, he argues that humans have failed in their freedom before God. This has given rise to the impression of quasi-mechanical modes of human behavior, which—if one is to preserve the insights of the second stage—must be seen as rooted in man's self-enslavement and not in any naturally determined biological processes. According to Schwager, Girard has conceded ambiguities in this particular regard and has spoken of the need for theological supplementation.[117] Dialogue between the two scholars over decades has led Girard to embrace the teachings of Original Sin explicitly in recent writings. Schwager himself, in a work published before his death in 2004, incorporates insights from the mimetic theory and the theory of evolution into his understanding of Original Sin.[118] Likewise, the English theologian James Alison has used the lens of the mimetic theory to examine the concept of Original Sin; his study looks at the issue of hominization in this context in such a way that it fully reconciles Girard's anthropological thesis and the possibility of freedom at the dawn of civilization.[119]

Grace, Resurrection, and the Holy Spirit

Alison's *The Joy of Being Wrong: Original Sin through Easter Eyes* underlines in convincing fashion the importance of grace and the resurrection for the understanding of Original Sin. He argues that only after experiencing reconciliation and salvation are humans capable of realizing their entanglement in sin, and of liberating themselves from its clutches. Alison's book raises the question of whether this deeper connection between grace and sin is itself also valid for Girard's theory. Again, however, one must not be deceived by first impressions: Tobin Siebers, a scholar of literature and himself a former student of Girard, claimed in 1988—despite Girard's own personal religious conviction—that the mimetic theory was incompatible with grace, arguing instead that Girard refers to the concept in a merely metaphoric sense. Instances of this, Siebers argues, can be found in *Deceit, Desire and the Novel* where Girard speaks of the "miraculous descent of novelistic grace" that manifests itself in the great European novels as a "conversion in death" (*Deceit, Desire and the Novel*, 309–310).[120] Such attempts to understand Girard as a quasi-humanist philosopher, however, overlook the fact that his discreet approach towards overarching theological inquiries does not imply any systematic denial of grace. Girard's primary objective exists much more in an anthropological apologetics of biblical thought, or rather in displaying the plausibility of biblical revelation without having to revert to any rash theological presuppositions. He was so fully bound to this objective at the beginning of his career that almost no theological premises can be found in his early works; only in his later writings does one find explicit reference to any form of theology.

Girard's mimetic theory exhibits certain parallels to parts of Kant's *Religion within the Boundaries of Mere Reason*, where he emphasizes the presence of evil in humanity and offers a kind of anthropological apologetics that contains only irreligious, indirectly theological analysis.[121] Kant situates his apology within the realm of sociology and stresses that it does not belong to theology.[122] All parallels between Kant and Girard, however, vanish when the notion of grace enters the realm of inquiry. According to Kant, man must overcome depravity using "*his own* power" in order to return to his origins in the good:[123] "The human being must make or have made himself into whatever he is or should become in a moral sense, good or evil."[124] Kant's "moral religion" remains within the limits of reason and allows no room for the influence of grace.[125] The mimetic theory, meanwhile, lends an entirely different meaning to grace. According to Girard, culture, which is rooted in the scapegoat mechanism, is a closed system that radically excludes the possibility of overcoming violence from the inside: "No system of thought is truly capable of creating the thought capable of destroying it," he argues in *The Scapegoat* (207).[126] With regard to man's inability to overcome societal violence on his own, Girard stresses in *Things Hidden since the Foundation of the World* that Jesus must come from outside the human world to free man from his entanglement in violence.[127] In Girard's eyes, the "Peace that the world gives" (John 14:27) is based on the structural violence of the scapegoat mechanism, whereas the nonviolent "Peace of God," which "surpasses all understanding," comes from outside the human realm (Philippians 4:7).[128] Only with the help of the grace of God, thus, can humanity free itself from the dungeon of scapegoat logic.[129] Grace is the boundary of Girard's anthropological apologetics, in particular where he demonstrates that it is essential for overcoming the scapegoat mechanism. The primary example for this is found in the Passion, in which Girard sees grace as the enabling factor for the break from the victimage mechanism. As the Jews and pagans come together in the persecution of Jesus, even the disciples are unable to withstand the mimetic attraction of the mob. They either desert or deny their master. With this, according to Girard's thesis of the scapegoat mechanism, all necessary conditions for the emergence of a new myth are met. The fate of Jesus, however, is portrayed not by myth, but rather by the Gospels, which break through the pattern of mythical violence and are the product of a small number of people who, in the end, were able to resist the mob's attraction. This "protesting minority" (*I See Satan*, 188) is formed among the disciples of Jesus who, after the crucifixion, come to realize their own involvement in the persecution of an innocent victim and subsequently change their point of view. Girard argues that grace—the outer boundary of his anthropological apologetics—is what enabled this reversal. In contrast to Kant, the mimetic theory transcends the realm of mere reason and incorporates the mystery of grace that led to the reversal of the disciples' point of view. In Girard's eyes, it is ultimately the resurrection of Jesus that enabled them to escape the mimetic pull of the persecutors and thus to adopt the perspective of the innocent victim:

> During the Passion, the little group of Jesus' last faithful followers was already more than half-possessed by the violent contagion against Jesus. Where did they suddenly find the strength to oppose the crowd and the Jerusalem authorities? . . . Until now I have always been able to find plausible responses to the questions posed in this book within a purely commonsensical and "anthropological" context. This time, however, *it is impossible.* To break the power of mimetic unanimity, we must postulate a power superior to violent contagion. If we have learned one thing in this study, it is that none exists on the earth. . . . The Resurrection is not only a miracle, a prodigious transgression of natural laws. It is the spectacular sign of the entrance into the world of a power superior to violent contagion. By contrast to the latter it is a power not at all hallucinatory or deceptive. Far from deceiving the disciples, it enables them to recognize what they had not recognized before and to reproach themselves for their pathetic flight in the preceding days. (*I See Satan*, 188–189)[130]

The two examples of this reversal to which Girard refers most frequently are those of Peter and Paul.[131] Both apostles realize through grace that they complied with the persecutors of Jesus. For Peter, it is the glance he exchanges with Jesus when he is taken captive in the temple of the high priests (Luke 22:61); for Paul, it is Jesus's words, "Saul, Saul, why do you persecute me?" (Acts 9:4). Girard sees these retrospective realizations as crucial not only for Peter and Paul, but also for the entire Christian tradition: "The Resurrection empowers Peter and Paul, as well as all believers after them, to understand that all imprisonment in sacred violence is violence done to Christ" (*I See Satan*, 191). This systematic insight, that the Resurrection of Jesus is prerequisite to Peter's conversion, is rooted deeply in the Christian tradition. El Greco, for instance, illustrates this idea at the end of the sixteenth century with "The Repentant Peter," a painting that depicts Peter shedding tears of regret, with Mary Magdalene in the background returning from the grave to announce the resurrection of Jesus.[132]

Girard combines his insights regarding grace and the Resurrection to form his conception of the Holy Spirit.[133] His analysis concentrates above all on the anthropologically explicable aspects of the Holy Spirit, as part of a greater attempt to give it a plausibility that stands beyond mere theology. He recalls the original meaning of the word *Paraclete* (Greek: "Holy Spirit"): "The principle meaning of *parakletos* is 'lawyer for the defense,' 'defender of the accused.' In place of looking for periphrases and loopholes to avoid this translation, we should prefer it to all others and marvel at its relevance. We should take with utmost seriousness the idea that the Spirit enlightens the persecutors concerning their acts of persecution. The Spirit discloses to individuals the literal truth of what Jesus said during his crucifixion: 'They don't know what they are doing.' We should also think of the God whom Job calls 'my defender'" (*I See Satan*, 189–190). While for Girard, Satan is a representative for the persecutory mob—as we will see in greater depth below—the Holy Spirit stands for the defense and protection of victims.

Self-Giving as Sacrifice

With regard to Girard's insights into the origins of archaic religion and their fundamental difference from the origins of the Judeo-Christian tradition, there is no issue more complex than that of sacrifice. Due to the fact that ritual sacrifice arises directly from the scapegoat mechanism, it is an inextricable element of archaic religions and therefore stands in direct opposition to biblical revelation. At the same time, however, the Christian tradition also refers to the crucifixion of Jesus as an explicit "sacrifice" and thus appears to be in line with, if not indistinguishable from, archaic religion. Likewise, the interpretations of the Christian sacrifice as being part of an eternal, nature-determining exchange of life and death [tr. *werden und vergehen*] tend to blur the fundamental difference between the Bible and myth. The sacrificial interpretation of natural processes is, namely, the product of a view that is rooted in the scapegoat mechanism and must not be identified with the biblical perspective.[134] Passages from the Bible that have been taken out of context, such as the verse regarding the grain of wheat that "bears much fruit" only if it dies (John 12:24), or romantic verses such as Goethe's "Die and have a new birth! / Life I praise through all the ages / Which for death in flames is yearning," have long warped the understanding of Christian sacrifice, which, from the contemporary perspective of the mimetic theory, is more than questionable.[135]

Girard struggled with the concept of "Christian sacrifice" for many years, and only in the later stages of his career—under the significant influence of Raymund Schwager—was he able to establish a position that clarifies the similarities and differences between archaic and Christian sacrifice. In the following, we will take a closer look at this position against the backdrop of the modern struggle with the complexity of sacrifice.

The Modern Rejection of Sacrifice

Under the influence of Judeo-Christian revelation, our contemporary world is marked by a fundamental rejection of sacrifice. This critical distance to sacrifice must be viewed first and foremost as a very positive fruit of biblical thinking; it is the unfolding of the biblical insight that God "desires steadfast love and not sacrifice, the knowledge of God rather than burnt-offerings" (Hosea 6:6; cf. Matthew 9:13; 12:7).

The modern liberal tradition identifies closely with this aversion to archaic sacrifice. One can observe a progression here from Thomas Hobbes at the beginning of modernity to contemporary thinkers such as John Rawls and Jürgen Habermas. According to Hobbes's understanding of natural law, "a man is forbidden to do, that, which is destructive of his life, or taketh away the means of preserving the same."[136] Self-preservation is the highest principle of this early liberalism. Even despite Hobbes's endorsement of war and his ensuing readiness to send citizens into battle, his identification with the notion of self-preservation is so manifest that he grants citizens the simultaneous right to elude such dangers brought about by the state. His strict adherence to self-preservation also forces him to reject Jesus's call for a unilateral concession in advance [tr. *einseitige Vorleistung*] found in the Sermon on the Mount, because nobody should "offer himself up as prey against his own will."[137] In a similar way to Hobbes, John Rawls also takes up the notion of sacrifice in his analysis of utilitarianism, arguing against any instance of sacrifice made in favor of the greater good: "Each person possesses an inviolability founded on justice that even the welfare of society as a whole cannot override. For this reason, justice denies that the loss of freedom for some is made right by a greater good shared by others. It does not allow that the sacrifices imposed on a few are outweighed by the larger sum of advantages enjoyed by many."[138] Likewise, Jürgen Habermas points out in several of his works that modern "rational morality puts its seal on the abolition of sacrifice."[139] In analyses of the death penalty, general conscription, tax liability, and compulsory education, he argues that the "normative core" of this "enlightenment culture . . . consists in the abolition of a publicly demanded *sacrificium* as an element of morality."[140]

In literature, one finds a distinct symbol for the modern rejection of sacrifice in Dostoyevsky's *The Brothers Karamazov*. Both Ivan and his brother Alyosha represent this critical stance—albeit in different ways—that has come to characterize our modern world. Ivan's revolt against God is ultimately based on the numerous instances of human cruelty against children that he collected over a period of many years. He attempts to provoke his brother Alyosha by asking him whether he would agree to the sacrifice of one single innocent child—if it were the single prerequisite for a world of complete harmony:

> "Tell me straight out, I call on you—answer me: imagine that you yourself are building the edifice of human destiny with the object of making people happy in the finale, of giving them peace and rest at last, but for that you must inevitably and unavoidably torture just one tiny creature, that same child who was beating her chest with her little fist, and raise your edifice on the foundation of her unrequited tears—would you agree to be the architect on such conditions?"[141]

Alyosha's response, "No, I would not agree," shows unequivocally that both brothers are one in their rejection of archaic sacrificial logic. In "The Legend of the Grand Inquisitor," Dostoyevsky further underscores the modern rejection of all cultures that are kept alive only by means of human sacrifice—in this case the sacrifices connected with the Inquisition.

This modern rejection of sacrificial practices corresponds to Girard's juxtaposition of archaic religions—in which ritual sacrifice was integral to the stabilization of cultural order—with Judeo-Christian revelation, which robbed the former of their legitimacy by uncovering the arbitrariness of the victimage mechanism. However, this initial difference between the sacrificial logic of both religions only sheds light on one side of the modern stance toward sacrifice. A further analysis delves deeper, thereby complicating this first dimension.

The Massacres of Modern Anti-Sacrificial Ideology

Even though the modern rejection of sacrifice finds its origins in biblical thinking, this does not yet mean that the full scope of revelation has taken on a determining role in the modern world. The biblical message has often only been received in fragmented fashion, which in turn has failed to bring about any real progress in comparison with archaic sacrificial cultures; in many cases it has even resulted in a worsening of the situation.[142]

The difficulty of overcoming the compulsion of sacrifice, despite the principal rejections of the practice that pervade the modern world, can be seen in the work of the liberal thinkers presented at the beginning of this section. Hobbes's philosophy offers a first example of the sacrificial consequences of anti-sacrificial liberalism. He is not only an early representative for liberal individualism, but also one of the prophets of the absolute state. What begins as anti-sacrificial individualism ends inexorably in the sacrificial ideology of the absolute state, which overruns the precise individualism it initially set out to establish.[143] Similarly, Jean-Pierre Dupuy uses the example of Rawls to show that his efforts to oppose sacrificial thought processes remain ultimately unsuccessful.[144] Rawls's theory is only plausible insofar as it excludes—from the outset—all situations that would necessitate sacrifice. In contrast to Rawls, meanwhile, Habermas does not fully exclude these tragic situations, and even conveys his moral admiration of those who follow the biblical imperative of love and make morally "unreasonable" sacrifices in the interest of one's neighbor. Such deeds, according to Habermas, represent the attempt "to counteract the effects of unjust suffering in cases of tragic complications or under barbarous living conditions that inspire our moral indignation."[145]

This rudimentary anti-sacrificial stance of the early liberal tradition has manifested itself in the modern world as a tendency for massacre. This is exhibited clearly, once again, by the literary example of Dostoyevsky's *The Brothers Karamazov*. Although Ivan and Alyosha both reject human sacrifice, the ways in which each respectively opposes the practice differ greatly. Ivan represents modern man not only through his dismissal of archaic logic, but also in his open rejection of the spirit of biblical revelation; in short, he has lost the connection to the spirit of Christ. Ivan rejects Jesus as a role model, for he sees himself as an autonomous being capable of creating a just world with his own powers. His ambition becomes his downfall, however, as he fails in his endeavor already within the circle of his own family.[146] As the ideological enunciator of the idea "everything is permitted," Ivan becomes the indirect murderer of his own father; Smerdyakov, the servant of the Karamazov house and Ivan's supposed half brother, is spurred by Ivan's ideology and commits the murder in his place.

Father Zossima, one of the great positive figures in Dostoyevsky's novel, conveys in his teachings that the proud attempt to create a just world without Christ can end only in bloodshed: "They hope to make a just order for themselves, but, having rejected Christ, they will end by drenching the earth with blood, for blood calls to blood, and he who draws the sword will perish by the sword. And were it not for Christ's covenant, they would annihilate one another down to the last two men on earth. And these last two, in their pride, would not be able to restrain each other either, so that the last would annihilate the next to last, and himself as well."[147] It is precisely these words that characterize Ivan's failed plan; despite his rejection of archaic sacrificial logic, he is unable to elude the temptation of sacrifice. His proud pursuit of autonomy renders him the spiritual father of a bloody, ultimately suicidal massacre that far transcends the violence of archaic sacrifice.

This literary reference to Ivan Karamazov is not without connection to the concrete problems facing our modern world. The extent to which the modern rejection of sacrifice can lead indirectly to massacre, i.e., the multiplication of sacrifice, can be seen most clearly in the confrontation of the Western world with the sacrificial culture of the Aztecs at the dawn of modernity. The conquering of Latin America was accompanied by massacres that were legitimized as the fight against human sacrifice. This topic was discussed extensively at a conference that Latin American liberation theologians and Girard organized in Brazil in 1990, with the German theologian Franz Hinkelammert rightly speaking there of an "anti-sacrificial—distinguished from 'non-sacrificial'—thinking" in his description of the Christian Occident. Hinkelammert describes the conquistadors' massacre of those making the original sacrifices a "new form of sacrifice, i.e. a sacrificial anti-sacrifice."[148] The French historian Tzvetan Todorov identifies this perverted form of sacrifice with the term "massacre" and differentiates it systematically from the violence of archaic sacrifice: "If religious murder is a sacrifice, massacre is an atheistic murder, and the Spaniards appear to have invented . . . precisely this type of violence, which we encounter in our own more recent past, whether on the level of individual violence or on that of violence perpetrated by states. It is as though the conquistadors obeyed the rule of Ivan Karamazov: 'Everything is permitted.'"[149] Todorov's bridge to Ivan Karamazov underlines the danger facing the modern world: Despite our distance from the sacrificial practices of traditional cultures, we are now faced with the greater peril of bringing about an exponential increase of this violence.

This modern dialectic of the quantitative increase of sacrifice is also at the heart of Roberto Calasso's cultural critique *The Ruin of Kasch*.[150] In several of the book's passages, Calasso refers to the veiled expansion of sacrifice in the modern world: "The first consequence of the eclipse of sacrifice will be that the world will be used without restraint, without limit, without any part being devoted to something else. But here, too, the end overlaps with the origin, like a reflection and hence reversed: once sacrifice is dissolved, the whole world reverts, unawares, to a great sacrificial workshop."[151]

The Dominion of the Antichrist: The "Other Totalitarianism"

Girard has thoroughly examined the modern perversion brought about by the biblical uncovering of the victimage mechanism.[152] He speaks here of the perversion of the Bible's knowledge of sacrifice [tr. *biblisches Opferwissen*] when this knowledge is used as an instrument for further, yet subtler persecution and violence. Girard's arguments are an indirect reference to the increasing virulent struggle in the modern world to be viewed as "the victim," which in the contemporary debate is also being interpreted as a radicalized "victimology" (*I See Satan*, 181). According to Girard, Nietzsche was correct in stating that persecution—in future generations—would only take place in the name of victims. Where Nietzsche simultaneously identifies biblical thinking with his conception of *ressentiment*, however, he overlooks that this new form of persecution is actually a perversion of biblical revelation. In Girard's words: "Resentment is merely an illegitimate heir, certainly not the father of Judeo-Christian Scripture" (*Job*, 108).

In biblical terms, Girard sees the New Testament figure of the Antichrist as the embodiment of the complexities facing the modern world (cf. 1 John 2:18, 22; 4:3; 2 John 1:7). However, Girard argues that this biblical figure must first be rid of its dramatic elements [tr. *entdramatisiert werden*] before it can be granted plausibility: "What does this word mean, *Antichrist*? It means that one will imitate Christ in a parodistic manner. It is an exact description of a world, our own, in which the most horrible acts of persecution are committed in the name of the fight against persecution" (*Quand ces choses commenceront*, 65). Girard refers to the persecutory system of Soviet Russia as one example of the modern dominion of the Antichrist, and also to the radical leftist movements gaining momentum around the world, which he describes as the "other totalitarianism" (*I See Satan*, 224).

Girard argues that there are two totalitarian dangers facing the modern world that simultaneously represent two different forms of neopaganism. The first danger, the extreme Right, is embodied by the philosophy of Nietzsche and the doctrines of National Socialism, which are both rooted in the illusory—yet no less dangerous—endeavor to return to a quasi-archaic sacrificial culture. The Holocaust is a clear example of the quantitative increase of sacrifice, which, despite its atrocious surge in violence, was unable to bring about the social accord established by sacrifice in archaic communities.[153] Girard differentiates this receding form of totalitarianism from another form, which he argues is rooted in a radicalization of the biblical concern for victims, and thus ultimately opposed—all the more—to the Christian spirit: "This other totalitarianism presents itself as the liberator of humanity. In trying to usurp the place of Christ, the powers imitate him in the way a mimetic rival imitates his model in order to defeat him. They denounce the Christian concern for victims as hypocritical and a pale imitation of the authentic crusade against oppression and persecution for which they would carry the banner themselves" (*I See Satan*, 180–181). According to Girard, the "pagan practices" that accompany this form of totalitarianism include "abortion, euthanasia, sexual undifferentiation, Roman circus games galore but without real victims, etc." (*I See Satan*, 181). The proponents of this ideology seek the abolishment of the Ten Commandments and all other prohibitions in the effort to enable the boundless fulfillment of desire. This unbridling of desire appears at first legitimate; as the range of consumer products expands, mimetic rivalry among humans logically diminishes. However, one look at the consequences of mass consumerism on the environment and nature shows that this form of totalitarianism merely shifts the problem elsewhere; a complete unbridling of desire, in other words, threatens a sacrifice of nature in its entirety.[154]

The Christian Sacrifice of Self-Giving

The path from archaic sacrificial cultures to modern massacre is not inescapable, however. Biblical revelation offers a way out of this dilemma that is no mere act of reason—or merely "better" insight—but is also itself connected with a form of sacrifice that we can call *self-giving*. This concept implies a renunciation of those objects of desire that typically result in mimetic rivalry, on the one hand, and a renunciation of the violence connected with the ensuing conflict, on the other hand. A literary instance of this form of Christian sacrifice is found in the figure of Alyosha Karamazov, who rejects archaic sacrificial logic without, however, following his brother and becoming a prophet of massacre. Alyosha's refusal of sacrifice is rooted in his self-giving to Jesus. The youngest of the Karamazov brothers sees the world as founded on the sacrifice of Christ, who "gave his innocent blood for all and for everything."[155] As the novel's overarching motto, Dostoyevsky chooses the Gospel verse of the "grain of wheat" (John 12:24), which functions as a leitmotiv in numerous key passages.[156] This symbol refers directly to a form of sacrifice based above all on the overcoming of pride and the prevention of sacrifice as a means of coping with one's own shortcomings. What Dostoyevsky implies here is the sacrifice of self-giving, which fosters the possibility of a humane life in the face of inhumane conflict.[157]

Another significant biblical instance of self-giving can be found in the Servant of Yahweh's songs of lament. The third song (Isaiah 50:4–7) dwells on the Servant's nonviolent conduct, which ultimately forces his persecutors to change their viewpoint and recognize him as an innocent victim:[158]

> Morning by morning he wakens—
> wakens my ear
> to listen as those who are taught.

The Lord God has opened my ear,
and I was not rebellious,
I did not turn backwards.

I gave my back to those who struck me,
and my cheeks to those who pulled out the beard;

I did not hide my face
from insult and spitting.
The Lord God helps me.

Jesus takes a similar path in the Gospel accounts where he, too, decides in favor of nonviolence in the face of his tragic situation. The "sacrifices" of the Servant of Yahweh and Jesus both diverge fundamentally from the archaic logic of the scapegoat mechanism and the modern perversion of this logic. They are directed neither at a violent form of self-preservation nor at any masochistic yearning to inflict violence upon oneself. The Servant of Yahweh and Jesus give their lives to save those of others; this form of sacrifice, or self-giving, is directed entirely at the preservation of human life.

Girard examines the biblical attitude of self-giving most closely in his analysis of the Judgment of Solomon (1 Kings 3:16–28).[159] Two harlots, who live in the same house in which the infant son of one of the two is found dead, appear before the king to ask his judgment on whose son is the living son. As there are neither witnesses nor any form of evidence to help resolve the dispute, the just king proposes to cut the child in two and give each woman her equal half. Solomon's judgment is a figurative reference to the sacrificial core of archaic arbitration, which in this case—not atypical for the political conflict resolution practiced at the time—would have ended in the sacrifice of a living child. However, the good harlot, who proves in the end to be the true mother, sees through this violent logic and renounces her entitlement to half of the child in order to save its life. With this renunciation, she risks even her own life, for her concession could have been legally interpreted as proof of her previous lie. While human beings in similar situations of crisis—in which one must decide between the alternatives "kill or be killed"—generally would accept the death of the other, the good harlot risks both her life and her motherhood to save the child's life. The bad harlot, meanwhile, embodies the typical sacrificial logic: It is better for neither mother to receive the child, that it be killed and divided into two equal halves, than for her rival to emerge victorious. Ultimately, King Solomon decides in favor of the good harlot and awards her the child.

For Girard, the good harlot possesses the spirit of self-giving that one must not identify with archaic sacrificial logic: "The good harlot agrees to substitute herself for the sacrificial victim, not because she feels a morbid attraction to the role but because she has an answer to the tragic alternative: kill or be killed. The answer is: be killed, not as a result of masochism, or the 'death instinct,' but *so that the child will live*" (*Things Hidden*, 242). The attitude made visible in this example corresponds to the readiness for self-giving called for in the New Testament in the face of similar tragic situations. The Sermon on the Mount, for instance, is deeply influenced by this spirit of unconditional renunciation (*Things Hidden*, 198); where conflict breaks out between two humans, the Christian is called upon to take the nonviolent path and concede to the other. Only this way is there hope of truly ending the conflict without violence. This attitude can be found in John 15:12–13, where Jesus offers a concise summary of his teachings: "This is my commandment, that you love one another as I have loved you. No one has greater love than this, to lay down one's life for one's friends." With these words, Jesus not only summarizes his teachings but also refers indirectly to his own example. Faced with a radical crisis in which the decision must be made, "kill or be killed," Jesus gives his life on the cross for all humans in a singular display of self-giving.

While for the Christian tradition both the good harlot and Jesus stand in a certain way for self-sacrifice, Girard refused for a long time to equate this form of self-giving with sacrifice. In *Things Hidden since the Foundation of the World*, he expressly rejects any use of the term in connection with Jesus.[160] Girard's justification for this is significant. Firstly, he aims to protect Christianity against accusations of masochism, which have come most frequently, and vehemently, from psychoanalytic circles: "Far from being an exclusively Christian concept, which would form the summit of 'altruism' by contrast with an 'egoism' prone to sacrifice the other with gay abandon, self-sacrifice can serve to camouflage the forms of slavery brought into being by mimetic desire. 'Masochism' can also find expression in self-sacrifice, even if a person has no knowledge of this, and no wish to reveal it"

(*Things Hidden*, 236). Girard uses literary examples already in his early work to demonstrate how mimetic rivalry can lead to masochistic sacrifice. His book on Dostoyevsky, for instance, contains an abundance of such references.[161] Father Zossima, in *The Brothers Karamazov*, refers directly to the extreme readiness of humans for self-sacrifice—when exposed to the pull of mimetic influence. Zossima juxtaposes Christian "active love" with this masochistic form of "passionate love," which he claims is only interested in quick and sensational success: "Indeed, it will go as far as the giving even of one's life, provided it does not take long but is soon over, as on stage, and everyone is looking on and praising."[162]

The second, yet more significant reason for Girard's initial refusal to refer to Christian self-giving as "sacrifice" is found in his emphasis of the difference between biblical and archaic religion. In order to maintain his unequivocal rejection of modern theories that equate myth and Christianity, Girard strictly opposed using the same terminology to describe the two. Furthermore, he argued that the Christian tradition, with its reference to the "sacrifice" of Jesus, had adopted a position that failed to comprehend the message of the Gospels, even claiming to find misperceptions in the New Testament itself—for instance in the Epistle to the Hebrews (Hebrews 9:22–26; 10:11–14), where Jesus's death is interpreted in the context of Old Testament sacrifice.[163] Although the Epistle to the Hebrews does recognize Jesus's death as the "ultimate sacrifice," thus eliminating any return to primitive sacrifice, Girard argued that the author of these texts failed in conveying the actual singularity at the heart of the Christian Passion.

This original dismissal of the term "sacrifice" in connection with Christian self-giving is not a necessary conclusion of the mimetic theory. At around the same time Girard began his investigation of the Bible, the Swiss theologian Raymund Schwager was already working on his book *Must There be Scapegoats?*, which was published in 1978, the same year as Girard's *Things Hidden since the Foundation of the World*. In contrast to Girard, Schwager was able to render an interpretation of the Epistle to the Hebrews that both accorded with the traditional Christian terminology of sacrifice and expounded the intricate difference between the biblical and archaic conceptions of sacrifice.[164] Discussions that went on for years between the two scholars led to Girard's eventual revision of his earlier position,[165] which Girard explains in his article "Mimetic Theory and Theology," written on the occasion of Schwager's sixtieth birthday. Girard states that his revision in no way minimizes his emphasis on the crucial difference between archaic and biblical religion; however, he does concede that his rejection of the term "sacrifice" was influenced by the seductive liberal tendency—examined above—that proposes a circumvention of the complexity of sacrifice that ignores the real difficulty and danger of the concept. In his arguments, Girard harkens back to the judgment of Solomon in order to outline the different veiled forms of sacrifice and, at the same time, to reject the liberal "illusion" he previously harbored:

> One cannot accuse this text of minimizing the distance between the two types of sacrifice; however: despite seeing what makes them different, we must bring them together. We ourselves say that the [good Harlot] *sacrifices* rivalry for the sake of her own child (1), whereas the other *sacrifices* her child for the sake of rivalry (2). The text tells us that it is impossible to renounce this first sacrifice, i.e. the sacrifice of others and the violence against others, without taking on a risk. This risk is that implied by the second sacrifice, embodied by the sacrifice of Christ, who died for his friends. This falling back on the same word "sacrifice" puts an immediate stop to any "neutral" ground, i.e. one foreign to violence. Such a non-sacrificial lookout post, to which the wise and scholarly can permanently make claim in order to procure the truth with marginal cost, . . . remains an illusion.[166]

This new viewpoint with regard to the terminology of sacrifice enabled Girard to understand the crucifixion of Christ as a "divine re-employment of the scapegoat mechanism" (*Celui par qui le scandale arrive*, 80).[167] Under Schwager's influence, he also retracted his criticism of the Epistle to the Hebrews.[168] His earlier rejection of the term sacrifice, he writes, prevented him from fully recognizing the extent to which this text breaks from archaic logic in its depiction of the Crucifixion as the final overcoming of pagan ritual. The quotation from Psalm 40 included and analyzed in Hebrews 10:1–18, for instance, expresses a clear turning away from archaic sacrifice: "Sacrifices and offerings you have not desired, but a body you have prepared for me; in burnt-offerings and sin-offerings you have taken no pleasure. Then I said, 'See, God, I have come to do your will, O God'" (Hebrews 10:5–7; Psalm 40:7–9).

With this revised viewpoint of Christian sacrifice, Girard returns to a central topic of his first book, in which he describes the conversion of the great novelistic authors as a form of sacrifice. He stresses in *Deceit, Desire and the Novel* that authors as disparate as Proust and Dostoyevsky look to the Bible—in particular the verse of the "grain of wheat" (John 12:24)—to convey their spiritual conversion.[169] These novelists, Girard argues, first had to renounce their self-righteousness before they could experience the resurrection that led to the creation of their great novels. After his struggle with the terminology of sacrifice that went on for over a decade, Girard was finally able—in his book on Shakespeare—to describe the conversion of the great European authors as a form of Christian sacrifice, without relinquishing thereby his rejection of archaic sacrificial violence. The sacrifice implied by these authors takes the shape of a genuine self-criticism that prevents them from using other people as scapegoats. Girard's direct usage of the term "sacrifice" thus alludes to the paradoxical conversion at the heart of the concept: the substantial core of Christian sacrifice is "nonsacrificial" (*A Theater of Envy*, 339).

The Paradoxical Unity of All That Is Religious

Girard's terminological revision did not go unnoticed. Several scholars familiar with his work claimed that his reversal contradicted his fundamental critique of archaic sacrificial cultures. Most vehement was the opposition of Georg Baudler, a German theologian who accused Girard of identifying too closely with Schwager's position.[170] Baudler, however, was himself too heavily influenced by contemporary liberalism to comprehend the importance of Girard's revision for avoiding the liberal illusions that ignore the danger of such an unproblematic overcoming of sacrifice. One sees this in Baudler's claim that Girard and Schwager represent an "ultimately unbiblical anthropological pessimism."[171] This claim, as Girard's understanding of Original Sin quickly shows, is untenable.

One of Baudler's points of criticism, however, deserves more thorough analysis. He argues that Girard's emphasis on the singularity of the Bible counteracts contemporary interreligious dialogue.[172] This is a rather strange claim, especially considering that it comes in the context of Girard's revision of his conception of sacrifice—for this new viewpoint enables Girard to demonstrate not only the differences but also the fundamental unity of all religions. One of the great dangers of the mimetic theory is, namely, the radical devaluation and demonization of all archaic cultures, which, on account of their foundations in the scapegoat mechanism, appear to represent the exact opposite of biblical revelation. Such a black-and-white understanding of religion is made possible precisely by such viewpoints—e.g., Girard's earlier position—that see sacrifice as belonging merely to archaic religions and not Christianity. Baudler overlooks this problem in his attempt to sustain Girard's earlier rejection of the term "sacrifice" for the Christian Passion, and at the same time, to view all other religions of the axial age as categorically nonsacrificial. Baudler understands religion in merely black-and-white terms, a pitfall Girard attempts to overcome fundamentally for all religions, not just Christianity or other axial religions. He stresses that a theory bound to the uncovering of the scapegoat mechanism must be wary of the simple demonizations it can generate. Like Baudler, Girard recognizes the critical role of all axial religions vis-à-vis archaic sacrificial cultures, and also emphasizes that the Judeo-Christian tradition displays the most consummate overcoming of primitive sacrifice.[173] In contrast to Baudler, however, he is able to demonstrate similarities between these two types of religion and is thus able to speak of a unity among all religions. His argument for the differences between myth and the Bible, in other words, does not imply a necessary separation of these forms of religion. His usage of the term "sacrifice" for both allows him to establish the "paradoxical unity of all that is religious throughout human history" (*Celui par qui le scandale arrive*, 79): "This divine re-employment of the scapegoat mechanism seals the unity of human religiosity, which one can construe as a ghastly and weaseling path from the first to the second type of sacrifice. This is a path, however, which beyond Christ is unreachable."[174]

This emphasis on the paradoxical unity of religion is no mere addition with which Girard attempts to open his theory to dialogue with other religions, however; it is much more a reflection of the insight one can find in the same book in which he articulated his rejection of Christian sacrifice most unequivocally. In *Things Hidden since the Foundation of the World*, Girard observes not only the differences but also the fundamental similarities connecting all forms of religion. He notes that as much as the myths differ from the Gospels, both are ultimately directed at establishing social peace and therefore display a mysterious interconnectedness.[175] He argues that even archaic religion, in the face of its very rudimentary nature, was directed at the same transcendence from which the biblical religions originated.[176]

Girard's emphasis on the unity of all religions is yet further proof that his theory of culture represents the Augustinian ontology of peace, according to which "peace is the instinctive aim of all creatures," including even warmongers and robbers.[177] Thus, even the proud are incapable of eluding the natural law of peace, when, in perverse imitation of God, they impose their own peace on other human beings. In Augustine's eyes, despite all evil there is no being that does not know the love of peace: "For no creature's perversion is so contrary to nature as to destroy the very last vestiges of its nature." Even the mythical monster Cacus—who infamously devoured his victims in solitude, and whose name literally represents evil (Greek: *Kakos*, or "wicked")—is not excluded from having universal peaceful intentions. Moreover, Augustine questions whether a creature portrayed as "evil" as Cacus is could have ever existed, arguing that the poets exaggerated his truculence in order to praise Hercules's heroism all the more: "The existence of such a man, or half man, is discredited, as are many similar poetical fictions."

Just as Augustine refuses to demonize Cacus and stamp him as an eternal scapegoat, Girard also refuses to demonize archaic religions, stressing their fundamental desire for peace. In our modern world, we seem to have lost this confidence in the peaceful nature of creation. What's more, it is precisely the proclamations of man's peaceful nature that can lead to the demonization of certain persons and groups, if the promised harmony takes too long to materialize. In perfect emulation of mythical persecution, we conjure the existence of monsters like Cacus. Mozart's opera *The Magic Flute* illustrates this tendency to lay the blame for social conflict on monstrous creatures. In the final verses of Sarastro's famous aria on love, forgiveness, and the renunciation of revenge, he denies those that oppose these humanistic endeavors their very being:

> *Wen solche Lehren nicht erfreuen, / Verdienet nicht, ein Mensch zu sein.*
> [Those not impressed by such teachings, / Do not deserve to be human beings.][178]

The struggle implied here refers indirectly to the dangers of all modern struggles against evil. Where the "opponents" of humanity are denied their right to existence, one is faced with the threat of those massacres that far exceed the violence of all archaic sacrificial cultures.

Sacrificial Christianity and the Apocalyptical Reading of History

In the following section, we will take a closer look at Girard's interpretation of historical Christianity, as well as his understanding of the historical dynamic that, from its origins in biblical revelation, has driven the development of the modern world. Our discussion will focus above all on Girard's interpretation of the apocalyptical texts of the New Testament.

Sacrificial Christianity

In the face of the New Testament's complete uncovering of the scapegoat mechanism, the question poses itself of how—throughout the history of Christianity—events that essentially followed the pattern of original collective persecution so often took place: How, despite its radical opposition to mythical violence, could biblical revelation lead to a cultural tradition that radically persecuted minority groups such as Jews or witches? Girard's defense of the singularity of the Judeo-Christian tradition does not overlook these perversions of the biblical message; on the contrary, he examines these questions systematically in his analysis of what he terms *sacrificial Christianity* (*Things Hidden*, 224; *De la violence à la divinité*, 979: "christianisme sacrificiel").[179]

This form of "historical Christianity" (*Things Hidden*, 224) is characterized by a sacrificial interpretation of the Gospel Passion and the salvation of Jesus, whose death is read as a sacrifice equivalent to those found in archaic religions. One example of this is the theology—widespread throughout Christendom—that interprets the crucifixion of Jesus as a sacrifice that is ordered from on high to appease the wrath of God. Girard argues that this interpretation of biblical scripture has given rise to a culture that, despite its direct reference to these texts, shows no real divergence from conventional sacrificial cultures:

> Thanks to the sacrificial reading it has been possible for what we call Christendom to exist for ten or twenty centuries; that is to say, a culture has existed that is based, like all cultures (at least up to a certain point) on the mythological forms engendered by the founding mechanism. Paradoxically, in the sacrificial reading the Christian text itself provides the basis. Mankind relies upon a misunderstanding of the text that explicitly reveals the founding mechanism to re-establish cultural forms which remain sacrificial and to engender a society that, by virtue of this misunderstanding, takes its place in the sequence of all other cultures, still clinging to the sacrificial vision that the Gospel rejects. (*Things Hidden*, 181)[180]

Sacrificial Christianity enables its followers to project interpersonal violence onto God, thus relieving themselves of the responsibility for this violence, which is universal and equally distributed among mankind. However, if this responsibility is not maintained by humans, it can lead to a spiral of violence that ends in the arbitrary persecution of scapegoats—onto whom the violence is unloaded. The persecution of other groups is therefore one of the typical characteristics of sacrificial Christianity; the systematic persecution of Jews, heretics, and witches, as well as all inquisitions, crusades, and religious wars are the direct result of this decisive misunderstanding of biblical scripture.[181]

This massive unloading of collective violence—so typical of sacrificial Christianity—can also be observed in the conventional interpretation of the biblical apocalypse. Here, too, God is understood as the primeval father of apocalyptic destruction: It is not humans, but God who will initiate the impending violence.

However, this form of Christianity does not return completely to the level of the original myths. According to Girard, it can be characterized as a regression to Old Testament conceptions of sacrifice.[182] Although the Old Testament does establish the foundation for the eventual overcoming of mythical thinking, it does not offer in itself any final or unequivocal uncovering of the scapegoat mechanism, which causes Girard to view it as an intermediate form [tr. *Zwischenform*] between myth and the Gospels. Typically speaking, this intermediate form of Christianity reverses the interpretive order of the Old and New Testament; the Gospels, in other words, are not seen as the key to interpreting the Old Testament, but are rather read in the light of the latter.

The Modern World as Mimetic Crisis

Despite this regression in the form of a return to mythical patterns, sacrificial Christianity was ultimately unable to impede the influence of the biblical message. Of course, traces of the original founding violence still exist in modern society; however, these differ fundamentally from their mythical beginnings. According to Girard, Judeo-Christian revelation was most responsible for bringing about this difference. He argues that the biblical uncovering of the scapegoat mechanism made all archaic strategies of channeling violence obsolete, leading to the development of the modern world, which can be understood as a planetary mimetic crisis.[183] If the beginnings of human civilization were marked by a war of "all against all," the undermining of traditional means of channeling this violence logically implies a return to this violence. It comes as no surprise that on the threshold of modernity, a thinker such as Thomas Hobbes began to speak of the violent origin of human civilization.

This general thesis outlined here can be observed concretely in the collapse of traditional forms of social difference. One of the earliest surviving philosophical fragments of the Western world, Heraclitus's phrase regarding war as the "father of all things, which establishes difference between gods and man, the free and the slaves," is for Girard—as we have already seen—a philosophical formula for the scapegoat mechanism's culture-founding potency. Out of this potency, social differences arise that are there to prevent any future outbreak of mimetic crisis. Ancient slavery and the feudal system of the Middle Ages are two manifestations of social hierarchies that served to oppress mimetic conflict. The biblical uncovering of the founding murder, however, removes the roots of such social models, and makes it unfeasible for them to exist in the long term. The prophet Joel announces—already in the Old Testament—the outpouring of a spirit that will include both "male and female slaves" (Joel 2:29).[184] Later, Paul writes: "There is no longer Jew or Greek, there is no longer slave or free, there is no longer male and female; for all of you are one in Christ Jesus" (Galatians 3:28). The equality of all humans before God no longer allows any containment of rivalry by means of hierarchical difference. One may argue that hierarchical forms arose in the course of Christendom; however, these were essentially impervious to the biblical impulse of equality and can be understood today as a mere protraction of this impulse. With the dawn of modernity, these hierarchical differences collapsed, and the crisis of violence present at the foundation of civilization reemerged. Ulysses's speech in Shakespeare's *Troilus and Cressida* offers an enlightening example of this, and can be understood as the context for Hobbes's conception of man's primordial warlike state, as well as for his conception of human equality in which anyone can kill anyone else [tr. *jeder jeden töten kann*].

Globalization

The contemporary phenomenon of globalization is likewise directly connected to the modern nondifferentiation brought about by biblical revelation. Girard observes that sacrificial Christianity, despite its regression to more conventional forms of archaic culture, also harbors a universalist potential, which he refers to as the "germs of a planetary society" (*Things Hidden*, 249).[185] Contemporary globalization increasingly displays this critical impulse of the Bible. The biblical identification with persecuted victims brings with it a globalized world in which cultural differences lose their meaning and thus—in reaction to the increasing uniformity of the world—give rise to a universal hegemony of mimesis. Already at the end of the 1970s, Girard describes this coalescence of culture as the "main enigma of an unprecedented historical situation," arguing in *Things Hidden since the Foundation of the World* that globalization could mean the "death of all cultures."[186] He offers a more detailed explanation of this in *Quand ces choses commenceront*, where he describes Christianity as being accompanied by a "global homogenization and a certain uniformity of the planet" (91). Though this does not imply the disappearance of all social differences, it does involve a radical relativization of cultural variance: "Of course, human groups and the religions will always divide the world, and there will be borders; but what separates them fundamentally? What makes us different from the Muslim countries? The economic decisions we make, or our educational methods? The world's cultures are already united through the concepts they utilize, their systems of communication, and the goods they consume: We will soon even have a planetary language: English" (*Quand ces choses commenceront*, 95). One can argue thus that Girard's thesis stands in direct opposition to all theories—e.g., Samuel Huntington's—that argue for a contemporary or future "clash of civilizations."

Apocalyptical Reading of History

However, it would be false to see in Girard a naive apologist for globalization and modern nondifferentiation. For, together with these very positive developments, there are also great dangers that arise. In Girard's eyes, the modern world is at once both better and worse than its predecessors.[187] The biblical unmasking of the scapegoat mechanism—and the violent cultural forms that originate from it—does not lead automatically to paradise on earth, but rather to initial dangers even greater than those that previously existed. Jesus's mysterious words regarding the "sword" that he will bring into the world allude to the dangers brought about by the abolishment of the "peace" emanating from the founding murder: "Do not think that I have come to bring peace to the earth; I have not come to bring peace, but a sword" (Matthew 10:34).[188] In the dangers that accompany the unmasking of the scapegoat mechanism, Girard sees an apocalyptical aspect of the biblical message, which, in the truest sense of the word "revelation," possesses both a revelatory and destructive side.

This apocalyptical dimension of the biblical message is of central significance for the mimetic theory. As an apocalyptical thinker, however, Girard immediately arouses suspicion in the modern world.[189] Gunnar Heinsohn, for instance, accuses Girard of attempting to turn an "undeclared apocalyptical conviction"—based on a "private yearning for decline and destruction"—into a "general anthropology."[190] Just about every aspect of this critique is untenable. Girard can neither be accused of ever having concealed the apocalyptical dimension of his theory, nor does he display any morbid yearning for catastrophe. His first book contains an entire chapter on the "Dostoyevskian Apocalypse" (*Deceit, Desire and the Novel*, 256–289), and at the end of his second main work, he speaks of a possible "stunning, catastrophic comeback" of violence in the modern world (*Violence and the Sacred*, 307). In his later works, Girard returns time and again to the theme of the apocalypse.[191] His interest in the topic does not mean that he preaches impending doom, or that he secretly hopes for any act of divine revenge; the apocalyptical dimension of his thought is based much more on his refusal to ignore the apocalyptical texts of the New Testament, which in his eyes provide a clearer understanding of the modern world. He argues that a "radically Christian appropriation of history can only be apocalyptical" (*Things Hidden*,

250). Girard recognizes in the apocalyptical texts a convincing interpretation of the phenomena that came about as a result of the Bible's influence: "The Christian revelation clarifies not only everything that comes before it, the religion and culture of myth and ritual, but also everything that comes after, the history we are in the process of making, the ever-growing disintegration of archaic religion, the opening into a future joining all humankind into one world. It is more and more liberated from ancient forms of servitude, but by the same token, it is deprived of all sacrificial protection" (*I See Satan*, 184). From Girard's point of view, these apocalyptical prophesies speak of a danger created by man alone, and are nothing other than a rational forecast of the violence that human beings can exert on one another and their environment if they disregard the Bible's warning against vengeful thinking and, at the same time, possess no sacred protective mechanisms on which they can rely: "If men turn down the peace Jesus offers them—a peace which is not derived from violence and that, by virtue of this fact, passes human understanding, the effect of the Gospel revelation will be made manifest through violence, through a sacrificial and cultural crisis whose radical effect must be unprecedented since there is no longer any sacralized victim to stand in the way of its consequences" (*Things Hidden*, 203).[192] At the heart of Girard's analysis are the apocalyptical texts in the Gospels in which he sees an unequivocal emphasis of man's responsibility for "apocalyptical" violence: "In the Gospels, this violence is always brought home to men, and not to God." Consider the following example from the Gospel of Matthew that exhibits how humans—and not God—fill the world with war: "And you will hear of wars and rumors of wars; see that you are not alarmed; for this must take place, but the end is not yet. For nation will rise against nation, and kingdom against kingdom, and there will be famines and earthquakes in various places" (Matthew 24:6–7).[193]

Girard argues that our contemporary world offers a particularly clear picture of the apocalyptical dangers that accompany this biblical impulse. The biblical demystification of the world has given rise to modern science and technology—in particular, nuclear weapons, which have provided mankind with the capability to annihilate itself.[194] Girard also sees the environmental catastrophes that threaten a self-inflicted end to the world as confirmation of the Bible's apocalyptical prophesies: "To say that we are objectively in an apocalyptic situation is in no sense to 'preach the end of the world.' It is to say that mankind has become, for the first time, capable of destroying itself, something that was unimaginable only two or three centuries ago. The whole planet now finds itself, with regard to violence, in a situation comparable to that of most primitive groups of human beings, except that this time we are fully aware of it. We can no longer count on sacrificial resources based on false religions to keep this violence at bay" (*Things Hidden*, 260–261).

According to Girard, the apocalyptical situation in which the world finds itself has forced humans to take the biblical message of nonviolence seriously: "The definitive renunciation of violence, without any second thoughts, will become for us the condition *sine qua non* for the survival of humanity itself and for each one of us" (*Things Hidden*, 137).[195] The apocalyptical situation brought about by biblical revelation leaves mankind with the choice between the message of God—that is, the nonviolent love of one's enemy—and the self-extirpation of humanity [tr. *Selbstauslöschung der Menschheit*].

Sacrificial Christianity as the Katechon

From the perspective of all cultures rooted in myth, the apocalyptical force of biblical revelation appears as a "subversive force" (*A Theater of Envy*, 283), or a "subversive and shattering truth" (*Things Hidden*, 252). Jesus himself can only be perceived from this standpoint as a "destructive and subversive force" (*Things Hidden*, 216). We are accustomed to viewing Christianity as a conservative force, thus placing it on an intellectual level with the feudalist social order that existed up until the French Revolution. This judgment is far too superficial, however, as it overlooks the Bible's propensity to undermine the legitimacy of culture. Political thinkers such as Machiavelli, Hobbes, Rousseau, Nietzsche, Max Weber, Carl Schmitt, Eric Voegelin, and Hannah Arendt all recognize and express—in their own way—the explosive political force of the biblical message. The most profound expression is found in Dostoyevsky's legend of the Grand Inquisitor, which poignantly illustrates the dangers Jesus poses to culture. Ivan Karamazov's vision embodies an understanding of politics that is authoritarian and utilizes sacrifice to establish peace and order for the largest possible human population. At the conclusion of the tale, the Grand Inquisitor is brought face to face with Jesus—who listens silently to the Inquisitor's self-justification and acquiesces to his request to leave the world and not disturb its peace, order, and happiness. Whereas the Bible concludes with the call for the return of Christ

(Revelation 22:20), Dostoyevsky's legend ends with the fulfillment of the Inquisitor's wish that Jesus "go and do not come again . . . never, never!"[196] This petition of the Grand Inquisitor corresponds completely to the attitude implicit in all cultures that attempt to defend against the subversive force of the Bible. Sacrificial Christianity has resulted in a protraction of the Bible's culture-dismantling impetus. Girard frequently refers in his analysis of the biblical apocalypse to the *deferral* (*Things Hidden*, 251; *De la violence à la divinité*, 1004: "diffèrement") brought about by this impetus.[197] In Luke, he sees the concept addressed in the differentiation between the apocalypse that applies to Judaism, on the one hand, and the entire world, on the other (Luke 21:5–36).[198] Only after the entire world is encompassed by this biblical impetus can it be revealed in its full breadth. Before then, a sacrificial mechanism [tr. *Schutzmantel*] will be needed to catalyze its propagation throughout the world. Girard sees this process of globalization as a signal that the world is approaching the moment of global apocalypse. In reference to the Book of Revelation (Rev 20:1–6), he describes the contemporary situation as an "unbinding of Satan" (*I See Satan*, 186):[199] Sacrificial Christianity was able to defer this moment by enchaining Satan; it appears now that Satan has been set free in order—as Girard hopes—to meet his final downfall.

The enchaining of Satan in the Book of Revelation finds a significant equivalent in the biblical figure of the *Katéchon* (2 Thessalonians) to which Girard frequently refers in several of his later writings.[200] The katechon is described as a "restrainer" and regulatory force that, on the one hand, opposes the function of the satanic Antichrist and, on the other hand, delays the Second Coming of Christ yearned for by the early Christians: "That day will not come unless the rebellion comes first and the lawless one is revealed, the one destined for destruction. He opposes and exalts himself above every so-called god or object of worship, so that he takes his seat in the temple of God, declaring himself to be God. . . . You know what is now restraining him, so that he may be revealed when his time comes. For the mystery of lawlessness is already at work, but only until the one who now restrains it is removed" (2 Thessalonians 2:3–7). The restraining katechon is a paradoxical force that we can compare to the violent overcoming of violence in the scapegoat mechanism. The katechon, like the scapegoat mechanism, is composed of the same evil that it itself attempts to restrain. In the initial phase of the early Church, the Roman Empire was most often identified with the katechon. Dostoyevsky's Grand Inquisitor is an illustration of such a social order, as it stands in opposition to Christ in the name of Christ.

The figure of the katechon can help us better understand the contemporary political reality with its manifold divisions and antagonisms. To a certain extent, our system of national states shows that we are still living under the protection of katechontic order. However, we can observe at the same time the weakening of these forces. With the end of the Cold War and the advance of globalization, one can say that the era of the traditional nation-state is reaching its end. Those who fear the impending chaos that follows the weakening of traditional forms of politics will perhaps remain in support of katechontic order and implement all resources made available by sacrificial Christianity to preserve social harmony. An example of this is found in the political thought of Carl Schmitt, who openly professed a belief in the katechon and consequently identified with Dostoyevsky's Grand Inquisitor.[201] Girard's stance with regard to the figure of the katechon does not coincide with Schmitt's position, for Girard argues that the days of katechontic order are numbered, and that any attempt to stem the dissolution of order will only bring about totalitarianism and thus end in catastrophic tyranny.[202] For Girard, the Grand Inquisitor is the consummate model of such totalitarian resolutions.[203]

By contrast, Girard's position resonates most fully with that of Dietrich Bonhoeffer, who in direct opposition to Schmitt recognizes in the katechontic "restrainer" no immaculate power worthy of our trust, but rather a hegemonic ruler that is "not without guilt."[204] Bonhoeffer, like Girard, also believes that the katechon is not alone as it faces its impending downfall. For, even before the katechontic regulatory force, Bonhoeffer names the Church, which he argues is capable of saving itself from extinction by means of the "miracle of a new awakening of faith."[205] Bonhoeffer's differentiation between worldly katechontic forces and the Church's annunciation of the biblical message is not directed at any radical separation of the two, but rather espouses a new form of cooperation. He claims that the Church does not seek the eradication of these regulatory mechanisms—which actually seek reconciliation with the Church—but rather summons them to "conversion." The contemporary Church is no longer encumbered by political influence, and thus no longer forced to carry the burden of the katechon. For this reason, it now has the duty to bring the message of the Kingdom of

God to the world to show that peace between humans is possible without scapegoats or mutual external enemies.

Satan as Embodiment of the Mimetic Cycle

It is fitting at this point in our biblical analysis to provide a depiction of Girard's mimetic interpretation of Satan. In the course of his unfolding of the mimetic theory, Girard returns time and again to the concept of the devil, which he describes as the embodiment of both mimetic rivalry and the scapegoat logic examined above.[206] In his most recent systematic exposition, *I See Satan Fall Like Lightning*, the topic of Satan becomes the focus of a larger analysis of biblical revelation. The book elucidates the three essential aspects of Girard's mimetic theory, which are all bundled in the concept of the *mimetic cycle* (*I See Satan*, 32; *Je vois Satan*, 57: "cycle mimétique"). At the outset, there is the mimetic crisis that is generated by the spread of mimetic rivalry throughout the community. This gives rise to the collective violence of the scapegoat mechanism, which transforms the chaos of the crisis into a newly established order. The third moment consists of the divine epiphany—i.e., the mythical divinization of the victim—that veils the real violence behind the mob's persecution. According to Girard, these three moments of the mimetic cycle can also be described as the cycle of satanic violence.[207] We will now take a closer look at these moments in order to gain (1) an understanding of Girard's interpretation of Satan, and (2) a summary of the mimetic theory from the perspective of the Bible.

Satan and Scandal: The Trap of Mimetic Rivalry

The devil represents in biblical scripture not only a principle of order, as his title "ruler of this world" (John 12:31; 14:30; 16:11) would suggest. He is also, as his Greek name, *diábolos*—"he who throws across"—suggests, synonymous with chaos. As a generator of chaos, the devil embodies the kind of mimetic rivalry that transforms human beings into reciprocal enemies based on the mimetic dynamic of the model-obstacle. Girard describes this chaotic side of Satan in connection with Jesus's harsh rejection of Peter when he fails to comprehend the necessity of his teacher's imminent suffering: "Get behind me, Satan! You are a stumbling block to me; for you are setting your mind not on divine things but on human things" (Matthew 16:23). For Girard, the concept of scandal—Greek: *skándalon*, which also translates as "stumbling block," "obstacle," "pitfall," or "snare"—insinuates the New Testament insight into the deadly impasse of mimetic rivalry. He returns time and again in his writings to the extraordinary meaning found in this biblical concept:[208]

> Like the Hebrew word that it translates, "scandal" means, not one of those ordinary obstacles that we avoid easily after we run into it the first time, but a paradoxical obstacle that is almost impossible to avoid: the more this obstacle, or scandal, repels us, the more it attracts us. Those who are scandalized put all the more ardor in injuring themselves against it because they were injured before. . . . Understanding this strange phenomenon depends upon seeing in it what I have just described: the behavior of mimetic rivals who, as they mutually prevent each other from appropriating the object they covet, reinforce more and more their double desire, their desire for both the other's object of desire and for the desire of the other. Each consistently takes the opposite view of the other in order to escape their inexorable rivalry, but they always return to collide with the fascinating obstacle that each one has come to be for the other. Scandals are responsible for the false infinity of mimetic rivalry. They secrete increasing quantities of envy, jealousy, resentment, and hatred—all the poisons most harmful not only for the initial antagonists but also for all those who become fascinated by their rivalistic desires. (*I See Satan*, 16–17)

In the First Epistle of John, for instance, we read—in accordance with the mimetic theory—that hatred against one's brother is a necessary consequence of scandal: "Whoever loves a brother or sister lives in the light, and in such a person there is no cause for stumbling [*skándalon*]. But whoever hates another believer is in the darkness, walks in the darkness, and does not know the way to go, because the darkness has brought on blindness" (1 John 2:10–11).

Jesus's words to Peter display how scandal-inducing mimetic rivalry arises from that perverse form of imitation that is directed against the will of God. Peter admires Jesus merely as his earthly teacher, thus evoking the danger of mimetic rivalry should Peter begin to envy Jesus's earthly fame.

This biblical passage portrays the essence of Satan as that of a mimetic seducer who threatens to become a stumbling block for Jesus. The dangers of truncated, i.e., merely worldly mimetic desire, which Jesus exposes here as the essence of scandal, are referred to later in John—where Jesus confronts his opponents—as the consequence of false, satanic desire. Mimetic rivalry and satanic desire, thus, are for the New Testament one and the same: "If God were your Father, you would love me, for I came from God and now I am here. I did not come on my own, but he sent me. Why do you not understand what I say? It is because you cannot accept my word. You are from your father the devil, and you choose to do your father's desires" (John 8:42–44).

Satan's Divided Kingdom: The Paradoxical Order of the Scapegoat Mechanism

As much as the first stage of the mimetic cycle, the rivalry that leads to social crisis, is implied by the comparison of Satan to scandal, the second stage of the cycle—the overcoming of crisis and the restoration of order by means of the scapegoat mechanism—is all the more part of the New Testament's depiction of Satan. The devil is identical with that very form of mimesis which, by means of the victimage mechanism, brings about the overcoming of the mimetic crisis. Just as this collective violence turns an initial chaos into a new order, the devil—both "dragon of chaos" and "prince of this world"—is the incarnation of both chaos and order at the same time. Satan's regulatory power manifests itself in the moment the mimetically poisoned community suddenly unites against a single victim and cleanses itself of the rivalry that had threatened to destroy it. Girard points out an explicit reference in the Gospel of John—just after the above-mentioned passage referring to "false, satanic desire" where Jesus is confronted by those who seek his death—that demonstrates Satan's identification with this founding violence: "He was a murderer from the beginning" (John 8:44).[209]

The etymology of Satan's Hebraic name connects the devil with the scapegoat mechanism in a similar way. The term "Satan"—as is made clear above all in the Book of Job—translates as "the accuser" and thus corresponds to the incriminations that commence the persecution of scapegoats.[210] As accuser, the devil stands in diametric opposition to the Holy Spirit, the "defender of victims."

Just as the scapegoat mechanism is characterized by a fundamental paradox, in that it employs violence to overcome violence, satanic order is also intrinsically paradoxical. One is reminded here of Goethe's famous characterization of the devil in *Faust* where he refers to Mephistopheles as "part of that force which, always willing evil, always produces good."[211] The New Testament brings to light this fundamentally paradoxical nature where Jesus responds thus to the high priests' accusation that he drove out demons by Beelzebub:

> How can Satan cast out Satan? If a kingdom is divided against itself, that kingdom cannot stand. And if a house is divided against itself, that house will not be able to stand. And if Satan has risen up against himself and is divided, he cannot stand, but his end has come. (Mark 3:23–26)

At first glance, Jesus appears with these words to be proclaiming a mere cliché'd banality. On a deeper level, however, one sees that Jesus is consciously using the language of his opponents to demonstrate the paradoxical logic of Satan present in their persecutory thinking. For Girard, Jesus's figurative response in Mark 3:23 emphasizes Satan's double essence of order and disorder: "The Satan expelled is that one who foments and exasperates mimetic rivalries to the point of transforming the community into a furnace of scandals. The Satan who expels is this same furnace when it reaches a point of incandescence sufficient to set off the single victim mechanism. In order to prevent the destruction of his kingdom, Satan makes out of his disorder itself, at its highest heat, a means of expelling himself" (*I See Satan*, 34–35).[212] At the conclusion of the biblical passage quoted above, however, we already find reference to the prescribed circumvention of satanic violence: Satan's kingdom, intrinsically divided, will fail to endure and ultimately destroy itself. One finds here the link to Girard's apocalyptical reading of history, which was discussed in the previous section.

Satanic Transcendence: Archaic Religions, Powers, and Principalities

The third stage of the mimetic cycle concerns the divine epiphany that stems from the collective's divinization of persecuted victims. The scapegoat mechanism gives rise to mythical religions, which disguise the truth of the founding murder. This third stage corresponds to the New Testament characterization of Satan as the "father of lies" (John 8:44). He is identical with this deceptive mythologization that cleanses the founding murder of all real violence by retrospectively divinizing the murdered victims: "The origin of primitive and pagan gods," according to Girard, is analogous to the rising of a "false" or "satanic transcendence" (*I See Satan*, 69, 46). From the beginning, the social peace engendered by the founding murder is shrouded in religion, which clouds the fact that the community itself employed violence to bring it about; the empire of the "prince of this world" is perceived by the members of the community as a religiously legitimized social order.

Several passages in the New Testament describe the false peace intrinsic to this order, which passes itself off as being ordained by God, but in reality is a representation of satanic transcendence. Luke, for instance, speaks of "the powers of the heavens" that will be "shaken" by the coming of Christ (Luke 21:26). In the Epistles of Paul, the religiously disguised political order rooted in the scapegoat mechanism is identified with the concepts of "powers and principalities," with other metaphors elsewhere also pointing to their religious dimension (Ephesians 2:2: "the rule of the spirit of the power of the air"; 3:10: "the rulers and authorities of the heavenly places"). Girard returns in later works time and again to the topic of "powers and principalities," which he interprets using his theory of the founding murder.[213] In his eyes, they represent the order established by the scapegoat mechanism and can be observed even in our contemporary world: "The system of powers Satan has engendered is a concrete phenomenon, material and simultaneously spiritual, religious in a very special sense, efficacious and illusory at the same time. It is religion as illusion, which protects humans from violence and chaos by means of sacrificial rituals. Although this system is grounded in an illusion, its action in the world is real to the extent that idolatry, or false transcendence, commands obedience" (*I See Satan*, 96).

Satan's Fall: The Triumph of the Cross Reveals His Essence

Biblical revelation, in that it unearths the truth of the scapegoat mechanism, brings about the fall of Satan's empire and reveals his true nature. Together with revelation, according to the Gospel of Luke, Satan's dominion meets its end: "I saw Satan fall like lightning from heaven" (10:18).[214] For Girard as

well, the triumph of the cross is analogous to Satan's inevitable end.²¹⁵ Since
the Gospels are no new myth—which would have veiled the collective murder of Jesus—they identify with the innocent victim and shed light on the
workings of founding violence, thus robbing Satan of his very foundation.
Numerous passages in the New Testament describe this triumph of the cross;
by penetrating the accusation mechanism and taking the side of the victims
of collective violence, God brings about the fall of all cultures rooted in this
violence: "And when you were dead in trespasses and the uncircumcision of
your flesh, God made you alive together with him, when he forgave us all our
trespasses, erasing the record that stood against us with its legal demands. He
set this aside, nailing it to the cross. He disarmed the rulers and authorities
and made a public example of them, triumphing over them in it" (Colossians 2:13–15). The wisdom of God thus transforms Jesus's defeat on earth
into an ultimate, eternal triumph over Satan: "None of the rulers of this age
understood this; for if they had, they would not have crucified the Lord of
glory" (1 Corinthians 2:7–8).

Girard's mimetic interpretation of Satan explicates this significant
Christian topic in a way that avoids, on the one hand, readings of the devil
as an actually existing "anti-god" and, on the other hand, the common theological practice of dismissing the concept of Satan as mere superstition. Both
of these misperceptions must be avoided. Sigmund Freud's *Civilization and
Its Discontents* illustrates the first danger, in particular where Freud refers to
the primary function of the "Christian Devil" as an "excuse for God; in that
way he would be playing the same part as an agent of economic discharge as
the Jew does in the world of the Aryan ideal."²¹⁶ Such interpretations of the
devil as a real person or entity can transform him into a scapegoat that has
an exculpatory function not for God—as Freud argues—but rather for man
himself. Satan embodies both the mimetic rivalries and the ensuing reciprocal accusations of which humans attempt to cleanse themselves through the
process of victimization. As a personal entity, Satan expresses the presence of
real scapegoats, the victims of collective violence, as well as the real motive of
the persecutory mob.²¹⁷ In the end, the devil is nothing other than the mimesis that can be seen as the actual desiring subject involved in the mimetic
cycle. He embodies the mimetic dynamics at work between subject and
model—"Satan is *always someone*" (*I See Satan*, 46)—without ever assuming
any discrete personal being. He is pure mimesis or, in other words, the ape of

God. His essence is the absence of being, which attempts to nest itself in the mimetic relations of God's creatures.[218]

The second potential misperception connected with Satan is the superficial denial of the concept. As Baudelaire remarks, and justifiably so, this is itself a strategy of Satan: "Never, my brethren, forget, when you hear enlightenment vaunted, that the neatest trick of the devil is to persuade you that he does not exist."[219] Girard's mimetic reading neither denies the existence of Satan, nor does it transform him into a scapegoat that can be used as an instrument by humanity: "The interpretation that assimilates Satan to rivalistic contagion and its consequences enables us for the first time to acknowledge the importance of the prince of this world without also endowing him with personal being" (*I See Satan*, 45).

In a similar way to Girard, William Golding—in his novel *Lord of the Flies*, discussed at length above—traces Satan's essence back to the collective behavior of man. As is revealed by its title, which alludes to Goethe's Mephistopheles, Golding's novel delves into the essence of the devil and man's diabolical nature. The stranded children are frightened of an "evil" wild animal, which is supposedly roaming the forests of the island. This "lord of the flies," to whom the children are attracted with almost religious fascination, turns out to be the corpse of a fighter pilot who died in a crash landing. This realization, however, does not mean that the question of the satanic disappears from the novel. Golding delves deeper into the concept and ultimately traces it back to the mechanism of collective violence to which Simon, one of the group members, falls victim. And it is Simon, in the end, who, when asked whether he believes in the existence of the evil beast, responds thus: "Maybe there is a beast. . . . What I mean is . . . maybe it's only us."[220] Golding joins Girard here in identifying the human collective as the origin of the devil.

Deconstruction and the Truth of the Bible

In the concluding section of this chapter, we will examine Girard's understanding of the Bible against the backdrop of his analyses of postmodern philosophy. The paradoxical structure of cultural forms rooted in the scapegoat mechanism—made clear in the preceding section on Satan—makes a comparative analysis of the mimetic theory and deconstruction relevant here, for

the latter shows a distinct interest for all conceptions and philosophical systems possessing inherent paradoxes and aporias. While expounding his thesis
on the scapegoat mechanism, Girard discovered a close connection to the
then just-published writings of Jacques Derrida, and used central concepts of
deconstruction to draw parallels to his own work. Just as deconstruction uses
precise analysis to elaborate the untenable paradoxes of philosophical texts,
Girard recognized in biblical revelation a source for the deconstruction of
cultural order. This attempt on the part of Girard to establish convergence
between the mimetic theory and deconstruction has been reciprocated,
meanwhile, by the Italian philosopher Gianni Vattimo, who from the side
of deconstruction has moved in the direction of the mimetic theory. However, this proximity between the two stances is accompanied by significant
divergence, which has become increasingly apparent in recent years. While
for Derridean deconstruction there are no attainable factual truths on which
texts are based—because every act of comprehension is subject to interpretation and thus part of an extended textual concept that excludes the possibility of any "outside" [tr. *Außerhalb*]—Girard argues for a truth outside all
texts, which is the precondition for his type of deconstruction. This understanding of truth is the basis for Girard's exegesis of biblical revelation and
harkens back to the figural interpretation of texts that was fundamental for
the Christian tradition, displaying once more Girard's openness with regard
to the concept of transcendence.

Supplement and Scapegoat: Girard's Proximity to Deconstruction

The early works of Derrida provide for Girard—up to the present day—an
important philosophical confirmation of the mimetic theory. Of particular
significance is Derrida's insight into the logic of the "supplement," which he
reconstructed as an essential attribute of all Western metaphysics. Careful
textual analysis of major philosophers such as Plato, Rousseau, Kant, Hegel,
Husserl, and Saussure led the French poststructuralist to discover at the
heart of metaphysics a fundamental paradox. Using above all the example
of the relationship between writing and the spoken word, he expounded an
aporia that defined the entirety of Western philosophical thought. Derrida
argues that from Plato onwards, philosophical exposition was dominated by
the notion that writing—in relation to the spoken word—was subordinate,

secondary, and merely derivative. Whereas the spoken word stood for intuition, originality, and self-sufficiency, writing was viewed as merely a retrospective addition, a *supplement*. Derrida's deconstruction consists of precise analysis of such conceptual claims, in which he dissects their basic elements in order to show that they—in this case, the hierarchical superordination of speaking over writing—are ultimately untenable. At least for philosophical discourse, Derrida displays that the spoken word was from the beginning necessarily derived from the written argument. If the written word assumed at first the significance of a merely additional supplement, closer examination shows that this supplement is a speech-enabling element, thus threatening to supplant the origin to which it was previously subordinate. The apparently self-sufficient origins prove to be plagued by an emptiness and therefore in need of a supplement. Derrida claims that all philosophical assertions of origin can be deconstructed to their core as claims held together by fundamentally untenable contradictions. The supplement, thus, carries a threatening double entendre; it is "dangerous," as Rousseau—from whom Derrida borrows the term—rightly noted.[221] In contrast to the argument that Derridean deconstruction simply promotes the arbitrariness of free association, this method is much more concerned with expounding the paradoxical logic inherent in the interrelatedness of central concepts and arguments of Western thought.[222]

For Girard, Derrida's study of the logic of the supplement in Plato's *Phaedrus* dialogue is of central importance. "Plato's Pharmacy," published in 1968, sheds light on the complex nature of the supplement through an analysis of Plato's stance to the written word—a most ambivalent stance considering Plato's philosophy that combats the written argument. Plato alludes to this paradox in his dialogue *Phaedrus* by describing the written word explicitly as a *pharmakon*. In following with the ambivalent logic of the dangerous supplement, the written word, as *pharmakon*, also possesses two meanings [tr. *erweist sich als doppeldeutig*]. According to the double meaning of the Greek term, *pharmakon* is both remedy and poison at once.[223] Derrida shows—with an intuitive understanding of the wide linguistic scope of the Greek *pharmakon*—that this logic of the supplement can be demonstrated in the related concept of *pharmakós* as well.[224] This latter concept, completely avoided in Plato's dialogue—which Derrida expressly points out—implies the scapegoats that were sacrificed in Athens and other Greek cities to defend against crises.[225] The ambivalent logic of the *pharmakon* thus applies likewise to these sacrifices of Greek cathartic ritual. They, too, are a dangerous supplement, which must be expelled to stabilize order within the city. Just as writing can be a "remedy and a poison" for the spoken word, scapegoats, for the community, can be both evil monsters worthy of expulsion, and indispensable protectors worthy of honor: "The ceremony of the pharmakos is played . . . out on the boundary line between inside and outside, which it has as its function ceaselessly to trace and retrace. . . . The origin of difference and division, the pharmakos represents evil both introjected and projected. Beneficial insofar as he cures—and for that, venerated and cared for—harmful insofar as he incarnates the powers of evil—and for that, feared and treated with caution. Alarming and calming. Sacred and accursed."[226]

By referring to the actual practice of sacrifice in ancient Greece and its structural parallels to the logic of the supplement, Derrida enables Girard to bridge his theory of the scapegoat mechanism with Derridean deconstruction. In *Violence and the Sacred*, Girard takes up Derrida's deconstruction of Plato's philosophy, concluding that both philosophy and culture are altogether rooted in the scapegoat mechanism.[227] He radicalizes Derrida's thesis insofar as he takes the logic of the supplement out of the realm of mere textual interpretation and uses it to deconstruct all forms of cultural order. In a later essay, "Origins: A View from Literature," Girard argues that myths are far more influenced by Derrida's logic of the supplement than the philosophical texts through which he discovered his theory.[228] For Girard, the paradox of this logic is identical to the logic of the scapegoat mechanism, which implements violence in order to overcome the violence of social crisis. The paradox of Satan thus corresponds to the logic of the supplement; the ambivalence of katechontic Christendom, as well, is characterized by this paradoxical basic structure. It is no surprise, thus, that Girard reverts back to the concept of *différer*—French for both "to differentiate" and "to suspend"—in his description of the temporal suspension of the Bible's dissolution of culture, which was brought about by sacrificial Christianity.[229] For *différer* is closely related to the aesthetic concept of *différance*, which Derrida uses to define the complex relationship of law and violence in a way that bears distinct similarities to Girard's understanding of our katechontic culture that is impeding the apocalypse: "*Différance* is a force *différée-différante*."[230] Andrew J. McKenna, an American scholar of literature, points out these structural parallels between the mimetic theory and deconstruction in his comprehensive study *Violent Difference*.[231] From McKenna's perspective, Girard's theory can offer deconstruction an essential anthropological backing to help it from descending into mere nihilistic language games.

While Derrida himself never offered his position with regard to the mimetic theory, one finds in the Italian philosopher Gianni Vattimo an important postmodern thinker—with ties to Derrida—who has shown attempts at convergence with the mimetic theory. In a very personal book, *Belief*, Vattimo describes how Girard's interpretation of the Bible enabled his "nihilistic rediscovery of Christianity" that culminates in the love of one's neighbor.[232] Similar to the way Girard discovered an impulse in the Bible that undermines human culture, Vattimo recognized—under the influence of Heidegger—that the "history of Being has as a guiding thread the weakening of strong structures."[233] He sees this "weakening" as immediately connected with the incarnation of Christ, and explains this by means of Girard's insight into the radical difference between the Christian faith and the religions based on the victimage mechanism. Girard's thesis, in other words, allows Vattimo to see the incarnation of Christ as the "dissolution" of the "violent God," the "God of which Nietzsche spoke."[234] He also emphasizes together with Girard that the close relationship between religion and violence in historical Christianity was able to restrain and protract the biblical impulse significantly.

On the occasion of Girard's retirement ceremony, during which he was awarded emeritus status at Stanford University, Vattimo gave a lecture on the connections between Girard and Heidegger in which he praised the insights of the mimetic theory that enabled him to pursue the consummation of Heidegger's work.[235] Vattimo's lecture connects with Girard's analysis of Heidegger and is relevant for the present discussion insofar as the example of Heidegger can illuminate a central difference between Vattimo and Girard.[236] Girard's interest in Heidegger is based on the latter's reflection of the inherent paradoxes of the sacred, and because this German father of deconstruction recognizes the violent logic of Heraclitus at the core of Western thought.[237] Girard also endorses Heidegger's unequivocal differentiation between Johanine logos and the logos of Greek philosophy. He distances himself from Heidegger, however, where the German philosopher fails to recognize nonviolence as the essential difference at work in the New

Testament. Girard sees Heidegger's blindness in this regard as rooted in "profound but discreet animosity to Judaism and Christianity." However, he claims that Heidegger is still active "in spite of himself in the immense process of the revelation," insofar as his philosophy detects traces of the founding violence at the origin of culture. Vattimo, by contrast, sees in Heidegger's philosophy no mere indirect involvement in the process of revelation, but rather a full-on "transcription of the Judeo-Christian revelation."[238] With this claim, Vattimo uses Girard to transcend Girard insofar as he combines the mimetic theory with Heidegger's philosophy in a bid to portray Heidegger as a critic of violence. In a continuation of Heidegger's thought, Vattimo affirms the weakening of those "strong structures" that accompany a rethinking of being: "Being is the very principle of weakening."[239] Processes of dissolution, thus, are what Vattimo believes characterize modernity: "the dissolution of authoritarian political institutions, the dissolution of the belief in the ultimacy of consciousness, the dissolution of the very notion of reality." In *Belief,* Vattimo also incorporates classical concepts of theology into these processes of dissolution. He extends far beyond Girard by identifying a waning secularization—which will meet its end in the principle of Christian charity—with Nietzsche's proclamation of the death of God: "To move closer to the nihilistic rediscovery of Christianity, it is sufficient to go just a little bit beyond Girard by acknowledging that the natural sacred is violent not only insofar as the victim-based mechanism presupposes a divinity thirsty for vengeance, but also insofar as it attributes to such a divinity all the predicates of omnipotence, absoluteness, eternity and 'transcendence' with regard to humanity."[240] Such conclusions remain far from Girard's position. In contrast to Vattimo, Girard sees his mimetic theory as being in line with the tradition of major Church dogmas.[241] Another important difference between the two can be seen in Girard's distance from Heidegger, whom he interprets along with Nietzsche as a representative of neopaganism—and not, as Vattimo believes, any biblically inspired critic of violence.[242]

However, Girard's distance from deconstruction is not limited to such superficial differences with regard to the estimation of Christian dogma or Heidegger's relationship to the Bible. The central difference pertains more to the understanding of truth and the greater question of textual referentiality—that is, whether texts can refer to external reality or are confined to themselves on account of external reality's merely interpretive nature.

Facts, Not Only Interpretations: Girard's Rejection of Postmodern Nihilism

Despite all positive reference to deconstruction—above all to the early works of Derrida—it must be said that Girard explicitly distanced himself from the beginning from all postmodern theories that radically deny texts any reference to external reality and thus exclude the possibility of truth. Already in *Things Hidden since the Foundation of the World*, he expresses the necessity to undertake—in the Derridean sense of the term—a deconstruction of cultural institutions in order to understand their origins.[243] At the same time, however, he rejects Derrida's argument that there are no factual origins on which concepts can be based. Girard emphasizes, contrary to Heidegger and Derrida, that a return to Pre-Socraticism is insufficient to penetrate the core of Western metaphysics, arguing rather that this deconstruction must extend to its origins in archaic religion, i.e., the scapegoat mechanism. The discovery of the founding violence is at once a justification of deconstruction, but it is also, at the same time, its very threshold: "Once the mechanism of the surrogate victim has been recognized, the beginning and the end of the 'deconstruction' are at hand, since its accomplishment amounts also to a 'reconstruction' which begins at the common matrix" (Girard, *Things Hidden*, 62). Where the reference to real origins disappears, with all comprehension limited to mere inner-textual configurations, deconstruction is reduced to a mere reflection of archaic religion and threatens to degenerate into a nihilistic language game. It comes as no surprise, thus, that Girard praises "Plato's Pharmacy" most highly among Derrida's deconstructive readings, for it refers to actually practiced scapegoat rituals in ancient Greece.

Girard's critique of poststructuralist theory has increased over time. He vehemently opposes the negation of referentiality—the thesis that texts offer an infinite amount of equivalent interpretations—and the general renunciation of truth that follows from it.[244] His most virulent attack on postmodern nihilism is found in his article "Theory and Its Terrors," published in 1989, in which he reinforces his earlier, already critical stance towards Lévi-Strauss's structuralism.[245] Girard's disassociation from deconstruction, however, is more directed at Derrida's epigones teaching at American universities than the founder of deconstruction himself.[246] Even if Derrida argues in *Of Grammatology* that "there is nothing outside of the text," this is no reference to any necessary rejection of external reality, but rather to the interpretive context within which all external facts are embedded.[247] Still, Derrida does differentiate from Girard insofar as he juxtaposes the Nietzschean standpoint, the "affirmation of the freeplay of the world and without truth, without origin" with all interpretations that "[dream] of deciphering, a truth or an origin which is free from freeplay and from the order of the sign."[248] While Derrida consciously objects to deciding in favor of either alternative, because he attempts to conceive "of the common ground, and the différance of this irreducible difference,"[249] Girard proposes a genetic model that recognizes in the scapegoat mechanism the actual event from which the system of signs and language originates: "The sign is the reconciliatory victim" (*Things Hidden*, 103).[250]

In his critical analysis of Vattimo, Girard explains his defense of referentiality and his ensuing disassociation from deconstruction.[251] For Vattimo and several other postmodern representatives, it is Nietzsche's critique of positivism that builds the starting point for their rejection of referentiality: "Against positivism, which is left standing at the phenomenon 'there are only facts,' I would say: no, it is precisely facts that do not exist, only interpretations. We cannot determine a factum 'in-itself': it is perhaps nonsense to even want to do so."[252] In Girard's eyes, this aphorism lies well behind the great insight of Nietzsche regarding the difference between myth and the Bible—"Dionysos versus the Crucified"—where the German philosopher spoke of two different interpretations of the same fact. With that insight, which was vital for Girard's interpretation of scripture, Nietzsche transcended the sterility of nineteenth-century positivism without encouraging any postmodern arbitrariness [tr. *Beliebigkeit*]: "In our days the 'deconstructionists' reverse the positivist error. For them, only interpretation exists. They want to be more Nietzschean than Nietzsche. Instead of getting rid of problems of interpretation, they get rid of facts" (*I See Satan*, 214). The suppressing of facts covers up the crucial difference between myth and the Bible. Both interpretations speak of real acts of violence against persecuted victims. The truth of the Bible consists in its factual interpretation of that real event, which in myth is shrouded by a veil of lies. The all-important truth of the innocent victim is lost when texts are understood only as interpretations without reference to any factual reality. Girard insists in opposition to these nihilist proclivities that the "real deconstruction" must address and revive the "concern for victims" (*I See Satan*, 177). This concern demands, in the final analysis, that there also be facts and not only interpretations.

It is perhaps Girard's initial training as a historian that made him impervious to the nihilistic temptations of postmodernism and thus able to defy, out of concern for victims, the dissolution of all facts in interpretations. Time and again in the course of his work, he harkens back to historical examples in order to emphasize the relationship between texts and their real origins, a method he views as central for his interpretation of myth. A telling example of this is found in the way Girard handles medieval texts of persecution—discussed at length above—which refer to the real persecution of groups such as witches, heretics, and Jews. He is exuberant in his praise of the historians of the Middle Ages who "refuse to deny the reality of the witch-hunts" (*I See Satan*, 74–75).[253] In more recent works, he refers frequently to the Dreyfus affair at the end of the nineteenth century to stress the importance of real persecutions in the context of textual interpretation.[254] In the late nineteenth century, Captain Alfred Dreyfus was unjustly convicted of treason and banished to Devil's Island in the Atlantic, where he was placed in solitary confinement. A small group of French intellectuals fought for Dreyfus's exoneration against the overwhelming majority of people who were convinced of his guilt. Girard's emphasis of the possibility for truth in the postmodern era identifies with the Dreyfus supporters who were ultimately able to save the falsely incriminated captain: "If the supporters of Dreyfus had not fought for their point of view, if they had not suffered (at least some of them) for the truth, if they had admitted, as have some in our day, that to believe there is such a thing as truth is the fundamental sin—then Dreyfus would never have been vindicated, and the lie would have won the victory" (*I See Satan*, 146). The truth that Girard so strongly defends in his work is the truth of innocent victims, whose voice can be heard only when facts are not dissolved in interpretation. A short essay by the English historian Timothy Garton Ash—like Girard a strong opponent of postmodernism—contains an etymological reference that can illustrate just how much a deconstruction like Girard's, whose starting point is the uncovering of the founding murder, must be based on fact.[255] Ash writes that in the sixteenth and seventeenth centuries, the English term "fact" meant first and foremost an evil deed [tr. *böse Tat*] or crime, and that its German equivalent, *Tatsache*, referred to the *Tatort*, or the location where the crime took place.

Figura Christi: The Imitation of Divine Truth

Girard understands the mimetic theory as a form of deconstruction that, on the one hand, is carried by the insight into a real founding event—the scapegoat mechanism—and, on the other hand, not only serves the interpretation of texts but also incorporates the entirety of cultural order as such. This ambitious undertaking does not mean that Girard sees himself as the new "master thinker" whose theory stands above all others. He views his theory as part of a much more encompassing deconstruction. According to Girard, biblical revelation is a source for the demythologization or deconstruction of myth and all institutions and cultural forms that emanate from it.[256] Since the Bible—in contrast to myth—sheds light on the victimage mechanism, it undermines all cultures that can only exist in ignorance of their own foundations: "But [Jesus] looked at them and said, "What then does this text mean: 'The stone that the builders rejected has become the cornerstone'?" (Luke 20:17).[257] However, the deconstruction brought about by biblical revelation does not spare postmodern thinkers who themselves fight against it; in Girard's words, the critics of Western thought, like Heidegger, participate "in spite of [themselves] in the immense process of revelation" (*Things Hidden*, 273).

The unconditional truth for which Girard so vehemently fights in his criticism of postmodern nihilism is the biblical partisanship with victims, which finds most distinct expression in the examples of Joseph, Job, and of course Jesus Christ himself: "Through much struggle and suffering the supporters of Dreyfus achieved a triumph for a truth as absolute, intransigent, and dogmatic as Joseph's in his opposition to mythological violence" (*I See Satan*, 146).[258]

However, does Girard fall victim with this reference to the absolute truth of the Bible to a fundamentalist reading of this text? Such misgivings can easily be dismissed. The truth that Girard stresses in the Bible is found not in specific words or individual passages, as such, but rather in the overall trajectory of the text where the truth of a God emerges who stands for nonviolent love and in solidarity with the earth's persecuted victims. Girard's reading of the Bible connects with the figural interpretation that was essential for the authors of scripture and the medieval church fathers who based their exegeses on these writings. Just as these traditional interpretations understood the Old Testament as the prophetic annunciation of Christ, Girard too refers to such prefigurations and annunciations of Christ. In accordance with this traditional form of biblical interpretation, he designates those figures as disparate as the Old Testament brothers Joseph and Judah, the Servant of Yahweh, the good harlot of the Salomonic judgment, and Job all as *figura Christi*.[259] Due to the fact that over time the figural interpretation became increasingly absorbed in allegorical exegesis, which devolved into mere superficial parallels to figures and other characteristics taken out of their original context, these parallelisms were viewed by modern science as proof of the "backwardness" of Christianity. Girard's mimetic theory, however, is capable today of making the deep truth of the figural reading once again plausible;[260] the connection between the individual occurrences in the Old and New Testaments must be viewed against the backdrop of the uncovering of the victimage mechanism. Precisely because the unveiling of the founding murder begins in the Old Testament, it must be seen as inextricable from its final revelation in the Passion of Christ. One must heed the interpretation of the mimetic cycle, Girard argues, in order to recognize how the two testaments are related: "The truth of prophecy in the Christian sense appears from the moment mimetic processes are emphasized as such rather than characters treated as Christ figures" (*Job*, 166). The many Old Testament passages that are quoted in the Gospels are proof for Girard just how much both accounts are directed at revealing the scapegoat mechanism. For instance, the Psalm verses 35:19 and 69:5 quoted in John—"They hated me without a cause" (John 15:25)—criticize the collective persecution of innocent victims in the same way the Gospels show solidarity with Jesus.[261] The actual essence of biblical prophecy is therefore not just any imaginary prophecy, but rather the true reading of the processes of the mimetic cycle.[262]

If one pursues Girard's reference—found in a footnote in *Things Hidden since the Foundation of the World*—to Erich Auerbach's essay "Figura," one sees just how much the figural reading of the Bible resonates with central parts of the mimetic theory.[263] Auerbach differentiates between Christian figural interpretation and pagan allegory that emanated from it, stressing in a similar way to Girard the referentiality to external-textual reality. Auerbach sees the figural interpretation as characterized by a particular emphasis of the historicity of interconnected events, refusing—à la postmodern nihilism—to metamorphose all events in mere metanarrative signs: "Figural interpretation establishes a connection between two events or persons, the first of which signifies not only itself but also the second, while the second encompasses or fulfills the first. The two poles of the figure are separate in time, but both, being real events or figures, are within time, within the stream of historical life."[264] This preservation of historicity corresponds fully to Girard's adherence to facts.

However, the figural reading also coincides with the mimetic theory with regard to the notion that all factual events require one corresponding explanation. This can be seen in the second, equally important characteristic of figural interpretation, which Auerbach refers to as *figural prophecy*: "Figural prophecy implies the interpretation of one worldly event through another; the first signifies the second, the second fulfills the first. Both remain historical events; yet both, looked at in this way, have something provisional and incomplete about them; they point to one another and both point to something in the future, something still to come, which will be the actual, real, and definitive event."[265] While "tentative" modern historical interpretations view the event "in an unbroken horizontal process," in figural prophecy the interpretation "is always sought from above."[266] Every interpretation finds its ultimate certainty in God, who "is at all times present and knows no difference in time" [tr. *steht in Jederzeitlichkeit*]. God is the consummate truth, whose temporarily fragmented imitations build the figures of *imitatio veritas*, the imitation of divine truth. The vertical connection to God that constitutes the figural doctrine of prophecy corresponds to the importance of true transcendence for the mimetic theory. For Girard, interpretation directed at divine truth thus supersedes even his so-cherished referentiality. Where he differentiates between the biblical story of Joseph and the lies of the Oedipus myth, he demonstrates that this truth transcends the question of referentiality: "The essential truth of the Joseph story lies, not in its possible correspondence to facts outside the text, but in its critique of mythical expulsions" (*I See Satan*, 147). Girard's preference of truth over referentiality also finds equivalence in Auerbach's description of figural interpretation, where the shrouded fact of the event is "subordinated to an interpretation which is fully secured to begin with."[267] Here, Girard reconnects with Derrida's argument that all reality, from the outset, is subject to interpretation. Girard goes beyond Derrida, however, insofar as he recognizes in the Christian logic of divine truth—manifested in the figure of Christ—the true interpretation of all facts. Derrida, by contrast, is more cautious with his notion of "the truth." He sees himself as a "friend of truth" because he is cognizant that truth is necessary in order to attain certainty—even if one cannot possess it: "The truth . . . is impossible to be it, to be there, to have it; one must only be its friend."[268] Derrida is similarly cautious in his definition of the messianic principle—the insight that no society can exist without a minimum quantity of faith—in relation to the messianism of biblical revelation, which he argues is necessarily bound to an absolute and concrete event.[269]

Auerbach, meanwhile, in his comprehensive study *Mimesis*, uses the example of "the sacrifice of Isaac" as a prefiguration of "the sacrifice of Christ" to show that the connection between these two events cannot be understood in temporal or causal terms—that is, that a vertical interpretation is required: "The horizontal, that is the temporal and causal, connection of occurrences is dissolved; the here and now is no longer a mere link in an earthly chain of events, it is simultaneously something which has always been, and which will be fulfilled in the future; and strictly, in the eyes of God, it is something eternal, something omni-temporal, something already consummated in the realm of fragmentary earthly events."[270] Auerbach's demonstration of figural interpretation is made plausible in the light of Girard's mimetic theory; the "God of victims" (Girard, *Job*, 154) identifies eternally with the scapegoats of this world because divine truth is constituted by love and nonviolence. This divine truth is the transcendent light in which all factual events experience their ultimate interpretation. In the case of Isaac, it is the voice of God that prevents his sacrifice; in the case of Jesus, God himself becomes a victim, in order to make his eternal meaning visible to the world.

Figural interpretation, however, is not limited to this narrow circle of biblical events, but rather views all occurrences in the one divine light. For Dante, one of the great representatives of figural interpretation, a pagan such as Virgil is also included in God's plan.[271] The same is valid for the mimetic theory. Girard, like Dante, sees traces of divine truth not only in biblical thought; in connection with Simone Weil, he praises Antigone, for instance, as a *figura Christi* (*Things Hidden*, 244). And, in reference to Matthew 25:40—"Whatever you did for one of the least of these brothers of mine, you did for me"—Girard stresses that the partisanship of Christ encompasses all victims of persecution: "We find here the essence of specifically Judeo-Christian prophetic religion. It is closely related to the suffering that all collective persecutions produce, whatever their date in human history, whatever the ethnic, religious, or cultural attributes of the victims" (*I See Satan*, 128).

CHAPTER 6

Political Implications of the Mimetic Theory

A people should not inquire with any practical aim in view into the origin of the supreme authority to which it is subject, that is, a subject ought not to reason subtly for the sake of action about the origin of this authority, as a right to the obedience he owes. . . . Whether a state began with an actual contract of submission . . . or whether power came first and law arrived only afterwards, or even whether they should have followed in this order: for a people already subject to civil law these subtle reasonings are altogether pointless and, moreover, threaten a state with danger.

—Immanuel Kant, *Metaphysics of Morals*

As a theory of culture [tr. *Kulturtheorie*], the mimetic theory explains not only the genesis of archaic religions and the foundation of human civilization, but also the formation of major political institutions, which in Girard's eyes can be traced back to the scapegoat mechanism. In the following chapter, we will pursue the violent origins of political power, legal order, and war through analyses of sacred kingship, capital punishment, and archaic friend/enemy distinctions. These political institutions all bear traces of the collective violence that, according to Girard, forms the basis of human civilization.

Sacred Kingship as Origin of Political Power

Sacred kingship belongs to the most ancient political institutions of human civilization.[1] What is the connection between this political manifestation and the scapegoat mechanism? Our intuition tells us that the kingship represents the exact opposite of a scapegoat; the crown symbolizes the supreme political and often religious authority, whereas the scapegoat—the victim of banishment or murder—assumes the lowest fathomable position in the social hierarchy. Indeed, could there be any difference more extreme than that between king and the banished victim? This spontaneous assessment, however, remains too superficial. We see already in Girard's thesis concerning the foundation of archaic religion that the scapegoat, after being murdered by the mob, is transformed into a god and thereafter the community's most exalted master. After the murder, the mob awards its victim powers that a king or god are normally entitled to. The metaphysical distance between victim and king, in other words, is much less significant than one assumes at first glance. Let us now use the mimetic theory to elucidate this seemingly paradoxical proximity, and with it the origins of sacred kingship.

Girard claims that all institutions are rooted in the controlled repetition of the scapegoat mechanism. In ritual, the scapegoat mechanism is consciously repeated to restore and consolidate peace among the members of the community on a continual basis. This ritual repetition is characterized by the same misapprehension of the actual violence—on the part of the community—observed in the original scapegoat mechanism. Just as the mob's violence and the innocence of the victim remain hidden, the truth of the rite is disguised by the sacred in religious sacrifice. The sacrificial victim, as we saw above, is marked by the double transference; it is viewed initially as absolutely evil, that is, as responsible for the plight that has descended on the given society, and retroactively as absolutely benevolent, i.e., as a harbinger of peace that has rescued the community from its plight. It is impossible, however, for ritual to reproduce these intrinsically paradoxical moments in their full two-sidedness [tr. *Janusk, pfigkeit*]; this would merely result in the spread of confusion and instability within the community and thus contradict what it set out to achieve, namely, the establishment of clear order, strict differences, and social harmony. For this reason, one of the two moments of the double transference is always emphasized more strongly than the other. The other moment, initially neglected and relegated to the fringe of the rite, is eventually eradicated completely in order to enable the unfolding of an institution free of contradiction. From one culture to another, this process can manifest itself in many different ways, with each individual community focusing on either moment in its own way. In the end, the two moments—at first part of the same double process—are severed from one another and appear, free of contradiction, as absolutely separate and completely unrelated. Girard deconstructs this "cultural Platonism" (*Things Hidden*, 58), which interprets these human institutions as individual eternal forms, in that he traces their origins back to the scapegoat mechanism. By means of a "genetic model" (*Things Hidden*, 59; see also 100), he shows how these forms arose from one single ritual matrix.

After being chosen by the community—and before the actual slaughtering—the victim of ritual sacrifice possesses the prestigious status of "harbinger of peace" conferred upon the original scapegoat after being murdered by the community. It is thus not uncommon in primitive cultures that the victim chosen for ritual sacrifice is granted the highest social privileges before its impending murder. Girard points out two enlightening examples of this phenomenon. The first concerns the Tupinambá people, a cannibalistic tribe in northwest Brazil, which treated its victims, mostly captive tribal enemies, with extreme ambivalence.[2] On the one hand, the Tupinambá insulted and swore at their victims, as is to be expected with enemy prisoners. On the other hand, however, these captives also attracted the community's veneration, evidenced by its exaggeratedly high praise of their sexual performance. A second instance of such behavior can be observed among the Aztecs.[3] The victims chosen for sacrifice in Aztec communities were given the social status that is normally reserved only for gods or kings. The members of the community went to great ends to ensure that their last wishes were fulfilled; they bowed down before their future victims and attempted to touch their clothes.

Sacred Kingship

According to Girard, this reverence for the future victims of ritual sacrifice is central to the rise of kingship: "The king reigns only by virtue of his future death; he is no more and no less than a victim awaiting sacrifice, a condemned man about to be executed" (*Violence and the Sacred*, 107). If the victim, before its sacrificial death, is able to transform the community's veneration into real political power, we are confronted with the beginnings of kingship, or rather, in even more general terms, the beginnings of central political power. The stronger this power can develop, the longer the king's eventual sacrifice is delayed. Kingship is rooted in the reverence the community shows the victim during the "lapse of time before the sacrifice" (*Things Hidden*, 53), which is then transformed into political influence. This power can become so pronounced that ultimately, it is not the victim who is sacrificed, but rather a substitute, any arbitrary victim close to him. The more the king is able to resolve conflict within the community and keep internal rivalries in check, the less his sacrifice—or that of the surrogate—is necessary. The element of sacrifice is marginalized until it disappears completely, giving rise to a form of political sovereignty that shrouds the connection to the scapegoat mechanism and is responsible for our intuitive skepticism with regard to the connection between ritual sacrifice and kingship.

Numerous characteristics of sacred kingdoms can illustrate this general delineation of the origin of kingship. A first interesting instance is offered by the sovereign incest rites that can be observed in the enthronement ceremonies of several African kingdoms. In order to become king, the prince was forced to break one of the community's extreme taboos, namely, to commit incest with his mother or another forbidden female member of his tribe. Here we see that the king, as original sacrificial victim, also embodied the negative, criminal elements of the persecuted scapegoat. The most primeval of criminal accusations emerge in the phenomenon of sovereign incest, which, from the perspective of the mimetic theory, provide clear evidence of the violent origins of kingship.

The enthronement of kings is often accompanied by collective animosity against the king, or even violent acts, which likewise point to an original connection with the scapegoat mechanism. James G. Frazer, for instance, points out an example in Sierra Leone concerning the savage Timmes, who after electing their king collectively thrashed him prior to the coronation. Frazer adds that oftentimes the elected monarchs failed to survive these violent rites of passage.[4] Elias Canetti describes similar phenomena in his portrayal of African kingship. An example from a culture in Gabon shows how the government there began with a terrifying rite in which the new ruler was encircled by bloodthirsty subjects who dangerously closed in on him.[5] Canetti also mentions Nigerian enthronement rituals in which traces of the scapegoat mechanism can be clearly seen: "A newly elected king was made to run three times round a mound and, while doing so, was well buffeted [*mit Stößen und Faustschlägen traktiert*[6]] by the dignitaries."[7] Where Canetti describes the "the insults and blows that [the king] is subjected to before entering on his office" as an "intimation of what awaits him in the end,"[8] he refers to the fact that many African kings were ritually murdered after a certain period of rule—that their rule was in fact derived from a suspension of their eventual sacrifice.

Another reference to the connection between the scapegoat mechanism and kingship is found in the unwillingness of subjects in many cultures to become king, with the eventual "chosen one" forced with violence to take on the position. Girard mentions as an example a culture that determined its kings by means of a persecutory hunt, at the end of which the slowest member, the one caught, was eventually crowned.[9] This fear of being appointed king is not unfounded; in many cultures, kings were simply killed if they were unable to overcome crises such as droughts or bad harvests.

A further instance that displays the connection between the origin of kingship and the founding murder is found in the enthronement process of the Shilluk people of central Africa.[10] At the outset of the process, the society was split into a civil war–like structure, with one half set against the other in fierce rivalry. Surprisingly enough, the future king—arbitrarily chosen—always belonged to the defeated camp. At the final moment, when the elected victim faced the ultimate coup de grace, he was crowned king of the entire people.

Several examples also document the murder of surrogate victims who were sacrificed in place of the king.[11] Frazer points out an interesting case among Tibetan Buddhists.[12] For twenty-three days after the beginning of the Tibetan new year, a "Jalno" monk—and not the Dalai Lama—was entrusted with power over the Tibetan people. This substitute, however, often gained too much power himself and was replaced with another surrogate, the "King of the Years," who governed for only a few days before being murdered. Frazer rightly concludes from this series of surrogate leaders that the Dalai Lama himself originally died as a scapegoat.

Sovereignty in Thomas Hobbes

At first glance, one might be mistaken by thinking that the element of sacrifice, and with it the original connection to the scapegoat mechanism, has disappeared from the modern conception of political sovereignty, as the evolution of ritual has given rise to a seemingly pure idea of political rule. However, it is still possible to find sporadic traces of the scapegoat mechanism in these modern conceptions of sovereignty, as well as in the fates of individual political figures. A first example, formulated at the dawn of modernity, is found in Thomas Hobbes's conception of the sovereign.[13] One sees the structure of the mimetic snowballing of all against one, typical of the founding murder, in Hobbes's description of how the sovereign emanates from the social contract: "I Authorise and give up my Right of Governing my selfe, to this Man, or to this Assembly of men, on this condition, that thou give up, thy Right to him, and Authorise all his Actions in like manner."[14] The sovereign enters into binding agreement with nobody; he remains outside of all contracts and treaties. Like the original scapegoat, who was excluded from the community and seen as responsible both for the crisis and for its resolution, Hobbes describes his sovereign both as excluded from the community and as a figure in which its power is vested.[15] The sovereign is seen as above the law in the same way the scapegoat is perceived by the community as outside the social order. The king and the scapegoat, by means of their existence outside the law, are simultaneously the source of law for the community. The sovereign decrees laws to which he alone is not subject; the scapegoat—by being murdered for "violating" the community's still nonexistent prohibitions—provides retroactive justification for the laws that are put in place to prevent such future violations. The German political scientist Thomas Heerich rightly speaks here of an "underground correspondence between the sovereign and the outlaw" in Hobbesian thought.[16] Hobbes underscores the sovereign's scapegoat role particularly clearly where he speaks of the relationship between civil obedience and sovereign protection. He argues that the civil duty of obedience [tr. *Gehorsamsverpflichtung*] is only valid insofar as the ruler can provide protection for his subjects.[17] Civil obedience and sovereign protection, in other words, condition one another reciprocally. Of course, the creators of modern sovereignty initially intended for their power to be endless, but, as Hobbes argues, the "many seeds of a naturall mortality"—external wars and internal conflicts—turned the Leviathan into a merely "MORTALL GOD."[18] If we compare Hobbes's understanding of the conditions of obedience with older forms of the right to resistance, a distinct proximity between the sovereign and the scapegoat becomes apparent. The Germanic right to resistance was founded on the precise relationship of protection and obedience to which Hobbes refers.[19] If rulers were unable to protect their subjects from external or domestic enemies, they were killed. In situations of crisis, such as bad harvests or war, the sacrifice of the ruler was a common and accepted practice.

Carl Schmitt's Decisionism

In the twentieth century, Carl Schmitt pursued Hobbes's initial inquiry into the nature and roots of political sovereignty; we can find Schmitt's response on what sovereignty means in a brief and pointed formulation at the beginning of his essay *Political Theology*: "Sovereign is he who decides on the exception."[20] With this definition, Schmitt dedicates himself—under Hobbes's influence—to the doctrine of decisionism and, in a similar way to Girard, concentrates his analysis on situations of social exception. As Girard displays in his analysis of many disparate myths, social disorder and chaos precede the law and norm of human civilization.[21] Like Schmitt, Girard assumes that a decision—the scapegoat mechanism—builds the foundation of human culture. According to Girard, the Latin *decidere* carries even more distinct traces of the founding violence; the original meaning, "to cut off" or even "to cut the victim's throat," leaves no doubt as to the deeper connection between the decision and the scapegoat mechanism.[22] But it is not only Schmitt's decisionism that suggests the connection between sovereignty and the founding murder. His systematic emphasis of the exception—"The rule proves nothing; the exception proves everything"[23]—also alludes to the essence of the scapegoat mechanism, which Girard describes as a "model of the exception" (*Things Hidden*, 100) and the most rudimentary of all cultural symbols.[24] The community chooses its victim at random—as in a lottery—in order to overcome the general mayhem that has broken out. The member of the community who chooses the "shortest straw," in other words, must die so that the community can survive (*Things Hidden*, 100).

Schmitt names as a central example of decisionism the understanding of executive power found in the *Federalist Papers*, a collection of essays that comment on the United States Constitution.[25] While the legislative branch of the American government is based on the discussion and counsel of a larger assembly, Alexander Hamilton, one of the authors of the *Federalist Papers*, claims that the executive can only lie in the hands of a single person. The unity of command, Hamilton argues, is central: "Decision, activity, secrecy, and despatch will generally characterize the proceedings of one man in a much more eminent degree than the proceedings of any greater number; and in proportion as the number is increased, these qualities will be diminished."[26] What appears at first glance as a mere postulate of pragmatic policy emerges at closer analysis as the remains of archaic scapegoating mentality: Hamilton argues that executive power must belong, as much as possible, to one person—so that the people can attribute the mistakes of the government to a single responsible individual. A "plurality in the Executive" would make it impossible "to determine on whom the blame or the punishment of a pernicious measure, or series of pernicious measures, ought really to fall."[27] Hamilton goes on to say it is "far more safe there should be a single object for the jealousy and watchfulness of the people," concluding that "all multiplication of the Executive is rather dangerous than friendly to liberty."[28] One finds in Hamilton's reflections a shimmer of that ancient political wisdom that saw in the death of a single individual a way to save the entire community.

Wilhelm II: Emperor and Scapegoat

Traces of the scapegoat mechanism in the modern world are not only found in certain theoretical conceptions and positions, however; they can also be observed in the fates of individual rulers and political figures. The reign of German Emperor Wilhelm II, despite the apparent impossibility of such a notion, displays how archaic forms of sacred kingship extended even into the twentieth century. In a comprehensive analysis of Wilhelm II, Nicolaus Sombart makes use of sociological studies on sacred kingship to approach a better understanding of the role and function of Germany's final emperor.[29] With the help of Girard's mimetic theory, Sombart interprets Wilhelm II as having suffered the fate of a scapegoat.[30] He refers to Wilhelm's physical disability, his numerous political scandals, and finally his banishment and exile following Germany's defeat in the First World War. The public accusation that Wilhelm II was a homosexual who would endanger the future of Germany belonged to the earliest of a series of allegations that stamped the emperor as a victim: "In this way, and completely in accordance with the logic of the scapegoat mechanism, the Germans accused their emperor of the most egregious social transgression fathomable in Germany at the time."[31] Such accusations—among others—persuaded the German people at the end of World War I to shift the blame for the defeat of their nation onto the shoulders of this one man.

Wilhelm II is most certainly an extreme example of the remaining traces of the violent origin of political power in our contemporary world. Much weakened forms of this violence can be seen now and again in the fates of many politicians in Western democracies. The German journalist Rolf Zundel addresses this phenomenon in senior German politicians who, at the end of their careers, are confronted by experiences that recall the origins of political power:

> Just as King Lear goes through the experience of "disturbing" the new relations, our aging politicians—Adenauer lived it, Brandt articulated it—also are the "scapegoats" of their office. Everything that threatens to impede the success of the incoming politicians is blamed on those outgoing. Consider the German election in 1961, when the coalition partners of Adenauer's [Christian Democratic Union] ran the campaign "*Mit der Union, aber ohne Adenauer*" ["With the Union, but without Adenauer"]. Or the example of Willy Brandt, who at the end of his party leadership had become the embodiment of a failed political strategy to forge a majority alliance between the Social Democrats and the Greens. In this atmosphere, the illusion spreads: Once the scapegoat is expelled, all problems are solved.[32]

The Death Penalty as Origin of Legal Order

Using the example of the origin of sacred kingship, we were able to pursue the ritual unfolding of the founding violence in its increasing orientation on the positive transference of sacrifice, i.e., the divinization of the sacrificial victim. Of course, the negative transference, or the initial collective violence brought against the victim, also became more pronounced over the course of the development of ritual. This side of ritual led likewise to the establishment of a central political institution—capital punishment—that forms the most ancient core of legal order. The death penalty must be recognized as a significant political institution, even if this contradicts our modern belief that we could live in peace without it.

Capital Punishment and Legal Order

Dostoyevsky, for one, was still aware in the nineteenth century just how closely the death penalty was related to legal order. In his short story *The Dream of a Ridiculous Man*, he describes how written codes are inextricable from the concept of justice, arguing that sustainment of these codes would require a reinstitution of the guillotine.[33] For conservative thinkers such as Joseph de Maistre, Juan Donoso Cortés, or Carl Schmitt, the political importance of the death penalty was never called into question; capital punishment, they argue, is indispensable for stemming the community's internal violence. De Maistre demonstrates this with his glorification of the executioner, who possessed central political influence: "All greatness, all power, all subordination rest on the executioner. He is the terror and the bond of human association. Remove this mysterious agent from the world, and in an instant order yields to chaos: thrones fall, society disappears."[34] Donoso Cortés fights for similar reasons against the abolition of capital punishment for political crimes, for he fears that this would result in the long-term disappearance of all forms of punishment. Without the death penalty, he claims "the earth will become a hell" where "blood will then gush forth from the rocks."[35] With reference to the contemporary world, Donoso Cortés is equally unequivocal: "Wherever a people have abolished the death penalty, society has distilled blood through every pore."[36] If we consider the history of the modern world, we see that Donoso Cortés's warning is not completely unjustified. An author as unsuspecting as Albert Camus, who during his life fought against capital punishment,[37] shows in *The Rebel* how both the Russian and French revolutions began with protests against the death penalty and ended in utter bloodbath: "Scaffolds seemed to be the very altars of religion and injustice. The new faith could not tolerate them. But a moment comes when faith, if it becomes dogmatic, erects its own altars and demands unconditional adoration. Then scaffolds reappear and despite the altars, the oaths, the feasts, and the freedom of reason, the masses of the new faith must now be celebrated with blood."[38] Camus refers to the French journalist and revolutionary Jean-Paul Marat—who claimed that the initial intention was to "cut off a few heads to save a great number"—in an attempt to illustrate how the French Revolution transcended all quantitative boundaries of archaic sacrifice. Camus challenges Marat's claim with a reference to the 273,000 victims who were ultimately executed.[39] Even today, one can still see an explicit connection between political power and capital punishment. It comes as no surprise that the United States, in its role as a superpower and the world's sheriff, adheres to the death penalty within its own borders. Is there a connection here between the willingness to use military violence abroad and a continued domestic dependency on capital punishment?

The death penalty is thus no mere violent form of punishment of which the civilized world can simply rid itself; it is indeed the archaic basis of legal order. A critique of the death penalty, thus, implies a critique of the justice system in its entirety. While the reactionary thinkers mentioned above at least suspect the deeper connection between capital punishment and social order, the critics of the death penalty remain unaware of this more fundamental connection. One important exception, however, is the German philosopher Walter Benjamin, who refers explicitly in his essay "Critique of Violence" to the death penalty as the violent foundation of legal order. According to Benjamin, the opponents of the death penalty sensed, "perhaps without knowing why and probably involuntarily, that an attack on capital punishment assails not legal measure, not laws, but law itself in its origin."[40] Benjamin sees his thesis confirmed in the completely disproportionate "fact that the death penalty in primitive legal systems is imposed even for such crimes as offenses against property." He concludes:

"Its purpose is not to punish the infringement of law but to establish new law. For in the exercise of violence over life and death more than in any other legal act, law reaffirms itself."[41]

Insofar as Benjamin's analysis incorporates not only "law-sustaining," but also "law-engendering" violence, he directs his critique of violence at the very foundations of justice. In a similar way, Sigmund Freud speaks of justice originating from an act of collective violence; he argues in *Civilization and Its Discontents* that the primordial form of justice is the violence of the community against that of the individual.[42] With reference to Freud, German scholar Karl Bruno Leder traces the death penalty back to archaic sacrifice, thereby characterizing the criminal as the community's scapegoat.[43] Leder's reference to Oedipus as a paradigmatic instance of this displays close proximity to Girard's mimetic theory.[44] For Leder, the scapegoating nature of the death penalty is the strongest argument working against it: "The demand for the death penalty, both fundamentally and intrinsically, is not based on foreign guilt, but rather that of the community for which a scapegoat must be found. If the criminal is actually guilty of his crime—all the better; if he or she is innocent—it is of no matter. His role as scapegoat, as bearer of the community's guilt [*Schuldträger*], will make him sacred afterwards."[45] The German sociologist Wolfgang Sofsky builds on Leder's argument with his emphasis of the connection between the death penalty and human sacrifice: "It is impossible to overlook the relatedness of the death penalty with ancient practices of sacrifice. Order is restored to the community—which had fallen to pieces—via the most precious offering imaginable: the life of a human being. The killing protects the society insofar as it both averts future harm [*Unheil*] and disposes of injustices committed. The scaffold is the community's altar—on which sacrifices are made to the highest of all possible gods: the community itself."[46]

Origins of the Death Penalty in the Scapegoat Mechanism

All these diverse references can be elucidated using Girard's mimetic theory insofar as it exhibits that capital punishment has its origins in the scapegoat mechanism. According to Girard, the death penalty, as well as the entire apparatus of political punishment [tr. *das gesamte Strafwesen*], finds its source in the founding murder.[47] To support this thesis, he refers to the work of Louis Gernet, a French philologist who examined the origins of the death penalty in ancient Greece. For Gernet, there are two forms of capital punishment that appear to have no direct connection to one another. The first form is purely religious:

> [It is] a means of eliminating pollution. . . . It purifies the affected group, who are often partly or wholly absolved of responsibility for the newly spilt blood (this is true, at any rate, in the case of lapidation). The violent expulsion, the expulsion unto death of the unworthy or accursed individual, has an ancillary sense: that of *devotio*. Indeed, the killing seems in one sense to be an act of piety. It makes us think of those ancient ordinances which declare that the murder of an outlaw does not cause pollution, or of that prescription of Germanic law that makes such killing a civic duty. . . . Then, too, the victim himself fills a true religious function, a function parallel to the priest-kings who are also put to death. The religious function can be seen in the Latin term for these victims: *homo sacer*; as well as in the Greek term *pharmakos*.[48]

Girard praises the clarity with which Gernet describes the connection between capital punishment and the scapegoat mechanism: "There is no doubt that the death penalty is portrayed here as a direct extension of generative violence" (*Violence and the Sacred*, 298).

The second type of capital punishment Gernet observes is devoid of all religious elements. It is the *apagoge*, a popular form of instant lynching endorsed by the mob to punish *in flagrante delicti*. Gernet explains that the victims were mostly foreigners whose public execution would pose no direct danger to the cohesion of the community. For Girard, this second manifestation of the death penalty is even more closely related to the scapegoat mechanism than the first. Whereas the religious execution is already a form of regulatory ritualized violence—i.e., a controlled repetition of the founding murder—the immediate lynching of a victim is directly related to the original scapegoat murder. As this spontaneous lynching became increasingly systematized and legalized in Greek society, it gradually assumed the ritual form of capital punishment described in Gernet's text above. Both types of public execution are thus interconnected and offer a unique glimpse into how statutory punishment is rooted in the mechanism of founding violence.

As in the case of kingship, we can observe in the example of capital punishment both elements of the double transference of the scapegoat mechanism. The executed victims, perceived by the community as guilty criminals, represent in obvious fashion the initial negative transference. We see elements of the positive transference, too, however, in the veneration shown even to criminals awaiting execution. Very weakened forms of this veneration can be observed even in our contemporary age. One considers the French custom in which the prisoner sentenced to death was permitted a cigarette and a glass of rum, or the ritual of the "last meal" for death-row inmates on the day of their execution.[49]

One finds numerous references in traditional folk culture to criminals who were sacralized after their execution.[50] The remains of executed criminals (body parts, blood, etc.), as well as any arbitrary object (clothing, splinters from the gallows, the hangman's noose) with which they came into contact, were venerated as sacred relics.[51] In seventeenth-century England, contact with the hand of a freshly hanged criminal was an accepted cure for gout.[52] Another interesting example concerns the Sicilian cult of the *santi decollati*, or the "holy beheaded," who were venerated as protective gods.[53] Girard argues that the public execution of these criminals brought about the same sacred veneration experienced by the divinized victims of the scapegoat mechanism. The fact that the victims of individual cases of murder or suicide in these cultures were not consecrated in any way further underscores the connection between the death penalty and the scapegoat mechanism.

The example of the death penalty also offers a glimpse into the difficulties faced by Christianity as it attempted to extricate itself from the world of sacred religions. The Gospels' uncovering of the scapegoat mechanism meant that early Christians were forced to adopt a negative stance towards capital punishment. Indeed, in the first centuries after the death of Christ, one finds instances of such a Christian stance: Tertullian, Lactantius, Origen, Marcus Minucius Felix, and the Canons of Hippolytus all spoke out against the death penalty. With the beginning of the established Church and the building of a "Christian" culture, however, sacrificial readings of the Gospels that opposed this resistance to capital punishment became increasingly prevalent. The death penalty eventually became a fixed element of Christian culture. The Catholic Church, even in the twentieth century, fought against its abolishment.[54] This stance has changed in the last decades, with the Catholic

Church having publicly voiced its opposition to this form of punishment. Its increasing distance from political power has enabled it today to oppose the death penalty with ever more vigor.

The Origin of War and Political Friend/Enemy Relations

Wars and reciprocal enmity between groups, nation-states, or blocks of states seem to belong inexorably to the nature of politics. In the history of human civilization, we find endless evidence supporting the thesis that enmity is an intrinsic component of political relations.

Politics and Enmity

One finds a wealth of examples in Greek and Roman antiquity that corroborate this view. The most distinct of these is offered by Aeschylus's tragedy *The Eumenides*, in which the concept of friendship within the Greek *polis* is made possible by unanimous outward hostility:

> Give joy in return for joy,
> one common will for love,
> and hate with one strong heart:
> such union heals a thousand ills of man.

This is Aeschylus's concise description of the friend/enemy distinction that builds the constitutive core of the Greek *polis*.[55] These structures also characterize the political philosophy of Aristotle and Plato.[56] Emphasis on the friend/enemy distinction is not only typical of ancient thought, however; Eastern philosophies have been formed by it as well. The Taoism of Laozi, renowned above all for its peaceful stance, offers a prime example. The ideal of a world composed of small, fully independent nation-states is accompanied by the praise of enmity: "The greatest of all calamities is to attack and find no enemy."[57] Where enmity is absent, Laozi argues, people lose their capacity for charity, temperance, and restraint from competition.[58] Even modern Europe, if we consider the strained relations between nation-states during the nineteenth and twentieth centuries, was formed significantly by the friend/enemy distinction. A very potent form of political hostility developed during the Cold War, which came to light only after the fall of the Iron Curtain. Up until the Cold War—during the era of the traditional nation-state—it was Carl Schmitt who stressed the importance of the friend/enemy distinction most clearly. His definition found in the *Concept of the Political* has since become the standard: "The specific political distinction to which political actions and motives can be reduced is that between friend and enemy."[59] Due in large part to Schmitt's Nazi past, his understanding of the political was widely ignored and tabooed during the Cold War. However, thinkers so apparently innocent of such allegiances as Georg Simmel or Sigmund Freud nevertheless show that Schmitt's emphasis on the friend/enemy distinction was no exception in the atmosphere of early twentieth-century political thought; this formula penetrated a dimension of the political that Freud and Simmel both held as unchallengeable. Simmel proposed a "general sociological rule," according to which all social unity is preconditioned by hostility directed at an external enemy: "It is a fact of the greatest sociological importance, one of the few that holds almost without exception for group formations of every kind, that the shared opposition unifying against a third party works under all circumstances, and does so in fact with much greater certainty than does the shared friendly relationship with a third party."[60] Freud's observation places similar emphasis on the close connection between internal love and external enmity: "The advantage which a comparatively small cultural group offers of allowing [its aggression] an outlet in the form of hostility against intruders is not to be underestimated [*geringzuschätzen*]. It is always possible to bind together a considerable number of people in love, so long as there are other people left over to receive the manifestations of their aggressiveness."[61]

The end of the Cold War gave rise to the hope that the reunification of the East/West division represented the final manifestation of the friend/enemy distinction and the ultimate overcoming of political enmity. The fall of the Iron Curtain, however, failed to bring about this freedom, resulting instead in a world of civil wars.[62] In this new international environment, the American political scientist Samuel Huntington attempted to subsume the fundamental friend/enemy distinctions under his concept of the "clash of civilizations." Huntington's new understanding of political identity brought Schmitt's distinction back into the center of political thought: "We know who we are only when we know who we are not and often only when we know whom we are against."[63] The terror attacks against New York and Washington on September 11, 2001, brought so much attention to Huntington's reflections that even United Nations Secretary General Kofi Annan made explicit reference to the "clash of civilizations" in his reaction. Annan partly accepted Huntington's thesis in his recognition that mutual enemies form an essential characteristic of society, while calling on the world to distance itself from absolute—religious or national—identification with enmity: "The international community is defined not only by what it is for, but by what and whom it is against. The UN must have the courage to recognise that just as there are common aims, there are common enemies. . . . While the world must recognise that there are enemies common to all societies, it must equally understand that they are not, are never, defined by religion or national descent."[64]

The Origin of Political Enmity in the Scapegoat Mechanism

Do wars and friend/enemy relations belong necessarily to man's political nature, or can these, too, be deconstructed as cultural products and extensions of the scapegoat mechanism? Girard's mimetic theory contradicts all attempts to portray friend/enemy relations as a constitutional form of any clash of civilizations: "Primitive warfare takes place among proximate, neighboring groups, which is to say among men who cannot be distinguished objectively in terms of race, language, or cultural habits. There is no real difference between the external enemy and the internal friend, and it is difficult to imagine how an external pattern could account for the difference in behavior" (*Things Hidden*, 85–86).[65] Girard argues that violence is always originally an internal problem. The rivalries within the group are channeled by means of the scapegoat mechanism into violence against an external enemy, which leads to friend/enemy relations between groups. From the perspective of the mimetic theory, all warfare and political enmity arises from the scapegoat mechanism.

In order to understand the origin of warfare and friend/enemy relations, we must concentrate on religious ritual, in which the spontaneous and unconscious occurrence of the scapegoat mechanism is consciously repeated to rejuvenate the peace originally restored in the community. The scapegoat mechanism generates in the eyes of the community a difference between itself, on the one hand, and the scapegoat it expels or murders, on the other hand. Within the community, the scapegoat goes through a process of unconscious "alienation." The scapegoat is both outsider and divinity and thus completely detached from its original community. As god of the community, the scapegoat is completely foreign. The ritualized violence, which is nothing other than the controlled imitation of the original scapegoat mechanism, takes the foreignness of the scapegoat as its unquestionable starting point. If the scapegoat mechanism is the channeling of internal into external violence, then ritual violence is characterized from the beginning by this difference between the two types of hostility. Political enmity and warfare are therefore not eternal institutions, but rather represent—based on the ritual repetition of the scapegoat mechanism—a more advanced form of containing violence. Using the example of the Canadian Tsimshian tribe, Girard reflects on the original function of religio-ritual wars and, by extension, friend/enemy relations: "Ritual violence is always less internal than the original violence. In assuming a mythico-ritual character, violence tends toward the exterior, and this tendency in turn assumes certain sacrificial characteristics; it conceals the site of the original violence, thereby shielding it from this violence, and from the very knowledge of this violence, the elementary group whose very survival depends on the absolute triumph of peace. . . . In sum, the groups agree never to be completely at peace among themselves. We see here the principle behind all 'foreign' wars: aggressive tendencies that are potentially fatal to the cohesion of the group are redirected from within the community to outside it" (*Violence and the Sacred*, 249).

The Eumenides *(Aeschylus)*

Aeschylus's tragedy *The Eumenides* is particularly well suited to illustrate this transition from the scapegoat mechanism to forms of political enmity.[66] The vengeful Erinyes initially represent in this text the collective violence of the scapegoat mechanism. Just as the mob persecutes its scapegoat, the Erinyes chase their victim Orestes to avenge the murder of his mother, Clytemnestra:

> Nay, be sure, not Apollo nor
> Athena's might can save thee from

perishing, spurned and neglected, knowing
not where in thy soul is joy—a bloodless
victim of the powers below, a shadow of
thyself. What! Dost thou not even answer,
but scornest my words, thou victim fatted
and consecrate to me? At no altar shalt
thou be slain, but, living, shalt thou be my
feast.[67]

The goddess Athena intervenes and pacifies the Erinyes by persuading them
to function as blissful goddesses—as Eumenides—in their future service to
Athens. The pacification of the Erinyes does not mean, however, that their
violence is forever surmounted; it has simply been shifted from within the
city to outside it. Behind the goddesses' superficial conversion from vengeance to bliss stands the transformation of the Athenian civil war into collective violence against outside enemies. This finds expression in the chorus
of the Eumenides, which alludes to Schmitt's friend/enemy model discussed
above:

May faction, initiate of ill, ne'er
raise her loud voice within this city—this I
pray; and may the dust not drink the black
blood of its people and through passion
work ruinous slaughtering for vengeance to
the destruction of the State. Rather may
they return joy for joy in a spirit of common
love, and may they hate with one accord;
for therein lieth the cure of many an evil in
the world.[68]

The goddess Athena substantiates this outward channeling of internal violence where she speaks of the wars raging outside the city gates, which are to
dissolve Athens's civil war:

Upon this realm, my realm, do thou
cast no keen incentives to bloodshed,

> injurious to young hearts, maddening them
> with a fury not of wine; nor yet, plucking as
> it were the heart out of fighting-cocks,
> implant in my people the spirit of intestine
> war in mutual recklessness. Let their
> warring be with foreign foes—and without
> stint for him in whom there shall live a
> strong passion for renown; but of birds'
> battling with the home I will have naught.[69]

One can hear echoes of the political enmity grounded in the scapegoat mechanism in Athena's description of the Eumenides's future role as harbingers of peace. As forces directly related to the scapegoat mechanism, the Eumenides will be faced with the task of eliminating internal enemies, while Athena—the representative of a new form of politics—is concentrated completely on the war with external enemies:

> May it be godly men whose increase
> thou prosperest the more; for, like him that
> careth for the growing plant, I cherish the
> stock of these just men that bring no blight
> of sorrow. Such boons are thine to give; and
> for my part, I will not suffer this city to be
> unhonoured among men, this city victorious
> in the glorious contests of deadly war.[70]

Aeschylus's *Eumenides* exhibits how—in the attempt to channel violence outwardly—internal violence can be transformed into enmity and bellicose relations between collectives. In the background of this process, we find the scapegoat mechanism that forms the original channeling of collective violence against an excluded third party.

The Origin of War in the Scapegoat Mechanism

There is a wealth of anthropological evidence that supports Girard's thesis regarding the origin of warfare and political enmity in the scapegoat mechanism. As one example, he refers to the ritual cannibalism of the Tupinambá in Brazil.[71] There existed between the Tupinambá tribes a "permanent warlike state" that produced sufficient victims for each individual tribe to stem its internal violence.

A very similar phenomenon can be observed in the "flower wars" of the Aztecs, who were likewise fixed on winning prisoners for ritual sacrifice. Sacrifice was so central to Aztec culture that, in the absence of real conflicts, simulated "flower wars" were instigated in order to generate sacrificial victims.[72] An interesting example that sheds light on the violence-containing function of ritual can be found in Muslim tribal societies that, due to their lack of a central authority, are held together by a segmented structure.[73] Segmentation, in this sense, implies that every small tribe is set against an enemy tribe. The external pressure—manifested above all in the blood revenge between the groups—generates the cohesion that holds each tribe together. At the same time, however, these hostile groups unite against other, larger, and likewise segmented groups. Peace in these segmented communities is generated by predominant friend/enemy relations and is crystallized in the following Arabic proverb: "I against my brothers, my brothers and I against our cousins, my brothers, cousins and I against the world."[74] Rivalry and violence commence here on the most elementary level and are only overcome by hostility directed at external enemies.

Girard's rejection of the thesis that war and political hostilities represent eternal human institutions opens up significant ethical perspectives for the future. This rejection undermines all theories that define warfare and xenophobia as inexorable elements of human nature. His argument that these institutions are based in the scapegoat mechanism shows, namely, that all forms of interpersonal violence and hostility begin in the most elementary human relationships. The way out of violence and enmity must be found on these rudimentary levels. The Sermon on the Mount is one such example that exhibits this way to peace. The practice of reconciliation and the love of one's enemy must commence from the beginning in order to avoid eventual dependence on the institution of warfare or any other means of channeling violence outwardly. Wrath or words of insult against one's own brother pave the way that ultimately leads to the hell of war (cf. Matthew 5:21–22). While Girard—in accordance with the biblical perspective—traces political structures and institutions back to elementary forms of human coexistence,

Schmitt denies the Sermon on the Mount any political relevance, viewing the biblical call to love one's enemy as limited to the private realm and thus disconnected from the apparently insurmountable enmity that exists between human groups.[75]

CHAPTER 7

Mimetic Theory
and Gender

How can I forget that last look she cast toward me as the two guards who were holding her by the arms expelled her from my city of Corinth through the southern gate, after she had been led, as is customary with scapegoats, through the city streets, which were lined by a hate-frothing, screaming, spitting, fist-shaking mob?

—Christa Wolf, *Medea: A Modern Retelling*

Girard's analytical search for the victims of primitive social and political persecution shows similarities to feminist stances that take the victim status of women as a starting point for their critique of patriarchal society.[1] His method of textual interpretation, like the feminist method, can be characterized by a "hermeneutics of suspicion."[2]

Such parallels, however, should not cause one to understand the mimetic theory as any kind of feminist stance. Many feminists themselves accuse Girard of both sexism and patriarchalism.[3] Girardians, meanwhile, have criticized such feminist conceptions, emphasizing more the greater breadth of their own stance.[4] They argue that Girard's work stands for all victims and not just women. With that being said, the Girardians also argue that a

297

more encompassing feminist theory could be built on the approach used by the mimetic theory to uncover the structural violence of patriarchal society directed against women.

The question of the relation between the sexes with regard to Girard's mimetic theory is much more complex than one assumes at first glance. In the following chapter, we will discuss this issue using two questions based on Girard's main theoretical concepts: How do the genders relate with regard to (1) mimetic desire, and (2) the scapegoat mechanism?

Is Mimetic Desire Typically Masculine?

A central question in connection with Girard's works on mimetic desire is whether his concept merely explicates masculine desire, thus leaving out any analysis of the characteristics of feminine desire. This inquiry forms the basis of Toril Moi's critique of Girard.[5] She points out that in *Deceit, Desire and the Novel* he only addresses the works of male authors; it appears, Moi argues, as if Girard were of the opinion that women do not belong to the great novelistic authors of modern literature. Also, with the exception of Flaubert's Emma Bovary—whose desire displays the less interesting form of external mediation—only male protagonists are addressed in Girard's book. The great majority of the examples contained therein tell of men who compete and fight with one another over women—who are thus portrayed as mere objects of male desire.

Girard rejects such criticism. He argues that his theory is in no part gender specific, and that his concept of mimetic desire applies to both men and women in essentially the same way. He leaves the question open, however, whether this equality is based on the nature of desire, or whether it is itself already a product of mimetic desire.[6] In later writings and recent interviews, Girard has often stressed the wish to include a female author—Virginia Woolf—in this original study of desire, *Deceit, Desire and the Novel*. He praises *The Waves*, in particular, as a major "novelistic" work that contains deep insights into the workings of desire.[7] The novel is not only the work of a female author; it also focuses on characters (three male and three female) that, irrespective of gender, offer an enlightening study of mimetic desire.

In the attempt to defend his claim that desire is not gender specific,

Girard refers time and again to examples from literature. With regard to Toril Moi's aforementioned critique, Shakespeare's *Two Gentlemen of Verona* offers an example in which women function as mere passive objects of masculine rivalry. However, Shakespeare can demonstrate otherwise. In *A Midsummer Night's Dream*, all four main characters—two men and two women—are driven in identical ways by mimetic desire. Girard emphasizes that gender plays no role whatsoever in this play.[8]

Sigmund Freud's Theory of Narcissism

Girard's strongest rejection of gender specificity in desire is found in his critique of Sigmund Freud's theory of narcissism. In 1914, Freud published what would become a very influential treatise, *On Narcissism*, in which he differentiates between two principal types of sexual desire. He first names the *attachment* type, which takes the "mother" as the original object of its desire before developing further into a general "object-love." He differentiates this from the second, *narcissistic* type, which takes *itself* as its original object. These two types of sexual desire, according to Freud, are gender specific:

> Complete object-love of the attachment type is, properly speaking, characteristic of the male. It displays the marked sexual overevaluation which is doubtless derived from the child's original narcissism and thus corresponds to a transference of that narcissism to the sexual object. This sexual overevaluation is the origin of the peculiar state of being in love, a state suggestive of a neurotic compulsion, which is thus traceable to an impoverishment of the ego as regards libido in favor of the love-object. A different course is followed in the type of female most frequently met, which is probably the purest and truest one. With the onset of puberty, the maturing of the female sexual organs, which up till then have been in a condition of latency, seems to bring about an intensification of the original narcissism, and this is unfavorable to the development of a true object-choice with its accompanying sexual overevaluation. Women, especially if they grow up with good looks, develop a certain self-contentment which compensates them for the social restrictions that are imposed upon them in their choice of object. Strictly speaking, it is only themselves that such women love with an intensity comparable to that of the man's love for them. Nor does their

need lie in the direction of loving, but of being loved; and the man who
fulfils this condition is the one who finds favor with them. . . . Such women
have the greatest fascination for men, not only for aesthetic reasons, since
as a rule they are the most beautiful, but also because of a combination of
interesting psychological factors. For it seems very evident that another
person's narcissism has a great attraction for those who have renounced
part of their own narcissism and are in search of object-love. The charm
of a child lies to a great extent in his narcissism, his self-contentment and
inaccessibility, just as does the charm of certain animals which seem not
to concern themselves about us, such as cats and the large beasts of prey.
Indeed, even great criminals and humorists, as they are represented in
literature, compel our interest by the narcissistic consistency with which
they manage to keep away from their ego anything that would diminish
it. It is as if we envied them for maintaining a blissful state of mind—an
unassailable libidinal position which we ourselves have since abandoned.[9]

Freud is aware that his theory runs the risk of being understood as misogynistic. He explains, however, that his stance is free of any "tendency to depre-
ciate women," for it is based merely on a principal distinction, which must
not necessarily manifest itself in reality.[10]

For Girard, this protective claim remains insufficient; he views Freud's
stance as explicitly misogynistic.[11] His main criticism concerns the assumption that a "narcissistic" desire even exists, one that completely differentiates
from the normal, object-oriented desire.[12] He sees in both Freudian modes
of desire nothing other than two different manifestations of mimesis. Freud
himself alludes to the influence of mimesis, in particular where he mentions the "envy" that apparently belongs only to narcissistic human beings.
According to Girard, this envy is indeed very much present and belongs to
the core of mimetic desire;[13] moreover, he contends that Freud's two types
of desire are identical and can both be traced back to desire's mimetic roots.

Pseudonarcissism

Can one interpret Freud's narcissism mimetically? At first glance, the narcissist appears completely self-assured and indifferent vis-à-vis the others in
his or her presence. This indifference, however, is not based on authentic

disinterest in the opinion of others; it is merely the outer surface of a conscious or unconscious "strategy."[14] We are all familiar with the tips that mothers give their daughters—and today also their sons—to assist them in their search for romance, which are precisely based on this "indifference": To be attractive, one must never chase after the person one seeks to attract. Only the appearance of indifference can attract his or her interest.

Shakespeare's Cressida offers an illustrative example of the importance of outward indifference in love affairs. Her teachings of romance reveal to us the secret:

> Women are angels, wooing:
> Things won are done; joy's soul lies in the doing.
> That she beloved knows nought that knows not this:
> Men prize the thing ungain'd more than it is:
> That she was never yet that ever knew
> Love got so sweet as when desire did sue.
> Therefore this maxim out of love I teach:
> Achievement is command; ungain'd, beseech:
> Then though my heart's content firm love doth bear,
> Nothing of that shall from mine eyes appear.[15]

This knowledge, or some version of it, is found in every successful self-help book that promises happiness in love. The less interested we appear to our fellow human beings—and the more interesting we attempt thereby to make ourselves—the more the others around us imitate our narcissistic self-adoration. Humans, who perpetually seek the being that they themselves lack, are attracted precisely by those who appear to possess this plenitude of being [tr. *Seinsfülle*] intrinsically. They begin to imitate the other's narcissistic self-adoration and fall inexorably under the latter's spell. The narcissist, in turn, who originally feigned self-adoration as a mere strategy, begins to imitate the love directed at him, thereby fostering an authentic sense of self-love. However, this strategy works only as long as the other's love for the narcissist remains genuine; as soon as the disciple's love wears off, the narcissist must search for new subjects to admire him, for such love of oneself is impossible without external confirmation. According to Girard, all narcissism is thus merely a form of *pseudonarcissism* (*A Theater of Envy*, 105).[16]

According to Girard, Freud ultimately failed—despite his later criticism of his own concept of narcissism—to comprehend the essence of pseudonarcissism.[17] He argues that Freud was too heavily influenced by the beauty and indifference of the women that surrounded him, which rendered him an admirer of women and the victim of his own resentment. The great novelistic authors are for Girard far superior to Freud with regard to their understanding of pseudonarcissism. Cervantes, Proust, Dostoyevsky, and Shakespeare—as we saw above in the chapter on mimetic desire—all use animal metaphors that underscore the narcissistic elements of desire in their descriptions of desirable women. These metaphors, however, do not correspond to the objective nature of the women they illustrate, but rather much more to the feelings aroused when these women reject or show indifference to one's own desire.[18]

William Shakespeare

Shakespeare's plays offer striking criticism of Freud's theory of narcissism. The comedy *Twelfth Night*, for instance, tells the story of the duke Orsino's desperate love for the "narcissistic" countess Olivia.[19] Orsino's every effort to court Olivia, "yond sovereign cruelty," meets with cold and complete indifference. These constant rejections lead Orsino to develop an opinion of women similar to that of Freud. The duke denies women any capacity for true love, which he claims he alone can feel:

> There is no woman's sides
> Can bide the beating of so strong a passion
> As love doth give my heart; no woman's heart
> So big, to hold so much; they lack retention.
> Alas, their love may be call'd appetite,
> No motion of the liver, but the palate,
> That suffer surfeit, cloyment and revolt;
> But mine is all as hungry as the sea,
> And can digest as much. Make no compare
> Between that love a woman can bear me
> And that I owe Olivia.[20]

While Freud's analysis of the concept is limited to this thesis, Shakespeare goes one decisive step further in that he exposes Olivia's narcissism as a plain pseudonarcissism. In a bid to win Olivia as his wife, Orsino sends Viola—disguised as a man, Cesario—to deliver his marriage proposal. Viola, as a woman, shows no sexual interest in Olivia. Moreover, Viola is herself in love with Orsino, which further intensifies her indifference when delivering the duke's marriage proposal to Olivia. This radical indifference catches the proud countess by surprise and causes her to fall in love with "Cesario," or the disguised Viola. Olivia, the self-assured pseudo-narcissist who is accustomed to treating everyone around her with indifference, is brought to her knees by Viola's much greater indifference. Immediately after their first meeting, she falls so completely in love with her "Cesario" that she desperately sends a messenger to present him with a ring she hopes will bring the two together again:

> I do I know not what, and fear to find
> Mine eye too great a flatterer for my mind.
> Fate, show thy force: ourselves we do not owe.
> What is decreed must be—and be this so! [21]

All self-assurance collapses on itself as soon as a single desire genuinely resists the attraction of the narcissist. Shakespeare's knowledge of the deeper nature of narcissism—and thus his superiority to Freud—is made clear by the fact that, of all characters, Orsino is the one who expresses insight into the mimetic nature of desire. In his ponderings on his own desire, he indirectly describes the mysterious nature of Olivia's indifference. Once desire is fulfilled, it is often immediately extinguished:

> O spirit of love, how quick and fresh art thou,
> That, notwithstanding thy capacity,
> Receiveth as the sea. Nought enters there,
> Of what validity and pitch soe'er,
> But falls into abatement and low price
> Even in a minute. So full of shapes is fancy
> That it alone is high fantastical. [22]

On a deeper level, there is no real difference between Orsino and Olivia. The duke, like the countess, is an archetype of pseudonarcissism, for his insight into the rapid loss of value of fulfilled desires—the phenomenon of mimetically induced inflation—springs from his experiences in which he, too, cast aside those who desired him on account of his "superior" position. In his relationship to Olivia, Orsino is the subordinate of the two pseudo-narcissists. It is this sense of defeat that brings about his anti-feminine ressentiment.

The example of Orsino and Olivia supports Girard's thesis that there is no fundamental difference between male and female desire.[23] However, for those offended by the notion that a woman ultimately embodies pseudo-narcissism in this comedy, another of Shakespeare's plays can be referenced to exhibit Shakespeare's understanding of the pseudo-narcissistic potential of both sexes: Achilles is to *Troilus and Cressida* what Olivia is to *Twelfth Night*.[24]

Are Women Typical Scapegoats?

Girard's thesis rejecting the gender specificity of desire undermines all moral differentiations between man and woman. This emphasis on the equality of man and woman is untenable for our second inquiry regarding the role of women as the victims of oppression, which has been a major impetus for contemporary feminist criticism. Can the mimetic theory account for the culturally universal position of women as victims?[25]

In Girard's analyses of scapegoating phenomena, he emphasizes time and again that women, across all cultures, belong to the group of preferred scapegoats, that femininity is one of the main signs of a victim.[26] This can be traced back to two central factors differentiating women from men: (1) their lower position in society, and (2) their weaker physical strength. As the weaker sex, women were perpetually exposed to the higher risk of being selected as sacrificial victims.

Archaic Goddesses as Feminine Scapegoats

Girard's thesis that women in primitive societies, on account of their physical weakness, were more often the victims of primitive sacrifice has important consequences for the contemporary discussion regarding the role of women at the beginning of civilization. The observation that there were more goddesses than gods in archaic religions has led to conclusions that human civilization was originally matriarchal, or at least matrifocal. These cultures, it follows, were characterized by nonviolence and egalitarian relations between the sexes.[27] One classic example of such observations—which long held sway in anthropological circles—is offered by the Minoan civilization of Crete. However, the matriarchal thesis has been so increasingly criticized in the contemporary debate that anthropologists today only speak of religions and cultures as being determined by the mother symbol.[28] The fundamentally peaceful nature of such cultures has also been increasingly called into question, based on evidence discovered in the 1980s suggestive of human sacrifice dating back to the Minoan period.[29] Much speaks for the thesis that such cultures bearing the mother symbol were just as rooted in the victimage mechanism. Girard traces the frequent emergence of archaic goddesses back to the prevalence of original female scapegoats; in many myths, one finds instances of divinized women who functioned as sacrificial victims for their cultures.[30]

Medea *(Christa Wolf)*

The German author Christa Wolf uses Girard's mimetic theory to reinterpret the Medea myth in a radically new way. The foreign priestess from Colchis is not the murderer of her own children in this reading, but rather the persecuted victim of Corinth's rulers who attempt to pin the murders on her.[31] With her new vision of the Medea myth, Wolf casts a critical glance on our contemporary social crisis, in particular on its propensity—especially since the end of the Cold War—for scapegoating practices.[32] Even if Wolf—as Susanne Nordhofen rightly points out—lags behind Girard's theory, insofar as she succumbs to the modern temptation of exploiting the position of victims, her critical reinterpretation of the Medea myth represents a project that, from the feminist perspective, had already been called for by the mimetic theory. In a recent study, Chris Shea accuses Girard of consciously excluding Euripides's *Medea* from his analysis, despite the significant role this tragedy could have played in the uncovering of the scapegoat mechanism.[33]

The Mythical "Feminization" of Collective Violence

The scapegoat role of womankind—brought about by their relative physical weakness—can also be observed in an interesting and ubiquitous primitive phenomenon. When violent conflict between the tribal males threatened to escalate, women—as the weaker sex—often fled the violence and took refuge on the village periphery. Ethnological findings confirm this tendency distinctly. Girard refers here to the village structure prevailing in a South American tribe known as the Bororo.[34] At the center of the village, one found the men's house, to which no woman in the tribe was permitted access. The women lived exclusively in houses—they were not permitted to leave—built on the fringe of the circular village. While this strict immobility was earlier taken as evidence of a matriarchy, Girard rejects any interpretation of the predominant role of Bororo women and argues for their passive role in a community dominated by masculine violence. The exclusion of women from the violent heart of culture can also be seen in ancient Greece, where women were prohibited, for example, from slaughtering using knives. No evidence exists of any female *mageiros*, who were assigned the tasks of a butcher, sacrificial servant, and cook.[35] The noun itself, *mageiro*, possesses no female gender. Even during the Thesmophoria, the three-day sacrificial festival organized exclusively for Greek women, a man had to be called to perform the slaughtering of the sacrificial animals.

This tendency to exclude women from primitive cultural violence relates, albeit paradoxically, to the especially close relationship of women to collective violence portrayed in ancient myth. Countless are the mythical examples in which women are depicted as particularly bloodthirsty. These include the Germanic Valkyries, the Amazons, the vengeful Erinyes, the Maenads, and the Bacchae, who kill Pentheus in a rush of Dionysian intoxication.[36] Likewise, the prevalent primitive taboo of menstrual blood points to this mythical confluence of femininity and violence.[37]

Girard takes up the example of the violent Bacchae in his search for the roots of the mythical feminization [tr. *Verweiblichung*] of collective violence,[38] postulating a "mythological substitution of women for men in regard to violence" (*Violence and the Sacred*, 139).[39] In mythical narrative, women are portrayed as responsible for the violence that, in actuality, belongs to the males of the community. The sacrificial crisis that precedes the scapegoat mechanism enables this passing of responsibility, as the differences between the sexes are blurred in the social chaos.[40] After order is restored to the community by the scapegoat mechanism, a reinforced sexual differentiation sets in. In this process, women—as potential scapegoats—are more prone to be divinized and therefore held responsible for the entire occurrence. In the mythical representation of any "successful" episode of the scapegoat mechanism, it is always only the scapegoats who are portrayed as the active perpetrators. It must have proven advantageous for ensuring cultural stability to depict the community's less violent members as most prone to brutal violence. From the outset, as the weaker sex, women were less often involved in the community's violence and were chosen more frequently as sacrificial victims. This victim status made it easier for myths—and the culture to which they belonged—to attach an overabundance of violence to women and distance them from the society's actual structures of power and violence. Extensions of this mythical thinking reach into the societies of the present day.

Women as Preferred Bearers of Truth

The exclusion of women from the violent centers of primitive societies, however, also gave them a greater chance to see through the victimage processes on which these cultures were based. The role played by women in the Gospels points in this direction. On the one hand, they are excluded from the mimetic snowballing that leads essentially all of Jesus's followers to deny or abandon him, and, on the other hand, they are the first witnesses of his resurrection.[41] The great authors of European literature build on this theme in their works. For Shakespeare—to cite just one example—women are the preferred bearers of truth.[42] Hippolyta, and not Theseus, understands the mimetic dynamics at work in *A Midsummer Night's Dream*. Hermione, in *A Winter's Tale*, takes on a similar function. In the end, Shakespeare even sides with Cressida, who—in the face of standard interpretations of her perfidiousness—is ultimately more honest than Troilus.

Chronology

1923 Born December 25, in Avignon, France

1941 Baccalaureate in Philosophy at the Lycée of Avignon

1943 École des Chartes in Paris

1947 PhD with dissertation "La vie privée à Avignon dans la seconde moitie du XVe siècle"

1947 Emigration to the United States

1947 Instructor of French language and student of contemporary history at Indiana University

1950 Second doctorate with dissertation "The American Opinion of France in the Years 1940–1943"

1951 Marriage to Martha V. McCullough

1952   Instructor of French language and literature at Duke University

1953   Assistant Professor of French at Bryn Mawr College

1957   Associate Professor of French at Johns Hopkins University

1961   *Mensonge romantique et vérité romanesque*

1961   Professor of French at Johns Hopkins University

1963   *Dostoievski: Du double à l'unité*

1966   Co-organizer (with Richard Macksey and Eugenio Donato) of
        the international symposium "The Languages of Criticism and
        the Sciences of Man," in which leading thinkers such as Roland
        Barthes, Jacques Derrida, Lucien Goldmann, Jean Hyppolite,
        Jacques Lacan, Georges Poulet, Tzvetan Todorov, and Jean-Pierre
        Vernant took part

1968   Professor of Arts and Letters at the State University of New York
        (Buffalo)

1972   *La violence et le sacré*

1976   *Critique dans un souterrain*

1976   James M. Beall Professor of French and Humanities at Johns
        Hopkins University

1978   *"To Double Business Bound": Essays on Literature, Mimesis, and
        Anthropology*

1978   *Des choses cachées depuis la fondation du monde*

1981   Andrew B. Hammond Professor of French Language, Literature,
        and Civilization at Stanford University

1982   *Le bouc émissaire*

1985   *La route antique des hommes pervers*

1985   Honorary doctorate at Vrije Universiteit Amsterdam (The
       Netherlands)

1988   Honorary doctorate at Universität Innsbruck (Austria)

1990   Founding of the Colloquium on Violence and Religion

1991   *A Theater of Envy: William Shakespeare*

1994   *Quand ces choses commenceront . . . Entretiens avec Michel Treguer*

1995   Emeritus status at Stanford University

1996   *The Girard Reader*

1997   Honorary doctorate at Universiteit Antwerp (Belgium)

1998   Nonino Literary Prize, "A un maestro del nostro tempo" (Italy)

1999   *Je vois Satan tomber comme l'éclair*

2001   Honorary doctorate at Università degli Studi di Padova (Italy)

2001   *Celui par qui le scandale arrive*

2002   *La voix méconnue du réel: Une théorie des mythes archaïques et
       modernes*

2003   *Le sacrifice*

2003   Honorary doctorate at St. Mary's Seminary and University (US)

Notes

Preface

1. Roberto Calasso, *The Ruin of Kasch*, trans. William Weaver and Stephen Sartarelli (Cambridge, MA: Harvard University Press, 1994), 157–158.

2. Isaiah Berlin, *The Hedgehog and the Fox: An Essay on Tolstoy's View of History* (New York: Simon & Schuster, 1953), 51–52. See René Girard, *Deceit, Desire and the Novel: Self and Other in Literary Structure*, trans. Yvonne Freccero (Baltimore: Johns Hopkins University Press, 1966), 166–167.

3. Girard, *I See Satan Fall Like Lightning*, trans. James G. Williams (Maryknoll, NY: Orbis Books, 2001), 30.

4. Paul Dumouchel and Jean Pierre Dupuy, eds., *L'enfer des choses: René Girard et la logique de l'économie* (Paris: Édition du Seuil, 1979); Michel Aglietta and André Orléan, eds., *La violence de la monnaie* (Paris: Presses Universitaires de France, 1982); Ivan Illich, *Vom Recht auf Gemeinheit* (Reinbek bei Hamburg: Rowohlt, 1982); Marianne Gronemeyer, *Die Macht der Bedürfnisse: Überfluss und Knappheit* (Darmstadt: Wissenschaftliche Buchgesellschaft, 2002); Erich Kitzmüller, *Gewalteskalation oder neues Teilen*, Beiträge zur mimetischen Theorie (Thaur: Druck- und Verlagshaus Thaur, 1996); Jim Grote and John McGeeney, *Clever as Serpents: Business Ethics and Office Politics* (Collegeville, MN: Liturgical Press, 1997); Wolfgang Palaver, "Mimesis and Nemesis: The Economy as a Theological Problem," *Telos*, no. 117 (1999): 79–112; Mark R. Anspach, "Desired Possessions: Karl Polanyi, René Girard, and the Critique of the Market Economy," *Contagion: Journal of Violence, Mimesis, and Culture* 11 (2004): 181–188; Palaver and Petra Steinmair-Pösel, eds., *Passions in Economy, Politics, and the Media: In Discussion with Christian Theology*, Beiträge zur mimetischen Theorie (Vienna: LIT, 2005); Wilhelm Guggenberger, *Die List der Dinge: Sackgassen der Wirtschaftsethik in einer funktional differenzierten Gesellschaft*, Beiträge zur mimetischen Theorie (Vienna: LIT, 2007); André Orléan, *L'empire de la valeur: Refonder l'économie* (Paris: Seuil, 2011).

5. Andrew J. McKenna, "The Law's Delay: Cinema and Sacrifice," *Legal Studies Forum* 15 (1991): 199–213; Gerhard Larcher, "Gewalt—Opfer—Stellvertretung: Ästhetisch-theologische Spiegelungen im zeitgenössischen Film," in *Vom Fluch und Segen der Sündenböcke: Raymund Schwager zum 60. Geburtstag*, ed. Józef Niewiadomski and Wolfgang Palaver (Thaur: Kulturverlag, 1995), 179–198; Larcher et al., eds., *Visible Violence: Sichtbare und verschleierte Gewalt im Film. Beiträge zum Symposium "Film and Modernity: Violence, Sacrifice and Religion," Graz 1997*, Beiträge zur Mimetischen Theorie (Münster: LIT, 1998); Leo Karrer et al., eds., *Gewaltige Opfer: Filmgespräche mit René Girard und Lars von Trier*, Film und Theologie (Köln: KIM-Verlag, 2000); Dietmar Regensburger, "Religion(En) und Gewalt: Systematische Reflexionen zu einem aktuellen und brisanten Spannungsfeld im Lichte der mimetischen Theorie René Girards," in *Weltreligionen im Film: Christentum, Islam, Judentum, Hinduismus, Buddhismus*, ed. Joachim Valentin (Marburg: Schüren, 2002), 15–34.

Preface to the English Edition

1. René Girard and Michel Serres, *Le tragique et la pitié: Discours de réception de René Girard à l'Académie française et réponse de Michel Serres* (Paris: Le Pommier, 2007). See Serres, "Receiving René Girard into the Académie Française," in *For René Girard: Essays in Friendship and in Truth*, ed. Sandor Goodhart et al., Studies in Violence, Mimesis, and Culture (East Lansing: Michigan State University Press, 2009).

2. René Girard, *Wissenschaft und christlicher Glaube*, trans. Shivaun Heath (Tübingen: Mohr Siebeck, 2007).

3. René Girard, *Evolution and Conversion: Dialogues on the Origin of Culture. With Pierpaolo Antonello and João Cezar de Castro Rocha* (London: Continuum, 2008), 60–61. See Scott R. Garrels, "Imitation, Mirror Neurons, and Mimetic Desire: Convergence between the Mimetic Theory of René Girard and Empirical Research on Imitation," *Contagion: Journal of Violence, Mimesis, and Culture* 12–13 (2006): 47–86; Vittorio Gallese, "The Two Sides of Mimesis: Girard's Mimetic Theory, Embodied Simulation and Social Identification," *Journal of Consciousness Studies* 16, no. 4 (2009): 21–24; Garrels, ed., *Mimesis and Science: Empirical Research on Imitation and the Mimetic Theory of Culture and Religion*, Studies in Violence, Mimesis, and Culture (East Lansing: Michigan State University Press, 2011).

4. René Girard and Nathan Gardels, "Ratzinger Is Right: Interview with Nathan Gardels," *New Perspectives Quarterly* 22, no. 3 (2005): 46.

5. Pankaj Mishra, "What Would the Buddha Think?," *New Perspectives Quarterly* 22, no. 3 (2005): 53.

6. See Frederiek Depoortere, *Christ in Postmodern Philosophy: Gianni Vattimo, René Girard and Slavoj Zizek* (London: T & T Clark, 2008), 147; Jacob Nordhofen, *Durch das Opfer erlöst? Die Bedeutung der Rede vom Opfer Jesu Christi in der Bibel und bei René Girard*, Beiträge zur mimetischen Theorie (Vienna: LIT, 2008), 243–248.

7. *Contagion: Journal of Violence, Mimesis, and Culture* 9 (2000). See Michael Kirwan, *Girard and Theology*, Philosophy and Theology (London: T & T Clark, 2009), 120–131.

8. René Girard and Sandor Goodhart, "Mimesis, Sacrifice, and the Bible: A Conversation with Sandor Goodhart," in *Sacrifice, Scripture, and Substitution: Readings in Ancient Judaism and Christianity*, ed. Ann W. Astell and Sandor Goodhart (Notre Dame, IN: University of Notre Dame Press, 2011), 64.

9. Girard, *Evolution and Conversion*, 212–213. See René Girard, *Sacrifice*, trans. Matthew Pattillo

and David Dawson, Breakthroughs in Mimetic Theory (East Lansing: Michigan State University Press, 2011), xi–xii, 87–93; Girard and Goodhart, "Mimesis," 64.

10. René Girard, *Battling to the End: Conversations with Benoît Chantre*, trans. Mary Baker, Studies in Violence, Mimesis, and Culture (East Lansing: Michigan State University Press, 2010), 182–193; René Girard and Thomas Assheuer, "Jesus, unser Sündenbock: Interview mit Thomas Assheuer," *Die Zeit*, 23 March 2005; Girard and Robert Doran, "Apocalyptic Thinking after 9/11: An Interview," *SubStance: A Review of Theory & Literary Criticism* 37, no. 1 (2008); René Girard and Giulio Meotti, "René Girard's Accusation: Intellectuals Are the Castrators of Meaning," *Modern Age* 50, no. 2 (2008): 180–185; René Girard and Wolfgang Palaver, "The Bloody Skin of the Victim," in *The New Visibility of Religion: Studies in Religion and Cultural Hermeneutics*, ed. Michael Hoelzl and Graham Ward (London: Continuum, 2008), 64–66; René Girard and Henri Tincq, "'What Is Happening Today Is Mimetic Rivalry on a Global Scale.' Interview with Henri Tincq," *South Central Review* 19, no. 2–3 (2002).

11. Mark R. Anspach, "Violence against Violence: Islam in Comparative Context." In *Violence and the Sacred in the Modern World*, ed. Mark Juergensmeyer (London: Frank Cass, 1992); Robert G. Hamerton-Kelly, "Response to Qamar-Ul Huda," *Contagion: Journal of Violence, Mimesis, and Culture* 9 (2002): 99–104.

12. Wilhelm Guggenberger and Wolfgang Palaver, eds., *Im Wettstreit um das Gute: Annäherungen an den Islam aus der Sicht der mimetischen Theorie*, Beiträge zur mimetischen Theorie (Vienna: LIT, 2009).

Chapter 1. Life and Work of René Girard

1. Girard, *Deceit, Desire and the Novel*, 290–314. See René Girard, *A Theater of Envy: William Shakespeare* (Oxford: Oxford University Press, 1991), 339–40; Hugo Assmann, ed., *René Girard com teólogos da libertaçao: Um diálogo sobre ídolos e sacrifícios* (Petrópolis, Brazil: Vozes, 1991), 73–75; René Girard, *The Girard Reader* (New York: Crossroad Publishing Company, 1996), 283–286; Girard, *Mimesis and Theory: Essays on Literature and Criticism, 1953–2005* (Stanford, CA: Stanford University Press, 2008), 263–273.

2. Girard, *Mimesis and Theory*, 56–70. See René Girard, *"To Double Business Bound": Essays on Literature, Mimesis, and Anthropology* (Baltimore: Johns Hopkins University Press, 1978), 4–5; Girard, *Things Hidden since the Foundation of the World: Research Undertaken in Collaboration with J.-M. Oughourlian and G. Lefort*, trans. Stephen Bann and Michael Metteer (Stanford, CA: Stanford University Press, 1987), 393–398.

3. René Girard, *Resurrection from the Underground: Feodor Dostoevsky*, trans. James G. Williams (New York: Crossroad Publishing Co., 1997), 140. See Girard, *Oedipus Unbound: Selected Writings on Rivalry and Desire* (Stanford, CA: Stanford University Press, 2004), 23; *To Double Business Bound*, 5–6; *Mimesis and Theory*, 68–69, 94, 263–264, 272; *Battling to the End*, 205; John Freccero, *Dante: The Poetics of Conversion* (Cambridge, MA: Harvard University Press, 1986); E. Tyler Graham, "St. Augustine's Novelistic Conversion." *Contagion: Journal of Violence, Mimesis, and Culture* 5 (1998): 135–154.

4. Girard, *To Double Business Bound*, 9–35.

5. Girard, *Mimesis and Theory*, 56, 67; *To Double Business Bound*, 11–12; *Theater of Envy*, 298, 339.

6. Girard, *Theater of Envy*, 46, 297–298, 303, 339.

7. Girard, *Theater of Envy*, 256–270. See René Girard, *Quand ces choses commenceront . . . Entretiens avec Michel Treguer* (Paris: arléa, 1994), 34–36.

8. James Joyce, *Ulysses* (New York: Vintage Books, 1990), 184–218.

9. Joyce, *Ulysses*, 185.

10. Joyce, *Ulysses*, 189.

11. James Joyce, *Letters*, 3 vols. (New York: Viking Press, 1957).

12. See Assmann, ed., *René Girard*, 45–47; Michael Jakob, ed., "Gespräch mit René Girard," in *Aussichten des Denkens* (Munich: Wilhelm Fink Verlag, 1994), 155–176; René Girard and Rebecca Adams, "Violence, Difference, Sacrifice: A Conversation with René Girard," *Religion & Literature* 25, no. 2 (1993): 11–15; Girard and Richard Golsan, "Interview," in Richard J. Golsan, *René Girard and Myth: An Introduction* (New York: Garland Publishing, Inc., 1993), 129–149; Mark Anspach, ed., *René Girard, Cahiers de l'Herne* (Paris: Éditions de l'Herne, 2008), 13–43; Girard, *Quand ces choses commenceront*, 187–198; Girard, *The Girard Reader*, 1–6, 283–288; Girard, *Evolution and Conversion*.

13. Richard Macksey and Eugenio Donato, eds., *The Structuralist Controversy: The Languages of Criticism and the Sciences of Man* (Baltimore: Johns Hopkins University Press, 1979).

14. Geoffrey Bennington and Jacques Derrida, *Jacques Derrida*, Religion and Postmodernism (Chicago: University of Chicago Press, 1999), 330–331.

15. c/o Forschungsprojekt "Religion—Gewalt—Kommunikation—Weltordnung," Institut für systematische Theologie, Universität Innsbruck, Karl-Rahner-Platz 1, A-6020 Innsbruck/Austria.

16. See Girard, *Quand ces choses commenceront*, 190–194; *The Girard Reader*, 283–288; Assmann, ed., *René Girard*, 45–47, 73–75.

17. Carl von Clausewitz, *On War*, trans. M. Howard and P. Paret (Princeton, NJ: Princeton University Press, 1984), 77.

Chapter 2. Religion and Modernity

1. See Józef Niewiadomski, ed., *Eindeutige Antworten? Fundamentalistische Versuchung in Religion und Gesellschaft* (Thaur: Kulturverlag, 1989); Gilles Kepel, *The Revenge of God: The Resurgence of Islam, Christianity, and Judaism in the Modern World*, trans. Alan Braley (University Park: Pennsylvania State University Press, 1994); Heiner Bielefeldt and Wilhelm Heitmeyer, eds., *Politisierte Religion: Ursachen und Erscheinungsformen des modernen Fundamentalismus* (Frankfurt am Main: Suhrkamp, 1998).

2. See Peter Berger, "Globaler Pluralismus," *Conturen*, no. 3 (1997): 38–39.

3. See Wolfgang Palaver, "Die religiöse Dimension des Nationalismus," *Theologisch-praktische Quartalschrift* 142, no. 3 (1994).

4. See Franz-Xaver Kaufmann, *Religion und Modernität: Sozialwissenschaftliche Perspektiven* (Tübingen: J.C.B. Mohr, 1989), 16–18, 201–208, 244; Peter Berger, "Sociology: A Disinvitation?" *Society* 30, no. 1 (1992): 12–18; Otto Kallscheuer, *Gottes Wort und Volkes Stimme: Glaube, Macht, Politik* (Frankfurt am Main: Fischer Taschenbuch Verlag, 1994); José Casanova, "Religion und Öffentlichkeit: Ein Ost-/Westvergleich," *Transit*, no. 8 (1994); David Martin, "Säkularisierung in Europa—Glaubensvielfalt in Amerika: Zwei Ausnahmen und keine Regel?" *Transit*, no. 8 (1994):

42–52; David Yamane, "Secularization on Trial: In Defense of a Neosecularization Paradigm." *Journal for the Scientific Study of Religion* 36, no. 1 (1997): 109–122.

5. Martin van Creveld, *The Transformation of War* (New York: The Free Press, 1991), 215. See also 134–142, 203–204, 214. See Samuel Huntington, *The Clash of Civilizations and the Remaking of World Order* (New York: Simon & Schuster, 1996), 95–101.

6. Jean-Marie Guéhenno, *The End of the Nation-State*, trans. Victoria Elliott (Minneapolis: University of Minnesota Press, 1995), 91–101.

7. Benjamin Barber, *Jihad vs. McWorld* (New York: Ballantine Books, 1996).

8. See Walter Laqueur, *The New Terrorism: Fanaticism and the Arms of Mass Destruction* (New York: Oxford University Press, 1999), 127–155; Bruce Hoffman, *Inside Terrorism*, rev. ed. (New York: Columbia University Press, 2006), 130–181; Peter Waldmann, *Terrorismus: Provokation der Macht* (Munich: Gerling Akademie Verlag, 1998), 98–119; Mark Juergensmeyer, *Terror in the Mind of God: The Global Rise of Religious Violence* (Berkeley: University of California Press, 2001); Wolfgang Palaver, "Terrorismus: Wesensmerkmale, Entstehung, Religion," in *Religion erzeugt Gewalt—Einspruch! Innsbrucker Forschungsprojekt "Religion—Gewalt—Kommunikation—Weltordnung,"* ed. Raymund Schwager and Józef Niewiadomski (Münster: LIT, 2003), 217–232.

9. Eric Voegelin, *Modernity without Restraints: The Political Religions, the New Science of Politics, and Science, Politics, and Gnosticism,* in *The Collected Works of Eric Voegelin* (Columbia: University of Missouri Press, 2000), 19–73; Denis de Rougemont, *Journal d'Allemagne* (Paris: Gallimard, 1938); Rougemont, *The Devil's Share*, trans. H. Chevalier (New York: Pantheon Books, 1952), 76. See Denis Hollier, ed. *The College of Sociology, 1937–1939* (Minneapolis: University of Minnesota Press, 1988), 162–167.

10. Walter Benjamin, *Selected Writings*, vol. 1 (Cambridge, MA: Harvard University Press, 1996), 100–103.

11. See Julio de Santa Ana, "Sacralizações e sacrifícios nas práticas humanas," in *René Girard com teólogos da libertaçao: Um diálogo sobre ídolos e sacrifícios* (Petrópolis: Vozes, 1991), 121–152, 128–135; Norbert Bolz, "Kapitalistische Religion—Die Antike in Walter Benjamins Moderne," in *Die berechnende Vernunft: Über das Ökonomische in allen Lebenslagen* (Vienna: Picus Verlag, 1993), 253–269; Bolz, *Die Sinngesellschaft* (Düsseldorf: ECON, 1997), 147–152; Jochen Hörisch, *Ende der Vorstellung: Die Poesie der Medien* (Frankfurt am Main: Suhrkamp, 1999), 214–240 ("Permanenter Kultus—Medienreligiöser Kapitalismus"); Wolfgang Palaver, "Challenging Capitalism as Religion: Hans G. Ulrich's Theological and Ethical Reflections on the Economy," *Studies in Christian Ethics* 20, no. 2 (2007): 215–230.

12. See Józef Niewiadomski, *Herbergsuche: Auf dem Weg zu einer christlichen Identität in der modernen Kultur*, Beiträge zur Mimetischen Theorie (Münster: LIT, 1999), 149–166 ("Extra media nulla salus. Zum religiösen Anspruch der Medienkultur"); Thomas H. Böhm, *Religion durch Medien—Kirche in den Medien und die "Medienreligion": Eine problemorientierte Analyse und Leitlinien einer theologischen Hermeneutik* (Stuttgart: Verlag W. Kohlhammer, 2005).

13. Girard, *Deceit, Desire and the Novel*: (Tocqueville) 64, 120, 124, 137–138; (de Rougemont) 48, 108, 165, 177–178, 179, 192, 226, 285, 287.

14. Alexis de Tocqueville, *Democracy in America*, trans. Henry Reeve, Francis Bowen, and Phillips Bradley (New York: Vintage Books, 1990), 1:310. See also 2:22.

15. Marcel Gauchet, "Alexis de Tocqueville, l'Amérique et nous," *LIBRE: Politique—anthropologie—philosophie*, no. 7 (March 1980). See Gauchet, *Disenchantment*, 4, 15, 101–106, 159, 161–165, 199–200.

16. Gauchet, "Alexis de Tocqueville"

17. See David Martin, *Säkularisierung*.

18. Ulrich Beck, "Väter der Freiheit," in *Kinder der Freiheit* (Frankfurt am Main: Suhrkamp, 1997), 333–347; Beck, "Ursprung als Utopie: Politische Freiheit als Sinnquelle der Moderne," in *Kinder der Freiheit* (Frankfurt am Main: Suhrkamp, 1997), 385–387.

19. See Girard, "The Founding Murder in the Philosophy of Nietzsche," in *Violence and Truth: On the Work of René Girard*, ed. Paul Dumouchel (Stanford, CA: Stanford University Press, 1988), 227–246; René Girard and Wolfgang Palaver, *Gewalt und Religion: Ursache oder Wirkung?*, trans. Heide Lipecky and Andreas Leopold Hofbauer (Berlin: Matthes & Seitz, 2010); Girard, *Evolution and Conversion*, 255; Gianni Vattimo and René Girard, *Christianity, Truth, and Weakening Faith: A Dialogue*, trans. W. McCuaig (New York: Columbia University Press, 2010), 32, 91.

20. See Hollier, ed., *The College of Sociology, 1937–1939*; Klaus-Dieter Scheer, "Die aufgeschobene Theokratie: Zur politischen Theologie Carl Schmitts," in *Das Heilige: Seine Spur in der Moderne* (Frankfurt am Main: Athenäum, 1987), 441–442; Hans Mayer, *Ein Deutscher auf Widerruf: Erinnerungen I* (Frankfurt am Main: Suhrkamp, 1988), 236–243; Nicolaus Sombart, *Pariser Lehrjahre 1951–1954: Leçons de sociologie* (Frankfurt am Main: Fischer Taschenbuch Verlag, 1996), 342–349.

21. Girard, *To Double Business Bound*, 5–7 ("The Mimetic Desire of Paolo and Francesca").

22. Lucien Goldmann, *Towards a Sociology of the Novel*, trans. Alan Sheridan (London: Tavistock Publications, 1975), 1–17. See Girard, *Resurrection from the Underground*, 94; *To Double Business Bound*, viii, 200; Assmann, ed., *René Girard*, 74.

23. See Georg Lukács, *Die Theorie des Romans: Ein geschichtsphilosophischer Versuch über die Formen der großen Epik* (Munich: Deutscher Taschenbuch Verlag, 1994); Lukács, "Die Gegenwartsbedeutung des kritischen Realismus." In *Essays über Realismus* (Neuwied: Luchterhand, 1971), 457–603; Lukács, *Die Zerstörung der Vernunft*, Werke (Neuwied: Luchterhand, 1960).

24. Sigmund Freud, *Beyond the Pleasure Principle*, rev. ed., trans. James Strachey(New York: Liveright Publishing Corp., 1961), 23, 41, 43; Calasso, *Ruin of Kasch*, 186 ("The Demon of Repetition").

25. See George Steiner, *Real Presences* (Chicago: University of Chicago Press, 1989), 216–227.

26. Fyodor Dostoyevsky, *Demons*, trans. Richard Pevear and Larissa Volokhonsky, 1st ed. (New York: A.A. Knopf, 1994), 250 (II.I.I). See Girard, *Deceit, Desire and the Novel*, 189–190; *Resurrection from the Underground*, 102–103.

27. Dostoyevsky, *Demons*, 251 (II.I.I).

28. Dostoyevsky, *Demons*, 252 (II.I.I).

29. Dostoyevsky, *The Brothers Karamazov*, trans. Richard Pevear and Larissa Volokhonsky, 1st Vintage Classics ed. (New York: Vintage Books, 1991), 254 (II.V.V).

30. Dostoyevsky, *The Adolescent*, trans. Andrew R. MacAndrew (Garden City, NY: Doubleday, 1971), 389 (III.II.III).

31. Girard, *Deceit, Desire and the Novel*, 23, 76–82, 198–216. See also *Mimesis and Theory*, 56–70.

32. Marcel Proust, *Sodom and Gomorrah*, trans. C. K. Scott-Moncrieff and Terence Kilmartin (New York: Modern Library, 1993), 718–719.

33. Proust, *The Past Recaptured*, trans. Andreas Mayor (New York: Random House, 1981), 935.

34. Girard, *Deceit, Desire and the Novel*, 53–82, 119.

35. Ludwig Feuerbach, *The Essence of Christianity*, trans. George Eliot (New York: Harper, 1957), 271.

36. Dostoyevsky, *Notes from the Underground and The Gambler*, trans. Jane Kentish (Oxford: Oxford University Press, 1991), 47.

37. Dostoyevsky, *Demons* (II. I.VI). See Girard, *Deceit, Desire and the Novel*, 59–61, 162; *Resurrection from the Underground*, 86–87, 90.

38. Dostoyevsky, *Demons*, 419 (II.VIII).

39. For Hölderlin references, see Girard, *Violence and the Sacred*, trans. Patrick Gregory (Baltimore: Johns Hopkins University Press, 1977), 155–158; *Oedipus Unbound*, 36, 46–50; *To Double Business Bound*, 48–49, 56, 61–62, 79, 95; *Things Hidden*, 315, 403; *Battling to the End*, 120–130. For Nietzsche references, see Girard: *To Double Business Bound*, 48–49, 61–83, 93 ("Strategies of Madness: Nietzsche, Wagner und Dostoyevsky"); *Things Hidden*, 309–310, 315, 403; Girard and Palaver, *Gewalt und Religion*; Girard/Sergio Benvenuto, "Psychoanalysis and Mimetic Theory: Difference and Identity: A Conversation with Sergio Benvenuto in Collaboration with Maurizio Meloni," *Journal of European Psychoanalysis*, no. 14 (2002): 23–25.

40. Friedrich Hölderlin, *Sämtliche Werke und Briefe in drei Bänden* (München: Carl Hanser Verlag, 1992), 690–691.

41. Hölderlin, *Sämtliche Werke*, 1:490–491. See Girard, *Violence and the Sacred*, 157–158.

42. Nietzsche, *Ecce Homo*, in *Basic Writings of Nietzsche*, trans. Walter Kaufmann (New York: Modern Library, 2000), 730. Translation corrected.

43. Nietzsche, *Ecce Homo* ("Why I am a destiny"), in *Basic Writings*, 791.

44. Giorgio Colli and Mazzino Montinari, eds., *Friedrich Nietzsche: Sämtliche Briefe. Kritische Studienausgabe in 8 Bänden*. Band 8: *Januar 1887–Januar 1889* (München: Deutscher Taschenbuch Verlag, 1986), 572–573.

45. Max Scheler, *On the Eternal in Man*, trans. Bernard Noble (New York: Harper, 1961), 399.

46. Girard, *Resurrection from the Underground*, 122–130.

47. See *The Girard Reader*, 209.

48. Albert Camus, *The Rebel*, trans. Anthony Bower (London: Penguin Classics, 2000), 11.

49. Camus, *The Rebel*, 115.

50. Camus, *The Rebel*, 66.

51. Camus, *The Rebel*, 270.

52. Camus, *The Rebel*, 269–270.

53. Camus, *The Rebel*, 258–264.

54. See Girard, *Deceit, Desire and the Novel*, 278–279; *Resurrection from the Underground*, 120–121.

55. Girard, *To Double Business Bound*, 9–35 ("Camus's Stranger Retried"). See also *Deceit, Desire and the Novel*, 269–272; *Oedipus Unbound*, 16–18; Girard and Adams, "Violence, Difference, Sacrifice," 14.

56. Camus, *The Fall*, trans. Justin O'Brien (New York: Vintage, 1956), 24–25, 28, 117–118, 142.

57. Girard, *To Double Business Bound*, 34. See also *Things Hidden*, 224; *A Theater of Envy*, 339; *I See Satan*, 158; Anspach, ed., *René Girard*, 200.

58. Girard, *Deceit, Desire and the Novel*, 271–272.

59. See Girard, *Deceit, Desire and the Novel*, 2–3.

60. Robert G. Hamerton-Kelly, ed., *Violent Origins*, 108, 215–220; *Violence and the Sacred*, 89–92, 274–308; *Things Hidden*, 3–7. See James G. Williams, *The Bible, Violence, and the Sacred: Liberation from the Myth of Sanctioned Violence* (San Francisco: HarperSanFrancisco, 1991), 14–20.

61. See Jean-Pierre Dupuy and Francisco J. Varela, eds., "Understanding Origins: An Introduction," in *Understanding Origins: Contemporary Views on the Origin of Life, Mind and Society* (Dordrecht: Kluwer Academic Publishers, 1992), 1–25.

62. E. E. Evans-Pritchard, *Theories of Primitive Religion* (Oxford: Clarendon Press, 1965), 104–105.

63. Bruce Chilton, *The Temple of Jesus: His Sacrificial Program within a Cultural History of Sacrifice* (University Park: Pennsylvania State University, 1992), 39–40; Josef Drexler, *Die Illusion des Opfers: Ein wissenschaftlicher Überblick über die wichtigsten Opfertheorien ausgehend vom deleuzianischen Polyperspektivismusmodell*, Münchener ethnologische Abhandlungen (München: Akademischer Verlag, 1993), 1–8, 88–96, 152–183.

64. See Drexler, *Die Illusion des Opfers*, 92; Williams, *The Bible, Violence, and the Sacred*, 18–19.

65. See Raymund Schwager, "Rückblick auf das Symposium," in *Dramatische Erlösungslehre: Ein Symposion*, ed. J. Niewiadomski and W. Palaver (Innsbruck: Tyrolia, 1992), 338–384.

66. See Mark Juergensmeyer, ed., *Violence and the Sacred in the Modern World* (London: Frank Cass, 1992).

67. *Contagion: Journal of Violence, Mimesis, and Culture* 4 (Spring 1997); Wolfgang Palaver, "Carl Schmitt on Nomos and Space," *Telos*, no. 106 (1996): 105–127.

68. Girard, *Celui par qui le scandale arrive* (Paris: Desclée de Brouwer, 2001), 8, 15–43; *Evolution and Conversion*, 237–238; *Battling to the End*, 211–217; Girard and Henri Tincq, "'What Is Happening Today Is Mimetic Rivalry on a Global Scale': Interview with Henri Tincq," *South Central Review* 19, no. 2–3 (2002), 22–27; Girard and Doran, "Apocalyptic Thinking," 20–32.

Chapter 3. Mimetic Desire

1. René Girard and Michael Jakob, "Gespräch mit René Girard," in *Aussichten des Denkens* (Munich: Wilhelm Fink Verlag, 1994), 165.

2. Antje Vollmer, *Heißer Frieden: Über Gewalt, Macht und das Geheimnis der Zivilisation* (Köln: Kiepenheuer & Witsch, 1995), 109–115. See Vollmer, "Gibt es Gemeinschaft ohne Sündenböcke?" *Zeitschrift für Missionswissenschaft und Religionswissenschaft* 83 (2001): 263–276.

3. See Girard, *De la violence à la divinité*, Bibliothèque Grasset (Paris: Bernard Grasset, 2007), 14–15; *Violence and the Sacred*, 145; *Things Hidden*, 95, 260, 414; *Theater of Envy*, 16, 18; *The Girard Reader*, 10; *I See Satan*, 11, 184; *Evolution and Conversion*, 75–76; *Celui par qui le scandale arrive*, 17, 40; "Violence and Religion," 180–181; Gianni Vattimo and René Girard, *Christianity, Truth, and Weakening Faith: A Dialogue*, trans. William McCuaig (New York: Columbia University Press, 2010), 59–60; Girard and Meotti, *René Girard's Accusation*, 181.

4. Gunnar Heinsohn, *Die Erschaffung der Götter: Das Opfer als Ursprung der Religion*

(Reinbek bei Hamburg: Rowohlt, 1997), 30–33; Hanna Gekle, "Aggression," in *Handbuch religionswissenschaftlicher Grundbegriffe*, ed. Hubert Cancik, Burkhard Gladigow, and Matthias Laubscher (Stuttgart: Verlag W. Kohlhammer, 1988), 405–406; Kurt Hübner, "Die Moderne Mythos-Forschung—Eine noch nicht erkannte Revolution," *Berliner Theologische Zeitschrift* 6 (1989): 11; Edmund Arens, "Dramatische Erlösungslehre aus der Perspektive einer theologischen Handlungstheorie," in *Dramatische Erlösungslehre: Ein Symposion*, ed. Józef Niewiadomski and Wolfgang Palaver (Innsbruck: Tyrolia, 1992), 170–171; Eugen Biser, "Ein überbrückendes Schlußwort," *Theologische Revue* 90 (1994): 367–368; Jean Greisch, "Homo Mimeticus: Kritische Überlegungen zu den anthropologischen Voraussetzungen von René Girards Opferbegriff," in *Zur Theorie des Opfers: Ein interdisziplinäres Gespräch*, ed. Richard Schenk (Stuttgart-Bad Cannstatt: frommann-holzboog, 1995), 44–46; Georg Baudler, *Die Befreiung von einem Gott der Gewalt: Erlösung in der Religionsgeschichte von Judentum, Christentum und Islam* (Düsseldorf: Patmos Verlag, 1999), 77–78; Barbara Ehrenreich, *Blood Rites: Origins and History of the Passions of War*, 1st ed. (New York: Metropolitan Books, 1997), 39; Jörg Dierken, "Gott und Gewalt: Ethisch-religiöse Aspekte eines zentralen Phänomens von Vergesellschaftung," *Zeitschrift für Missionswissenschaft und Religionswissenschaft* 83 (1999): 282, 286; Christoph Lienkamp, "Gewalt und Religion: Zwei Möglichkeiten einer nicht-totalisierenden religiösen Ordnung," *Orientierung* 65 (2001): 212. See Norbert Copray, "Interview mit Hubert Cancik," *Börsenblatt für den deutschen Buchhandel* 19 (1991): 813.

5. Walter Burkert, *Homo Necans: The Anthropology of Ancient Greek Sacrificial Ritual and Myth*, trans. Peter Bing (Berkeley: University of California Press, 1983), 1, 19–20, 23; *Anthropologie des religiösen Opfers* (München: Carl Friedrich von Siemensstiftung, 1983), 20, 25, 33–34; "The Problem of Ritual Killing," in *Violent Origins: Walter Burkert, René Girard, and Jonathan Z. Smith on Ritual Killing and Cultural Formation*, ed. Robert G. Hamerton-Kelly (Stanford, CA: Stanford University Press, 1987), 151, 159, 169–170.

6. Girard, *Deceit, Desire and the Novel*, 2. See Girard, *Resurrection from the Underground*, 150; Paisley Livingston, *Models of Desire: René Girard and the Psychology of Mimesis* (Baltimore: Johns Hopkins University Press, 1992), 11.

7. Girard, *Violence and the Sacred*, 146. See Girard, *Deceit, Desire and the Novel*, 222–223; *I See Satan*, 15; *Evolution and Conversion*, 56–58; *Celui par qui le scandale arrive*, 17–18; Eugene Webb, *Philosophers of Consciousness: Polanyi, Lonergan, Voegelin, Ricoeur, Girard, Kierkegaard* (Seattle: University of Washington Press, 1988), 184–185; Richard J. Golsan, *René Girard and Myth: An Introduction* (New York and London: Garland Publishing, Inc.), 3.

8. See Girard, *Things Hidden*, 16–18, 248; *The Girard Reader*, 290–291.

9. See *The Girard Reader*, 64; *I See Satan*, 16.

10. Girard, *Deceit, Desire and the Novel*, 16–17, 24, 27–29, 34, 38–39, 43, 51, 56, 105–106, 111, 158, 169–170, 177, 183, 212–213, 249, 257–259, 266, 270–271, 273, 278, 283.

11. Girard, *Resurrection from the Underground*, 91–95, 155–156; *To Double Business Bound*, 133; Assmann, ed., *René Girard*, 74. See Jean-Michel Oughourlian, *The Puppet of Desire: The Psychology of Hysteria, Possession, and Hypnosis*, trans. Eugene Webb (Stanford, CA: Stanford University Press, 1991), 112–113; Charles Taylor, *Sources of the Self: The Making of the Modern Identity* (Cambridge, MA: Harvard University Press, 1989), 127–142.

12. Dostoyevsky, *Brothers Karamazov*, 642 (IV.XI.IX).

13. Gunter Gebauer and Christoph Wulf, *Mimesis: Culture—Art—Society*, trans. Don Reneau (Berkeley: University of California Press, 1995), 144–148.

14. See Girard, *Resurrection from the Underground*, 94; Assmann, ed., *René Girard*, 71; Oughourlian, *Puppet*, 1–27; Robert G. Hamerton-Kelly, *The Gospel and the Sacred: Poetics of Violence in Mark* (Minneapolis: Fortress, 1994), 189–195; Gil Bailie, "The Vine and Branches Discourse: The Gospel's Psychological Apocalypse," *Contagion: Journal of Violence, Mimesis, and Culture* 4 (1997); James Alison, *The Joy of Being Wrong: Original Sin through Easter Eyes* (New York: Crossroad Publishing Co., 1998), 12, 27–33.

15. Aristotle, *Politics*, in *The Basic Works of Aristotle*, ed. Richard McKeon (New York: Modern Library, 2001), 1129, 1182, (1253a, 1278b).

16. Thomas Hobbes, *Leviathan* (Cambridge: Cambridge University Press, 1991), 119 (ch. 17); Hobbes, *The Elements of Law Natural and Politic*, part 1, *Human Nature* (Oxford: Oxford University Press, 1994), 105–106 (I.XIX.5); Hobbes, *On the Citizen*, trans. Richard Tuck and Michael Silverthorne (New York: Cambridge University Press, 1998), 21–22 (De cive I.2), 71–72 (De cive v.5). See Girard, *Theater of Envy*, 227–229; *Quand ces choses commenceront*, 29; *I See Satan*, 8; "Victims," 132.

17. See John Milbank, *Theology and Social Theory: Beyond Secular Reason* (Oxford: Basil Blackwell, 1990), 13; Palaver, "Schmitt's Critique of Liberalism," *Telos*, no. 102 (1995): 43–46.

18. Immanuel Kant, *Idea for a Universal History with a Cosmopolitan Aim: A Critical Guide*, ed. Amélie Oksenberg Rorty and James Schmidt, trans. Allen W. Wood (Cambridge: Cambridge University Press, 2009), 15.

19. Aristotle, *Nicomachean Ethics*, in *Basic Works of Aristotle*, 1058–1059 (1155a); Thomas Aquinas, *Summa Contra Gentiles*, vol. 3, trans. the English Dominican Fathers (London: Burns, Oates and Washburn, 1928), 177 (III), 54 (IV); Hobbes, *On the Citizen*, 3–4 (De cive, Epistle dedicatory).

20. Augustine, *Concerning the City of God against the Pagans*, trans. Henry Bettenson (New York: Penguin Books, 2003), 508 (XII, 28).

21. Girard, *Deceit, Desire and the Novel*, 2; *Violence and the Sacred*, 146; *Things Hidden*, 95, 283–284; *I See Satan*, 15.

22. See Girard, *I See Satan*, 7–10; *Celui par qui le scandale arrive*, 85, 118.

23. See Girard, *Quand ces choses commenceront*, 28.

24. See Assmann, ed., *René Girard*, 50, 57–59, 69–70; Girard, *I See Satan*, 10–11.

25. Girard, *Violence and the Sacred*, 33–36, 118, 218–222; *Things Hidden*, 3–79, 96; Girard and Meotti, *Accusation*, 182.

26. Girard, *Things Hidden*, 95.

27. Camille Paglia, *Sexual Personae: Art and Decadence from Nefertiti to Emily Dickinson* (New York: Vintage Books, 1991), 1–39.

28. Paglia, *Sexual Personae*, 2, 23. See Paglia, *Sex, Art, and American Culture* (New York: Vintage Books, 1992), 105.

29. Girard, *Things Hidden*, 255–256, 442; *The Scapegoat*, 53, 205; *Job*, 16–17, 129; *Theater of Envy*, 322; *Quand ces choses commenceront*, 69, 117; *Celui par qui le scandale arrive*, 17; Assmann, ed., *René Girard*, 27.

30. Jean-Jacques Rousseau, *The Discourses and Other Political Writings*, trans. Victor Gourevitch (Cambridge: Cambridge University Press, 1997), 154–155.

31. Rousseau, *Discourses*, 155. See Rousseau, *Emile; or On Education*, trans. Allan Bloom (New York: Basic Books, 1979), 214.

32. Rousseau, *Discourses*, 165.

33. Rousseau, *Discourses*, 155.

34. Aristotle, *Poetics*, in *The Basic Works of Aristotle*, 1457 (1448b). See Girard, *Things Hidden*, 1.

35. See Girard, *Things Hidden*, 8; *Evolution and Conversion*, 139–140.

36. Walter Benjamin, *Selected Writings*, Vol. 2, 694–698 ("Doctrine of the Similar"), here 694. See also 720–722 ("On the Mimetic Faculty").

37. Friedrich August von Hayek, *The Fatal Conceit: The Errors of Socialism*, The Collected Works of F. A. Hayek (Chicago: University of Chicago Press, 1989), 21. See also Hayek, *The Fatal Conceit*, 12, 18; Hayek, *The Constitution of Liberty* (London: Routledge, 1999), 74; Jean-Pierre Dupuy, *Libéralisme et justice sociale: Le sacrifice et l'envie*, Pluriel (Paris: Hachette-littératures, 1997), 242, 266–276; Dupuy, "Mimesis and Social Autopoiesis: A Girardian Reading of Hayek," *Paragrana: Internationale Zeitschrift für Historische Anthropologie* 4, no. 2 (1995): 192–201.

38. Livingston, *Models*, xvi.

39. Erich Auerbach, *Mimesis: The Representation of Reality in Western Literature*, trans. Willard R. Trask (Princeton, NJ: Princeton University Press, 2003), 515.

40. See Girard, *Things Hidden*, 7, 15–18; *To Double Business Bound*, 90, 104–105, 201; *Quand ces choses commenceront*, 28–29, 35–36; Girard, *Celui par qui le scandale arrive*, 20.

41. Girard, *Celui par qui le scandale arrive*, 20.

42. Plato, *The Republic*, trans. Allan David Bloom (New York: Basic Books, 1991), 71 (393c).

43. Plato, *The Republic*, 74 (395c).

44. See Gebauer and Wulf, *Mimesis*, 326–327.

45. Plato, *The Republic*, 290 (606d).

46. Also see Girard, *Things Hidden*, 17–18.

47. Plato, *The Republic*, 95–96 (416d–e), 143–144 (464b–d).

48. Plato, *The Republic*, 290 (607a). See Plato, *The Laws of Plato*, trans. Thomas L. Pangle (New York: Basic Books, 1980), 190 (Nomoi 801a); Hans-Georg Gadamer, "Plato und die Dichter," in *Griechische Philosophie I, Gesammelte Werke* (Tübingen: J.C.B. Mohr [Paul Siebeck], 1985), 206; Eric Voegelin, *Order and History III: Plato and Aristoteles*, Collected Works of Eric Voegelin (Columbia: University of Missouri Press, 2000), 185–188; Peter Sloterdijk, "Erwachen im Reich der Eifersucht: Notiz zu René Girards anthropologischer Sendung," in René Girard, *Ich sah den Satan vom Himmel fallen wie einen Blitz* (Munich: Carl Hanser Verlag, 2002), 247.

49. Plato, *The Republic*, 179–180 (500b–c).

50. See Girard, *Things Hidden*, 8; *Celui par qui le scandale arrive*, 20–21.

51. Aristotle, *Poetics*, in *The Basic Works of Aristotle*, 1458 (1448b). See McKenna, "Aristotle's Theater of Envy: Paradox, Logic, and Literature," in *Philosophical Designs for a Socio-Cultural Transformation: Beyond Violence and the Modern Era*, ed. Tetsuji Yamamoto (Boulder, CO: Rowman & Littlefield Publishers, 1998), 633.

52. Aristotle, *Poetics*, in *The Basic Works of Aristotle*, 1460 (1449b). See Girard, *Violence and the*

Sacred, 290–296; *Theater of Envy*, 221–222, 280; *I See Satan*, 37–38, 51, 78; René Girard, "Die Einheit von Ethik und Ästhetik im Ritual," in *Ethik der Ästhetik*, ed. Christoph Wulf, Dietmar Kamper, and Hans Ulrich Gumbrecht (Berlin: Akademie Verlag, 1994), 71–73; Gebauer and Wulf, *Mimesis*, 56–57.

53. Thomas Hobbes, *Leviathan* 87 (ch. 13). See Girard, "Victims, Violence and Christianity," *The Month* 259, no. 1564 (1998): 132.

54. See Girard, *Things Hidden*, 29, 35; *Theater of Envy*, 186; *De la violence à la divinité*, 745.

55. Girard, *Deceit, Desire and the Novel*, 2, 83.

56. Shakespeare, *Coriolanus*, IV, iv, 12–22, in *The Complete Signet Classic Shakespeare*, ed. Sylvan Barnet (New York: Harcourt Brace Jovanovich, 1972).

57. See Girard, *Theater of Envy*, 8–20; Gebauer and Wulf, *Mimesis*, 101–103.

58. Shakespeare, *Two Gentlemen of Verona*, II, iv, 145 and 151–3.

59. Shakespeare, *Two Gentlemen of Verona*, II, iv, 192–208.

60. See Girard, *Theater of Envy*, 21–28.

61. See Girard, *Deceit, Desire and the Novel*, 14–15.

62. See Girard, *Deceit, Desire and the Novel*, 1–3; Cesáreo Bandera, *Mímesis conflictiva: Ficción literaria y violencia en Cervantes y Calderón* (Madrid: Gredos, 1975); Bandera, *The Humble Story of Don Quixote: Reflections on the Birth of the Modern Novel* (Washington, DC: Catholic University of America Press, 2006); Golsan, *Girard*, 2–4.

63. Miguel de Cervantes Saavedra, *Don Quixote*, trans. John Ormsby (New York: Norton, 1981), 178 (I.XV).

64. Cervantes, *Don Quixote*, 189 (I.XXVI).

65. Cervantes, *Don Quixote*, 58 (I.VII).

66. See Girard, *Deceit, Desire and the Novel*, 5.

67. Gustave Flaubert, *Madame Bovary*, trans. Geoffrey Wall (London: Penguin, 2003), 34–35 (I.VI).

68. Flaubert, *Madame Bovary*, 150–151 (II.IX).

69. Flaubert, *Madame Bovary*, 271 (III.VI). See Girard, *Deceit, Desire and the Novel*, 63–64.

70. See Girard, *Deceit, Desire and the Novel*, 4–6; Golsan, *Girard*, 9–13.

71. Stendhal, *The Red and the Black*, trans. Robert Martin Adams. 2nd ed. (New York: W.W. Norton, 2008), 57 (ch. 10).

72. Stendhal, *The Red and the Black*, 48 (ch. 8). See Golsan, *Girard*, 5.

73. Stendhal, *The Red and the Black*, 48 (ch. 9), 75 (ch. 15).

74. See Girard, *Deceit, Desire and the Novel*, 17–40; Golsan, *Girard*, 13–15.

75. Marcel Proust, *Swann's Way*, trans. Lydia Davis (New York: Viking, 2003), 195–396 ("Swann in Love").

76. Proust, *Swann's Way*, 368.

77. Proust, *Swann's Way*, 395–396.

78. Proust, *Swann's Way*, 245.

79. Proust, *Swann's Way*, 281.

80. Proust, *The Past Recaptured*, trans. Andreas Mayor (New York: Random House, 1981), Vol. 3, 420–421. See Girard, *Deceit, Desire and the Novel*, 47–48.

81. Proust, *Within a Budding Grove*, trans. C. K. Scott-Moncrieff and Terence Kilmartin (New York: Modern Library, 1992), 1–298 ("Madame Swann at Home"). See Girard, *Deceit, Desire and the Novel*, 33–39.

82. Proust, *Within a Budding Grove*, 27.

83. Proust, *Within a Budding Grove*, 28.

84. Proust, *Within a Budding Grove*, 37.

85. Proust, *Within a Budding Grove*, 39.

86. Proust, *Within a Budding Grove*, 71–72.

87. Proust, *Within a Budding Grove*, 28.

88. See Girard, *Deceit, Desire and the Novel*, 41–48; Golsan, *Girard*, 15–21.

89. See Girard, *Deceit, Desire and the Novel*, 45–51; *Resurrection from the Underground*, 47–52, 147–150.

90. Dostoyevsky, *The Eternal Husband*, in *The Short Stories of Dostoevsky*, trans. Constance Garnett (New York: Dial Press, 1946), 56.

91. Sigmund Freud, "Dostoyevsky and Parricide," in *Sigmund Freud: Writings on Art and Literature*, trans. James Strachey (Stanford, CA: Stanford University Press, 1997), 242.

92. Girard, *Deceit, Desire and the Novel*, 47; *To Double Business Bound*, 49–57; *Things Hidden*, 338–347; *Resurrection from the Underground*, 148.

93. See Dostoyevsky, *Brothers Karamazov*, 143–153 (I.III.X).

94. Dostoyevsky, *Eternal Husband*, 83.

95. Dostoyevsky, *Eternal Husband*, 125–126.

96. Dostoyevsky, *Eternal Husband*, 126.

97. Dostoyevsky, *Eternal Husband*, 83.

98. See Dostoyevsky, *Eternal Husband*, 82, 84.

99. See Girard, *Deceit, Desire and the Novel*, 46.

100. Cervantes, *Don Quixote*, 249–285 (I.XXXIII–XXXV). See Girard, *Deceit, Desire and the Novel*, 48–52, 98; Girard and Palaver, *Gewalt und Religion*, 42–50.

101. Tocqueville, *Democracy in America*, 1:137–138. See Girard, *Deceit, Desire and the Novel*, 120; Wolfgang Palaver, "Gleichheit als Sprengkraft? Zum Einfluß des Christentums auf die Entwicklung der Demokratie," in *Verweigerte Mündigkeit? Politische Kultur und Kirche*, ed. Józef Niewiadomski (Thaur: Kulturverlag, 1989), 213–214.

102. Vollmer, *Heißer Frieden*, 180.

103. Heraclitus, *Fragments*, trans. T. M. Robinson (Toronto: University of Toronto Press, 1987), 37 (B 53). See Girard, *Violence and the Sacred*, 88.

104. See Tocqueville, *Democracy in America*, 1:7.

105. Wolfgang Sofsky, "Das Gesetz des Gemetzels," *Die Zeit*, 2 April 1998, 54. See also Sofsky, *Traktat über die Gewalt* (Frankfurt am Main: S. Fischer, 1996), 181.

106. Misha Glenny, *The Fall of Yugoslavia: The Third Balkan War* (New York: Penguin Books, 1994), 171–172.

107. Michael Ignatieff, "The Balkan Tragedy," *New York Review of Books* 40, no. 9 (1993): 3. See also Ignatieff, *The Warrior's Honor: Ethnic War and the Modern Conscience* (London: Metropolitan Books, 1998), 34–71.

108. Michael Ignatieff, *Blood and Belonging: Journeys into the New Nationalism* (New York: Farrar, Straus and Giroux, 1994), 28.

109. Huntington, *Clash of Civilizations*, 254.

110. See Huntington, *Clash of Civilizations*, 176–177, 210, 233, 245, 250, 256, 258, 264–265, 317.

111. See Girard, *Violence and the Sacred*, 249; *Violent Origins*, 219; *I See Satan*, 53.

112. Sigmund Freud, *Civilization and Its Discontents*, in *The Freud Reader*, ed. Peter Gay, trans. James Strachey (New York: W.W. Norton, 1989), 751. See Freud, *Group Psychology and the Analysis of the Ego*, trans. James Strachey (New York: Norton, 1975), 42.

113. Sigmund Freud, *Moses and Monotheism*, trans. Katherine Jones, International Psycho-Analytical Library (London: Hogarth Press, 1951), 146.

114. Freud and Gay, *The Freud Reader*, 751.

115. Aquinas, *Summa Contra Gentiles*, III.132.

116. Thomas Hobbes, *Behemoth or the Long Parliament* (Chicago: University of Chicago Press, 1990), 32.

117. Adam Smith, *The Theory of Moral Sentiments*, Glasgow Edition of the Works and Correspondence of Adam Smith (Indianapolis: Liberty Fund, 1984), 230–231.

118. Georg Simmel, *Sociology: Inquiries into the Construction of Social Forms*, vol. 1, trans. Anthony J. Blasi, Anton K. Jacobs, and Mathew J. Kanjirathinkal (Leiden: Brill, 2009), 248–249. See also *Simmel on Culture: Selected Writings*, trans. David Frisby and Mark Ritter (Thousand Oaks, CA: Sage, 1997), 233–245 ("On the Psychology of Money").

119. See Donald Harman Akenson, *Small Differences: Irish Catholics and Irish Protestants, 1815–1922* (Montreal: McGill-Queen's University Press, 1988), 149; Byron Bland, "Marching and Rising: The Rituals of Small Differences and Great Violence," *Contagion: Journal of Violence, Mimesis, and Culture* 4 (1997).

120. See Girard, *Resurrection from the Underground*, 57–58; *Violence and the Sacred*, 155; *To Double Business Bound*, 89–90, 114–115; *Theater of Envy*, 332–333; *Quand ces choses commenceront*, 46, 73, 110–111; *I See Satan*, 20.

121. See Girard, "Introduction," in Roel Kaptein, *On the Way of Freedom. With the Cooperation of Duncan Morrow* (Dublin: Columba Press, 1993), 9.

122. See Girard, *Things Hidden*, 299–302, 307, 338, 389; *Theater of Envy*, 333; Dupuy, "Le signe et l'envie," in *L'enfer des choses: René Girard et la logique de l'économie*, ed. Paul Dumouchel and Jean-Pierre Dupuy (Paris: Édition du Seuil, 1979), 76–85; Günther Ortmann, *Regel und Ausnahme: Paradoxien sozialer Ordnung* (Frankfurt am Main: Suhrkamp, 2003), 147–148.

123. Rolf Haubl, *Neidisch sind immer nur die anderen: Über die Unfähigkeit, zufrieden zu sein* (Munich: Verlag C.H. Beck, 2001), 268. See Girard, *Deceit, Desire and the Novel*, 105; Dupuy, "Le signe," 46–47.

124. Dupuy, "Le signe," 92.

125. See Girard, *Deceit, Desire and the Novel*, 93, 103–104; *Violence and the Sacred*, 155; *To Double Business Bound*, 118; *Things Hidden*, 298, 300–301; *Theater of Envy*, 332.

126. Immanuel Kant, *Anthropology from a Pragmatic Point of View*, trans. Robert B. Louden (Cambridge: Cambridge University Press, 2006), 142–143.

127. Simmel, "The Philosophy of Fashion," in *Simmel on Culture: Selected Writings*, trans. David Frisby and Mark Ritter (Thousand Oaks, CA: Sage, 1997), 188–189. See René König, *Kleider und Leute: Zur Soziologie der Mode* (Frankfurt am Main: Fischer Bücherei, 1967), 70–71.

128. See Dupuy, "Le signe et l'envie," 79.

129. Simmel, *On Culture*, 189.

130. Simmel, *On Culture*, 194.

131. Simmel, *On Culture*, 194.

132. Simmel, *On Culture*, 194.

133. See Girard, *The Girard Reader*, 214; *I See Satan*, 27.

134. Simmel, *On Culture*, 195.

135. See Girard, *Deceit, Desire and the Novel*, 25–26, 33–37, 46, 67–76, 218–225; Dupuy, "Le signe," 67–68.

136. Girard, *Deceit, Desire and the Novel*, 75–76.

137. Girard, *Deceit, Desire and the Novel*, 70–74.

138. Girard, *Deceit, Desire and the Novel*, 70, 221. See König, *Kleider*, 77–79, 104–107.

139. See Girard, *Deceit, Desire and the Novel*, 59, 221, 298, 300; *The Girard Reader*, 268; René Girard, "Die Einheit von Ethik und Ästhetik im Ritual," in *Ethik der Ästhetik*, ed. Christoph Wulf, Dietmar Kamper, and Hans Ulrich Gumbrecht, 69–74 (Berlin: Akademie Verlag, 1994), 70; Henri Bergson, *Creative Evolution*, trans. Arthur Mitchell (Lanham, MD: University Press of America, 1983); see also Bergson, *The Two Sources of Morality and Religion*, trans. R. Ashley Audra and Cloudesley Brereton (Notre Dame, IN: University of Notre Dame Press, 1977); Jean-Paul Sartre, *Being and Nothingness: A Phenomenological Essay on Ontology*, trans. Hazel E. Barnes (New York: Pocket Books, 1966).

140. See Burton Mack, "Introduction: Religion and Ritual," in *Violent Origins: Walter Burkert, René Girard, and Jonathan Z. Smith on Ritual Killing and Cultural Formation*, ed. Robert G. Hamerton-Kelly (Stanford, CA: Stanford University Press, 1987), 13–14; Livingston, *Models*, 5; Eugene Webb, *The Self Between: From Freud to the New Social Psychology of France* (Seattle: University of Washington Press, 1993), 229.

141. Girard and Adams, "Violence," 14–15. See René Girard, "Existentialism and Criticism," in *Yale French Studies*, no. 9 (1955). Also quoted in Jean-Paul Sartre, *Sartre: A Collection of Critical Essays*, ed. E. Kern (Englewood Cliffs, NJ: Prentice-Hall, 1962), 121–128.

142. Sartre, *Being and Nothingness*, 85–90.

143. Sartre, *Being and Nothingness*, 58, 63, 102, 109–110, 116.

144. Sartre, *Being and Nothingness*, 90, 652, 592, 615, 625–626.

145. Sartre, *Being and Nothingness*, 652.

146. Girard, *Quand ces choses commenceront*, 162–163.

147. Sartre, *Being and Nothingness*, 59.

148. Michel Contat and Michel Rybalka, eds., *The Writings of Jean-Paul Sartre*, vol. 2, *Selected Prose* (Evanston, IL: Northwestern University Press, 1974), 67.

149. Sartre, *War Diaries: Notebooks from a Phoney War, November 1939–March 1940*, trans. Quintin Hoare (London: Verso, 1999), 110–111.

150. Jean-Paul Sartre, *Anti-Semite and Jew*, trans. George Joseph Becker (New York: Schocken Books, 1948), 53–54.

151. Sartre, *Anti-Semite and Jew*, 109.

152. See Girard, *Deceit, Desire and the Novel*, 53, 73, 185; *To Double Business Bound*, 3; *Violence and the Sacred*, 148, 170; *Things Hidden*, 296, 321, 333–334; René Girard, *Job: The Victim of His People*, trans. Yvonne Freccero (Stanford, CA: Stanford University Press, 1987), 50; *Theater of Envy*, 4, 42–43, 141, 147; *Quand ces choses commenceront*, 28; *De la violence à la divinité*, 11.

153. Johann Wolfgang von Goethe, *The Sorrows of Young Werther*, trans. Burton Pike (New York: Modern Library, 2004), 71–72. See Achterhuis, *Het rijk van de schaarste: Van Thomas Hobbes tot Michel Foucault* (Utrecht: Ambo/Baarn, 1988), 111–112.

154. Sartre, *Being and Nothingness*, 221–430.

155. Sartre, *Being and Nothingness*, 262. See also 221–222, 280–281; Jean-Paul Sartre, *Existentialism Is a Humanism* (New Haven: Yale University Press, 2007), 41–42; Alain Finkielkraut, *Der eingebildete Jude*, trans. Hainer Kober (Frankfurt am Main: Fischer Taschenbuch Verlag, 1984), 17, 28–29, 34, 167–168.

156. Sartre, *Being and Nothingness*, 650. See Sartre, *War Diaries*, 110; Josef Pieper, *Faith, Hope, Love*, trans. Richard Winston, Clara Winston, and Mary Francis McCarthy (San Francisco: Ignatius Press, 1997), 179.

157. Sartre, *Being and Nothingness*, 243–244, 251. See Sartre, *Existentialism*, 41–42.

158. Sartre, *Being and Nothingness*, 283. See also 250, 273, 275, 297, 413.

159. Sartre, *War Diaries*, 110; Peter Bürger, *Das Verschwinden des Subjekts: Eine Geschichte der Subjektivität von Montaigne bis Barthes* (Frankfurt am Main: Suhrkamp, 1998), 184.

160. Girard, *Deceit, Desire and the Novel*, 282–288. See *Job*, 62–63; *Quand ces choses commenceront*, 159.

161. Dostoyevsky, *Brothers Karamazov*, 642 (IV.XI.IX).

162. Dostoyevsky, *Brothers Karamazov*, 120 (I.III.V), 155 (I.III.XI).

163. Proust, *Swann's Way*, 301. See Girard, *Mimesis and Theory*, 191–193.

164. Heinrich von Kleist, "On the Marionette Theater," in *German Romantic Criticism*, ed. A. Leslie Willson (New York: Continuum, 1982), 238–244. See Palaver, "Gott oder mechanischer Gliedermann? Die religiöse Problematik in Kleists Essay *über das Marionettentheater*," in *Kleist zur Gewalt: Transdisziplinäre Perspektiven*, ed. Gianluca Crepaldi, Andreas Kriwak, and Thomas Pröll (Innsbruck: Innsbruck University Press, 2011), 45–62.

165. Kleist, "On the Marionette Theater," 243–244.

166. Rousseau, *Discourses*, 102, 137–138, 153–154, 235–236; Rousseau, *Emile*, 223; Rousseau, *Rousseau, Judge of Jean-Jacques, Dialogues*, trans. Judith R. Bush, Christopher Kelly, and Roger D. Masters (Hanover, NH: University Press of New England, 1990), 112–114.

167. Alexandre Kojève, *Introduction to the Reading of Hegel: Lectures on the Phenomenology of Spirit*, trans. James H. Nichols Jr. (New York: Basic Books, 1969), 387, 434; Leo Strauss and Alexandre Kojève, *On Tyranny* (Toronto: Maxwell Macmillan International, 1991), 255. See Jacob Taubes, "Ästhetisierung der Wahrheit im Posthistoire," in *Streitbare Philosophie: Margherita von Brentano zum 65. Geburtstag*, ed. Gabriele Althaus and Irmingard Staeuble (Berlin: Metropol, 1988), 41–46; Lutz Niethammer, *Posthistoire: Ist die Geschichte zu Ende?* (Reinbek bei Hamburg: rowohlts enzyklopädie, 1989), 79–82; Francis Fukuyama, *The End of History and the Last Man* (New York: Avon Books, 1993), 311, 387; Martin Meyer, *Ende der Geschichte?* (Munich: Carl Hanser Verlag, 1993), 105–107, 184–185.

168. Friedrich Nietzsche, *Sämtliche Werke: Kritische Studienausgabe in 15 Einzelbänden*, ed. Giorgio Colli and Mazzino Montinari (Berlin: Walter de Gruyter, 1988), vol. 3: 467–469 (*Die fröhliche Wissenschaft*, Nr. 109), 521 (Nr. 276), 570 (Nr. 341); vol. 5: 74–75 (*Jenseits von Gut und Böse*, 55, 56); vol. 6: 297, 335, 363 (*Ecce homo*, "Warum ich so klug bin," 10, "Also sprach Zarathustra," 1, "Der Fall Wagner," 4); vol. 6: 436 (*Nietzsche contra Wagner*; Epilogue, 1); vol. 13: 492–493 (Nachgelassene Fragmente, Frühjahr-Sommer 1888, 16[32]); Nietzsche, *Briefe* (vol. 6), 199–200 (Brief vom 5. Juni 1882 an F. Overbeck). See Girard, *Deceit, Desire and the Novel*, 274–279; *To Double Business Bound*, 26, 61–83 ("Strategies of Madness: Nietzsche, Wagner and Dostoyevsky").

169. Claude Lévi-Strauss, *Tristes Tropiques*, trans. John Weightman and Doreen Weightman (New York: Penguin Books, 1992), 373–415 ("The Return"); Lévi-Strauss, *The Savage Mind* (Chicago: University of Chicago Press, 1966), 245–269 ("History and Dialectic"); Lévi-Strauss, *Totemism*, trans. Rodney Needham (Boston: Beacon Press, 1963), 69–71, 99–102; Lévi-Strauss, *The Raw and the Cooked*, trans. John and Doreen Weightman (New York: Harper & Row, 1969), 53; Lévi-Strauss, *The Naked Man*, trans. John and Doreen Weightman (New York: Harper & Row, 1981), 625–695 ("Finale"); Lévi-Strauss, *Structural Anthropology*, vol. 2, trans. Monique Layton (New York: Basic Books, 1963), 33–43 ("Jean-Jacques Rousseau, Founder of the Sciences of Man"). See Girard, *Things Hidden*, 124, 414; *To Double Business Bound*, 158–159, 166–175 ("Differentiation and Reciprocity in Lévi-Strauss and Contemporary Theory"); *The Scapegoat*, 74–75; Jacques Derrida, "Structure, Sign, and Play in the Discourse of the Human Sciences," in *The Structuralist Controversy: The Languages of Criticism and the Sciences of Man*, ed. Richard Macksey and Eugenio Donato (Baltimore: Johns Hopkins University Press, 1972), 264; Calasso, *Ruin of Kasch*, 201–205; Renate Schlesier, *Kulte, Mythen und Gelehrte: Anthropologie der Antike seit 1800* (Frankfurt am Main: Fischer Taschenbuch Verlag, 1994), 243–267.

170. Ulrich Horstmann, *Das Untier: Konturen einer Philosophie der Menschenflucht* (Frankfurt am Main: Suhrkamp, 1985), 113–114. See Michel Serres, *La Traduction*, Hermès (Paris: Éditions de Minuit, 1974), 73–104. Girard, *Things Hidden*, 409–415.

171. Freud, "On Narcissism: An Introduction." In *The Freud Reader*, 554–555.

172. Sartre, *Being and Nothingness*, 55–58. See Girard, *Deceit, Desire and the Novel*, 105–107.

173. Kleist, "On the Marionette Theater," 241.

174. Girard, *Deceit, Desire and the Novel*, 71, 197, 234, 240, 254, 273; *To Double Business Bound*, 12, 18–19, 30.

175. Girard, *Deceit, Desire and the Novel*, 158.

176. See Girard, *Quand ces choses commenceront*, 162–163.

177. Girard, *Deceit, Desire and the Novel*, 159; *Resurrection from the Underground*, 57–58.

178. See Milbank, *Theology*, 320–321; John Milbank, "Stories of Sacrifice," *Contagion: Journal of Violence, Mimesis, and Culture* 2 (1995): 92, 100.

179. Sartre, *Being and Nothingness*, 364.

180. Jean-Paul Sartre, *No Exit, and Three Other Plays*, trans. Stuart Gilbert (New York: Vintage International, 1989), 59.

181. Sartre, *Anti-Semite and Jew*, 114.

182. Sartre, *Anti-Semite and Jew*, 36.

183. Charles K. Bellinger, *The Genealogy of Violence: Reflections on Creation, Freedom, and Evil* (Oxford: Oxford University Press, 2001), 72–74.

184. Bellinger, *Genealogy of Violence*, 74.

185. Søren Kierkegaard, *Upbuilding Discourses in Various Spirits*, trans. Howard V. and Edna H. Hong (Princeton, NJ: Princeton University Press, 1993), 167–169. See Bellinger, *Genealogy of Violence*, 75.

186. Kierkegaard, *Upbuilding Discourses*, 169.

187. Kierkegaard, *The Concept of Anxiety: A Simple Psychologically Orienting Deliberation on the Dogmatic Issue of Hereditary Sin*, trans. Albert Anderson and Reidar Thomte (Princeton, NJ: Princeton University Press, 1980); See Bellinger, *Genealogy of Violence*, 34–39.

188. Kierkegaard, *Eighteen Upbuilding Discourses*, trans. Howard V. Hong and Edna H. Hong (Princeton, NJ: Princeton University Press, 1992), 136.

189. See Hamerton-Kelly, *Sacred Violence: Paul's Hermeneutic of the Cross* (Minneapolis: Fortress Press, 1992), 166–170.

190. Augustine, *Confessions*, trans. Garry Wills (New York: Penguin Books, 2006), 3 (I, 1). See Hamerton-Kelly, *Sacred Violence*, 168; Pieter Tijmes, "Die Intuitionen René Girards," in *Die Macht der Differenzen: Beiträge zur Hermeneutik der Kultur*, ed. Reinhard Düssel, Geert Edel, and Ulrich Schödlbauer (Heidelberg: SYNCHRON, Wissenschafts-Verlag der Autoren, 2001), 135.

191. Pieper, *Love*, 218.

192. See Bellinger, *Genealogy of Violence*, 74; Hamerton-Kelly, *Sacred Violence*, 166–168.

193. Sartre, *Being and Nothingness*, 467–470; 538.

194. Sartre, *Being and Nothingness*, 290.

195. Sartre, *Being and Nothingness*, 263.

196. Sartre, *Being and Nothingness*, 288–289.

197. Sartre, *Being and Nothingness*, 290.

198. Girard, *Deceit, Desire and the Novel*, 58–59.

199. Girard, *To Double Business Bound*, 5–6. See Girard, *Resurrection from the Underground*, 140.

200. See Girard, *Theater of Envy*, 296; *Celui par qui le scandale arrive*, 141.

201. See Avital Wohlman, "René Girard et Saint Augustin: Anthropologie et theologie," *Recherches*

Augustiniennes 20 (1985): 257–303; Stanislaw Budzik, "Perversa imitatio Die: Zum Begriff der Erbsünde bei Augustinus und Schwager," in *Vom Fluch und Segen der Sündenböcke: Raymund Schwager zum 60. Geburtstag,* ed. Józef Niewiadomski and Wolfgang Palaver (Thaur: Kulturverlag, 1995), 100–102; Alison, *Joy of Being Wrong,* 293–295; Graham, "Novelistic Conversion."

202. Augustine, *Confessions,* 121 (VI, 13).

203. Augustine, *Confessions,* 10 (I, 11).

204. Augustine, *Confessions,* 13 (I, 15). See also 22–23 (I, 30).

205. Augustine, *Confessions,* 13 (I, 16); 20–21 (I, 28); 22–23 (I, 30); 30 (II, 7); 44 (III, 6).

206. Augustine, *Confessions,* 36–37 (II, 16–17).

207. Augustine, *Confessions,* 61 (IV, 1).

208. Augustine, *Confessions,* 75 (IV, 21).

209. Augustine, *Confessions,* 75 (IV, 21).

210. Augustine, *Confessions,* 75 (IV, 23).

211. Augustine, "*Concerning the City of God against the Pagans,* trans. Henry Bettenson (New York: Penguin Books, 2003), 594 (XV, ch. 1). See Girard, *Deceit, Desire and the Novel,* 58; *Job,* 155; *I See Satan,* 17.

212. Augustine, *Concerning the City of God,* 571–573 (XIV, ch. 13); 593–594 (XIV, ch. 28).

213. Augustine, *On Free Choice of the Will,* trans. Thomas Williams (Indianapolis: Hackett Publishing Co., 1993), 122 (3.25.76); Augustine, *On Christian Belief,* trans. Matthew O'Connell, in *Works of Saint Augustine,* part 1, vol. 8 (Hyde Park, NY: New City Press, 2005), 87 (XLV, 84); Augustine, *Confessions,* 67 (II, 14), 247–248 (X, 59); Augustine, *City of God,* 866–869 (XIX, ch. 12).

214. Augustine, *City of God,* 324 (VIII, ch. 17).

215. Augustine, *City of God,* 310 (VIII, ch. 8).

216. Augustine, *On Christian Doctrine,* trans. D. W. Robertson (New York: Macmillan, 1958), 9–10 (I, 4); Augustine, *The Trinity,* in *Works of Saint Augustine,* ed. John E. Rotelle, trans. Edmund Hill (Brooklyn, NY: New City Press, 1991), 294 (X, 10); Augustine, *City of God,* 458–459 (XI, ch. 25).

217. Augustine, *City of God,* 599 (XV, ch. 4).

218. Augustine, *City of God,* 600 (XV, ch. 4).

219. Augustine, *City of God,* 600 (XV, ch. 5).

220. Augustine, *On Christian Belief,* 88 (XLV, 85, 242).

221. Augustine, *City of God,* 601 (XV, ch. 6).

222. Augustine, *On Christian Belief,* 88 (XLVI.86.243).

223. Thomas Aquinas, *Summa Theologiæ,* trans. Thomas Gilby, vol. 44 (New York: Black Friars; McGraw-Hill, 1972), 43 (II–IIae 36.2).

224. Aquinas, *Summa Contra Gentiles,* III.135. See also S.132.

225. Dante Alighieri, *Divine Comedy,* vol. 2, trans. Mark Musa (New York: Penguin Books, 1985), 162–163 (XV, 49–57).

226. Blaise Pascal, *Pensées: Thoughts on Religion and Other Subjects*, trans. William Finlayson Trotter (New York: Washington Square Press, 1965), 120 (425).

227. Max Scheler, *Formalism in Ethics and Non-Formal Ethics of Values: A New Attempt toward the Foundation of an Ethical Personalism*, trans. Manfred S. Frings and Roger L. Funk, 5th rev. ed. (Evanston, IL: Northwestern University Press, 1973), 93.

228. Max Scheler, *Formalism in Ethics*, 94.

229. See Gronemeyer, *Macht der Bedürfnisse*, 86–88.

230. See Achterhuis, *Rijk van de Schaarste*, 136–137, 141.

231. Girard, *Deceit, Desire and the Novel*, 17, 168, 173, 228, 259, 268; *Things Hidden*, 309; *To Double Business Bound*, 221–222.

232. See Palaver, *Politik und Religion bei Thomas Hobbes: Eine Kritik aus der Sicht der Theorie René Girards*, Innsbrucker Theologische Studien (Innsbruck: Tyrolia, 1991), 40–45.

233. Hobbes, *The Elements of Law Natural and Politic*, part 1, *Human Nature*; part 2, *De Corpore Politico* (Oxford: Oxford University Press, 1994), 59 (1.IX.21).

234. Goethe, *The Sorrows of Young Werther*, 72; see also 74.

235. Dostoyevsky, *Notes from the Underground*, 57.

236. Hobbes, *Elements of Law*, 59–60 (1.IX.21).

237. Leo Strauss, *The Political Philosophy of Hobbes: Its Basis and Its Genesis*, trans. Elsa M. Sinclair (Chicago: University of Chicago Press, 1963), 11–29, 110–112, 130, 132–133, 150, 166–167, 169. See Girard, *Deceit, Desire and the Novel*, 6–7, 14–15.

238. Hobbes, *Elements of Law*, 50–51 (1.IX.1); Hobbes, *On the Citizen*, 21–24 (De cive 1.2); Hobbes, *Leviathan*, 42–43 (ch. 6), 54 (ch. 8), 72 (ch. 11), 205 (ch. 27); Thomas Hobbes, *Man and Citizen: De Homine and De Cive*, trans. Charles T. Wood, T.S.K. Scott-Craig, and Bernard Gert (Indianapolis: Hackett Publishing Co., 1991), 58 (De homine XII.6), 60–61 (De homine XII.9). See Voegelin, *Modernity without Restraints*.

239. Hobbes, *Elements of Law*, 51 (1.IX.1); Hobbes, *Leviathan*, 42–43 (ch. 6). See Victoria Kahn, "Hobbes, Romance, and the Contract of Mimesis," *Political Theory* 29, no. 1 (2001): 4–29.

240. Hobbes, *Leviathan*, 119 (ch. 17). See Hobbes, *Elements of Law*, 105 (1.XIX.5); Hobbes, *On the Citizen*, 71 (De cive V.5).

241. See Girard, *Deceit, Desire and the Novel*, 56–58; *Resurrection from the Underground*, 51, 54–55, 61, 124–125, 139–140; *Theater of Envy*, 4, 10, 101, 148, 171, 197, 298, 326.

242. Hobbes, *Leviathan*, 220–221 (ch. 28). See Strauss, *Political Philosophy of Hobbes*, 13; *Job* 41:25–26.

243. Stephen Holmes, "Introduction," in Thomas Hobbes, *Behemoth or the Long Parliament* (Chicago: University of Chicago Press, 1990), xvii. See also xxvii–xxxiv; Hobbes, *Behemoth*, 4, 22–23, 30, 32, 89, 107, 109, 169, 176.

244. Hobbes, *Elements of Law*, 163–164 (II.XXVII.3).

245. Hobbes, *Leviathan*, 62 (ch. 10). See Hobbes, *Man and Citizen*, 48–49 (De homine XI.6).

246. Hobbes, *Leviathan* 63, (ch. 10).

247. Hobbes, *Leviathan*, 70, (ch. 11). See also 54 (ch. 8).

248. Hobbes, *Elements of Law*, 45 (I.VII.7).

249. Voegelin, *Modernity without Restraints*, 238–239.

250. Voegelin, *Modernity without Restraints*, 239.

251. See Hobbes, *Leviathan*, 46 (ch. 6), 70 (ch. 11). See Voegelin, *Modernity without Restraints* 235–236; Palaver, *Politik*, 47.

252. Voegelin, *Modernity without Restraints*, 238.

253. See Niklas Luhmann, *Die Wirtschaft der Gesellschaft*, 2nd ed. (Frankfurt am Main: Suhrkamp, 1996), 183.

254. Benedict de Spinoza, *Tractatus Theologico-Politicus*, in *The Chief Works of Benedict de Spinoza*, trans. Robert Harvey Monro Elwes (London: G. Bell and Sons, 1883), 289 (§5).

255. Spinoza, *Ethics*, in *The Chief Works of Benedict de Spinoza*, 148 (III, 27).

256. Spinoza, *Ethics*, 151 (III, 31).

257. Spinoza, *Ethics*, 152 (III, 31).

258. Spinoza, *Ethics*, 152 (III, 32).

259. Spinoza, *Ethics*, 152 (III, 32).

260. Johann Wolfgang von Goethe, *The Autobiography of Johann Wolfgang von Goethe*, trans. John Oxenford, 2 vols. (Chicago: University of Chicago Press, 1974), 261–262.

261. Goethe, *Autobiography*, 180. See Girard and Palaver, *Gewalt und Religion*, 41–51.

262. See Achterhuis, *Rijk van de Schaarste*, 142; Robert Hamerton-Kelly, "Popular Sovereignty and the Sacred: A Mimetic Reading of Rousseau's Doctrine of the General Will," *Paragrana: Internationale Zeitschrift für Historische Anthropologie* 4, no. 2 (1995), 240; Tzvetan Todorov, *Life in Common: An Essay in General Anthropology*, trans. Katherine Golsan and Lucy Golsan (Lincoln: University of Nebraska Press, 2001), 38.

263. Rousseau, *Emile*, 213. Cf. Rousseau, *Discourses*, 152–153, 165–167, 170–171, 184, 187, 199; Rousseau, *Judge of Jean-Jacques*, 9–11, 112–114.

264. Proust, *The Past Recaptured*, trans. Andreas Mayor (New York: Random House, 1981), 932. See Girard, *Deceit, Desire and the Novel*, 59, 298; *Mimesis and Theory*, 39, 62, 68, 72, 74.

265. Rousseau, *Discourses*, 166. See also 131–132, 154, 157, 162, 197–199.

266. Rousseau, *Judge of Jean-Jacques*, 112.

267. Rousseau, *Discourses*, 184.

268. See Pascal, *Pensées*, 100, 430, 455, 472, 483, 485, 492, 545, 556; Iring Fetscher, *Rousseaus politische Philosophie: Zur Geschichte des demokratischen Freiheitsbegriffs* (Frankfurt am Main: Suhrkamp, 1993), 65–75; McKenna, "Pascal, Order, and Difference," *Religion & Literature* 25, no. 2 (1993): 55–75.

269. Rousseau, *Discourses*, 127, 138–139, 149, 159, 187; Rousseau, *Emile*, 39–40.

270. Rousseau, *Emile*, 221.

271. Rousseau, *Emile*, 221, 290; Rousseau, *Judge of Jean-Jacques*, 119.

272. Rousseau, *Emile*, 184–186. See Rousseau, *Judge of Jean-Jacques*, 118.

273. See Girard, *Deceit, Desire and the Novel*, 265; *Resurrection from the Underground*, 96–97; Gebauer and Wulf, *Mimesis*, 294; Bailie, "Vine and Branches," 134–135, 138.

274. Rousseau, *Reveries of the Solitary Walker*, trans. Russell Goulbourne (Oxford: Oxford University Press, 2011), 55–56. See Rousseau, *Emile*, 293.

275. See Girard, *Resurrection from the Underground*, 40, 65, 96–97, 99.

276. See Girard, *To Double Business Bound*, 48–49, 79.

277. Rousseau, *The Social Contract and Discourses*, trans. G.D.H. Cole, J. H. Brumfitt, and John C. Hall (London: Dent, 1990), 53. See Achterhuis, *Rijk van de Schaarste*, 42.

278. Rousseau, *Discourses*, 152–154. See also 166–167, 171, 218, 228 (Letter to Philopolis); Rousseau and Johann Gottfried Herder, *On the Origin of Language*, trans. John H. Moran and Alexander Gode (Chicago: University of Chicago Press, 1986), 32 (ch. 9); Rousseau, *Emile*, 221–223.

279. Rousseau, *Social Contract*, 127–128, 152; Rousseau, *Emile*, 213, 218–229, 233, 290; Rousseau, *Judge of Jean-Jacques*, 112–118.

280. Rousseau, *Judge of Jean-Jacques*, 112.

281. Rousseau, *Emile*, 220–223.

282. Rousseau, *Confessions*, trans. Angela Scholar (Oxford: Oxford University Press, 2000), 10. See Bailie, "Vine and Branches," 134–135.

283. Rousseau, *Confessions*, 18–20. See Hans Robert Jauß, *Ästhetische Erfahrung und literarische Hermeneutik* (Frankfurt am Main: Suhrkamp, 1997), 236–237.

284. Rousseau, *Judge of Jean-Jacques*, 116–118.

285. See Jauß, *Ästhetische Erfahrung*, 232–243; Jeremiah Alberg, *A Reinterpretation of Rousseau: A Religious System*, foreword by René Girard (New York: Palgrave Macmillan, 2007).

286. Immanuel Kant, *The Metaphysics of Morals*, trans. Mary J. Gregor (Cambridge: Cambridge University Press, 1996), 206 (Doctrine of the Elements of Ethics §36). See Helmut Schoeck, *Der Neid: Eine Theorie der Gesellschaft* (Freiburg: Verlag Karl Alber, 1966), 193–195.

287. Kant, *Religion within the Boundaries of Mere Reason*, trans. Allen W. Wood and George Di Giovanni (Cambridge: Cambridge University Press, 1998), 51; See Kant, *Schriften zur Geschichtsphilosophie* ("Ausgewählte Reflexionen aus dem Nachlaß") (Stuttgart: Philipp Reclam jun., 1985).

288. Kant, *Idea for a Universal History with a Cosmopolitan Aim: A Critical Guide*, ed. Amélie Oksenberg Rorty and James Schmidt, trans. Allen W. Wood (Cambridge: Cambridge University Press, 2009), 15.

289. Kant, "Universal History," 13.

290. Kant, *Religion*, 51.

291. Kant, "Universal History," 14.

292. Johann Wolfgang von Goethe, *Faust*, trans. Stuart Pratt Atkins (Cambridge, MA: Insel Publishers Boston, 1984), 36 (I.1336).

293. Kant, "Universal History," 14.

294. See Girard, *Deceit, Desire and the Novel*, 11–13.

295. Max Scheler, *Ressentiment*, trans. Lewis B. Coser and William W. Holdheim (Milwaukee, WI: Marquette University Press, 1994), 35.

296. Scheler, *Ressentiment*, 36.

297. Scheler, *Ressentiment*, 37. See Goethe, *Torquato Tasso*, trans. Alan Brownjohn (London: Angel Books, 1985), 59–67 (II, iii, 1196–1408).

298. Hans Magnus Enzensberger, *Civil Wars: From L.A. to Bosnia*, trans. Piers Spence and Martin Chalmers (New York: The New Press, 1994), 11.

299. Enzensberger, *Civil Wars*, 12–13.

300. Enzensberger, *Civil Wars*, 11.

301. See Enzensberger, *Civil Wars*, 29–30, 40.

302. See Enzensberger, *Civil Wars*, 36–37.

303. Enzensberger, *Civil Wars*, 38.

304. See Carl Schmitt, *Ex Captivitate Salus: Erfahrungen der Zeit 1945/47* (Köln: Greven Verlag, 1950), 26, 56–57.

305. See Carl Schmitt, *The Leviathan in the State Theory of Thomas Hobbes: Meaning and Failure of a Political Symbol*, trans. George Schwab and Erna Hilfstein (Chicago: University of Chicago Press, 2008), 21, 47.

306. Carl Schmitt, *The Nomos of the Earth in the International Law of the Jus Publicum Europaeum*, trans. G. L. Ulmen (New York: Telos Press, Ltd., 2006), 142.

307. See Wolfgang Palaver, *Die mythischen Quellen des Politischen: Carl Schmitts Freund-Feind-Theorie*, Beiträge zur Friedensethik (Stuttgart: Verlag W. Kohlhammer, 1998).

308. Carl Schmitt, *The Concept of the Political*, trans. George Schwab (Chicago: University of Chicago Press, 2007), 27.

309. Schmitt, *Ex Captivitate Salus*, 89–90.

310. See Georg Wilhelm Friedrich Hegel, *Phenomenology of Spirit*, trans. Arnold Miller (Oxford: Clarendon Press, 1977), 127–136.

311. See Niethammer, *Posthistoire*, 74; Piet Tommissen, "Kojèves Hegel-Seminar: Hintergrund und Teilnehmer," in *Schmittiana: Beiträge zu Leben und Werk Carl Schmitts*, ed. Piet Tommissen, Band 6 (Berlin: Duncker & Humblot, 1998).

312. See Williams, *The Bible, Violence, and the Sacred*, 260; Livingston, *Models of Desire*, 7. See René Girard, *Battling to the End: Conversations with Benoît Chantre*, trans. Mary Baker (East Lansing: Michigan State University Press, 2010), 30; Webb, *The Self Between*, 116.

313. Kojève, *Introduction to the Reading of Hegel*, 3.

314. Kojève, *Introduction*, 5.

315. Kojève, *Introduction*, 6.

316. Kojève, *Introduction*, 40.

317. See Kojève, *Introduction*, 5, 13–14, 37–38, 135, 225.

318. Kojève, *Introduction*, 40–41.

319. See Meyer, *Ende der Geschichte?*, 55.

320. See Meyer, *Ende der Geschichte?*, 123–127; Francis Fukuyama, *The End of History and the Last Man* (New York: Avon Books, 1993), 203.

321. See Fukuyama, *End of History*, 203.

322. See Fukuyama, *End of History*, part 3, "The Struggle for Recognition," 143–208.

323. See Fukuyama, *End of History*, 57–60, 76, 83, 144, 155, 162–166, 255, 371. See Strauss, *The Political Philosophy of Hobbes*, 57–58, 105.

324. Enzensberger, *Civil Wars*, 38–39.

325. See Fukuyama, *End of History*, part 5, "The Last Man," 287–339.

326. See Fukuyama, *End of History*, 302.

327. Girard, *Deceit, Desire and the Novel*, 110–111.

328. Girard, *Quand ces choses commenceront*, 124. See Girard and Markus Müller, "Interview with René Girard," *Anthropoetics: The Electronic Journal of Generative Anthropology*, no. 1 (1996): 7.

329. See Girard, *Deceit, Desire and the Novel*, 110; *Violence and the Sacred*, 154, 306–307; *To Double Business Bound*, 89, 201, 203, 218; *Things Hidden*, 15, 265, 320, 423; *Theater of Envy* 51–52; Raymund Schwager, *Must There Be Scapegoats? Violence and Redemption in the Bible*, trans. Maria L. Assad (San Francisco: Harper & Row, 1987), 35–40; Hamerton-Kelly, *Sacred Violence*, 199–207; Alison, *Joy of Being Wrong*, 39–40.

330. See Girard, *Things Hidden*, 283–284; *Quand ces choses commenceront*, 45–46; Girard and Müller, "Interview," 9, 11; Francis Fukuyama, *Our Posthuman Future: Consequences of the Biotechnology Revolution* (New York: Farrar, Straus and Giroux, 2002), 45.

331. Assmann, ed., *René Girard*, 48.

332. Palaver, *Die mythischen Quellen des Politischen*, 54–55.

333. Girard, *Deceit, Desire and the Novel*, 4–5. See Girard, *Things Hidden*, 320; *Battling to the End*, 30–31; Hamerton-Kelly, *Sacred Violence*, 19; James Alison, *Raising Abel: The Recovery of the Eschatological Imagination* (New York: Crossroad Publishing Co., 1996), 186.

334. Alexandre Kojève, *Introduction à la lecture de Hegel: Leçons sur la phénoménologie de l'esprit. Professées de 1933 à 1939 à l'École des Hautes-Études réunies et publiées Raymond Queneau* (Paris: Gallimard, 1947), 266.

335. Hegel, *Phenomenology of Spirit*, 263–409 (ch. 6: "Spirit"); Kojève, *Introduction to the Reading of Hegel*, 70; Kojève, "Hegel, Marx, and Christianity," *Interpretation: A Journal of Political Philosophy* 1, no. 1 (1970): 39.

336. Kojève, "Hegel, Marx, and Christianity," 39.

337. Hegel, *Phenomenology of Spirit*, 158–160; Kojève, *Introduction to the Reading of Hegel*, 55–57, 258, 335; Kojève, *Introduction à la lecture de Hegel*, 66–73.

338. Strauss and Kojève, *On Tyranny*, 255. See Meyer, *Ende*, 185.

339. See Meyer, *Ende der Geschichte?*, 81.

340. Dostoyevsky, *Demons*, 232–239 (II.I.VI); *Brothers Karamazov*, 634–650 (IV.XI.IX).

341. Kojève, *Introduction to the Reading of Hegel*, 241, 257, 265.

342. Kojève, *Introduction to the Reading of Hegel*, 248; Kojève, *Hegel, Marx, and Christianity*, 28. See Dostoyevsky, *Demons*, 620–623 (III.VI.II).

343. Kojève, *Introduction à la lecture de Hegel*, 66; Kojève, *Introduction to the Reading of Hegel*, 54.

344. Dostoyevsky, *Brothers Karamazov*, 257–258 (II.V.V.).

345. See Meyer, *Ende der Geschichte?*, 83–84.

346. Girard, *Resurrection from the Underground*, 90.

347. Girard, *Deceit, Desire and the Novel*, 274–279; *Resurrection from the Underground*, 104–105.

348. See Girard, *Deceit, Desire and the Novel*, 112, 158, 182; *To Double Business Bound*, 3.

349. Girard, *Violence and the Sacred*, 143–168; *Things Hidden*, 283–298.

350. See Girard, *Things Hidden*, 8–9; *To Double Business Bound*, 201; *The Girard Reader*, 10.

351. Frans de Waal, *Good Natured: The Origins of Right and Wrong in Humans and Other Animals* (Cambridge, MA: Harvard University Press, 2003), 71–72.

352. De Waal, *Good Natured*, 71.

353. See Livingston, "Girard and the Origin of Culture," in *Understanding Origins: Contemporary Views on the Origin of Life, Mind and Society*, ed. Jean-Pierre Dupuy and Francisco J. Varela (Dordrecht: Kluwer Academic Publishers, 1992), 98–101; Lee Alan Dugatkin, The Imitation Factor: Evolution beyond the Gene (New York: The Free Press, 2000).

354. See Girard, *To Double Business Bound*, 203; Girard and Müller, "Interview," 11.

355. Girard, *Things Hidden*, 295.

356. Girard, *To Double Business Bound*, 89.

357. Goethe, *The Sorrows of Young Werther*, 124.

358. Cervantes, *Don Quixote*, 142–151 (I, 21). See Girard, *Deceit, Desire and the Novel*, 239–240; *Things Hidden*, 16.

359. Stendhal, *On Love*, trans. Vyvyan Beresford Holland and C. K. Scott-Moncrieff (New York: Liveright Publishing Corporation, 1947), 6. See also 53–55; Girard, *Deceit, Desire and the Novel*, 19, 39, 41, 78–79, 87; *Mimesis and Theory*, 187–189.

360. Girard, *Things Hidden*, 283, 296–297.

361. See Girard, *Deceit, Desire and the Novel*, 83–95, 282–289, 294–295; *Things Hidden*, 296–297, 387; *The Girard Reader*, 290.

362. Karl Marx, *Capital: A Critique of Political Economy*, vol. 1, trans. Ben Fowkes (Harmondsworth, UK: Penguin, 1976), 163–164. See Andrew Feenberg, "Fetishism and Form: Erotic and Economic Disorder in Literature," in *Violence and Truth: On the Work of René Girard*, ed. Paul Dumouchel (Stanford, CA: Stanford University Press, 1988); Achterhuis, *Rijk van de Schaarste*, 218–219; Santa Ana, *Sacralizações*, 133; Michael J. Shapiro, *Reading the Postmodern Polity: Political Theory as Textual Practice* (Minneapolis: University of Minnesota Press, 1992), 54–67 ("Political Economy and Mimetic Desire in *Babette's Feast*"); Césáreo Bandera, *The Sacred Game: The Role of the Sacred in the Genesis of Modern Literary Fiction* (University Park: Pennsylvania State University Press, 1994), 264–267.

363. See Girard, *Deceit, Desire and the Novel*, 222–223.

364. Girard, *Things Hidden*, 295. See Dupuy, "Le signe," 41–42, 74–75.

365. Hobbes, *Leviathan*, 88 (ch. 13). See Wolfgang Palaver, *Politik und Religion bei Thomas Hobbes: Eine Kritik aus der Sicht der Theorie René Girards*, Innsbrucker Theologische Studien (Innsbruck: Tyrolia, 1991), 41; Fukuyama, *End of History*, 154–155.

366. Girard, *Things Hidden*, 16; *Theater of Envy*, 17.

367. Shakespeare, *Hamlet*, IV, iv, 18–19.

368. Shakespeare, *Hamlet*, IV, iv, 47–56. See Girard, *Theater of Envy*, 277.

369. See Ekkehard Krippendorff, *Politik in Shakespeares Dramen: Historien, Römerdramen, Tragödien* (Frankfurt am Main: Suhrkamp, 1992), 380–381, 388–389.

370. See Girard, *Things Hidden*, 334.

371. See Girard, *Things Hidden*, 304, 328–329.

372. Girard, *Things Hidden*, 330–331.

373. Girard, *Things Hidden*, 333.

374. See Girard, *Deceit, Desire and the Novel*, 7–8, 42, 81; *Resurrection from the Underground*, 117; *Violence and the Sacred*, 181, 182, 187–189; *Things Hidden*, 26, 266, 311, 321, 335, 348–349, 368, 390, 397, 416; *The Scapegoat*, 130, 132, 135, 172, 194; *Job*, 50, 86, 93; *Theater of Envy*, 346; *The Girard Reader*, 291–292.

375. Franz Kafka, "Before the Law," in *The Metamorphosis, In the Penal Colony, and Other Stories*, trans. Joachim Neugroschel (New York: Scribner Paperback Fiction, 2000), 249–251. See also Kafka, *The Trial*, trans. Willa and Edwin Muir (New York: Schocken Books, 1995), 213–220; Girard, *Deceit, Desire and the Novel*, 7–8; *Violence and the Sacred*, 189; Bruce Bassoff, "The Model as Obstacle: Kafka's 'The Trial,'" in *To Honor René Girard: Presented on the Occasion of his Sixtieth Birthday by Colleagues, Students, and Friends*, ed. Alphonse Juilland (Saratoga, CA: Anma Libri, 1986).

376. Girard, *Violence and the Sacred*, 181–182; *Things Hidden*, 290–294, 295, 304, 311, 329, 335, 362; *To Double Business Bound*, 96. See Freud, *The Ego and the Id*, in *The Freud Reader*, 646–647; Freud, *Group Psychology and the Analysis of the Ego*, trans. James Strachey (New York: Norton, 1975), 46–47; Gregory Bateson, *Steps to an Ecology of Mind: Collected Essays in Anthropology, Psychiatry, Evolution, and Epistemology* (San Francisco: Chandler Publishing Co., 1972), 201–227 ("Toward a Theory of Schizophrenia"), 244–378 ("Minimal Requirements for a Theory of Schizophrenia"), 271–278 ("Double Bind, 1969"); Simon Simonse, "Mimesis, Schismogenesis, and Catastrophe Theory: Gregory Bateson as a Forerunner of Mimetic Theory: With a Demonstration of His Theory on Nilotic Regicide," *Synthesis: An Interdisciplinary Journal* 1, no. 1 (1995): 147–172.

377. Girard, *Deceit, Desire and the Novel*, 99.

378. Goethe, *The Sorrows of Young Werther*, 47.

379. See Girard, *Deceit, Desire and the Novel*, 15, 101, 107; Jean-Pierre Dupuy, "Self-Reference in Literature," *Poetics* 18 (1989): 506.

380. Stendhal, *The Red and the Black*, 15–16 (ch. 3).

381. Stendhal, *The Red and the Black*, 18 (ch. 4).

382. Stendhal, *The Red and the Black*, 23 (ch. 5).

383. See Girard, *Deceit, Desire and the Novel*, 172; Dupuy, "Self-Reference," 506.

384. See Girard, *Things Hidden*, 35, 299–305, 416; *Theater of Envy*, 49, 66–67, 146, 340; *The Girard Reader*, 291; Oughourlian, *Puppet*, 15, 17. See Alison, *Joy of Being Wrong*, 27–33.

385. See Girard, *I See Satan*, 22.

386. See Girard, *Violence and the Sacred*, 148.

387. The translation found in *Things Hidden* for this concept, "conflictual mimesis," has been changed here to correspond more closely to the French original, "mimésis de l'antagoniste," and to avoid potential ambiguity. The term "conflictual mimesis" also appears in *Violence and the Sacred* (187), but in this case the French original is "mimésis conflictuelle." (Translator's note)

388. Charles Baudelaire, "Cake." In *Paris Spleen: Little Poems in Prose*, trans. Keith Waldrop (Middletown, CT: Wesleyan University Press, 2009), 29–30. See Girard and Palaver, *Gewalt und Religion*, 52.

389. Girard, *Deceit, Desire and the Novel*, 99–100, 105–106; *Violence and the Sacred*, 159.

390. Proust, *Within a Budding Grove*, 304–305. See Girard, *Deceit, Desire and the Novel*, 100; *Things Hidden*, 301; Dupuy, "Le signe," 52.

391. See Girard, *Things Hidden*, 320–321.

392. Girard, *Deceit, Desire and the Novel*, 287; *Things Hidden*, 415.

393. See Girard, *To Double Business Bound*, 201.

394. Dostoyevsky, *Brothers Karamazov*, 642, 648 (IV.XI.IX). See Goethe, *Faust*, 36 (I.1334–1344).

Chapter 4. The Scapegoat Mechanism as Origin of Culture

1. See Girard, *Deceit, Desire and the Novel*, 99.

2. Girard, *To Double Business Bound*, 136–154; *I See Satan*, 52.

3. See Girard, *Violence and the Sacred*, 31; *To Double Business Bound*, 137–138; *The Scapegoat*, 12–14, 43–44; *Theater of Envy*, 161.

4. Heinsohn, *Erschaffung*, 51–52, 78–82, 92–93.

5. See Girard, *Quand ces choses commenceront*, 38–48.

6. See Girard, *Violence and the Sacred*, 39–67.

7. See Girard, *Theater of Envy*, 6, 160–199.

8. Sophocles, *Oedipus the King*, in *The Three Theban Plays*, trans. Robert Fagles (New York: Penguin Books, 1984), 160 (22–30).

9. See Girard, *Oedipus Unbound*, 52, 73, 75, 85–89, 96–102; *Violence and the Sacred*, 76–78; *To Double Business Bound*, 137–138.

10. Sophocles, *Oedipus the King*, 164 (100–101).

11. Hobbes, *Leviathan*, 89 (ch. 13).

12. Heinrich von Kleist, "The Earthquake in Chile," in *Six German Romantic Tales*, trans. Ronald Taylor (London: Angel Books, 1985), 56–69. See Girard, "Mythos."

13. Kleist, "The Earthquake in Chile," 57–58.

14. Kleist, "The Earthquake in Chile," 64.

15. Kleist, "The Earthquake in Chile," 63.

16. Dostoyevsky, *Crime and Punishment*, trans. Jessie Senior Coulson (Oxford: Oxford University Press, 1998), 523–524. See Girard, *Deceit, Desire and the Novel*, 281; *To Double Business Bound*, 138–140.

17. Theodor Storm, *The Dykemaster*, trans. Denis Jackson (London: Angel Books, 1996), 106. See Wolfgang Palaver, "Hauke Haien—Ein Sündenbock? Theodor Storms Schimmelreiter aus der Perspektive der Theorie René Girards," in *Religion—Literatur—Künste: Aspekte eines Vergleichs*, ed. Peter Tschuggnall (Anif/Salzburg: Verlag Ursula Müller-Speiser, 1998), 231.

18. See Girard, *Violence and the Sacred*, 49–50.

19. Shakespeare, *Troilus and Cressida*, I, iii, 101–134. See Girard, *Violence and the Sacred*, 50–51; *To Double Business Bound*, 140–143; *Theater of Envy*, 160–166.

20. Shakespeare, *Troilus and Cressida*, I, iii, 85–101.

21. See Girard, *Violence and the Sacred*, 56–58, 61–64; Matthew Schoffeleers, "Twins and Unilateral Figures in Central and Southern Africa: Symmetry and Asymmetry in the Symbolization of the Sacred," *Journal of Religion in Africa* 21, no. 4 (1991), 345–372.

22. See Girard, *Violence and the Sacred*, 45–46; *Oedipus Unbound*, 36, 46–50, 55, 57, 59, 73, 80–81, 87, 90; Hölderlin, *Sämtliche Werke Bd. II*, 309–316 ("Anmerkungen zum Oedipus"), 369–376 ("Anmerkungen zur Antigonä").

23. See Girard, *Theater of Envy*, 50–56; "Myth and Ritual"; Anspach, ed., *René Girard*, 200–201.

24. Shakespeare, *A Midsummer Night's Dream*, II, ii, 94–99.

25. Shakespeare, *A Midsummer Night's Dream*, II, i, 203–210.

26. Shakespeare, *A Midsummer Night's Dream*, III, ii, 226.

27. Shakespeare, *A Midsummer Night's Dream*, II, I, 230–233.

28. See Girard, *Violence and the Sacred*, 161; *Things Hidden*, 300–303.

29. Girard, *Violence and the Sacred*, 160.

30. Shakespeare, *A Midsummer Night's Dream*, IV, i, 190–193.

31. Girard, *Violence and the Sacred*, 164–166; *Things Hidden*, 35.

32. Girard, *Violence and the Sacred*, 166–168; *Things Hidden*, 35; *Theater of Envy*, 61–62.

33. See Palaver, *Politik*, 47–58; Girard, *Theater of Envy*, 227–229; *I See Satan*, 8–9; "Victims," 132.

34. Emile Durkheim, *The Elementary Forms of the Religious Life*, trans. J. W. Swain (New York: The Free Press, 1965), 258–259; see also 241, 249–250, 269; Girard, *To Double Business Bound*, 163; *Quand ces choses commenceront*, 47; "Disorder and Order in Mythology," paper presented at the Stanford International Symposium (Saratoga, CA: Anma Libri, 1981), 86.

35. Girard, *Things Hidden*, 26–27; *Theater of Envy*, 186.

36. See Girard, *Things Hidden*, 33, 130–134; *To Double Business Bound*, xiii; *The Scapegoat*, 40; *Violent Origins*, 73–78; *I See Satan*, 154–160.

37. See Girard, *I See Satan*, 28.

38. See Girard, *Violence and the Sacred*, 21, 118, 136, 232, 237, 259, 310–311, 317; *Things Hidden*, 33, 34–35, 164, 443; *The Scapegoat*, 55–56; *The Girard Reader*, 70; *Evolution and Conversion*, 81–88.

39. See Girard, *Deceit, Desire and the Novel*, 249; *Violence and the Sacred*, 92, 116–118, 136, 146, 176–183, 189, 209, 310–311; *To Double Business Bound*, 218; *Things Hidden*, 34, 356, 359; *The Scapegoat*, 142, 172; *Theater of Envy*, 18, 312; René Girard and Thomas F. Bertonneau, "The Logic of the Undecidable: An Interview," *Paroles Gelées*, no. 5 (1987): 18–19; Girard, Benvenuto, and Meloni, "Psychoanalysis," 13; Oughourlian, *Puppet of Desire*, 18–19.

40. See Acts 3:17; Girard, *The Scapegoat*, 110–111; *I See Satan*, 40, 148, 190.

41. See Girard, *Things Hidden*, 78, 100; Girard and Palaver, *Gewalt und Religion*.

42. Girard, *Things Hidden*, 35.

43. Adolf Ellegard Jensen, *Myth and Cult among Primitive Peoples*, trans. Marianna Tax Choldin and Wolfgang Weissleder (Chicago: University of Chicago Press, 1963), 95.

44. See Girard, *Violence and the Sacred*, 85–88, 265–266; *Things Hidden*, 23–47, 178, 218, 227, 233–234; *To Double Business Bound*, 142; *The Scapegoat*, 166, 196; *Job*, 111, 120; *Theater of Envy*, 341; *The Girard Reader*, 202–203; *I See Satan*, 45, 69, 96–98, 99–100, 130–131; René Girard, "Is There Anti-Semitism in the Gospels?" *Biblical Interpretation*, no. 3 (1993): 350. See also Durkheim, *The Elementary Forms*, 253, 261.

45. See Durkheim, *The Elementary Forms*, 455–461.

46. For tremendum and fascination, see Rudolf Otto, *The Idea of the Holy*, tr. John W. Harvey (London: Oxford University Press, 1923), 12–24, 31–40.

47. See Girard, *Things Hidden*, 19–23; *The Scapegoat*, 139–140; *Job*, 91–108.

48. See Chilton, *Temple of Jesus*, 23; Markwart Herzog, "Religionstheorie und Theologie René Girards," *Kerygma und Dogma* 38, no. 2 (1992): 129.

49. See Girard, *Things Hidden*, 215; *The Girard Reader*, 275.

50. See Girard, *Oedipus Unbound*; *Violence and the Sacred*, 68–88; Golsan, *René Girard*, 39–43.

51. Sophocles, *Oedipus the King*, 178 (346–349).

52. Sophocles, *Oedipus the King*, 179 (350–353).

53. Sophocles, *Oedipus the King*, 195 (628).

54. Sophocles, *Oedipus the King*, 244 (1410–1412).

55. See Girard, *The Scapegoat*, 122–123; *Job*, 39–40; Sandor Goodhart, *Sacrificing Commentary: Reading the End of Literature* (Baltimore: Johns Hopkins University Press, 1996), 13–41 ("Oedipus and Laius's Many Murderers").

56. Kleist, "Earthquake in Chile," 63. See Girard, "Mythos und Gegenmythos: Zu Kleist 'Das Erdbeben in Chile,'" in *Positionen der Literaturwissenschaft: Acht Modellanalysen am Beispiel von Kleists "Das Erdbeben in Chile,"* ed. David E. Wellbery (Munich: Verlag C.H. Beck, 2001), 141.

57. Girard, "Mythos," 142–143; *Violence and the Sacred*, 243; *Things Hidden*, 39, 114. See Alison, *Joy of Being Wrong*, 250–251; Lévi-Strauss, *The Raw and the Cooked*, 51.

58. Kleist, "The Earthquake in Chile," 62. See Girard, "Mythos," 145.

59. Kleist, "The Earthquake in Chile," 69–70.

60. Dostoyevsky, *Crime and Punishment*, 524. See Girard, *To Double Business Bound*, 144.

61. See Palaver, "Haien."

62. Storm, *Dykemaster*, 115.

63. Livy, *Books 1–2*, Loeb Classical Library, vol. 1, trans. B. O. Foster (Cambridge, MA: Harvard University Press, 1919), 59 (I.XVI). See Girard, *The Scapegoat*, 89.

64. Plutarch, *Lives in Eleven Volumes*, Loeb Classical Library, vol. 1, trans. Bernadotte Perrin (Cambridge, MA: Harvard University Press, 1967), 175 (XXVII: Romulus). See Girard, *The Scapegoat*, 89.

65. See René Girard and Giuseppe Fornari, *La vittima e la folla: Violenza del mito e cristianesimo* (Santi Quaranta: Treviso, 1998), 97–103; Girard, *I See Satan*, 49–81; Girard, "Stone"; Wolfgang Stegemann, "Der Tod Jesu als Opfer? Anthropologische Aspekte seiner Deutung im Neuen Testament," in *Abschied von der Schuld? Zur Anthropologie und Theologie von Schuldbekenntnis, Opfer und Versöhnung*, ed. Richard Riess (Stuttgart: Verlag W. Kohlhammer, 1996), 134–136.

66. Philostratus, *The Life of Apollonius of Tyana*, Loeb Classical Library, vol. 1, trans. Christopher Jones (Cambridge, MA: Harvard University Press, 2005), 339–341 (IV.X).

67. See Girard, *Things Hidden*, 83, 171–173; *Quand ces choses commenceront*, 179–186; Girard and Fornari, *La vittima e la folla*, 95–131.

68. William Golding, *Lord of the Flies* (New York: Coward-McCann, 1962), 20–21.

69. Golding, *Lord of the Flies*, 178.

70. Golding, *Lord of the Flies*, 181.

71. Golding, *Lord of the Flies*, 182.

72. See Achterhuis, *Rijk van de Schaarste*, 51–52; Mark Anspach, "The Making of a Meta-God: Sacrifice and Self-Transcendence in Vedic Mythology," *Paragrana: Internationale Zeitschrift für Historische Anthropologie* 4, no. 2 (1995): 117–118; Gil Bailie, *Violence Unveiled: Humanity at the Crossroads* (New York: Crossroad, 1995), 64–66.

73. See Girard, *Violence and the Sacred*, 193–222; *Quand ces choses commenceront*, 157–160; S. Freud, *Totem and Taboo*, 176; Maurizio Meloni, "A Triangle of Thoughts: Girard, Freud, Lacan," *Journal of European Psychoanalysis*, no. 14 (2002): 38–42.

74. Girard, *Violence and the Sacred*, 217–218. See *De la violence à la divinité*, 587–590; *Things Hidden*, 24–25, 65, 96–97, 124; *To Double Business Bound*, 163; *The Scapegoat*, 88, 178; *The Girard Reader*, 260–261.

75. Girard, *Violence and the Sacred*, 197; *Things Hidden*, 25; *Violent Origins*, 121, 247–249.

76. Jensen, *Die Getötete Gottheit: Weltbild Einer Frühen Kultur* (Stuttgart: Kohlhammer, 1966). See also Jensen, *Myth and Cult*, 162–189; Girard, *Violence and the Sacred*, 91–92; Theodor Ahrens et al., "Religion und Gewalt: Ein Seminarbericht," in *Zwischen Regionalität und Globalisierung: Studien zu Mission, Ökumene und Religion* (Ammersbek bei Hamburg: Verlag an der Lottbek, 1997), 375–376, 408.

77. Jensen, *Gottheit*, 125. See also 34, 92.

78. Arthur Maurice Hocart, *The Life-Giving Myth, and Other Essays* (London: Methuen, 1952); Hocart, *Social Origins* (London: Watts, 1954); Hocart, *Kings and Councillors: An Essay in the Comparative Anatomy of Human Society* (Chicago: University of Chicago Press, 1970).

79. Lucien Scubla, "Réciprocité rituelle et subordination politique," in *Logiques de la réciprocité* (Paris: Centre de recherche en épistemologie appliquée, 1985), 119–273.

80. See Wolfgang Palaver, "Violence and Religion: Walter Burkert and René Girard in Comparison," *Contagion: Journal of Violence, Mimesis, and Culture* 17 (2010): 121–137.

81. Burkert, *Homo Necans*, 2–3.

82. Burkert, *Homo Necans*, 10–13.

83. Mircea Eliade, *Patterns in Comparative Religion*, trans. R. Sheed (Lincoln: University of Nebraska Press, 1996), 359.

84. Mircea Eliade, *Patterns*, 399–400.

85. Mircea Eliade, *A History of Religious Ideas*, vol. 1, *From the Stone Age to the Eleusinian Mysteries*, trans. W. R. Trask (Chicago: University of Chicago Press, 1978), 72.

86. See Girard, *I See Satan*, 83, 86.

87. Girard, *Violence and the Sacred*, 213, 259, 298; *Violent Origins*, 125; *Theater of Envy*, 228; *Quand ces choses commenceront*, 40, 46–47; *I See Satan*, 93; "Victims," 133; René Girard and Mark Anspach, "Mark: A Response: Reflections from the Perspective of Mimetic Theory," in *Violence and the Sacred in the Modern World*, ed. M. Juergensmeyer (London: Routledge, 1992), 147.

88. Girard, *Violence and the Sacred*, 306–308; *Things Hidden*, 65, 70, 82; *To Double Business Bound*, 162–163; *Quand ces choses commenceront*, 46–47; *I See Satan*, 99–100. See Tyler E. Graham, "The Danger of Durkheim: Ambiguity in the Theory of Social Effervescence," *Religion* 37, no. 1 (2007): 26–38.

89. Jacob Burckhardt, *Über das Studium der Geschichte* (Munich: Verlag C.H. Beck, 1982), 175–176, 256–257, 309, 401; Peter von Matt, *Die tintenblauen Eidgenossen: Über die literarische und politische Schweiz* (Munich: Hanser, 2001), 96–103.

90. Jacob Burckhardt, *Reflections on History*, trans. Marie Donald Hottinger (London: G. Allen & Unwin, Ltd., 1943), 34. See Burckhardt, *Über das Studium der Geschichte*, 175.

91. See Palaver, *Politik*, 61–83; Girard and Anspach, "Mark: A Response," 147; Robert Hamerton-Kelly, "Popular Sovereignty and the Sacred: A Mimetic Reading of Rousseau's Doctrine of the General Will," *Paragrana: Internationale Zeitschrift für Historische Anthropologie* 4, no. 2 (1995): 215–244.

92. Hobbes, *Leviathan*, 99 (ch. 14).

93. Hobbes, *Leviathan*, 99 (ch. 14).

94. Livy, 85 (I.XXIV).

95. Burkert, *Homo Necans*, 35.

96. See Emile Durkheim, *Professional Ethics and Civic Morals*, trans. C. Brookfield (London: Routledge, 1992), 175–176, 182–183, 186.

97. Rousseau, *Social Contract*, 207 (II.4).

98. Rousseau, *Social Contract*, 213–217 (II.7), 298–308 (IV.8).

99. Rousseau, *The Plan for Perpetual Peace, On the Government of Poland, and Other Writings on History and Politics*, trans. C. Kelly and J. Bush (Hanover, NH: Dartmouth College Press, 2005), 158–159. See Paolo Prodi, *Das Sakrament der Herrschaft: Der politische Eid in der*

Verfassungsgeschichte des Okzidents, trans. Judith Elze (Berlin: Duncker & Humblot, 1997), 395–399.

100. See Louis Dumont, *Essays on Individualism: Modern Ideology in Anthropological Perspective* (Chicago: University of Chicago Press, 1986), 103.

101. Rousseau, *Social Contract*, 203 (11.3). See Rousseau, *Emile*, 39–40.

102. Hannah Arendt, *On Revolution* (Harmondsworth: Penguin Books, 1990), 77. See Schmitt, *Concept of the Political*, 29; Palaver, *Quellen*, 44–45.

103. See Girard, *Violence and the Sacred*, 306–308; *Things Hidden*, 102; Schwager, *Scapegoats*, 28–29.

104. Girard, *Things Hidden*, 38, 146, 159, 161; *The Girard Reader*, 203; *I See Satan*, 83–85.

105. Girard, *Violence and the Sacred*, 94, 306; *The Girard Reader*, 274; *I See Satan*, 82; *Sacrifice*, 36–47; Girard and Müller, "Interview," 11.

106. *Rgveda Samhita*, trans. Svami Satya Prakash Saravasvati and Satyakam Vidyalankar, vol. XIII (New Delhi: Veda Pratishthana, 1987), 4487 (book 10, hymn 90, lines 9–14).

107. Heraclitus, *Fragments*, 37 (B 53). See Girard, *Violence and the Sacred*, 88.

108. See Durkheim, *The Elementary Forms*, 23–25, 488–491; *Professional Ethics*, 149–158, 161–163.

109. Mircea Eliade, *The Sacred and the Profane: The Nature of Religion*, trans. W. R. Trask (San Diego: Harcourt, 1998), 20–65; *Patterns in Comparative Religion*, trans. R. Sheed (Lincoln: University of Nebraska Press, 1996), 367–387.

110. Mircea Eliade, *The Sacred and the Profane*, 54–58.

111. See Paul Piccone, "The Crisis of Liberalism and the Emergence of Federal Populism," *Telos*, no. 89 (1991): 7–44; Massimo Cacciari, *Gewalt und Harmonie: Geo-Philosophie Europas*, trans. Günter Memmert (Munich: Carl Hanser Verlag, 1995); Gary Ulmen, "Toward a New World Order: Introduction to Carl Schmitt's 'The Land Appropriation of a New World,'" *Telos*, no. 109 (1997): 3–27.

112. Schmitt, *Nomos of the Earth*, 42–55.

113. See Wolfgang Palaver, "Carl Schmitt on Nomos and Space," *Telos*, no. 106 (1996): 105–127; Palaver, "Globalisierung und Opfer: Carl Schmitts Lehre vom Nomos," in *Das Opfer—Aktuelle Kontroversen: Religions-politischer Diskurs im Kontext der mimetischen Theorie. Deutsch-Italienische Fachtagung der Guardini Stiftung in der Villa Vigoni 18.-22. Oktober 1999*, ed. Bernhard Dieckmann (Münster: LIT, 2001).

114. Schmitt, *Nomos of the Earth*, 74. See also 73.

115. Hannah Arendt, *The Human Condition* (Chicago: University of Chicago Press, 1998), 63–64. See Arendt, *On Revolution*, 12, 186–187, 275, 281.

116. Arendt, *Human Condition*, 64.

117. See Wolfgang Palaver, "Foundational Violence and Hannah Arendt's Political Philosophy," *Paragrana: Internationale Zeitschrift für Historische Anthropologie* 4, no. 2 (1995): 166–76.

118. See Kurt Klusemann, *Das Bauopfer: Eine ethnographisch-prähistorische-linguistische Studie* (Graz: Selbstverlag der Verfassers, 1919); Durkheim, *Professional Ethics*, 149–158; Jensen, *Myth and Cult*, 169, 173; Burkert, *Homo Necans*, 39.

119. See also *Things Hidden*, 163–167; *I See Satan*, 91–92.

120. Klusemann, *Bauopfer*, 5.

121. See Armin Ehrenzweig, "Kain und Lamech," *Zeitschrift für die Alttestamentliche Wissenschaft* 35 (1915): 1.

122. See Klusemann, *Bauopfer*, 8.

123. Heinrich Harrer, *Geister und Dämonen: Magische Abenteure in fernen Ländern* (Frankfurt am Main: Ullstein, 1969), 196–197.

124. Patrick Tierney, *The Highest Altar: The Story of Human Sacrifice* (New York: Viking, 1989), 203. See also 367.

125. *Tiroler Tageszeitung* (31 October/1 November 1987), 21.

126. See Palaver, "Haien," 224, 227–229.

127. Storm, *Dykemaster*, 88–89.

128. Storm, *Dykemaster*, 63.

129. Storm, *Dykemaster*, 116.

130. Thomas Mann, *Joseph and His Brothers*, trans. H. T. Lowe-Porter (New York: Alfred A. Knopf, 1948), 155, 184.

131. See Mann, *Joseph and His Brothers*, 215–216; Thomas Mann, *Essays*, Bd. 5: *Deutschland und die Deutschen 1938–1945* (Frankfurt am Main: Fischer Taschenbuch Verlag, 1996), 199.

132. See Girard, *Things Hidden*, 105.

133. Girard, *The Scapegoat*, 26–27, 33–35.

134. Burckhardt, *Reflections on History*, 34. See also *Studium der Geschichte*, 257.

135. Von Matt, *Eidgenossen*, 100.

136. See Lévi-Strauss, *Savage Mind*.

137. See Girard, *Things Hidden*, 105–125; *To Double Business Bound*, 178–198 ("Violence and Representation in the Mythical Text"); *Violent Origins*, 95, 100–105, 132f; Golsan, *René Girard*, 69–78.

138. Lévi-Strauss, *Totemism*, 19.

139. Lévi-Strauss, *Totemism*, 25–26.

140. Lévi-Strauss, *Totemism*, 26; *The Raw and the Cooked*, 52.

141. Lévi-Strauss, *Totemism*, 27.

142. Lévi-Strauss, *Naked Man*, 793. See also 667–684.

143. See Girard, *Things Hidden*, 28–29, 38, 60; *To Double Business Bound*, 155–177 ("Differentiation and Reciprocity in Lévi-Strauss and Contemporary Theory"); *The Girard Reader*, 225; Girard, "From Ritual to Science," *Configurations*, no. 8 (2000): 172–173; Girard and Benvenuto, "Psychoanalysis," 13–14, 21–22.

144. Girard, *The Scapegoat*, 54–56.

145. Lucien Scubla, *Lire Lévi-Strauss: Le déploiement d'une intuition* (Paris: Éditions Odile Jacob, 1998).

146. Peter Hassler, *Menschenopfer bei den Azteken? Eine quellen- und ideologiekritische Studie* (Bern: Peter Lang Verlag, 1992); Hassler, "Die Lüge des Hernán Cortés," In *Die Zeit* no. 38 (18 September 1992): 20 (international edition).

147. See Girard, *The Scapegoat*, 63; *Quand ces choses commenceront*, 97.

148. Hassler, "Lüge."

149. Hassler, *Menschenopfer*, 241.

150. Hassler, *Menschenopfer*, 172. See Gilberto Da Silva, *Am Anfang war das Opfer: René Girard aus Afroindiolateinamerikanischer Perspektive* (Münster: LIT, 2001), 92–98; Girard, *The Scapegoat*, 57–65.

151. Hassler, *Menschenopfer*, 170.

152. See Hassler, *Menschenopfer*, 223–227.

153. See Williams, *The Bible, Violence, and the Sacred*, 21–24.

154. See Girard, *I See Satan*, 64.

155. See Girard, *Violent Origins*, 191–235.

156. See Girard, *Things Hidden*, 105–138; *The Scapegoat*, 1–99; *To Double Business Bound*, 178–198; *Violent Origins*, 73–105; *The Girard Reader*, 118–141; Golsan, *René Girard*, 61–84.

157. Quoted in Girard, *The Scapegoat*, 2.

158. See Girard, *The Scapegoat*, 17–21; *I See Satan*, 26, 73.

159. Girard, *The Scapegoat*, 25.

160. See Girard, *The Scapegoat*, 76–95; *Theater of Envy*, 216; *The Girard Reader*, 219.

161. See Freud, *Studienausgabe*, Bd. 9: 493 ("Der Mann Moses und die monotheistische Religion").

162. See Girard, *Things Hidden*, 100, 247; *The Scapegoat*, 160, 162, 200; *Job*, 38, 161, 165; *Quand ces choses commenceront*, 15; Hamerton-Kelly, *Sacred Violence*, 16; Golsan, *René Girard*, 68.

163. Girard, *The Scapegoat*, 57–65; See Georges Bataille, *The Accursed Share: An Essay on General Economy*, vol. 1, *Consumption*, trans. R. Hurley (New York: Zone Books, 1988), 47–49.

164. See Girard, *Violence and the Sacred*, 70, 105, 126, 128–129, 134, 135–136, 255, 291–292; *Things Hidden*, 151–152; *The Scapegoat*, 61, 64; *Job*, 58; *Theater of Envy*, 222; *Quand ces choses commenceront*, 199; "Myth and Ritual," 205.

165. See Girard, *Things Hidden*, 25; *Job*, 45.

Chapter 5. Biblical Revelation and Christianity

1. See Girard, *Things Hidden*, 139–280 (book 2, "The Judaeo-Christian Scriptures"); *The Scapegoat*, 100–212; *Job*; Raymund Schwager, *Scapegoats*, 43–227; Williams, *Bible*; Golsan, *Girard*, 85–105; Hamerton-Kelly, *Sacred Violence*; *Gospel*.

2. See René Girard, *Je vois Satan tomber comme l'éclair* (Paris: Bernard Grasset, 1999), 10–12.

3. See Paul Wendland, "Jesus als Saturnalien-Koenig," *Hermes: Zeitschrift für Klassische Philologie* 33, no. 1 (1898): 175–179.

4. James George Frazer, *The Golden Bough: A Study in Magic and Religion*, part 6, *The Scapegoat*

(London: MacMillan Press, Ltd., 1913), 413–414. See also 412–423 ("The Crucifixion of Christ"); also quoted in Girard, *Things Hidden*, 168.

5. See Girard and Bertonneau, "Logic," 9; Girard and Golsan, "Interview," 130; Assmann, ed., *René Girard*, 50.

6. See Girard, *I See Satan*, 172–173; *The Girard Reader*, 243–261; *Quand ces choses commenceront*, 197–198; *Battling to the End*, 125, 129–130; "Founding Murder"; Girard and Vattimo, *Weakening Faith*, 67–68. Tobin Siebers, *The Ethics of Criticism* (Ithaca, NY: Cornell University Press, 1988), 124–158.

7. Friedrich Nietzsche, *The Will to Power*, trans. Walter Kaufmann and R. J. Hollingdale (New York: Random House, 1967), 543.

8. Girard and Jakob, "Gespräch," 175.

9. Nietzsche, *Will to Power*, 141–142. See Nietzsche, *Sämtliche Werke*, vol. 13:218–220 (Nachgelassene Fragmente, Frühjahr 1888 14[5]). See Girard, *Quand ces choses commenceront*, 18–19; *I See Satan*, 174; "Founding Murder," 244; Max Weber, *Ancient Judaism*, trans. Hans H. Gerth and Don Martindale (Glencoe, IL: Free Press, 1952).

10. See Girard, *The Scapegoat*, 148; *Quand ces choses commenceront*, 198.

11. Weber, *Ancient Judaism*, 5, 145, 233, 374–375, 379.

12. Weber, *Ancient Judaism*, 374.

13. Weber, *Ancient Judaism*, 375.

14. Weber, *Ancient Judaism*, 375.

15. Weber, *Ancient Judaism*, 3–5, 47, 255–260, 369–371, 376, 379, 382, 423–424. See Weber, *Economy and Society: An Outline of Interpretive Sociology*, vol. 3, trans. Ephraim Fischoff (New York: Bedminster Press, 1968), 299–304.

16. Girard, *Things Hidden*, 147; *To Double Business Bound*, 226; *Theater of Envy*, 281; *I See Satan*, 148.

17. See Paul Duff and Joseph Hallman, "Murder in the Garden? The Envy of the Gods in Genesis 2 and 3," *Contagion: Journal of Violence, Mimesis, and Culture* 3 (1996), 197; Alison, *Joy of Being Wrong*, 246–247.

18. See Girard, *Violence and the Sacred*, 218–222; *The Scapegoat*, 178; "Disorder," 80–82.

19. See Alison, *Raising Abel*, 44; Rüdiger Safranski, *Das Böse oder Das Drama der Freiheit* (Munich: Carl Hanser Verlag, 1997), 23.

20. See Girard, *Things Hidden*, 142; *To Double Business Bound*, 156, 186; Aidan Carl Mathews, "Knowledge of Good and Evil: The Work of René Girard," in *To Honor René Girard: Presented on the Occasion of His Sixtieth Birthday by Colleagues, Students, and Friends*, ed. Alphonse Juilland (Saratoga, CA: Anma Libri, 1986), 23–24; McKenna, *Violence and Difference: Girard, Derrida, and Deconstruction* (Urbana and Chicago: University of Illinois Press, 1992), 51–52.

21. See Alison, *Raising Abel*, 49–56; Alison, *Joy of Being Wrong*, 94–102.

22. Giuseppe Fornari, "Towards a Biblical Anthropology of Violence: Acquisitive Imitation and Violence in Original Sin," *Bulletin of the Colloquium on Violence & Religion*, no. 14 (1998).

23. See Girard, *Things Hidden*, 112; *Violent Origins*, 79–89, 94–95, 100–104, 112, 117–119, 129–132; Eliade, *Patterns*, 265–330; Jensen, *Myth and Cult*, 90–95.

24. See Girard, *The Scapegoat*, 107.

25. See Hamerton-Kelly, *Sacred Violence*, 95–96; Duff and Hallman, "Murder," 198; Schwager, *Banished from Eden: Original Sin and Evolutionary Theory in the Drama of Salvation*, trans. James G. Williams (Leominster: Gracewing, 2006), 90.

26. Girard, *Things Hidden*, 142, 275; Schwager, *Banished from Eden*, 89–90.

27. See Duff and Hallman, "Murder," 188–192.

28. See Norbert Lohfink, "Altes Testament—Die Entlarvung der Gewalt," in *Weltgestaltung und Gewaltlosigkeit*, ed. Norbert Lohfink and Rudolf Pesch (Düsseldorf: Patmos Verlag, 1978), 54–55; Lohfink, "Wie sollte Man das Alte Testament auf die Erbsünde hin befragen?," in *Zum Problem der Erbsünde: Theologische und philosophische Versuche*, ed. Norbert Lohfink, Alexander Sand, Georg Scherer, and Wilhelm Breuning (Essen: Ludgerus, 1981), 43–45.

29. See Schwager, *Scapegoats*, 63, 66, 72; Palaver, *Politik*, 161–164; Stuart Lasine, "Levite Violence, Fratricide, and Sacrifice in the Bible and Later Revolutionary Rhetoric," in *Curing Violence*, ed. Mark I. Wallace and Theophus H. Smith (Sonoma, CA: Polebridge Press, 1994), 214–219.

30. See Girard, *Violence and the Sacred*, 14; *Things Hidden*, 143, 239; *Quand ces choses commenceront*, 74–75; Lohfink, "Altes Testament—Die Entlarvung der Gewalt," 51–52; André Lascaris, "Opfere weder Isaak noch dich selbst," in *Isaak wird wieder geopfert: Die "Bindung Isaaks" als Symbol des Leidens Israels. Versuche einer Deutung*, ed. Willem Zuidema (Neukirchen-Vluyn: Neukirchener Verlag, 1987), 146–179; Peter Tschuggnall, *Das Abraham-Opfer als Glaubensparadox. Bibeltheologischer Befund—Literarische Rezeption—Kierkegaards Deutung* (Frankfurt am Main: Peter Lang, 1990), 13–58; Georg Baudler, *Töten oder Lieben: Gewalt und Gewaltlosigkeit in Religion und Christentum* (Munich: Kösel, 1994), 188–217; Micha Brumlik, "Die Aufhebung des Menschenopfers in der Isaak- und Iphigenieerzählung," in *Das Opfer: Religionsgeschichtliche, theologische und politische Aspekte*, ed. Dietrich Neuhaus (Frankfurt am Main: Haag + Herrchen Verlag, 1998).

31. Girard, *Things Hidden*, 275.

32. See Girard, *Theater of Envy*, 324–325; *Quand ces choses commenceront*, 54–55; *I See Satan*, 21; Schwager, *Scapegoats*, 74, 79, 178; Schwager, "Mimesis und Freiheit," *Zeitschrift für Katholische Theologie* 107 (1985): 367–368; Lohfink, "Entlarvung," 56; Oughourlian, *Puppet*, 21–27; Mathews, *Knowledge*, 25–26; Hamerton-Kelly, *Sacred Violence*, 91–97; Bailie, *Violence Unveiled*, 137; Alison, *Joy of Being Wrong*, 246.

33. Kierkegaard, *Concept of Anxiety*, 32; Hamerton-Kelly, *Sacred Violence*, 107; Alison, *Joy of Being Wrong*, 149.

34. Augustine, *On Genesis*, in *The Works of Saint Augustine*, part 1, vol. 13, trans. Edmund Hill (Brooklyn, NY: New City Press, 1990), 364 (8:14, 31), 360–366 (11:14, 18–11:15, 20). See Augustine, *Expositions of the Psalms, 51–72*, in *The Works of Saint Augustine*, part 3, vol. 17, trans. Maria Boulding (Hyde Park, NY: New City Press, 1999), 420–421 (Psalm 70: 6–7); Thomas Aquinas, *Summa Theologiae*, 149–163 (II–IIae).

35. See Schwager, *Scapegoats*, 68–69, 221; Lohfink, "Erbsünde," 37–39.

36. See Girard, *Theater of Envy*, 324–325; Mathews, *Knowledge*, 27; Hamerton-Kelly, *Sacred Violence*, 94–96; Schwager, *Banished from Eden*, 16; Bailie, *Violence Unveiled*, 138; Alison, *Joy of Being Wrong*, 133–134.

37. Safranski, *Böse*, 28–31.

122. Girard, *I See Satan*, 3.

123. Kant, *Religion*, 71.

124. Kant, *Religion*, 65.

125. Kant, *Religion*, 71. See Palaver, "Mimesis and Scapegoating in the Works of Hobbes, Rousseau and Kant," *Contagion: Journal of Violence, Mimesis, and Culture* 10 (2003): 144–146; Heinz Dieter Kittsteiner, *Listen der Vernunft: Motive geschichtsphilosophischen Denkens* (Frankfurt am Main: Fischer Taschenbuch Verlag, 1998), 73–84.

126. See Livingston, *Models*, 133–134.

127. Girard, *Things Hidden*, 215–223.

128. Girard, *Things Hidden*, 203–204; *I See Satan*, 186; *Celui par qui le scandale arrive*, 74; "Gospels," 30; Girard and Vattimo, *Weakening Faith*, 106.

129. Assmann, ed., *René Girard*, 74. See *The Girard Reader*, 286; Anspach, ed., *René Girard*, 123; Ludwig Ecker, *Zwischen Recht und Vergebung: Der Beitrag der Theorie René Girards zur Beschreibung christlicher Existenz* (Linz: Verlagsatelier Wagner, 1999), 105–106.

130. Girard, *Things Hidden*, 194, 231, 234–235; *The Scapegoat*, 162–163; *Theater of Envy*, 339–342; *Quand ces choses commenceront*, 137–138, 171; *The Girard Reader*, 286; *I See Satan*, 173; *Mimesis and Theory*, 272–273; *Celui par qui le scandale arrive*, 109–110; "Gospels," 31; René Girard, "Reconciliation, Violence and the Gospel," in *Film and Modernity: Violence, Sacrifice and Religion*, ed. G. Larcher, F. Grabner, and Ch. Wessely (Münster: Thaur, 1997), 218–221; Girard and Vattimo, *Weakening Faith*, 104–105; Józef Niewiadomski, "Transzendenz und Menschwerdung. Transformationskraft des Opfers im Fokus österlicher Augen," in *Das Opfer—Aktuelle Kontroversen: Religions-politischer Diskurs im Kontext der Mimetischen Theorie. Deutsch-Italienische Fachtagung der Guardini Stiftung in der Villa Vigoni 18.-22. Oktober 1999*, ed. Bernhard Dieckmann (Münster: LIT, 2001), 293–306.

131. See Girard, *I See Satan*, 190–191; *The Girard Reader*, 123; *Battling to the End*, 103, 112, 216; René Girard, "Violence Renounced: Response," in *Violence Renounced: René Girard Biblical Studies and Peacemaking*, ed. W. M. Swartley (Telford, PA: Pandora Press, 2000), 309; Anspach, ed., *René Girard*, 123; Girard, "Reconciliation," 216–221; Girard and Vattimo, *Weakening Faith*, 105.

132. See title cover: Józef Niewiadomski and Nikolaus Wandinger, eds. *Dramatische Theologie im Gespräch: Symposion/Gastmahl zum 65. Geburtstag von Raymund Schwager*. Beiträge zur Mimetischen Theorie (Münster: LIT, 2003).

133. See Girard, *Things Hidden*, 194; *The Scapegoat*, 198–212; *Job*, 154, 158, 164–165; *Quand ces choses commenceront*, 77–78; *The Girard Reader*, 201, 206–207; *I See Satan*, 189–190; *Celui par qui le scandale arrive*, 99–103; Girard and Vattimo, *Weakening Faith*, 105.

134. See Niewiadomski, "Konturen einer Theologie der Eucharistie," in *Faszinierendes Geheimnis: Neue Zugänge zur Eucharistie in Familie, Schule und Gemeinde*, ed. Matthias Scharer and Józef Niewiadomski (Innsbruck: Tyrolia-Verlag, 1999), 95–96.

135. Goethe, *West-Eastern Divan*, trans. J. Whaley (London: Wolff, 1974), 25–26 ("Blessed Longing"). See Girard, *I See Satan*, 82–83; Baudler, *Töten*, 56.

136. Hobbes, *Leviathan*, 91 (ch. 14). See Palaver, *Politik*, 124–126.

137. Hobbes, *Leviathan: Sive de Materia, Forma, et Potestate Civitatis Ecclesiasticae et Civilis*, Thomae Hobbes Malmesburiensis Opera Philosophica Quae Latine Scripsit Omnia in Unum Corpus (London: Bohn, 1841), 103.

138. John Rawls, *A Theory of Justice* (Cambridge, MA: Belknap Press, 2005), 3–4. See Jean-Pierre Dupuy, "The Self-Deconstruction of the Liberal Order," *Contagion: Journal of Violence, Mimesis, and Culture* 2 (1995): 10–14.

139. Jürgen Habermas, *Justification and Application: Remarks on Discourse Ethics*, trans. Ciaran Cronin (Cambridge, MA: MIT Press, 1993), 34 (translation corrected).

140. Jürgen Habermas, *The Postnational Constellation: Political Essays*, trans. Max Pensky (Cambridge, MA: MIT Press, 2001), 101. See Habermas, *Time of Transitions*, trans. Ciaran Cronin and Max Pensky (Cambridge: Polity, 2006), 166.

141. Dostoyevsky, *The Brothers Karamazov*, 245 (II.V.IV).

142. See Girard, *The Scapegoat*, 116.

143. See Dumont, *Individualism*, 81–83; Hugo Assmann and Franz Hinkelammert, *Götze Markt*, trans. Horst Goldstein (Düsseldorf: Patmos Verlag, 1992), 155.

144. Dupuy, "The Self-Deconstruction of the Liberal Order," 12–13.

145. Habermas, *Justification and Application*, 35. See Habermas, *Transitions*, 166.

146. See Dieckmann, *Judas als Sündenbock*, 311–312.

147. Dostoyevsky, *The Brothers Karamazov*, 318 (II.VI.III).

148. Quoted in Assmann, ed., *René Girard*, 171. See also 42–45, 168.

149. Tzvetan Todorov, *The Conquest of America*, 144–145.

150. See Raymund Schwager, "Schöpfung und Opfer: Roberto Calasso und René Girard," in *Das Opfer—Aktuelle Kontroversen: Religions-politischer Diskurs im Kontext der mimetischen Theorie, Deutsch-Italienische Fachtagung der Guardini Stiftung in der Villa Vigoni 18.-22. Oktober 1999*, ed. Bernhard Dieckmann (Münster: LIT, 2001), 19–35; Giuseppe Fornari, "Dionysos, die Natur und die evangelische Differenz," in *Das Opfer—Aktuelle Kontroversen: Religions-politischer Diskurs im Kontext der mimetischen Theorie, Deutsch-Italienische Fachtagung der Guardini Stiftung in der Villa Vigoni 18.-22. Oktober 1999*, ed. Bernhard Dieckmann, Beiträge zur mimetischen Theorie (Münster: LIT, 2001).

151. Calasso, *Ruin of Kasch*, 138. See also 136, 156; Palaver, "Globalisierung," 181–189.

152. See Anspach, ed., *René Girard*, 123–124; Girard, *Job*, 108; *The Girard Reader*, 209, 275; *Quand ces choses commenceront*, 64–65, 114; *I See Satan*, 180–181; *Celui par qui le scandale arrive*, 118; Girard and Palaver, *Gewalt und Religion*, 60–63; Girard and Meotti, *Accusation*, 181; Bailie, *Violence Unveiled*, 22–24; Taylor, "Notes on the Sources of Violence: Perennial and Modern," in *Beyond Violence: Religious Sources for Social Transformation in Judaism, Christianity and Islam*, ed. James L. Heft (Ashland, OH: Fordham University Press, 2004), 63–64, 67–68; Taylor, *A Secular Age* (Cambridge, MA: Belknap Press, 2007), 683–684, 707–709.

153. See Girard, *Things Hidden*, 128–129.

154. See Jacques Attali, *Millennium: Gewinner und Verlierer in der Kommenden Weltordnung*, trans. Bernd Rüther (Düsseldorf: ECON Verlag, 1992), 88–93; Kitzmüller, *Gewalteskalation*, 15–53.

155. Dostoyevsky, *The Brothers Karamazov*, 246 (II.V.IV).

156. Dostoyevsky, *The Brothers Karamazov*, 1, 285 (II.VI.I), 309 (II.VI.II). See Girard, *Deceit, Desire and the Novel*, 311.

157. See Dostoyevsky, *The Brothers Karamazov*, 524 (II.VI.III); Dieckmann, *Judas*, 312–314.

158. See Schwager, *Scapegoats*, 126–129.

159. See Girard, *Things Hidden*, 237–245; *Celui par qui le scandale arrive*, 77–80; *Evolution and Conversion*, 214–217; Girard and Adams, *Violence*, 29–30; McKenna, *Violence and Difference*, 206–211.

160. See Girard, *Things Hidden*, 240–243.

161. See Girard, *Resurrection from the Underground*, 37, 41, 45, 50–51, 88.

162. Dostoyevsky, *The Brothers Karamazov*, 58 (I.II.IV).

163. See Girard, *Things Hidden*, 227–231; Assmann, ed., *René Girard*, 42–43, 166–168; Eugene Webb, "Girard, Sacrifice, and Religious Symbolism," *Journal of European Psychoanalysis*, no. 14 (2002): 63–64.

164. See Schwager, *Scapegoats*, 200–204.

165. See Girard, *Quand ces choses commenceront*, 15, 171; *Evolution and Conversion*, 216–217; *De la violence à la divinité*, 28, 1001; Girard and Vattimo, *Weakening Faith*, 92–93; Anspach, ed., *René Girard*, 125–142; Raymund Schwager, *Jesus in the Drama of Salvation: Toward a Biblical Doctrine of Redemption*, trans. James G. Williams and Paul Haddon (New York: Crossroad Publishing Co., 1999), 187–189; Wolfgang Palaver, "Die Bedeutung von Stellvertretung für eine theologische Sozialethik: Ein Beitrag aus der Sicht der mimetischen Theorie René Girards," in *Stellvertretung: Theologische, philosophische und kulturelle Aspekte*, Band 1: *Interdisziplinäres Symposion Tübingen 2004*, ed. J. Christine Janowski, Bernd Janowski, Hans P. Lichtenberger, and Anette Krüger (Neukirchen-Vluyn: Neukirchener, 2006), 213–26.

166. Girard, "Mimetische Theorie und Theologie," 27–28.

167. See Girard, "Violence Renounced," 319; Schwager, *Scapegoats*, 200–214.

168. See Girard, *The Scapegoat*, 200; *Celui par qui le scandale arrive*, 115–116; Girard and Adams, "Violence, Difference, Sacrifice," 28–29; Chilton, *Temple of Violence*, 155–159; Michael Hardin, "Sacrificial Language in Hebrews: Reappraising René Girard," in *Violence Renounced: René Girard, Biblical Studies, and Peacemaking*, ed. Willard M. Swartley (Telford, PA: Pandora Press, 2000), 103–119; Loren L. Johns, "'A Better Sacrifice' or 'Better Than Sacrifice'? Response to Michael Hardin's 'Sacrificial Language in Hebrews,'" in *Violence Renounced: René Girard, Biblical Studies, and Peacemaking*, ed. Willard M. Swartley (Telford, PA: Pandora Press, 2000), 120–131.

169. See Girard, *Deceit, Desire and the Novel*, 317–322.

170. Georg Baudler, "Jesus—der vollkommene Sündenbock? Zu René Girards Revision seines Opferbegriffs," *Lebendiges Zeugnis* 52, no. 3 (1997). See Baudler, *Befreiung*, 63–79.

171. Baudler, *Befreiung*, 78.

172. See Baudler, *Befreiung*, 79.

173. See Girard and Müller, "Interview," 3.

174. Girard, "Mimetische Theorie und Theologie," 28. See Girard, *Quand ces choses commenceront*, 170; Girard and Vattimo, *Weakening Faith*, 99–100.

175. Girard, *De la violence à la divinité*, 1170–1171; *Things Hidden*, 401–402. See also *De la violence à la divinité*, 1211–1213; *Things Hidden*, 444–445.

176. See Girard, *Quand ces choses commenceront*, 142–143; René Girard and David Cayley, "The

Scapegoat: René Girard's Anthropology of Violence and Religion," *Canadian Broadcasting Corporation Radio Interviews* (Toronto: CBS, 2001), 31–32.

177. Augustine, *City of God*, 867–869 (XIX, ch. 12).

178. Wolfgang Amadeus Mozart/Emanuel Schikaneder, *Die Zauberflöte*, II, 12.

179. See Girard, *Things Hidden*, 224–262; *The Scapegoat*, 126; Bellinger, *Genealogy*, 108–111.

180. See Girard, *Things Hidden*, 224, 249–250.

181. See Girard, *Things Hidden*, 224, 245; *Quand ces choses commenceront*, 115; *I See Satan*, 26; Anthony W. Bartlett, *Cross Purposes: The Violent Grammar of Christian Atonement* (Harrisburg, PA: Trinity Press International, 2001).

182. Girard, *Things Hidden*, 227, 252.

183. See Girard, *Deceit, Desire and the Novel*, 92; *Violence and the Sacred*, 206, 318; *To Double Business Bound*, 82; *Things Hidden*, 288–289; *The Scapegoat*, 101, 191; *Quand des choses commenceront*, 91; *I See Satan*, 165–166, 184.

184. Girard, *Quand ces choses commenceront*, 92.

185. See Girard, *Quand ces choses commenceront*, 23, 91, 95; *I See Satan*, 165, 177, 184.

186. See Girard, *Things Hidden*, 441; *To Double Business Bound*, 118.

187. See Girard, *Quand ces choses commenceront*, 24, 100; *I See Satan*, 165.

188. See Girard, *I See Satan*, 159; *The Girard Reader*, 209, 254–255.

189. See Girard, *Theater of Envy*, 228.

190. Heinsohn, *Erschaffung*, 174. See Greisch, "Homo mimeticus," 57–59.

191. See Girard, *Things Hidden*, 185–190, 195, 200–205, 253–262; *To Double Business Bound*, 227; *Theater of Envy*, 282–283, 286, 289, 293, 295–296; *Quand ces choses commenceront*, 24, 100, 133–134; *I See Satan*, 184; *Battling to the End*; Girard and Palaver, *Gewalt und Religion*, 63–65, 68–72; Girard and Doran, "Apocalyptic Thinking," 20–32; Girard and Meotti, "René Girard's Accusation," 183; Robert Hamerton-Kelly, ed., *Politics and Apocalypse*, Studies in Violence, Mimesis, and Culture (East Lansing: Michigan State University Press, 2007); Wolfgang Palaver et al., eds., *Aufgeklärte Apokalyptik: Religion, Gewalt und Frieden im Zeitalter der Globalisierung*, Edition Weltordnung—Religion—Gewalt (Innsbruck: Innsbruck University Press, 2007); Palaver, "Im Zeichen des Opfers: Die apokalyptische Verschärfung der Weltlage als Folge des Monotheismus," in *Westliche Moderne, Christentum und Islam: Gewalt als Anfrage an monotheistische Religionen*, ed. Wolfgang Palaver, Roman A. Siebenrock, and Dietmar Regensburger (Innsbruck: Innsbruck University Press, 2008), 151–176.

192. See Girard, *Theater of Envy*, 282.

193. See Girard, *Things Hidden*, 193; *Battling to the End*, 110–116; Girard and Vattimo, *Weakening Faith*, 31.

194. Girard, *Things Hidden*, 255; *Theater of Envy*, 286; René Girard and Thomas F. Bertonneau, "The Logic of the Undecidable: An Interview," *Paroles Gelées*, no. 5 (1987): 14; Girard and Palaver, *Gewalt und Religion*, 64–65.

195. See Girard, *Things Hidden*, 197, 258; *Theater of Envy*, 282; *Celui par qui le scandale arrive*, 43.

196. Dostoyevsky, *The Brothers Karamazov*, 262. See Girard, *Resurrection from the Underground*, 134.

197. Girard, *Things Hidden*, 203, 251, 288–289; *To Double Business Bound*, 227; *The Scapegoat*, 13, 16, 94, 110, 191; *Theater of Envy*, 282–283; *Quand ces choses commenceront*, 63–64; *I See Satan*, 186.

198. Girard, *Things Hidden*, 251. See also 205.

199. See Girard, *Quand ces choses commenceront*, 102; *I See Satan*, 185–186.

200. See René Girard and Giuseppe Fornari, *La vittima e la folla: Violenza del mito e cristianesimo* (Treviso: Santi Quaranta, 1998), 165–166; *I See Satan*, 186; *Celui par qui le scandale arrive*, 148–150, 153–154; Wolfgang Palaver, "Hobbes and the Katéchon: The Secularization of Sacrificial Christianity," *Contagion: Journal of Violence, Mimesis, and Culture* 2 (1995): 57–74.

201. Carl Schmitt, *Roman Catholicism and Political Form*, trans. G. L. Ulmen (Westport, CT: Greenwood Press, 1996), 32. See Schmitt, *Nomos of the Earth*, 59–60; Schmitt, *Glossarium: Aufzeichnungen der Jahre 1947–1951* (Berlin: Duncker & Humblot, 1991), 63; Wolfgang Palaver, "Order out of Chaos in the Theories of Carl Schmitt and René Girard," *Synthesis* 1 (1994): 100–106.

202. See Girard, *Things Hidden*, 128–129, 286; *To Double Business Bound*, 82; Norbert Bolz, *Das Wissen der Religion: Betrachtungen eines religiös Unmusikalischen* (Munich: Wilhelm Fink, 2008), 61–73.

203. See Girard, *Resurrection from the Underground*, 123.

204. Dietrich Bonhoeffer, *Ethics*, trans. Neville Horton Smith (New York: Macmillan Publishing Co., 1965), 108.

205. Bonhoeffer, *Ethics*, 108.

206. See Girard, *Deceit, Desire and the Novel*, 192; *Resurrection from the Underground*, 133; *Oedipus Unbound*, 68–69; *Things Hidden*, 161–163; *The Scapegoat*, 184–197; *The Girard Reader*, 194–210, 293; *Quand ces choses commenceront*, 78, 102, 139; *I See Satan*, 32–46, 68–69, 86–87; *Celui par qui le scandale arrive*, 90–94; Anspach, ed., *René Girard*, 119–124; Schwager, *Banished from Eden*, 143–165.

207. See Girard, *I See Satan*, 104.

208. See Girard, *Oedipus Unbound*, 68–70, 73–75, 79–86, 92–94; *Things Hidden*, 162, 416–431; *The Scapegoat*, 132–133, 157–159, 183, 191–193; *Theater of Envy* 189, 295, 324, 340–342; *The Girard Reader*, 198–199, 215–216; *I See Satan*, 7–31; *Celui par qui le scandale arrive*, 94–97; Anspach, ed., *René Girard*, 119–121; Hamerton-Kelly, *Gospel*, 46–48, 108–111; David McCracken, "Scandal and Imitation in Matthew, Kierkegaard, and Girard," *Contagion: Journal of Violence, Mimesis, and Culture* 4 (1997): 146–162.

209. See Girard, *Things Hidden*, 161–163; *The Girard Reader*, 204; *I See Satan Fall Like Lightning*, 39–44.

210. See Girard, *Job*, 3, 138, 156, 158–159, 164; *The Girard Reader*, 201; *I See Satan*, 35–36, 41.

211. Goethe, *Faust*, 36 (I.1336).

212. See Girard, *The Scapegoat*, 184–197.

213. See Girard, *Things Hidden*, 190–196; *The Girard Reader*, 202–203, 206–208; *Quand ces choses commenceront*, 93; *I See Satan*, 95–100; "Is There Anti-Semitism in the Gospels?," 350–351; Hamerton-Kelly, *Sacred Violence*, 156–158; Walter Wink, *Engaging the Powers: Discernment and Resistance in a World of Domination* (Minneapolis: Fortress Press, 1992), 65–85.

214. Luke passage quoted from the New International Version Bible.

215. See Girard, *Things Hidden*, 191–194; *The Girard Reader*, 205–210; *I See Satan*, 137–153.

216. Gay, ed., *The Freud Reader*, 755.

217. See Girard, *I See Satan*, 45–46, 69.

218. See Girard, *The Scapegoat*, 194; *I See Satan*, 41, 45, 69.

219. Charles Baudelaire, "Generous Gambler," in *Paris Spleen: Little Poems in Prose*, translated by Keith Waldrop (Middletown, CT: Wesleyan University Press, 2009), 60.

220. Golding, *Lord of the Flies*, 103. See Johann Wolfgang von Goethe, *Faust*, trans. Stuart Pratt Atkins (Cambridge, MA: Insel Publishers Boston, 1984), 36 (I.1334).

221. Rousseau, *Confessions*, 106. See Rousseau, *Emile*, 360; Jacques Derrida, *Of Grammatology*, trans. Gayatri Chakravorty Spivak (Baltimore: Johns Hopkins University Press, 1997), 141–164. Jonathan Culler, *On Deconstruction: Theory and Criticism after Structuralism* (Ithaca, NY: Cornell University Press, 1989), 102–106; McKenna, *Violence and Difference*, 77–78.

222. See Culler, *On Deconstruction*, 109–110.

223. See Derrida, *Dissemination*, trans. Barbara Johnson (Chicago: University of Chicago Press, 1981), 95–117; Culler, *On Deconstruction*, 142–144; McKenna, *Violence and Difference*, 27–40; James G. Williams, "On Job and Writing: Derrida, Girard, and the Remedy-Poison," *Scandinavian Journal of the Old Testament* 7, no. 1 (1993): 34–39.

224. See Derrida, *Dissemination*, 128–134.

225. See Frazer, *Golden Bough*, 598–606.

226. See Derrida, *Dissemination*, 133.

227. Girard, *Violence and the Sacred*, 196–197. See also *To Double Business Bound*, 105, 168, 175, 220–210; Girard and Adams, "Violence," 17–19.

228. See René Girard, "Origins: A View from the Literature," in *Understanding Origins: Contemporary Views on the Origin of Life, Mind and Society*, ed. F. J. Varela and J. P. Dupuy (Dordrecht: Kluwer Academic Publishers, 1992), 27–42; Golsan, *René Girard*, 77–78.

229. See Girard, *Things Hidden*, 203, 251, 253, 287; *To Double Business Bound*, 222; *The Scapegoat*, 13, 16, 94; *Celui par qui le scandale arrive*, 32–33; Derrida, *Margins of Philosophy*, trans. Alan Bass (Brighton, Sussex: Harvester, 1982), 7–9; Siebers, *Language*, 208–213; Culler, *On Deconstruction*, 97; Lutz Ellrich, "Gewalt und Zeichen: René Girard," in *Von Michel Serres bis Julia Kristeva*, ed. Joseph Jurt (Freiburg: Rombach Verlag, 1999), 82; Walter Seitter, "Katechontiken im 20: Jahrhundert nach Christus," *Tumult*, no. 25 (2001): 127.

230. Jacques Derrida, "Force of Law: The 'Mystical Foundation of Authority,'" *Cardozo Law Review* 11, no. 5–6 (1990): 929.

231. See McKenna, *Violence and Difference*, 1–115.

232. Gianni Vattimo, *Belief*, trans. Luca D'Isanto and David Webb (Stanford, CA: Stanford University Press, 1999), 34, 36–37, 40–41; Vattimo, *Beyond Interpretation: The Meaning of Hermeneutics for Philosophy*, trans. David Webb (Stanford, CA: Stanford University Press, 1997), 50–51; Vattimo, *Tecnica ed esistenza: Una mappa filosofica del Novecento* (Milan: Mondadori, 2002), 99–100; Stefano Tomelleri, "Ressentiment und Dekonstruktion," in *Das Opfer—Aktuelle Kontroversen: Religions-politischer Diskurs im Kontext der mimetischen Theorie. Deutsch-Italienische Fachtagung der Guardini Stiftung in der Villa Vigoni 18.-22. Oktober 1999*, ed. Bernhard Dieckmann (Münster: LIT, 2001), 281–292; Niewiadomski, "Transzendenz."

233. Vattimo, *Belief*, 36.

234. Vattimo, *Belief*, 39.

235. See Girard and Vattimo, *Weakening Faith*, 78–87.

236. See Martin Heidegger, *Being and Time*, trans. John MacQuarrie and Edward Robinson. Library of Philosophy and Theology (London: SCM Press, 1962), 41–49 (§6: "The Task of Destroying the History of Ontology").

237. See Girard, *Things Hidden*, 263–274; Girard and Bertonneau, "Logic," 12–13; Martin Heidegger, *An Introduction to Metaphysics*, trans. Ralph Manheim (New Haven, CT: Yale University Press, 1959), 97–135.

238. Girard and Vattimo, *Weakening Faith*, 80. See Vattimo, *Belief*, 36.

239. Girard and Vattimo, *Weakening Faith*, 85.

240. Gianni Vattimo, *Belief*, 38–39.

241. See Girard, *Quand ces choses commenceront*, 15, 150–153; *The Girard Reader*, 288; Girard and Vattimo, *Weakening Faith*, 92.

242. See Girard, *Job*, 151; *The Girard Reader*, 283; *I See Satan*, 175–176; Girard and Bertonneau, "Logic," 10–13; Girard and Palaver, *Gewalt und Religion*, 56–59.

243. See Girard, *Things Hidden*, 62–65; *De la violence à la divinité*, 775–779.

244. See Girard, *The Scapegoat*, 124; *The Girard Reader*, 288; *I See Satan*, 70, 73–75, 112, 116, 144, 146; Girard and Golsan, "Interview," 132–133, 141; Girard and Adams, *Violence*, 19–20; René Girard and Michael Jakob, "Gespräch mit René Girard," in *Aussichten des Denkens*, ed. Michael Jakob (Munich: Wilhelm Fink Verlag, 1994), 158–160; Assmann, ed., *René Girard*, 41–42, 69.

245. Girard, *Mimesis and Essays on Theory*, 194–213. See Girard and Meotti, "René Girard's Accusation"; Golsan, *René Girard*, 107–110.

246. See Girard, *Mimesis and Theory*, 201–203; Girard and Jakob, "Gespräch," 158; McKenna, *Violence and Difference*, 60–61; Golsan, *René Girard*, 107.

247. Derrida, *Of Grammatology*, 158. See Peter Engelmann, "Einführung: Postmoderne und Dekonstruktion. Zwei Stichwörter zur zeitgenössischen Philosophie," in *Postmoderne und Dekonstruktion: Texte französischer Philosophen der Gegenwart*, ed. Peter Engelmann (Stuttgart: Philipp Reclam jun., 1990), 20–21.

248. Derrida, "Structure, Sign, and Play," 264–265.

249. Derrida, "Structure, Sign, and Play," 265. See Williams, *Bible*, 20–21.

250. See Girard, *Violence and the Sacred*, 234–235; *Things Hidden*, 99–104; *The Scapegoat*, 193; Eric Gans, *The Origin of Language: A Formal Theory of Representation* (Berkeley: University of California Press, 1981); Williams, *Bible*, 20–25; McKenna, *Violence and Difference*, 66–115.

251. See Girard and Vattimo, *Weakening Faith*, 88–108.

252. Nietzsche, *Sämtliche Werke*, vol. 12:315 (Nachgelassene Fragmente; Ende 1886–Frühjahr 1887 7[60]). See Vattimo, *Beyond Interpretation*, 105.

253. See Girard, *The Girard Reader*, 134.

254. Girard, *The Girard Reader*, 263, 267; *I See Satan*, 145–146; *Celui par qui le scandale arrive*, 175.

255. Timothy Garton Ash, "On the Frontier," *New York Review of Books* 49, no. 17 (2002): 60.

256. See Girard, *Violence and the Sacred*, 66; *Things Hidden* 191, 247, 429; *The Girard Reader*, 137–138; "Mythology," 116; "Victims," 134; Goodhart, *Sacrificing Commentary*, 183.

257. See Girard, *Things Hidden*, 178–179, 428–429; *The Scapegoat*, 117; *The Girard Reader*, 138.

258. See Girard, *I See Satan*, 186–187; *Things Hidden*, 427; *Job*, 98.

259. See Girard, *Things Hidden*, 205–206, 221, 226, 241, 244, 263, 274; *The Scapegoat*, 101–104, 116–117; *Job*, 165–166; *Quand ces choses commenceront*, 52–53; *I See Satan*, 127–130.

260. See Raymund Schwager, *Der Wunderbare Tausch: Zur Geschichte und Deutung der Erlösungslehre* (Munich: Kösel, 1986), 29–31.

261. See Girard, *The Scapegoat*, 102; *I See Satan*, 128.

262. See Girard, *Things Hidden*, 211; *The Scapegoat*, 157–161; *I See Satan*, 129.

263. Girard, *Things Hidden*, 454; *Evolution and Conversion*, 180–182. See Erich Auerbach, "Figura," in *Scenes from the Drama of European Literature*, trans. Ralph Manheim (Gloucester, MA: Peter Smith, 1973), 11–76; Auerbach, *Mimesis*, 18–19, 51–52, 74–77.

264. Auerbach, "Figura," 53.

265. Auerbach, "Figura," 58.

266. Auerbach, "Figura," 59.

267. Auerbach, "Figura," 81.

268. Jacques Derrida, *Politics of Friendship*, trans. George Collins (London: Verso, 1997), 43.

269. See Jacques Derrida, *Deconstruction in a Nutshell: A Conversation with Jacques Derrida* (New York: Fordham University Press, 1997), 20–25, 156–180.

270. Auerbach, *Mimesis*, 74.

271. See Auerbach, "Figura," 63–71; Auerbach, *Mimesis*, 184–195.

Chapter 6. Political Implications of the Mimetic Theory

1. See Girard, *Violence and the Sacred*, 103–116, 299–306; *Things Hidden*, 48–68; *Job*, 86–108; *The Girard Reader*, 269–272; *I See Satan*, 92; Palaver, *Politik*, 217–223; Simon Simonse, *Kings of Disaster: Dualism, Centralism and the Scapegoat King in the Southeastern Sudan* (Leiden: E.J. Brill, 1992); Bailie, *Violence Unveiled*, 123–126.

2. Girard, *Violence and the Sacred*, 274–278.

3. Girard, *Violence and the Sacred*, 301.

4. Frazer, *Golden Bough*, 146.

5. Elias Canetti, *Crowds and Power*, trans. Carol Stewart (New York: Viking Press, 1962), 411.

6. Elias Canetti, *Masse und Macht* (Frankfurt am Main: Fischer, 1980), 463.

7. Canetti, *Crowds and Power*, 414.

8. Canetti, *Crowds and Power*, 418.

9. See Girard, *Things Hidden*, 58; Frazer, *Golden Bough*, 146; S. Freud, *Studienausgabe*, Bd, 9: 338 ("Totem und Tabu").

10. See Girard, *Things Hidden*, 65.

11. See Girard, *Violence and the Sacred*, 302; *Things Hidden*, 53; Geo Widengren, *Religionsphänomenologie*, trans. Rosmarie Elgnowski (Berlin: Walter de Gruyter, 1969), 309–310.

12. Frazer, *Golden Bough*, 583–585. See Girard, *Things Hidden*, 53.

13. See Palaver, *Politik*, 78–83.

14. Hobbes, *Leviathan*, 120 (ch. 17).

15. See Paul Dumouchel, "Hobbes: La course à la souveraineté," in *To Honor René Girard: Presented on the Occasion of his Sixtieth Birthday by Colleagues, Students, and Friends*, ed. Alphonse Juilland, Stanford French and Italian Studies (Saratoga, CA: Anma Libri, 1986), 176.

16. Thomas Heerich, *Transformation des Politikkonzepts von Hobbes zu Spinoza: Das Problem der Souveränität* (Würzburg: Königshausen & Neumann, 2000), 55.

17. Hobbes, *Leviathan*, 153 (ch. 21).

18. Hobbes, *Leviathan*, 153 (ch. 21), 120 (ch. 17).

19. See Fritz Kern, *Gottesgnadentum und Widerstandsrecht im frühen Mittelalter: Zur Entwicklungsgeschichte der Monarchie* (Darmstadt: Wissenschaftliche Buchgesellschaft, 1962), 318.

20. Carl Schmitt, *Political Theology: Four Chapters on the Concept of Sovereignty*, trans. George Schwab (Chicago: University of Chicago Press, 2005), 5.

21. Girard, "Disorder." See Wolfgang Palaver, "A Girardian Reading of Schmitt's *Political Theology*," *Telos*, no. 93 (1992): 51–58; Palaver, "Order out of Chaos," 89–100.

22. See Girard, *To Double Business Bound*, 105; *Things Hidden*, 237; *The Scapegoat*, 114; Joachim Schickel, *Gespräche Mit Carl Schmitt* (Berlin: Merve Verlag, 1993), 71–72.

23. Schmitt, *Political Theology*, 15.

24. See Williams, *Bible*, 20–25.

25. See Carl Schmitt, *The Crisis of Parliamentary Democracy*, trans. Ellen Kennedy (Cambridge, MA: MIT Press, 1988), 56–57.

26. James Madison, Alexander Hamilton, and John Jay, *The Federalist Papers* (Harmondsworth, England: Penguin Books, 1987), 403 (no. 70).

27. Madison, Hamilton, and Jay, *Federalist Papers*, 405–406 (no. 70).

28. Madison, Hamilton, and Jay, *Federalist Papers*, 407 (no. 70).

29. Nicolaus Sombart, *Wilhelm II: Sündenbock und Herr der Mitte* (Berlin: Verlag Volk & Welt, 1996), 94–98.

30. Sombart, *Wilhelm II*, 205–228.

31. Sombart, *Wilhelm II*, 218.

32. Rolf Zundel, "Der Schwere Abschied: Vom Leiden der Politiker nach dem Entzug von Macht, Öffentlichkeit, Apparat und Wirkungsmöglichkeiten," *Die Zeit*, 7 April 1989, 45–46.

33. Dostoyevsky, "The Dream of a Ridiculous Man," in *The Short Stories of Dostoyevsky*, 610.

34. Quoted in Isaiah Berlin, *The Crooked Timber of Humanity: Chapters in the History of Ideas* (New York: Vintage Books, 1992), 117.

35. Juan de Donoso Cortés, *Essay on Catholicism, Liberalism and Socialism: Considered in Their Fundamental Principles*, trans. Madeleine Vinton Goddard (Albany, NY: Preserving Christian Publications, Inc., 1991), 292. See Carl Schmitt, "A Pan-European Interpretation of Donoso Cortés," *Telos*, no. 125 (2002): 110.

36. Donoso Cortés, *Essay on Catholicism*, 288–289.

37. See Albert Camus, *Reflections on the Guillotine: An Essay on Capital Punishment*, trans. Richard Howard (Michigan City, IN: Fridtjof-Karla Publications, 1960); Brigitte Sändig, "'. . . Etwas Stärkeres als alle Rechtsprechung': Camus und die Todesstrafe," *Orientierung* 64 (2000): 215–219.

38. Camus, *The Rebel*, 87; Sofsky, *Traktat über Die Gewalt*, 120.

39. Camus, *The Rebel*, 94.

40. Benjamin, "Critique of Violence," in *Selected Writings*, vol. 1, 285–286.

41. Benjamin, "Critique of Violence," 286.

42. Gay, ed., *The Freud Reader*, 741–742. See Freud and Einstein, *Why War?*, 2.

43. Karl Bruno Leder, *Todesstrafe: Ursprung, Geschichte, Opfer* (Munich: Meyster, 1980), 63–65.

44. Leder, *Todesstrafe*, 74–75.

45. Leder, *Todesstrafe*, 301.

46. Wolfgang Sofsky, *Traktat*, 124.

47. See Girard, *Violence and the Sacred*, 297–299; *I See Satan*, 84; Bailie, *Violence Unveiled*, 78–85; Smith, Brian K., "Capital Punishment and Human Sacrifice," *Journal of the American Academy of Religion* 68, no. 1 (2000): 3–25.

48. Louis Gernet, *Anthropologie de la Grèce antique*, Textes à l'appui (Paris: F. Maspero, 1968), quoted in Girard, *Violence and the Sacred*, 298.

49. See Girard, *Things Hidden*, 53.

50. See Leder, *Todesstrafe*, 266–267.

51. See Herzog, *Religionstheorie*, 123.

52. See Keith Thomas, *Religion and the Decline of Magic: Studies in Popular Beliefs in Sixteenth- and Seventeenth-Century England* (Harmondsworth, UK: Penguin, 1985), 242.

53. See Markwart Herzog, "Hingerichtete Verbrecher als Gegenstand der Heiligenverehrung: Zum Kontext von René Girard," *Geist und Leben* 65 (1992): 367–386.

54. See Johannes Ude, "*Du sollst nicht töten!*" (Dornbirn: Mayer, 1948), 91.

55. Hugh Lloyd-Jones, ed., *Aeschylus in Two Volumes*, vol. 2, *Agamemnon, Libation-Bearers, Eumenides, Fragments* (Cambridge, MA: Harvard University Press, 1983), 984–986. See Christian Meier, *Die Entstehung des Politischen bei den Griechen* (Frankfurt am Main: Suhrkamp, 1995), 207–214; Palaver, *Die mythischen Quellen des Politischen*, 36–37.

56. Plato, *Republic*, 149–151 (469a–471c); Aristotle, *Politics*, 1128–1129 (1252b), 1285–1286 (1327b). See Reinhart Koselleck, "Zur historisch-politischen Semantik asymmetrischer Gegenbegriffe," in

Vergangene Zukunft: Zur Semantik geschichtlicher Zeiten (Frankfurt am Main: Suhrkamp, 1995), 219–220.

57. Laozi and Arthur Waley, *The Way and Its Power: A Study of the Tao Tě Ching and Its Place in Chinese Thought* (New York: Grove Press, 1958), 228 (ch. 69).

58. See Laozi and Waley, *The Way and Its Power*, 25 (ch. 67).

59. Schmitt, *Concept of the Political*, 26.

60. Simmel, *Sociology: Inquiries into the Construction of Social Forms*, 539–540.

61. Gay, ed., *The Freud Reader*, 751. Strachey's translation of "*geringzuschätzen*" is changed here from "despised" to "underestimated." (Translator's note.)

62. Enzensberger, *Civil Wars*.

63. Huntington, *Clash of Civilizations*, 21.

64. Kofi Annan, "United We Stand against Terror, Divided We Fail," *The Guardian*, 22 September 2001.

65. See Girard, *Violence and the Sacred*, 249; *Violent Origins*, 219; *I See Satan*, 53; Lewis Mumford, *The City in History: Its Origins, Its Transformations, and Its Prospects* (New York: Harcourt, Inc., 1989), 24–25, 41–42. See also Raymond Aron, *Peace and War: A Theory of International Relations* (New Brunswick, NJ: Transaction Publishers, 2003), 362–365.

66. Girard, *Job*, 146–154; Palaver, *Die mythischen Quellen des Politischen*, 38–45.

67. Aeschylus, *Eumenides*, in *Aeschylus in Two Volumes*, vol. 2, *Agamemnon, Libation-Bearers, Eumenides, Fragments*, trans. H. Lloyd-Jones and Herbert Weir Smyth (Cambridge, MA: Harvard University Press, 1983), 299–305. See Girard, *Job*, 148.

68. Aeschylus, *Eumenides*, 378–387.

69. Aeschylus, *Eumenides*, 858–866.

70. Aeschylus, *Eumenides*, 910–915.

71. See Girard, *Violence and the Sacred*, 274–280.

72. See Bataille, *Accursed Share*, 49; Mumford, *City*, 41; Anthony Giddens, *The Nation-State and Violence* (Berkeley: University of California Press, 1987), 72; Creveld, *Transformation*, 140, 150–151; Calasso, *The Ruin of Kasch*, 136.

73. See Ernest Gellner, *Muslim Society* (Cambridge: Cambridge University Press, 1981), 40–44.

74. Gellner, *Muslim Society*, 69.

75. See Girard, *Resurrection from the Underground*, 59, 139–140; *Things Hidden*, 136–137, 197, 258; Schmitt, *Concept of the Political*, 29–30.

Chapter 7. Mimetic Theory and Gender

1. See Susan Nowak, "The Girardian Theory and Feminism: Critique and Appropriation," *Contagion: Journal of Violence, Mimesis, and Culture* 1 (1994): 20–24; Schwager, "Rückblick," 354.

2. Nowak, "The Girardian Theory," 20–21; M. Reineke, *Sacrificed Lives*, 65–102; R. G. Hamerton-Kelly, *Violence*, 55.

3. See Nowak, "The Girardian Theory," 24–26; Toril Moi, "The Missing Mother: The Oedipal Rivalries of René Girard," *Diacritics: A Review of Contemporary Criticism* 12, no. 2 (1982): 29–30; Sarah Kofman, "The Narcissistic Woman: Freud and Girard," *Diacritics: A Review of Contemporary Criticism* 10, no. 3 (1980): 36–45; Luce Irigaray, "Women, the Sacred, Money," in *Sexes and Genealogies* (New York: Columbia University Press, 1993), 73–88; Golsan, *René Girard*, 113–115.

4. See Nowak, "The Girardian Theory," 26–28; Hamerton-Kelly, *Sacred Violence*, 47–48, 54–56; Schwager, "Rückblick," 355.

5. See Moi, "The Missing Mother."

6. See Girard and Golsan, "Interview," 139, 141.

7. See Girard, *Quand ces choses commenceront*, 162–163; *Mimesis and Theory*, 192; Girard and Golsan, "Interview," 133–134; Girard and Palaver, *Gewalt und Religion*, 38–39; Bailie, *Vine*, 135–139; William A. Johnsen, *Violence and Modernism: Ibsen, Joyce, and Woolf* (Gainesville: University Press of Florida, 2003), 108–138; Simon De Keukelaere, "What Is Deviated Transcendency? Woolf's *The Waves* as a Textbook Case," *Contagion: Journal of Violence, Mimesis, and Culture* 12–13 (2006): 195–218.

8. See Girard, *A Theater of Envy*, 35–36.

9. Freud, *On Narcissism*, 554–555.

10. Freud, *On Narcissism*, 555.

11. See Girard, *Things Hidden*, 377–378; Girard and Golsan, "Interview," 142–146; Golsan, *René Girard*, 114–115.

12. See Girard, *Things Hidden*, 367–382; *Mimesis and Theory*, 175–193.

13. See Webb, *Self*, 110–111.

14. See Girard, *Things Hidden*, 371; *A Theater of Envy*, 107, 149.

15. Shakespeare, *Troilus and Cressida*, I, ii, 293–302. See Girard, *A Theater of Envy*, 125.

16. See Girard, *To Double Business Bound*, 57–59; *Things Hidden*, 356–392, 403; *A Theater of Envy*, 100–111, 143, 146, 197; *Mimesis and Theory*, 175–193; Girard and Bertonneau, "Logic," 18; Dupuy, "Totalization and Misrecognition," in *Violence and Truth: On the Work of René Girard*, ed. Paul Dumouchel (Stanford, CA: Stanford University Press, 1988), 77; Dupuy, *Self-Reference*, 494; Meloni, *Triangle*, 35–38.

17. See Girard, *A Theory of Envy*, 104.

18. See Girard, *Things Hidden*, 382–392; *To Double Business Bound*, 57–59.

19. See Girard, *A Theater of Envy*, 106–120.

20. Shakespeare, *Twelfth Night*, II, iv, 93–103. See Girard, *A Theater of Envy*, 115–116.

21. Shakespeare, *Twelfth Night*, I, v, 306–309.

22. Shakespeare, *Twelfth Night*, I, i, 9–15.

23. See Girard, *Things Hidden*, 337; *A Theater of Envy*, 116.

24. See Girard, *A Theater of Envy*, 141–151; Golsan, *René Girard*, 115.

25. See Girard and Golsan, "Interview," 141–142.

26. See Girard, *Violence and the Sacred*, 141–142; *Things Hidden*, 221–222; *The Scapegoat*, 19, 49

27. See Riane Eisler, *The Chalice and the Blade: Our History, Our Future* (San Francisco: Harper & Row, 1987).

28. See Georg Baudler, *Erlösung vom Stiergott: Christliche Gotteserfahrung im Dialog mit Mythen und Religionen* (Munich: Kösler, 1989), 321; Brigitte Röder, Juliane Hummel, and Brigitte Kunz, *Göttinnendämmerung: Das Matriarchat aus archäologischer Sicht* (Munich: Droemer Knaur, 1996).

29. See Baudler, *Erlösung*, 336–339; Schwager, "Rückblick," 365; Christa Wolf, *Voraussetzungen einer Erzählung: Kassandra. Frankfurter Poetik Vorlesungen* (Darmstadt: Luchterhand, 1983), 58–69; Eisler, *Chalice*, 360–362.

30. See Girard, *The Scapegoat*, 49; *The Girard Reader*, 118–141, 276; Baudler, *Erlösung*, 166–177; Knud Rasmussen, *The Netsilik Eskimos: Social Life and Spiritual Culture*, Report of the Fifth Thule Expedition, 1921–24, vol. 8, no. 1–2 (Copenhagen: Nordisk Forlag, 1931), 225–229.

31. Christa Wolf, *Medea: A Modern Retelling*, trans. John Cullen, 1st ed. (New York: Nan A. Talese, 1998), 139, 161. See Susanne Nordhofen, "Christa Wolfs Medea: Mythos und Tragödie im Licht der mimetischen Theorie," in *Das Opfer—Aktuelle Kontroversen: Religions-politischer Diskurs im Kontext der mimetischen Theorie. Deutsch-Italienische Fachtagung der Guardini Stiftung in der Villa Vigoni 18.–22. Oktober 1999*, ed. Bernhard Dieckmann (Münster: LIT, 2001).

32. Christa Wolf, "Warum Medea? Gespräch mit Petra Kammamann am 25.1.1996." In *Christa Wolfs Medea: Voraussetzungen zu einem Text*, ed. M. Hochgeschurz (Munich: Deutscher Taschenbuch Verlag, 2000), 75.

33. See Chris Shea, "Victims on Violence: 'Different Voices' and Girard," in *Curing Violence*, ed. Mark I. Wallace and Theophus H. Smith (Sonoma, CA: Polebridge Press, 1994), 258.

34. See Girard, *Violence and the Sacred*, 140–141; *The Girard Reader*, 276; Claude Lévi-Strauss, *Tristes tropiques*, trans. J. Weightman and D. Weightman (New York: Penguin Books, 1992), 215–229.

35. Marcel Detienne, "The Violence of Wellborn Ladies: Women in the Thesmophoria," in *The Cuisine of Sacrifice among the Greeks*, ed. Marcel Detienne and Jean-Pierre Vernant (Chicago: University of Chicago Press, 1989), 143.

36. See Girard, *Job*, 29, 147–152.

37. See Girard, *Violence and the Sacred*, 33–36.

38. Girard, *Violence and the Sacred*, 139–142. See Irigaray, *Women*, 124.

39. See Girard, *A Theater of Envy*, 60; *Violent Origins*, 101–102.

40. See Girard, *Violence and the Sacred*, 127, 141.

41. See Girard, *I See Satan*, 125; *The Girard Reader*, 275–77.

42. See Girard, *A Theater of Envy*, 66–70, 324; Girard and Golsan, "Interview," 142.

Bibliography

Achterhuis, Hans. *Het Rijk van de schaarste: Van Thomas Hobbes tot Michel Foucault.* Utrecht: Ambo/Baarn, 1988.

Aeschylus. *Aeschylus in Two Volumes.* Vol. 2, *Agamemnon, Libation-Bearers, Eumenides, Fragments.* Translated by H. Lloyd-Jones and H. Weir Smyth. Cambridge, MA: Harvard University Press, 1983.

Aglietta, Michel, and André Orléan. *La violence de la monnaie.* Paris: Presses Universitaires de France, 1982.

Ahrens, Theodor, Justus Freytag, Fred Gardiner, and Tim Schramm. "Religion und Gewalt: Ein Seminarbericht." In *Zwischen Regionalität und Globalisierung: Studien zu Mission, Ökumene und Religion*, edited by Theodor Ahrens, 369–408. Ammersbek bei Hamburg: Verlag an der Lottbek, 1997.

Akenson, Donald Harman. *Small Differences: Irish Catholics and Irish Protestants, 1815–1922: An International Perspective.* Montreal: McGill-Queen's University Press, 1988.

Alberg, Jeremiah. *A Reinterpretation of Rousseau: A Religious System.* Foreword by René Girard. New York: Palgrave Macmillan, 2007.

Alighieri, Dante. *Divine Comedy.* Vol. 2, *Purgatory.* Translated by Mark Musa. New York: Penguin Books, 1985.

Alison, James. *The Joy of Being Wrong: Original Sin through Easter Eyes.* Foreword by S. Moore. New York: Crossroad Publishing Co., 1998.

———. *Raising Abel: The Recovery of the Eschatological Imagination.* New York: Crossroad, 1996.

Annan, Kofi A. "United We Stand against Terror, Divided We Fail," *The Guardian*, 22 September 2001.

———. "Vereint gegen den Terrorismus." *Frankfurter Allgemeine Zeitung*, 22–23 September 2001, 3.

Anspach, Mark R. "Desired Possessions: Karl Polanyi, René Girard, and the Critique of the Market Economy." *Contagion: Journal of Violence, Mimesis, and Culture* 11 (2004): 181–188.

———. "The Making of a Meta-God: Sacrifice and Self-Transcendence in Vedic Mythology." *Paragrana: Internationale Zeitschrift für Historische Anthropologie* 4, no. 2 (1995): 117–125.

———, ed. *René Girard*, Cahiers de l'Herne. Paris: Éditions de l'Herne, 2008.

———. "Violence against Violence: Islam in Comparative Context." In *Violence and the Sacred in the Modern World*, edited by Mark Juergensmeyer, 9–29. London: Frank Cass, 1992.

Aquinas, Saint Thomas. *Summa Contra Gentiles.* Translated by the English Dominican Fathers. Vol. 3. London: Burns, Oates and Washburn, 1928.

———. *Summa Theologiæ.* Translated by Thomas Gilby. Vol. 44. New York: Black Friars; McGraw-Hill, 1972.

Arendt, Hannah. *The Human Condition.* 2nd ed. Chicago: University of Chicago Press, 1998.

———. *On Revolution.* Harmondsworth, UK: Penguin Books, 1990.

Arens, Edmund. "Dramatische Erlösungslehre aus der Perspektive einer theologischen Handlungstheorie." In *Dramatische Erlösungslehre: Ein Symposion*, edited by Józef Niewiadomski and Wolfgang Palaver, 165–77. Innsbruck: Tyrolia, 1992.

Aristotle. *The Basic Works of Aristotle.* Edited by Richard McKeon. Modern Library Classics. New York: Modern Library, 2001.

Aron, Raymond. *Peace and War: A Theory of International Relations.* New Brunswick, NJ: Transaction Publishers, 2003.

Ash, Timothy Garton. "On the Frontier." *New York Review of Books* 49, no. 17 (2002): 60–61.

Assmann, Hugo, ed. *René Girard com teólogos da libertaçao: Um diálogo sobre ídolos e sacrifícios.* Petrópolis, Brazil: Vozes, 1991.

Assmann, Hugo, and Franz J. Hinkelammert. *Götze Markt.* Translated by Horst Goldstein. Düsseldorf: Patmos Verlag, 1992.

Attali, Jacques. *Millennium: Gewinner und Verlierer in der kommenden Weltordnung.* Translated by Bernd Rüther. Düsseldorf: ECON Verlag, 1992.

Auerbach, Erich. "Figura." In *Gesammelte Aufsätze zur romanischen Philologie*, 55–92. Bern: Francke Verlag, 1967.

———. *Mimesis. Dargestellte Wirklichkeit in der abendländischen Literatur.* 8th ed. Bern, Stuttgart: Francke Verlag, 1988.

———. *Mimesis: The Representation of Reality in Western Literature.* Translated by Willard R. Trask. Princeton, NJ: Princeton University Press, 2003.

———. *Scenes from the Drama of European Literature: Six Essays.* Translated by Ralph Manheim. Gloucester, MA: Peter Smith, 1973.

Augustine. *Concerning the City of God against the Pagans.* Translated by Henry Bettenson. Penguin Classics. New York: Penguin Books, 2003.

———. *Confessions.* Translated by Garry Wills. New York: Penguin Books, 2006.

———. *Expositions of the Psalms, 51–72*. Translated by Maria Boulding. In *The Works of Saint Augustine*, part 3, vol. 17. Hyde Park, NY: New City Press, 1999.

———. *On Christian Belief*. Translated by Matthew O'Connell. In *The Works of Saint Augustine*, part 1, vol. 8. Hyde Park, NY: New City Press, 2005.

———. *On Christian Doctrine*. Translated by D. W. Robertson. 1st ed. The Library of Liberal Arts. New York: Macmillan, 1958.

———. *On Free Choice of the Will*. Translated by Thomas Williams. Indianapolis: Hackett Publishing Co., 1993.

———. *On Genesis*. Translated by Edmund Hill. In *The Works of Saint Augustine*, part I, vol. 13. Brooklyn, NY: New City Press, 1990.

———. *The Trinity*. Translated by Edmund Hill. In *The Works of Saint Augustine*, edited by John E. Rotelle. Brooklyn, NY: New City Press, 1991.

Bailie, Gil. "The Vine and Branches Discourse: The Gospel's Psychological Apocalypse." *Contagion: Journal of Violence, Mimesis, and Culture* 4 (1997): 120–145.

———. *Violence Unveiled: Humanity at the Crossroads*. New York: Crossroad, 1995.

Bandera, Cesáreo. *The Humble Story of Don Quixote: Reflections on the Birth of the Modern Novel*. Washington, DC: Catholic University of America Press, 2006.

———. *Mímesis conflictiva: Ficción literaria y violencia en Cervantes y Calderón*. Madrid: Gredos, 1975.

———. *The Sacred Game: The Role of the Sacred in the Genesis of Modern Literary Fiction*. University Park: Pennsylvania State University Press, 1994.

Barber, Benjamin R. *Jihad vs. McWorld*. 1st Ballantine Books ed. New York: Ballantine Books, 1996.

Bartlett, Anthony W. *Cross Purposes: The Violent Grammar of Christian Atonement*. Harrisburg, PA: Trinity Press International, 2001.

Bassoff, Bruce. "The Model as Obstacle: Kafka's 'The Trial.'" In *To Honor René Girard: Presented on the Occasion of His Sixtieth Birthday by Colleagues, Students, and Friends*, edited by Alphonse Juilland, 299–315. Saratoga, CA: Anma Libri, 1986.

Bataille, Georges. *The Accursed Share: An Essay on General Economy*. Vol. 1, *Consumption*. Translated by Robert Hurley. New York: Zone Books, 1988.

Bateson, Gregory. *Steps to an Ecology of Mind: Collected Essays in Anthropology, Psychiatry, Evolution, and Epistemology*. Chandler Publications for Health Sciences. San Francisco: Chandler Publishing Co., 1972.

Baudelaire, Charles. *Paris Spleen: Little Poems in Prose*. Translated by Keith Waldrop. Middletown, CT: Wesleyan University Press, 2009.

Baudler, Georg. *Die Befreiung von einem Gott der Gewalt: Erlösung in der Religionsgeschichte von Judentum, Christentum und Islam*. Düsseldorf: Patmos Verlag, 1999.

———. *Erlösung vom Stiergott: Christliche Gotteserfahrung im Dialog mit Mythen und Religionen*. München: Kösler, 1989.

———. "Jesus—der vollkommene Sündenbock? Zu René Girards Revision seines Opferbegriffs." *Lebendiges Zeugnis* 52, no. 3 (1997): 212–223.

———. *Töten oder Lieben: Gewalt und Gewaltlosigkeit in Religion und Christentum*. Munich: Kösel, 1994.

———. *Ursünde Gewalt: Das Ringen um Gewaltfreiheit*. Düsseldorf: Patmos, 2001.

Bauer, Joachim. *Warum ich fühle, was du fühlst: Intuitive Kommunikation und das Geheimnis der Spiegelneurone*. 7th ed. Munich: Wilhelm Heyne Verlag, 2007.

Beck, Ulrich. "Ursprung als Utopie: Politische Freiheit als Sinnquelle der Moderne." In *Kinder der Freiheit*, edited by Ulrich Beck, 382–401. Frankfurt am Main: Suhrkamp, 1997.

———. "Väter der Freiheit." In *Kinder der Freiheit*, edited by Ulrich Beck, 333–381. Frankfurt am Main: Suhrkamp, 1997.

Bellinger, Charles K. *The Genealogy of Violence: Reflections on Creation, Freedom, and Evil*. Oxford: Oxford University Press, 2001.

Benjamin, Walter. *Selected Writings. Volume 1: 1913–1926*. Edited by M. Bullock and M. W. Jennings. Cambridge: The Belknap Press of Harvard University Press, 1996.

———. *Selected Writings. Volume 2: 1927–1934*. Translated by Rodney Livingstone and others. Cambridge: The Belknap Press of Harvard University Press, 1999.

Bennington, Geoffrey, and Jacques Derrida. *Jacques Derrida*. Religion and Postmodernism. Chicago: University of Chicago Press, 1999.

Berger, Peter L. "Globaler Pluralismus." *Conturen*, no. 3 (1997): 33–45.

———. "Sociology: A Disinvitation?" *Society* 30, no. 1 (1992): 12–18.

Bergson, Henri. *Creative Evolution*. Translated by Arthur Mitchell. Lanham, MD: University Press of America, 1983.

———. *The Two Sources of Morality and Religion*. Translated by R. Ashley Audra and Cloudesley Brereton. Notre Dame, IN: University of Notre Dame Press, 1977.

Berlin, Isaiah. *The Crooked Timber of Humanity: Chapters in the History of Ideas*. New York: Vintage Books, 1992.

———. *The Hedgehog and the Fox: An Essay on Tolstoy's View of History*. New York: Simon & Schuster, 1953.

Bielefeldt, Heiner, and Wilhelm Heitmeyer, eds. *Politisierte Religion: Ursachen und Erscheinungsformen des modernen Fundamentalismus*. Frankfurt am Main: Suhrkamp, 1998.

Biser, Eugen. "Ein überbrückendes Schlußwort." *Theologische Revue* 90 (1994): 367–368.

Bland, Byron. "Marching and Rising: The Rituals of Small Differences and Great Violence." *Contagion: Journal of Violence, Mimesis, and Culture* 4 (1997): 101–119.

Bödefeld, Axel. ". . . Und du bist weg!" *Bullying in Schulklassen als Sündenbock-Mechanismus*. Beiträge zur mimetischen Theorie. Vienna: LIT, 2006.

Böhm, Thomas H. *Religion durch Medien—Kirche in den Medien und die "Medienreligion." Eine problemorientierte Analyse und Leitlinien einer theologischen Hermeneutik*. Stuttgart: Verlag W. Kohlhammer, 2005.

Bolz, Norbert. *Das Wissen der Religion: Betrachtungen eines religiös Unmusikalischen*. Munich: Wilhelm Fink, 2008.

———. *Die Sinngesellschaft*. Düsseldorf: ECON, 1997.

———. "Kapitalistische Religion—Die Antike in Walter Benjamins Moderne." In *Die berechnende*

Vernunft: Über das Ökonomische in allen Lebenslagen, edited by Wolfgang Müller-Funk, 253–269. Vienna: Picus Verlag, 1993.

Bolzano, Klaus. *Die Neidgesellschaft: Warum wir anderen nichts gönnen*. Vienna: Goldegg Verlag, 2007.

Bonhoeffer, Dietrich. *Ethics*. Translated by Neville Horton Smith. New York: Macmillan Publishing Co., 1965.

Brumlik, Micha. "Die Aufhebung des Menschenopfers in der Isaak- und Iphigenieerzählung." In *Das Opfer: Religionsgeschichtliche, theologische und politische Aspekte*, edited by Dietrich Neuhaus, 51–65. Frankfurt am Main: Haag + Herrchen Verlag, 1998.

Budzik, Stanislaw. "Perversa Imitatio Dei: Zum Begriff der Erbsünde bei Augustinus und Schwager." In *Vom Fluch und Segen der Sündenböcke: Raymund Schwager zum 60. Geburtstag*, edited by József Niewiadomski and Wolfgang Palaver, 93–109. Thaur: Kulturverlag, 1995.

Burckhardt, Jacob. *Reflections on History*. Translated by Marie Donald Hottinger. London: G. Allen & Unwin, Ltd., 1943.

———. *Über das Studium der Geschichte*. Munich: Verlag C.H. Beck, 1982.

———. *Weltgeschichtliche Betrachtungen: Über geschichtliches Studium. Mit einem Nachwort von J. Fest*. Basel: Schwabe Verlag & Co. AG, 1993.

Bürger, Peter. *Das Verschwinden des Subjekts: Eine Geschichte der Subjektivität von Montaigne bis Barthes*. Frankfurt am Main: Suhrkamp, 1998.

Burkert, Walter. *Anthropologie des religiösen Opfers. Die Sakralisierung der Gewalt*. München: Carl Friedrich von Siemensstiftung, 1983.

———. *Homo Necans: The Anthropology of Ancient Greek Sacrificial Ritual and Myth*. Translated by Peter Bing. Berkeley: University of California Press, 1983.

———. "The Problem of Ritual Killing." In *Violent Origins: Walter Burkert, René Girard, and Jonathan Z. Smith on Ritual Killing and Cultural Formation*, edited by Robert G. Hamerton-Kelly, 149–176. Stanford, CA: Stanford University Press, 1987.

Cacciari, Massimo. *Gewalt und Harmonie: Geo-Philosophie Europas*. Translated by Günter Memmert. Munich: Carl Hanser Verlag, 1995.

Calasso, Roberto. *The Ruin of Kasch*. Translated by William Weaver and Stephen Sartarelli. Cambridge, MA: Harvard University Press, 1994.

Camus, Albert. *The Fall*. Translated by Justin O'Brien. 1st American ed. New York: Vintage, 1956.

———. *The Rebel*. Translated by Anthony Bower. Penguin Classics ed. London: Penguin Books, 2000.

———. *Reflections on the Guillotine: An Essay on Capital Punishment*. Translated by Richard Howard. Michigan City, IN: Fridtjof-Karla Publications, 1960.

———. *The Stranger*. Translated by Matthew Ward. 1st Vintage International ed. New York: Vintage International, 1989.

Canetti, Elias. *Crowds and Power*. Translated by Carol Stewart. New York: Viking Press, 1962.

Canetti, Elias. *Masse und Macht*. Frankfurt am Main: Fischer, 1980.

Casanova, José. "Religion und Öffentlichkeit: Ein Ost-/Westvergleich." *Transit*, no. 8 (1994): 21–41.

Cervantes Saavedra, Miguel de. *Don Quixote*. Translated by John Ormsby. A Norton Critical Edition. New York: Norton, 1981.

Chilton, Bruce. *The Temple of Jesus: His Sacrificial Program within a Cultural History of Sacrifice.* University Park: Pennsylvania State University, 1992.

Clausewitz, Carl von. *On War.* Translated by Michael Howard and Peter Paret. Princeton, NJ: Princeton University Press, 1984.

Contat, Michel, and Michel Rybalka, eds. *The Writings of Jean-Paul Sartre.* Vol. 2, *Selected Prose.* Northwestern University Studies in Phenomenology & Existential Philosophy. Evanston, IL: Northwestern University Press, 1974.

Copray, Norbert. "Interview mit Hubert Cancik." *Börsenblatt für den deutschen Buchhandel* 19 (Theologie) (1991): 812–813.

Creveld, Martin van. *The Transformation of War.* New York: The Free Press, 1991.

Culler, Jonathan. *On Deconstruction: Theory and Criticism after Structuralism.* Ithaca, NY: Cornell University Press, 1989.

Da Silva, Gilberto. *Am Anfang war das Opfer: René Girard aus Afroindiolateinamerikanischer Perspektive.* Münster: LIT, 2001.

De Keukelaere, Simon. "What Is Deviated Transcendency? Woolf's *The Waves* as a Textbook Case." *Contagion: Journal of Violence, Mimesis, and Culture* 12–13 (2006): 195–218.

Depoortere, Frederiek. *Christ in Postmodern Philosophy: Gianni Vattimo, René Girard and Slavoj Zizek.* London: T & T Clark, 2008.

Derrida, Jacques. *Deconstruction in a Nutshell: A Conversation with Jacques Derrida.* New York: Fordham University Press, 1997.

———. *Dissemination.* Translated by Barbara Johnson. Chicago: University of Chicago Press, 1981.

———. "Force of Law: The 'Mystical Foundation of Authority.'" *Cardozo Law Review* 11, no. 5–6 (1990): 919–1045.

———. *Margins of Philosophy.* Translated by Alan Bass. Brighton, Sussex: Harvester, 1982.

———. *Of Grammatology.* Translated by Gayatri Chakravorty Spivak. Baltimore: Johns Hopkins University Press, 1997.

———. *Politics of Friendship.* Translated by George Collins. London: Verso, 1997.

———. "Structure, Sign, and Play in the Discourse of the Human Sciences." In *The Structuralist Controversy: The Languages of Criticism and the Sciences of Man,* edited by Richard Macksey and Eugenio Donato, 247–272. Baltimore: Johns Hopkins University Press, 1972.

Detienne, Marcel. "The Violence of Wellborn Ladies: Women in the Thesmophoria." In *The Cuisine of Sacrifice among the Greeks,* edited by Marcel Detienne and Jean-Pierre Vernant, 129–147. Chicago: University of Chicago Press, 1989.

Dieckmann, Bernhard, ed. *Das Opfer—Aktuelle Kontroversen: Religions-politischer Diskurs im Kontext der mimetischen Theorie. Deutsch-Italienische Fachtagung der Guardini Stiftung in der Villa Vigoni 18.–22. Oktober 1999.* Beiträge zur mimetischen Theorie. Münster: LIT, 2001.

———. *Judas als Sündenbock: Eine verhängnisvolle Geschichte von Angst und Vergeltung.* Munich: Kösel, 1991.

Dierken, Jörg. "Gott und Gewalt: Ethisch-religiöse Aspekte eines zentralen Phänomens von Vergesellschaftung." *Zeitschrift für Missionswissenschaft und Religionswissenschaft* 83 (1999): 277–291.

Donoso Cortés, Juan de. *Essay on Catholicism, Liberalism and Socialism: Considered in Their Fundamental Principles.* Translated by Madeleine Vinton Goddard. Albany, NY: Preserving Christian Publications, 1991.

Dostoyevsky, Fyodor. *The Adolescent.* Translated by Andrew R. MacAndrew. 1st ed. Garden City, NY: Doubleday, 1971.

———. *The Brothers Karamazov.* Translated by Richard Pevear and Larissa Volokhonsky. 1st Vintage Classics ed. New York: Vintage Books, 1991.

———. *Crime and Punishment.* Translated by Jessie Senior Coulson. Oxford: Oxford University Press, 1998.

———. *Demons.* Translated by Richard Pevear and Larissa Volokhonsky. 1st ed. New York: A.A. Knopf, 1994.

———. *Notes from the Underground and The Gambler.* Translated by Jane Kentish. Oxford: Oxford University Press, 1991.

———. *The Short Stories of Dostoevsky.* Translated by Constance Garnett. New York: Dial Press, 1946.

Drexler, Josef. *Die Illusion des Opfers: Eine wissenschaftlicher Überblick über die wichtigsten Opfertheorien ausgehend vom Deleuzianischen Polyperspektivismusmodell.* Münchener Ethnologische Abhandlungen. Munich: Akademischer Verlag, 1993.

Duff, Paul, and Joseph Hallman. "Murder in the Garden? The Envy of the Gods in Genesis 2 and 3." *Contagion: Journal of Violence, Mimesis, and Culture* 3 (1996): 183–200.

Dugatkin, Lee Alan. *The Imitation Factor: Evolution beyond the Gene.* New York: The Free Press, 2000.

Dumont, Louis. *Essays on Individualism: Modern Ideology in Anthropological Perspective.* Chicago: University of Chicago Press, 1986.

Dumouchel, Paul. "Hobbes: La course à la souveraineté." In *To Honor René Girard: Presented on the Occasion of His Sixtieth Birthday by Colleagues, Students, and Friends,* edited by Alphonse Juilland, 153–176. Stanford French and Italian Studies. Saratoga, CA: Anma Libri, 1986.

———. "Violence et non-violence." *Esprit* 60, no. 12 (1981): 153–160.

Dumouchel, Paul, and Jean Pierre Dupuy. *L'enfer des choses: René Girard et la logique de l'économie.* Paris: Édition du Seuil, 1979.

Dunne, John S. *The Peace of the Present: An Unviolent Way of Life.* Notre Dame, IN: University of Notre Dame Press, 1991.

Dupuy, Jean Pierre. "Le signe et l'envie." In *L'enfer des choses: René Girard et la logique de l'économie* by Paul Dumouchel and Jean-Pierre Dupuy, 15–134. Paris: Édition du Seuil, 1979.

Dupuy, Jean-Pierre. *Libéralisme et justice sociale: Le sacrifice et l'envie.* Pluriel. Paris: Hachette-littératures, 1997.

———. "Mimesis and Social Autopoiesis: A Girardian Reading of Hayek." *Paragrana: Internationale Zeitschrift für Historische Anthropologie* 4, no. 2 (1995): 192–214.

———. "The Self-Deconstruction of the Liberal Order." *Contagion: Journal of Violence, Mimesis, and Culture* 2 (1995): 1–16.

———. "Self-Reference in Literature." *Poetics* 18 (1989): 491–515.

———. "Totalization and Misrecognition." In *Violence and Truth: On the Work of René Girard*, edited by Paul Dumouchel, 75–100. Stanford, CA: Stanford University Press, 1988.

Dupuy, Jean-Pierre, and Francisco J. Varela. "Understanding Origins: An Introduction." In *Understanding Origins: Contemporary Views on the Origin of Life, Mind and Society*, edited by Jean-Pierre Dupuy and Francisco J. Varela, 1–25. Dordrecht: Kluwer Academic Publishers, 1992.

Durkheim, Emile. *The Elementary Forms of the Religious Life*. Translated by Joseph Ward Swain. New York: The Free Press, 1965.

———. *Professional Ethics and Civic Morals*. Translated by Cornelia Brookfield. 2nd ed. London: Routledge, 1992.

Ecker, Ludwig. *Zwischen Recht und Vergebung: Der Beitrag der Theorie René Girards zur Beschreibung christlicher Existenz*. Linz: Verlagsatelier Wagner, 1999.

Ehrenreich, Barbara. *Blood Rites: Origins and History of the Passions of War*. 1st ed. New York: Metropolitan Books, 1997.

Ehrenzweig, Armin. "Kain und Lamech." *Zeitschrift für die Alttestamentliche Wissenschaft* 35 (1915): 1–11.

Eisler, Riane. *The Chalice and the Blade: Our History, Our Future*. San Francisco: Harper & Row, 1987.

Eliade, Mircea. *A History of Religious Ideas*. Vol. 1, *From the Stone Age to the Eleusinian Mysteries*. Translated by Willard R. Trask. Chicago: University of Chicago Press, 1978.

———. *Patterns in Comparative Religion*. Translated by Rosemary Sheed. Lincoln: University of Nebraska Press, 1996.

———. *The Sacred and the Profane: The Nature of Religion*. Translated by Willard R. Trask. San Diego: Harcourt, 1987.

Ellrich, Lutz. "Gewalt und Zeichen: René Girard." In *Von Michel Serres bis Julia Kristeva*, edited by Joseph Jurt, 57–85. Freiburg: Rombach Verlag, 1999.

Elshtain, Jean Bethke. *Augustine and the Limits of Politics*. Notre Dame, IN: Notre Dame University Press, 1995.

Engelmann, Peter. "Einführung: Postmoderne und Dekonstruktion. Zwei Stichwörter zur zeitgenössischen Philosophie." In *Postmoderne und Dekonstruktion: Texte französischer Philosophen der Gegenwart*, edited by Peter Engelmann, 5–32. Stuttgart: Philipp Reclam jun., 1990.

Enzensberger, Hans Magnus. *Civil Wars: From L.A. to Bosnia*. Translated by Piers Spence and Martin Chalmers. New York: The New Press, 1994.

Evans-Pritchard, E. E. *Theories of Primitive Religion*. Oxford: Clarendon Press, 1965.

Feenberg, Andrew. "Fetishism and Form: Erotic and Economic Disorder in Literature." In *Violence and Truth: On the Work of René Girard*, edited by Paul Dumouchel, 134–151. Stanford, CA: Stanford University Press, 1988.

Fetscher, Iring. *Rousseaus politische Philosophie: Zur Geschichte des demokratischen Freiheitsbegriffs*. 7th ed. Frankfurt am Main: Suhrkamp, 1993.

Feuerbach, Ludwig. *Das Wesen des Christentums*. Stuttgart: Philipp Reclam, 2002.

———. *The Essence of Christianity*. Translated by George Eliot, The Library of Religion and Culture. New York: Harper, 1957.

Finkielkraut, Alain. *Der eingebildete Jude*. Translated by Hainer Kober. Frankfurt am Main: Fischer Taschenbuch Verlag, 1984.

Flaubert, Gustave. *Madame Bovary*. Translated by Geoffrey Wall. Penguin Classics. London: Penguin, 2003.

Fleming, Chris. *René Girard: Violence and Mimesis*. Cambridge: Polity, 2004.

Fornari, Giuseppe. "Dionysos, die Natur und die evangelische Differenz." In *Das Opfer—Aktuelle Kontroversen: Religions-politischer Diskurs im Kontext der mimetischen Theorie. Deutsch-Italienische Fachtagung der Guardini Stiftung in der Villa Vigoni 18.-22. Oktober 1999*, edited by Bernhard Dieckmann, 37–58. Münster: LIT, 2001.

———. "Towards a Biblical Anthropology of Violence: Acquisitive Imitation and Violence in Original Sin." *Bulletin of the Colloquium on Violence & Religion*, no. 14 (1998): 6–7.

Frazer, James George. *The Golden Bough: A Study in Magic and Religion*. London: Macmillan 1913; Oxford: Oxford University Press, 1998.

Freccero, John. *Dante: The Poetics of Conversion*. Cambridge, MA: Harvard University Press, 1986.

Freud, Sigmund. *Beyond the Pleasure Principle*. Translated by James Strachey. Rev. ed. International Psycho-Analytical Library. New York: Liveright Publishing Corp., 1961.

———. *Group Psychology and the Analysis of the Ego*. Translated by James Strachey. New York: Norton, 1975.

———. *Moses and Monotheism*. Translated by Katherine Jones. International Psycho-Analytical Library. London: Hogarth Press, 1951.

———. *Totem and Taboo: Some Points of Agreement between the Mental Lives of Savages and Neurotics*. Translated by James Strachey. The Standard Edition of the Complete Psychological Works of Sigmund Freud. New York: W.W. Norton, 1989.

———. *Writings on Art and Literature*. Translated by James Strachey. Stanford, CA: Stanford University Press, 1997.

Freud, Sigmund, and Albert Einstein. *Why War?* An International Series of Open Letters. Paris: International Institute of Intellectual Co-operation, League of Nations, 1933.

Freud, Sigmund, and Peter Gay. *The Freud Reader*. Translated by James Strachey. New York: W.W. Norton, 1989.

Fukuyama, Francis. *The End of History and the Last Man*. New York: Avon Books, 1993.

———. *Our Posthuman Future: Consequences of the Biotechnology Revolution*. New York: Farrar, Straus and Giroux, 2002.

Fustel de Coulanges, Numa Denis. *The Ancient City: A Study on the Religion, Laws, and Institutions of Greece and Rome. With a New Foreword by Arnaldo Momigliano and S. C. Humphreys*. Baltimore: Johns Hopkins University Press, 1980.

Gadamer, Hans-Georg. "Plato und die Dichter." In *Griechische Philosophie I*, 187–211. Tübingen: J.C.B. Mohr (Paul Siebeck), 1985.

Gallese, Vittorio. "The Two Sides of Mimesis: Girard's Mimetic Theory, Embodied Simulation and Social Identification." *Journal of Consciousness Studies* 16, no. 4 (2009): 21–44.

Gans, Eric. *The Origin of Language: A Formal Theory of Representation*. Berkeley: University of California Press, 1981.

———. *The Scenic Imagination: Originary Thinking from Hobbes to the Present Day*. Stanford, CA: Stanford University Press, 2008.

Garrels, Scott R. "Imitation, Mirror Neurons, and Mimetic Desire: Convergence between the Mimetic Theory of René Girard and Empirical Research on Imitation." *Contagion: Journal of Violence, Mimesis, and Culture* 12–13 (2006): 47–86.

———, ed. *Mimesis and Science: Empirical Research on Imitation and the Mimetic Theory of Culture and Religion*. Studies in Violence, Mimesis, and Culture. East Lansing: Michigan State University Press, 2011.

Gauchet, Marcel. "Alexis de Tocqueville, l'Amérique et nous." *LIBRE: Politique—anthropologie— philosophie*, no. 7 (1980): 43–120.

———. *The Disenchantment of the World: A Political History of Religion*. Translated by Oscar Burge. Princeton, NJ: Princeton University Press, 1999.

Gebauer, Gunter. "Größenphantasien des Sports." In *Sport—Eros—Tod*, edited by Gerd Hortleder and Gunter Gebauer, 216–230. Frankfurt am Main: Suhrkamp, 1986.

Gebauer, Gunter, and Christoph Wulf. *Mimesis: Culture—Art—Society*. Translated by Don Reneau. Berkeley: University of California Press, 1995.

———. *Mimesis. Kultur—Kunst—Gesellschaft*. Reinbek bei Hamburg: rowohlts enzyklopädie, 1992.

Gekle, Hanna. "Aggression." In *Handbuch religionswissenschaftlicher Grundbegriffe*, edited by Hubert Cancik, Burkhard Gladigow and Matthias Laubscher, 394–406. Stuttgart: Verlag W. Kohlhammer, 1988.

Gellner, Ernest. *Muslim Society*. Cambridge: Cambridge University Press, 1981.

Gernet, Louis. *Anthropologie de la Grèce antique*. Textes à l'appui. Paris: F. Maspero, 1968.

Giddens, Anthony. *The Nation-State and Violence*. Berkeley: University of California Press, 1987.

Girard, René. "Are the Gospels Mythical?" *First Things: A Monthly Journal of Religion & Public Life*, no. 62 (1996): 27–31.

———. *Battling to the End: Conversations with Benoît Chantre*. Translated by Mary Baker. Studies in Violence, Mimesis, and Culture. East Lansing: Michigan State University Press, 2010.

———. *Celui par qui le scandale arrive*. Paris: Desclée de Brouwer, 2001.

———. "Das Evangelium legt die Gewalt bloß." *Orientierung* 38, no. 5 (1974): 53–56.

———. *De la violence à la divinité*. Bibliothèque Grasset. Paris: Bernard Grasset, 2007.

———. *Deceit, Desire and the Novel: Self and Other in Literary Structure*. Translated by Yvonne Freccero. Baltimore: Johns Hopkins University Press, 1966.

———. "Der Grundlegende Mord im denken Nietzsches." In *Das Heilige: Seine Spur in der Moderne*, edited by Dietmar Kamper and Christoph Wulf, 255–274. Frankfurt am Main: Athenäum, 1987.

———. "Die Einheit von Ethik und Ästhetik im Ritual." In *Ethik der Ästhetik*, edited by Christoph Wulf, Dietmar Kamper, and Hans Ulrich Gumbrecht, 69–74. Berlin: Akademie Verlag, 1994.

———. "Disorder and Order in Mythology." Paper presented at the Stanford International Symposium, Saratoga, California. Saratoga, CA: Anma Libri 1981.

———. *Evolution and Conversion: Dialogues on the Origin of Culture*. With Pierpaolo Antonello and João Cezar de Castro Rocha. London: Continuum, 2008.

———. "Existentialism and Criticism." *Yale French Studies*, no. 16 (1955): 45–52.

———. "The First Stone." *Renascence* 52 (1999): 5–17.

———. "The Founding Murder in the Philosophy of Nietzsche." In *Violence and Truth: On the Work of René Girard*, edited by Paul Dumouchel. Stanford, CA: Stanford University Press, 1988.

———. "From Ritual to Science." *Configurations*, no. 8 (2000): 171–185.

———. *The Girard Reader.* New York: Crossroad Publishing Co., 1996.

———. *I See Satan Fall Like Lightning.* Translated by James G. Williams. Maryknoll, NY: Orbis Books, 2001.

———. "Is There Anti-Semitism in the Gospels?" *Biblical Interpretation* 1, no. 3 (1993): 339–352.

———. *Je vois Satan tomber comme l'éclair.* Paris: Bernard Grasset, 1999.

———. *Job: The Victim of His People.* Translated by Yvonne Freccero. Stanford, CA: Stanford University Press, 1987.

———. *Mimesis and Theory: Essays on Literature and Criticism, 1953–2005.* Edited by R. Doran. Stanford, CA: Stanford University Press, 2008.

———. "Mimetische Theorie und Theologie." In *Vom Fluch und Segen der Sündenböcke: Raymund Schwager zum 60. Geburtstag,* edited by Józef Niewiadomski and Wolfgang Palaver, 15–29. Thaur: Kulturverlag, 1995.

———. "Mythology, Violence, Christianity." *Paragrana: Internationale Zeitschrift für Historische Anthropologie* 4, no. 2 (1995): 103–116.

———. "Mythos und Gegenmythos: Zu Kleist 'Das Erdbeben in Chili.'" In *Positionen der Literaturwissenschaft: Acht Modellanalysen am Beispiel von Kleists "Das Erdbeben in Chili,"* edited by David E. Wellbery, 130–148. Munich: Verlag C. H. Beck, 2001.

———. *Oedipus Unbound: Selected Writings on Rivalry and Desire.* Edited and with an Introduction by M. R. Anspach. Stanford, CA: Stanford University Press, 2004.

———. "Origins: A View from the Literature." In *Understanding Origins: Contemporary Views on the Origin of Life, Mind and Society,* edited by F. J. Varela and J. P. Dupuy, 27–42. Dordrecht: Kluwer Academic Publishers, 1992.

———. *Quand ces choses commenceront . . . Entretiens avec Michel Treguer.* Paris: arléa, 1994.

———. "Reconciliation, Violence and the Gospel." In *Film and Modernity: Violence, Sacrifice and Religion,* edited by G. Larcher, F. Grabner, and Ch. Wessely. Graz: Thaur, 1997.

———. *Resurrection from the Underground: Feodor Dostoevsky.* Translated by James G. Williams. New York: Crossroad Publishing Co., 1997.

———. *Sacrifice.* Translated by Matthew Pattillo and David Dawson. Breakthroughs in Mimetic Theory. East Lansing: Michigan State University Press, 2011.

———. *Le sacrifice.* Paris: Bibliothèque nationale de France, 2003.

———. *The Scapegoat.* Translated by Yvonne Freccero. Baltimore: Johns Hopkins University Press, 1986.

———. *A Theater of Envy: William Shakespeare.* Oxford: Oxford University Press, 1991.

———. *Things Hidden since the Foundation of the World: Research Undertaken in Collaboration with*

J.-M. Oughourlian and G. Lefort. Translated by Stephen Bann and Michael Metteer. Stanford, CA: Stanford University Press, 1987.

———. *"To Double Business Bound": Essays on Literature, Mimesis, and Anthropology.* Baltimore: Johns Hopkins University Press, 1978.

———. "Victims, Violence and Christianity." *The Month* 259, no. 1564 (1998): 129–135.

———. *Violence and the Sacred.* Translated by Patrick Gregory. Baltimore: Johns Hopkins University Press, 1977.

———. "Violence Renounced: Response." In *Violence Renounced: René Girard Biblical Studies and Peacemaking*, edited by W. M. Swartley, 308–320. Telford, PA: Pandora Press, 2000.

———. "Violence and Religion." In *Das Gewaltpotential des Monotheismus und der dreieine Gott*, edited by Peter Walter, 180–190. Freiburg: Herder, 2005.

———. *Wissenschaft und christlicher Glaube.* Translated by Shivaun Heath. Tübingen: Mohr Siebeck, 2007.

Girard, René, and Rebecca Adams. "Violence, Difference, Sacrifice: A Conversation with René Girard." *Religion & Literature* 25, no. 2 (1993): 11–33.

Girard, René, and Mark Anspach. "Mark: A Response: Reflections from the Perspective of Mimetic Theory." In *Violence and the Sacred in the Modern World*, edited by M. Juergensmeyer. London: Routledge, 1992.

Girard, René, and Thomas Assheuer. "Jesus, unser Sündenbock: Interview mit Thomas Assheuer." *Die Zeit* 13 (23 March 2005): 49.

Girard, René, Sergio Benvenuto, and Maurizio Meloni. "Psychoanalysis and Mimetic Theory: Difference and Identity." *Journal of European Psychoanalysis* 14 (2002): 3–25.

Girard, René, and Thomas F. Bertonneau. "The Logic of the Undecidable: An Interview." *Paroles Gelées*, no. 5 (1987): 1–24.

Girard, René, and David Cayley. "The Scapegoat: René Girard's Anthropology of Violence and Religion." In *Canadian Broadcasting Corporation Radio Interviews.* Toronto: CBS, 2001.

Girard, René, and Robert Doran. "Apocalyptic Thinking after 9/11: An Interview." *SubStance: A Review of Theory & Literary Criticism* 37, no. 1 (2008): 20–32.

Girard, René, and Giuseppe Fornari. *La vittima e la folla: Violenza del mito e cristianesimo.* Treviso: Santi Quaranta, 1998.

Girard, René, and Nathan Gardels. "Ratzinger Is Right: Interview with Nathan Gardels." *New Perspectives Quarterly* 22, no. 3 (2005): 43–48.

Girard, René, and Richard. J. Golsan, "Interview." In Richard J. Golsan, *René Girard and Myth: An Introduction*, 129–149. New York: Garland Publishing, Inc., 1993.

Girard, René, and Sandor Goodhart. "Mimesis, Sacrifice, and the Bible: A Conversation with Sandor Goodhart." In *Sacrifice, Scripture, and Substitution: Readings in Ancient Judaism and Christianity*, edited by Ann W. Astell and Sandor Goodhart, 39–69. Notre Dame, IN: University of Notre Dame Press, 2011.

Girard, René, and Michael Jakob. "Gespräch mit René Girard." In *Aussichten des Denkens*, edited by Michael Jakob, 155–176. Munich: Wilhelm Fink Verlag, 1994.

Girard, René, and Giulio Meotti. "René Girard's Accusation: Intellectuals Are the Castrators of Meaning." *Modern Age* 50, no. 2 (2008): 180–185.

Girard, René, and Markus Müller. "Interview with René Girard." *Anthropoetics: The Electronic Journal of Generative Anthropology*, no. 1 (1996).

Girard, René, and Wolfgang Palaver. "The Bloody Skin of the Victim." In *The New Visibility of Religion: Studies in Religion and Cultural Hermeneutics*, edited by Michael Hoelzl and Graham Ward, 59–67. London: Continuum, 2008.

Girard, René, and Wolfgang Palaver. *Gewalt und Religion: Ursache oder Wirkung?* Translated by Heide Lipecky and Andreas Leopold Hofbauer. Berlin: Matthes & Seitz, 2010.

Girard, René, and Michel Serres. *Le tragique et la pitié: Discours de réception de René Girard à l'Académie française et réponse de Michel Serres.* Paris: Le Pommier, 2007.

Girard, René, and Henri Tincq. "'What Is Happening Today Is Mimetic Rivalry on a Global Scale': Interview with Henri Tincq." *South Central Review* 19, no. 2–3 (2002).

Glenny, Misha. *The Fall of Yugoslavia: The Third Balkan War.* New York: Penguin Books, 1994.

Goethe, Johann Wolfgang von. *The Autobiography of Johann Wolfgang Von Goethe.* Translated by John Oxenford. 2 vols. Chicago: University of Chicago Press, 1974.

———. *Faust.* Translated by Stuart Pratt Atkins. Cambridge, MA: Insel Publishers Boston, 1984.

———. *The Sorrows of Young Werther.* Translated by Burton Pike. New York: Modern Library, 2004.

———. *Torquato Tasso.* Translated by Alan Brownjohn. Angel Classics ed. London: Angel Books, 1985.

———. *West-Eastern Divan.* Translated by J. Whaley. London: Wolff, 1974.

Golding, William. *Lord of the Flies.* New York: Coward-McCann, 1962.

Goldmann, Lucien. *Towards a Sociology of the Novel.* Translated by Alan Sheridan. London: Tavistock Publications, 1975.

Golsan, Richard J. *René Girard and Myth: An Introduction.* Theorists of Myth. New York and London: Garland Publishing, Inc., 1993.

Goodhart, Sandor. "'*Al Lo-Chamas Asah* (Although He Had Done No Violence)': René Girard and the Innocent Victim." In *Violence Renounced: René Girard, Biblical Studies and Peacemaking*, edited by Willard M. Swartley, 157–177. Telford, PA: Pandora Press, 2000.

———. *Sacrificing Commentary: Reading the End of Literature.* Baltimore: Johns Hopkins University Press, 1996.

Graham, E. Tyler. "The Danger of Durkheim: Ambiguity in the Theory of Social Effervescence." *Religion* 37, no. 1 (2007): 26–38.

Graham, Tyler. "St. Augustine's Novelistic Conversion." *Contagion: Journal of Violence, Mimesis, and Culture* 5 (1998): 135–154.

Graves, Robert von Ranke. *The Greek Myths.* Complete and unabridged ed. Mt. Kisco, NY: Moyer Bell, 1988.

Greisch, Jean. "Homo Mimeticus: Kritische Überlegungen zu den anthropologischen Voraussetzungen von René Girards Opferbegriff." In *Zur Theorie des Opfers: Ein interdisziplinäres Gespräch*, edited by Richard Schenk, 27–63. Stuttgart-Bad Cannstatt: frommann-holzboog, 1995.

Gronemeyer, Marianne. *Die Macht der Bedürfnisse: Überfluss und Knappheit*. Darmstadt: Wissenschaftliche Buchgesellschaft, 2002.

Grote, Jim, and John McGeeney. *Clever as Serpents: Business Ethics and Office Politics*. Collegeville, MN: Liturgical Press, 1997.

Guggenberger, Wilhelm. *Die List der Dinge: Sackgassen der Wirtschaftsethik in einer funktional differenzierten Gesellschaft*. Beiträge zur mimetischen Theorie. Wien: LIT, 2007.

Guggenberger, Wilhelm, and Wolfgang Palaver, eds. *Im Wettstreit um das Gute*: *Annäherungen an den Islam aus der Sicht der mimetischen Theorie*. Beiträge zur mimetischen Theorie. Vienna: LIT, 2009.

Guéhenno, Jean-Marie. *The End of the Nation-State*. Translated by Victoria Elliott. Minneapolis: University of Minnesota Press, 1995.

Haag, Ernst. "Die Botschaft vom Gottesknecht: Ein Weg zur Überwindung der Gewalt." In *Gewalt und Gewaltlosigkeit im Alten Testament*, edited by Norbert Lohfink, 159–213. Freiburg: Herder, 1983.

Habermas, Jürgen. *Justification and Application: Remarks on Discourse Ethics*. Translated by Ciaran Cronin. Cambridge, MA: MIT Press, 1993.

———. *The Postnational Constellation: Political Essays*. Translated by Max Pensky. Cambridge, MA: MIT Press, 2001.

———. *Time of Transitions*. Translated by Ciaran Cronin and Max Pensky. Cambridge: Polity, 2006.

Hallman, Joseph M. "Am I Born a Sinner? Augustine of Hippo and René Girard." *Irish Theological Quarterly* 59, no. 2 (1993): 81–93.

Hamerton-Kelly, Robert G., ed. *The Gospel and the Sacred: Poetics of Violence in Mark*. Minneapolis: Fortress, 1994.

———. *Politics and Apocalypse*. Studies in Violence, Mimesis, and Culture. East Lansing: Michigan State University Press, 2007.

———. "Popular Sovereignty and the Sacred: A Mimetic Reading of Rousseau's Doctrine of the General Will." *Paragrana: Internationale Zeitschrift für Historische Anthropologie* 4, no. 2 (1995): 215–244.

———. "Response to Qamar-Ul Huda." *Contagion: Journal of Violence, Mimesis, and Culture* 9 (2002): 99–104.

———. *Sacred Violence: Paul's Hermeneutic of the Cross*. Minneapolis: Fortress Press, 1992.

Hamerton-Kelly, Robert G., ed. *Violent Origins: Walter Burkert, René Girard, and Jonathan Z. Smith on Ritual Killing and Cultural Formation*. Stanford: Stanford University Press, 1987.

Hardin, Michael. "Sacrificial Language in Hebrews: Reappraising René Girard." In *Violence Renounced: René Girard, Biblical Studies, and Peacemaking*, edited by Willard M. Swartley, 103–119. Telford, PA: Pandora Press, 2000.

Harrer, Heinrich. *Geister und Dämonen: Magische Abenteure in fernen Ländern*. Frankfurt am Main: Ullstein, 1969.

Hassler, Peter. "Die Lüge des Hernán Cortés." *Die Zeit* 38 (18 September 1992): 20 (international edition).

———. *Menschenopfer bei den Azteken? Eine quellen- und ideologiekritische Studie*. Bern: Peter Lang Verlag, 1992.

Haubl, Rolf. *Neidisch sind immer nur die anderen: Über die Unfähigkeit, zufrieden zu sein.* Munich: Verlag C. H. Beck, 2001.

Hayek, Friedrich August. *The Constitution of Liberty.* London: Routledge, 1999.

Hayek, Friedrich August von. *The Fatal Conceit: The Errors of Socialism.* The Collected Works of F. A. Hayek. Chicago: University of Chicago Press, 1989.

Heerich, Thomas. *Transformation des Politikkonzepts von Hobbes zu Spinoza: Das Problem der Souveränität.* Würzburg: Königshausen & Neumann, 2000.

Hegel, Georg Wilhelm Friedrich. *Phenomenology of Spirit.* Translated by Arnold Miller. Oxford: Clarendon Press, 1977.

Heidegger, Martin *Being and Time.* Translated by John MacQuarrie and Edward Robinson. Library of Philosophy and Theology. London: SCM Press, 1962.

——. *An Introduction to Metaphysics.* Translated by Ralph Manheim. New Haven, CT: Yale University Press, 1959.

Heinsohn, Gunnar. *Die Erschaffung der Götter: Das Opfer als Ursprung der Religion.* Reinbek bei Hamburg: Rowohlt, 1997.

Heraclitus. *Fragments.* Translated by T. M. Robinson. Toronto: University of Toronto Press, 1987.

Herzog, Markwart. "Hingerichtete Verbrecher als Gegenstand der Heiligenverehrung: Zum Kontext von René Girard." *Geist und Leben* 65 (1992): 367–386.

——. "Religionstheorie und Theologie René Girards." *Kerygma und Dogma* 38, no. 2 (1992): 105–137.

Hobbes, Thomas. *Behemoth or the Long Parliament.* Chicago: University of Chicago Press, 1990.

——. *The Elements of Law Natural and Politic.* Part 1, *Human Nature*; part 2, *De Corpore Politico. With Three Lives.* Oxford: Oxford University Press, 1994.

——. *Leviathan.* Cambridge: Cambridge University Press, 1991.

——. *Leviathan, Sive de Materia, Forma, et Potestate Civitatis Ecclesiasticae et Civilis.* Thomae Hobbes Malmesburiensis Opera Philosophica Quae Latine Scripsit Omnia in Unum Corpus. London: Bohn, 1841.

——. *Man and Citizen: De Homine and De Cive.* Translated by Charles T. Wood, T.S.K. Scott-Craig, and Bernard Gert. Indianapolis: Hackett Publishing Co., 1991.

——. *On the Citizen.* Translated by Richard Tuck and Michael Silverthorne. Cambridge Texts in the History of Political Thought. New York: Cambridge University Press, 1998.

Hocart, Arthur Maurice. *The Life-Giving Myth, and Other Essays.* London: Methuen, 1952.

——. *Social Origins.* London: Watts, 1954.

——. *Kings and Councillors: An Essay in the Comparative Anatomy of Human Society.* Chicago: University of Chicago Press, 1970.

Hoffman, Bruce. *Inside Terrorism.* Rev. ed. New York: Columbia University Press, 2006.

Hölderlin, Friedrich. *Sämtliche Werke und Briefe.* 3 vols. Munich: Carl Hanser Verlag, 1992.

Hollier, Denis, ed. *The College of Sociology, 1937–1939.* Theory and History of Literature. Minneapolis: University of Minnesota Press, 1988.

Holmes, Stephen. "Introduction." In *Behemoth or the Long Parliament* by Thomas Hobbes. Chicago: University of Chicago Press, 1990.

Hörisch, Jochen. *Ende der Vorstellung: Die Poesie der Medien.* Frankfurt am Main: Suhrkamp, 1999.

Horstmann, Ulrich. *Das Untier: Konturen einer Philosophie der Menschenflucht.* Frankfurt am Main: Suhrkamp, 1985.

Hübner, Kurt. "Die Moderne Mythos-Forschung—Eine noch nicht erkannte Revolution." *Berliner Theologische Zeitschrift* 6 (1989): 8–21.

Huntington, Samuel P. *The Clash of Civilizations and the Remaking of World Order.* New York: Simon & Schuster, 1996.

Ignatieff, Michael. "The Balkan Tragedy." *New York Review of Books* 40, no. 9 (1993): 3–5.

——. *Blood and Belonging: Journeys into the New Nationalism.* 1st American ed. New York: Farrar, Straus and Giroux, 1994.

——. "Human Rights: The Midlife Crisis." *New York Review of Books* 46, no. 9 (1999): 58–62.

——. *The Warrior's Honor: Ethnic War and the Modern Conscience.* London: Metropolitan Books, 1998.

Illich, Ivan. *Vom Recht auf Gemeinheit.* Reinbek bei Hamburg: Rowohlt, 1982.

Irigaray, Luce. "Women, the Sacred, Money." In *Sexes and Genealogies*, 73–88. New York: Columbia University Press, 1993.

Jakob, Michael. "Gespräch mit René Girard." In *Aussichten des Denkens.* Munich: Wilhelm Fink Verlag, 1994.

Jauß, Hans Robert. *Ästhetische Erfahrung und literarische Hermeneutik.* 2nd ed. Frankfurt am Main: Suhrkamp, 1997.

Jensen, Adolf Ellegard. *Die getötete Gottheit: Weltbild einer frühen Kultur.* Stuttgart: Kohlhammer, 1966.

——. *Myth and Cult among Primitive Peoples.* Translated by Marianna Tax Choldin and Wolfgang Weissleder. Chicago: University of Chicago Press, 1963.

Johns, Loren L. "'A Better Sacrifice' or 'Better Than Sacrifice'? Response to Michael Hardin's 'Sacrificial Language in Hebrews.'" In *Violence Renounced: René Girard, Biblical Studies, and Peacemaking*, edited by Willard M. Swartley, 120–131. Telford, PA: Pandora Press, 2000.

Johnsen, William A. *Violence and Modernism: Ibsen, Joyce, and Woolf.* Gainesville: University Press of Florida, 2003.

Joyce, James. *Letters.* 3 vols. New York: Viking Press, 1957.

——. *Ulysses.* First Vintage International Edition ed. New York: Vintage Books, 1990.

Juergensmeyer, Mark. *Terror in the Mind of God: The Global Rise of Religious Violence.* Berkeley: University of California Press, 2001.

——, ed. *Violence and the Sacred in the Modern World.* London: Frank Cass, 1992.

Kafka, Franz. *The Metamorphosis, In the Penal Colony, and Other Stories.* Translated by Joachim Neugroschel. 1st Scribner Paperback Fiction ed. New York: Scribner Paperback Fiction, 2000.

——. *The Trial.* Translated by Willa Muir and Edwin Muir. Definitive ed. New York: Schocken Books, 1995.

Kahn, Victoria. "Hobbes, Romance, and the Contract of Mimesis." *Political Theory* 29, no. 1 (2001): 4–29.

Kallscheuer, Otto. *Gottes Wort und Volkes Stimme: Glaube, Macht, Politik.* Frankfurt am Main: Fischer Taschenbuch Verlag, 1994.

Kant, Immanuel. *Anthropology from a Pragmatic Point of View.* Translated by Robert B. Louden. Cambridge Texts in the History of Philosophy. Cambridge: Cambridge University Press, 2006.

———. *Idea for a Universal History with a Cosmopolitan Aim: A Critical Guide.* Translated by Allen W. Wood. Edited by Amélie Oksenberg Rorty and James Schmidt. Cambridge: Cambridge University Press, 2009.

———. *The Metaphysics of Morals.* Translated by Mary J. Gregor. Cambridge Texts in the History of Philosophy. Cambridge: Cambridge University Press, 1996.

———. *Religion within the Boundaries of Mere Reason and Other Writings.* Translated by Allen W. Wood and George Di Giovanni. Cambridge Texts in the History of Philosophy. Cambridge: Cambridge University Press, 1998.

———. *Schriften zur Geschichtsphilosophie.* Stuttgart: Philipp Reclam jun., 1985.

Kaptein, Roel. *On the Way of Freedom. With the Cooperation of Duncan Morrow.* Dublin: The Columba Press, 1993.

Karrer, Leo, Charles Martig, and Eleonore Näf, eds. *Gewaltige Opfer: Filmgespräche mit René Girard und Lars von Trier.* Film und Theologie. Köln: KIM-Verlag, 2000.

Kaufmann, Franz-Xaver. *Religion und Modernität: Sozialwissenschaftliche Perspektiven.* Tübingen: J.C.B. Mohr (Paul Siebeck), 1989.

Kepel, Gilles. *The Revenge of God: The Resurgence of Islam, Christianity, and Judaism in the Modern World.* Translated by Alan Braley. University Park: Pennsylvania State University Press, 1994.

Kern, Fritz. *Gottesgnadentum und Widerstandsrecht im frühen Mittelalter: Zur Entwicklungsgeschichte der Monarchie.* 3rd ed. Darmstadt: Wissenschaftliche Buchgesellschaft, 1962.

Kierkegaard, Søren. *The Concept of Anxiety: A Simple Psychologically Orienting Deliberation on the Dogmatic Issue of Hereditary Sin.* Translated by Albert Anderson and Reidar Thomte. Princeton, NJ: Princeton University Press, 1980.

———. *Eighteen Upbuilding Discourses.* Translated by Howard V. Hong and Edna H. Hong. Kierkegaard's Writings. Princeton, NJ: Princeton University Press, 1992.

———. *Upbuilding Discourses in Various Spirits.* Translated by Howard V. Hong and Edna H. Hong. Kierkegaard's Writings. Princeton, NJ: Princeton University Press, 1993.

Kirwan, Michael. *Discovering Girard.* London: Darton, Longman & Todd, 2004.

———. *Girard and Theology.* Philosophy and Theology. London: T & T Clark, 2009.

Kittsteiner, Heinz Dieter. *Listen der Vernunft: Motive geschichtsphilosophischen Denkens.* Frankfurt am Main: Fischer Taschenbuch Verlag, 1998.

Kitzmüller, Erich. *Gewalteskalation oder neues Teilen*, Beiträge zur mimetischen Theorie. Thaur: Druck- und Verlagshaus Thaur, 1996.

Kleist, Heinrich von. "On the Marionette Theater." In *German Romantic Criticism*, edited by A. Leslie Willson, 238–244. New York: Continuum, 1982.

Kleist, Heinrich von, Ludwig Tieck, and E.T.A. Hoffmann. *Six German Romantic Tales.* Translated by
    Ronald Taylor. London: Angel Books, 1985.

Klusemann, Kurt. *Das Bauopfer: Eine ethnographisch-prähistorische-linguistische Studie.* Graz:
    Selbstverlag der Verfassers, 1919.

Kofman, Sarah. "The Narcissistic Woman: Freud and Girard." *Diacritics: A Review of Contemporary
    Criticism* 10, no. 3 (1980): 36–45.

Kojève, Alexandre. "Hegel, Marx, and Christianity." *Interpretation: A Journal of Political Philosophy* 1,
    no. 1 (1970): 21–42.

———. *Introduction to the Reading of Hegel; Lectures on the Phenomenology of Spirit.* Translated by
    James H. Nichols Jr. New York: Basic Books, 1969.

———. *Introduction à la lecture de Hegel: Leçons sur la phénoménologie de l'esprit. Professées de 1933 à
    1939 à l'École des Hautes-Études réunies et publiées Raymond Queneau.* Paris: Gallimard, 1947.

Koselleck, Reinhart. "Zur historisch-politischen Semantik asymmetrischer Gegenbegriffe." In
    Vergangene Zukunft: Zur Semantik geschichtlicher Zeiten, 211–259. Frankfurt am Main: Suhrkamp,
    1995.

König, René. *Kleider und Leute: Zur Soziologie der Mode.* Frankfurt am Main: Fischer Bücherei, 1967.

Krippendorff, Ekkehard. *Politik in Shakespeares Dramen: Historien, Römerdramen, Tragödien.* Frankfurt
    am Main: Suhrkamp, 1992.

Künzli, Arnold. *Gotteskrise: Fragen zu Hiob: Lob des Agnostizismus.* Reinbek bei Hamburg: rowohlts
    enzyklopädie, 1998.

Laozi, and Arthur Waley. *The Way and Its Power: A Study of the Tao Tě Ching and Its Place in Chinese
    Thought.* New York: Grove Press, 1958.

Laqueur, Walter. *The New Terrorism: Fanaticism and the Arms of Mass Destruction.* New York: Oxford
    University Press, 1999.

Larcher, Gerhard. "Gewalt—Opfer—Stellvertretung: Ästhetisch-theologische Spiegelungen im
    zeitgenössischen Film." In *Vom Fluch und Segen der Sündenböcke: Raymund Schwager zum 60.
    Geburtstag,* edited by Józef Niewiadomski and Wolfgang Palaver, 179–198. Thaur: Kulturverlag,
    1995.

Larcher, Gerhard, Franz Grabner, and Christian Wessely, eds. *Visible Violence: Sichtbare und verschleierte
    Gewalt im Film. Beiträge zum Symposium "Film and Modernity: Violence, Sacrifice and Religion,"
    Graz 1997.* Beiträge zur mimetischen Theorie. Münster: LIT, 1998.

Lascaris, André. "Die Einmaligkeit Jesu." In *Dramatische Erlösungslehre: Ein Symposion,* edited by Józef
    Niewiadomski and Wolfgang Palaver, 213–226. Innsbruck: Tyrolia, 1992.

———. "Opfere weder Isaak noch dich selbst." In *Isaak wird wieder geopfert: Die "Bindung Isaaks"
    als Symbol des Leidens Israels. Versuche einer Deutung,* edited by Willem Zuidema, 146–179.
    Neukirchen-Vluyn: Neukirchener Verlag, 1987.

Lasine, Stuart. "Levite Violence, Fratricide, and Sacrifice in the Bible and Later Revolutionary Rhetoric."
    In *Curing Violence,* edited by Mark I. Wallace and Theophus H. Smith, 204–229. Sonoma, CA:
    Polebridge Press, 1994.

Leder, Karl Bruno. *Todesstraf: Ursprung, Geschichte, Opfer.* Munich: Meyster, 1980.

Lévi-Strauss, Claude. *The Naked Man.* Translated by John and Doreen Weightman. 1st American ed.
    Introduction to a Science of Mythology. New York: Harper & Row, 1981.

———. *The Raw and the Cooked.* Translated by John and Doreen Weightman. Introduction to a
    Science of Mythology. New York: Harper & Row, 1969.

———. *The Savage Mind.* Nature of Human Society Series. Chicago: University of Chicago Press, 1966.

———. *Structural Anthropology.* Translated by Monique Layton. Vol. 2. New York: Basic Books, 1963.

———. *A World on the Wane.* Translated by John Russell. New York: Criterion Books, 1961.

———. *Totemism.* Translated by Rodney Needham. Boston: Beacon Press, 1963.

———. *Tristes Tropiques.* Translated by John Weightman and Doreen Weightman. New York: Penguin
    Books, 1992.

Lewis, C. S. *The Four Loves.* London: Harper Collins Publishers, 2002.

Lienkamp, Christoph. "Gewalt und Religion: Zwei Möglichkeiten einer nicht-totalisierenden religiösen
    Ordnung." *Orientierung* 65 (2001): 209–212.

Livingston, Paisley. "Girard and the Origin of Culture." In *Understanding Origins: Contemporary Views
    on the Origin of Life, Mind and Society,* edited by Jean-Pierre Dupuy and Francisco J. Varela,
    91–110. Dordrecht: Kluwer Academic Publishers, 1992.

———. *Models of Desire: René Girard and the Psychology of Mimesis.* Baltimore: Johns Hopkins
    University Press, 1992.

Livy. *Books 1–2.* Translated by B. O. Foster. Vol. 1. Loeb Classical Library. Cambridge, MA: Harvard
    University Press, 1919.

Lloyd-Jones, Hugh, ed. *Aeschylus in Two Volumes.* Vol. 2, *Agamemnon, Libation-Bearers, Eumenides,
    Fragments* (Cambridge, MA: Harvard University Press, 1983.

Lohfink, Norbert. "Altes Testament—Die Entlarvung der Gewalt." In *Weltgestaltung und
    Gewaltlosigkeit,* edited by Norbert Lohfink and Rudolf Pesch, 45–61. Düsseldorf: Patmos Verlag,
    1978.

———. "'Gewalt' als Thema Alttestamentlicher Forschung." In *Gewalt und Gewaltlosigkeit im Alten
    Testament,* edited by Norbert Lohfink, 15–50. Freiburg: Herder, 1983.

———. "Wie sollte man das Alte Testament auf die Erbsünde hin befragen?" In *Zum Problem der
    Erbsünde: Theologische und philosophische Versuche,* edited by Norbert Lohfink, Alexander Sand,
    Georg Scherer, and Wilhelm Breuning, 9–52. Essen: Ludgerus, 1981.

Luhmann, Niklas. *Die Wirtschaft der Gesellschaft.* 2nd ed. Frankfurt am Main: Suhrkamp, 1996.

Lukács, Georg. "Die Gegenwartsbedeutung des kritischen Realismus (1957)." In *Essays über Realismus,*
    457–603. Neuwied: Luchterhand, 1971.

———. *Die Theorie des Romans: Ein geschichtsphilosophischer Versuch über die Formen der großen Epik.*
    Munich: Deutscher Taschenbuch Verlag, 1994.

———. *Die Zerstörung der Vernunft.* Werke. Neuwied: Luchterhand, 1960.

Mack, Burton. "Introduction: Religion and Ritual." In *Violent Origins: Walter Burkert, René Girard,
    and Jonathan Z. Smith on Ritual Killing and Cultural Formation,* edited by Robert G. Hamerton-
    Kelly, 1–70. Stanford, CA: Stanford University Press, 1987.

Macksey, Richard, and Eugenio Donato, eds. *The Structuralist Controversy: The Languages of Criticism and the Sciences of Man*. Baltimore: Johns Hopkins University Press, 1979.

Madison, James, Alexander Hamilton, and John Jay. *The Federalist Papers*. Harmondsworth: Penguin Books, 1987.

Mann, Thomas. *Essays*. Bd. 5: *Deutschland und die Deutschen 1938–1945*. Frankfurt am Main: Fischer Taschenbuch Verlag, 1996.

———. *Joseph and His Brothers*. Translated by H. T. Lowe-Porter. New York: Alfred A. Knopf, 1948.

Marr, Andrew O.S.B. *Tools for Peace: The Spiritual Craft of St. Benedict and René Girard*. New York: iUniverse, Inc., 2007.

Martin, David. "Säkularisierung in Europa—Glaubensvielfalt in Amerika: Zwei Ausnahmen und keine Regel?" *Transit*, no. 8 (1994): 42–52.

Marx, Karl. *Capital: A Critique of Political Economy*. Translated by Ben Fowkes. Vol. 1. Harmondsworth: Penguin, 1976.

Mathews, Aidan Carl. "Knowledge of Good and Evil: The Work of René Girard." In *To Honor René Girard: Presented on the Occasion of His Sixtieth Birthday by Colleagues, Students, and Friends*, edited by Alphonse Juilland, 17–28. Saratoga, CA: Anma Libri, 1986.

Matt, Peter von. *Die tintenblauen Eidgenossen: Über die literarische und politische Schweiz*. Munich: Hanser, 2001.

Mayer, Hans. *Ein Deutscher auf Widerruf: Erinnerungen I*. Frankfurt am Main: Suhrkamp, 1988.

McCracken, David. "Scandal and Imitation in Matthew, Kierkegaard, and Girard." *Contagion: Journal of Violence, Mimesis, and Culture* 4 (1997): 146–162.

McKenna, Andrew J. "Aristotle's Theater of Envy: Paradox, Logic, and Literature." In *Philosophical Designs for a Socio-Cultural Transformation: Beyond Violence and the Modern Era*, edited by Tetsuji Yamamoto, 632–654. Boulder, CO: Rowman & Littlefield Publishers, 1998.

———. "The Law's Delay: Cinema and Sacrifice." *Legal Studies Forum* 15 (1991): 199–213.

———. "Pascal, Order, and Difference." *Religion & Literature* 25, no. 2 (1993): 55–75.

———. *Violence and Difference: Girard, Derrida, and Deconstruction*. Urbana and Chicago: University of Illinois Press, 1992.

Meier, Christian. *Die Entstehung des Politischen bei den Griechen*. 3. Aufl. ed. Frankfurt am Main: Suhrkamp, 1995.

Meloni, Maurizio. "A Triangle of Thoughts: Girard, Freud, Lacan." *Journal of European Psychoanalysis*, no. 14 (2002): 27–56.

Meyer, Martin. *Ende der Geschichte?* Munich: Carl Hanser Verlag, 1993.

Miggelbrink, Ralf. *Der Zorn Gottes: Geschichte und Aktualität einer ungeliebten biblischen Tradition*. Freiburg: Herder, 2000.

Milbank, John. "Stories of Sacrifice." *Contagion: Journal of Violence, Mimesis, and Culture*, no. 2 (1995): 75–102.

———. *Theology and Social Theory: Beyond Secular Reason*. Oxford: Basil Blackwell, 1990.

Mishra, Pankaj. "What Would the Buddha Think?" *New Perspectives Quarterly* 22, no. 3 (2005): 49–53.

Moi, Toril. "The Missing Mother: The Oedipal Rivalries of René Girard." *Diacritics: A Review of Contemporary Criticism* 12, no. 2 (1982): 21–31.

Mozart, Wolfgang Amadeus. *Die Zauberflöte: Eine große Oper in zwei Aufzügen.* Stuttgart: Phillip Reclam jun., 1991.

Mumford, Lewis. *The City in History: Its Origins, Its Transformations, and Its Prospects.* New York: Harcourt, Inc., 1989.

Musa, Mark, ed. *The Portable Dante.* New York: Penguin Books, 1995.

Müller-Funk, Wolfgang. *Kulturtheorie: Einführung in Schlüsseltexte der Kulturwissenschaften,* Utb. Tübingen: A. Francke Verlag, 2006.

Niethammer, Lutz. *Posthistoire: Ist die Geschichte zu Ende?* Reinbek bei Hamburg: rowohlts enzyklopädie, 1989.

Nietzsche, Friedrich. *Basic Writings of Nietzsche.* Translated by Walter Kaufmann. Modern Library ed. New York: Modern Library, 2000.

——— . *Sämtliche Briefe: Kritische Studienausgabe in 8 Bänden.* Band 8: *Januar 1887–Januar 1889.* Edited by Giorgio Colli and Mazzino Montinari. Munich: Deutscher Taschenbuch Verlag, 1986.

——— . *Sämtliche Werke: Kritische Studienausgabe in 15 Einzelbänden.* Edited by Giorgio Colli and Mazzino Montinari. Berlin: Walter de Gruyter, 1988.

——— . *The Will to Power.* Translated by Walter Kaufmann and R. J. Hollingdale. New York: Random House, 1967.

Niewiadomski, Józef, ed. *Eindeutige Antworten? Fundamentalistische Versuchung in Religion und Gesellschaft.* 3rd ed. Theologische Trends. Thaur: Kulturverlag, 1989.

——— . *Herbergsuche: Auf dem Weg zu einer christlichen Identität in der modernen Kultur,* Beiträge zur mimetischen Theorie. Münster: LIT, 1999.

——— . "Konturen einer Theologie der Eucharistie." In *Faszinierendes Geheimnis: Neue Zugänge zur Eucharistie in Familie, Schule und Gemeinde,* edited by Matthias Scharer and Józef Niewiadomski, 75–105. Innsbruck: Tyrolia-Verlag, 1999.

——— . "Transzendenz und Menschwerdung: Transformationskraft des Opfers im Fokus österlicher Augen." In *Das Opfer—Aktuelle Kontroversen: Religions-politischer Diskurs im Kontext der mimetischen Theorie. Deutsch-Italienische Fachtagung der Guardini Stiftung in der Villa Vigoni 18.-22. Oktober 1999,* edited by Bernhard Dieckmann, 293–306. Münster: LIT, 2001.

——— . "Vom Verfluchten zum Nichterwählten, aber doch verdammten Esau: Prädestinationsdilemma im Licht der Theorie von René Girard." In *Congresso Internazionale Su S. Agostino nel Xvi Centenario della Conversione.* Atti 3, 297–307. Rome, 1987.

Niewiadomski, Józef, and Nikolaus Wandinger, eds. *Dramatische Theologie im Gespräch: Symposion/ Gastmahl zum 65. Geburtstag von Raymund Schwager.* Beiträge zur mimetischen Theorie. Münster: LIT, 2003.

Nordhofen, Eckhard. "Vor der Bundeslade des Bösen." *Die Zeit,* 9 April 1993, 61–62.

Nordhofen, Jacob. *Durch das Opfer erlöst? Die Bedeutung der Rede vom Opfer Jesu Christi in der Bibel und bei René Girard.* Beiträge zur mimetischen Theorie. Vienna: LIT, 2008.

Nordhofen, Susanne. "Christa Wolfs Medea: Mythos und Tragödie im Licht der mimetischen Theorie." In *Das Opfer—Aktuelle Kontroversen: Religions-politischer Diskurs im Kontext der mimetischen*

Theorie. Deutsch-Italienische Fachtagung der Guardini Stiftung in der Villa Vigoni 18.–22. Oktober 1999, edited by Bernhard Dieckmann, 81–97. Münster: LIT, 2001.

Nowak, Susan. "The Girardian Theory and Feminism: Critique and Appropriation." *Contagion: Journal of Violence, Mimesis, and Culture* 1 (1994): 19–29.

Ojara, Pius, and Patrick Madigan. *Marcel, Girard, Bakhtin: The Return of Conversion*. Frankfurt am Main: Peter Lang, 2004.

Orléan, André. *L'empire de la valeur: Refonder l'économie*. Paris: Seuil, 2011.

Ortmann, Günther. *Regel und Ausnahme: Paradoxien sozialer Ordnung*. Frankfurt am Main: Suhrkamp, 2003.

Otto, Rudolf. *The Idea of the Holy: An Inquiry into the Non-Rational Factor in the Idea of the Divine and Its Relation to the Rational*. Translated by John W. Harvey. A Galaxy Book. London: Oxford University Press, 1923.

Oughourlian, Jean-Michel. *The Puppet of Desire: The Psychology of Hysteria, Possession, and Hypnosis*. Translated by Eugene Webb. Stanford, CA: Stanford University Press, 1991.

Paglia, Camille. *Sex, Art, and American Culture*. New York: Vintage Books, 1992.

———. *Sexual Personae: Art and Decadence from Nefertiti to Emily Dickinson*. New York: Vintage Books, 1991.

Palaver, Wolfgang. "Carl Schmitt on Nomos and Space." *Telos*, no. 106 (1996): 105–127.

———. "Challenging Capitalism as Religion: Hans G. Ulrich's Theological and Ethical Reflections on the Economy." *Studies in Christian Ethics* 20, no. 2 (2007): 215–230.

———. "Die Bedeutung von Stellvertretung für eine theologische Sozialethik: Ein Beitrag aus der Sicht der Mimetischen Theorie René Girards." In *Stellvertretung: Theologische, philosophische und kulturelle Aspekte*. Band 1: *Interdisziplinäres Symposion Tübingen 2004*, edited by J. Christine Janowski, Bernd Janowski, Hans P. Lichtenberger, and Anette Krüger, 213–226. Neukirchen-Vluyn: Neukirchener, 2006.

———. *Die mythischen Quellen des Politischen: Carl Schmitts Freund-Feind-Theorie*. Beiträge zur Friedensethik. Stuttgart: Verlag W. Kohlhammer, 1998.

———. "Die religiöse Dimension des Nationalismus." *Theologisch-praktische Quartalschrift* 142, no. 3 (1994): 225–233.

———. "Foundational Violence and Hannah Arendt's Political Philosophy." *Paragrana: Internationale Zeitschrift für Historische Anthropologie* 4, no. 2 (1995): 166–176.

———. "A Girardian Reading of Schmitt's *Political Theology*." *Telos*, no. 93 (1992): 43–68.

———. "Girards versteckte Distanz zur zeuzeitlichen Ontologisierung der Gewalt." In *Dramatische Theologie im Gespräch: Symposion/Gastmahl zum 65. Geburtstag von Raymund Schwager*, edited by Józef Niewiadomski and Nikolaus Wandinger, 113–126. Münster: LIT, 2003.

———. "Gleichheit als Sprengkraft? Zum Einfluß des Christentums auf die Entwicklung der Demokratie." In *Verweigerte Mündigkeit? Politische Kultur und Kirche*, edited by Józef Niewiadomski, 195–217. Thaur: Kulturverlag, 1989.

———. "Globalisierung und Opfer: Carl Schmitts Lehre vom Nomos." In *Das Opfer—Aktuelle Kontroversen: Religions-politischer Diskurs im Kontext der mimetischen Theorie*.

Deutsch-Italienische Fachtagung der Guardini Stiftung in der Villa Vigoni 18.-22. Oktober 1999, edited by Bernhard Dieckmann, 181–206. Münster: LIT, 2001.

———. "Gott oder mechanischer Gliedermann? Die religiöse Problematik in Kleists Essay *über das Marionettentheater.*" In *Kleist zur Gewalt: Transdisziplinäre Perspektiven,* edited by Gianluca Crepaldi, Andreas Kriwak, and Thomas Pröll, 45–62. Innsbruck: Innsbruck University Press, 2011.

———. "Hauke Haien—ein Sündenbock? Theodor Storms Schimmelreiter aus der Perspektive der Theorie René Girards." In *Religion—Literatur—Künste: Aspekte Eines Vergleichs,* edited by Peter Tschuggnall, 221–236. Anif/Salzburg: Verlag Ursula Müller-Speiser, 1998.

———. "Hobbes and the Katéchon: The Secularization of Sacrificial Christianity." *Contagion: Journal of Violence, Mimesis, and Culture* 2 (1995): 57–74.

———. "Im Zeichen des Opfers: Die apokalyptische Verschärfung der Weltlage als Folge des Monotheismus." In *Westliche Moderne, Christentum und Islam: Gewalt als Anfrage an monotheistische Religionen,* edited by Wolfgang Palaver, Roman A. Siebenrock, and Dietmar Regensburger, 151–176. Innsbruck: Innsbruck University Press, 2008.

———. "Kapitalismus als Religion." *Quart,* no. 3–4 (2001): 18–25.

———. "Mimesis and Nemesis: The Economy as a Theological Problem." *Telos,* no. 117 (1999): 79–112.

———. "Mimesis and Scapegoating in the Works of Hobbes, Rousseau and Kant." *Contagion: Journal of Violence, Mimesis, and Culture* 10 (2003): 126–148.

———. "Order out of Chaos in the Theories of Carl Schmitt and René Girard." *Synthesis* 1 (1994): 87–106.

———. *Politik und Religion bei Thomas Hobbes: Eine Kritik aus der Sicht der Theorie René Girards.* Innsbrucker Theologische Studien. Innsbruck: Tyrolia, 1991.

———. "Schmitt's Critique of Liberalism." *Telos,* no. 102 (1995): 43–71.

———. "Terrorismus: Wesensmerkmale, Entstehung, Religion." In *Religion erzeugt Gewalt—Einspruch! Innsbrucker Forschungsprojekt "Religion—Gewalt—Kommunikation—Weltordnung,"* edited by Raymund Schwager and Józef Niewiadomski, 217–232. Münster: LIT, 2003.

———. "Violence and Religion: Walter Burkert and René Girard in Comparison." *Contagion: Journal of Violence, Mimesis, and Culture* 17 (2010): 121–137.

Palaver, Wolfgang, Andreas Exenberger, and Kristina Stöckl, eds. *Aufgeklärte Apokalyptik: Religion, Gewalt und Frieden im Zeitalter der Globalisierung.* Edition Weltordnung—Religion—Gewalt. Innsbruck: Innsbruck University Press, 2007.

Palaver, Wolfgang, and Petra Steinmair-Pösel, eds. *Passions in Economy, Politics, and the Media: In Discussion with Christian Theology.* Beiträge zur mimetischen Theorie. Vienna: LIT, 2005.

Pascal, Blaise. *Pensées: Thoughts on Religion and Other Subjects.* Translated by William Finlayson Trotter. New York: Washington Square Press, 1965.

Philostratus. *The Life of Apollonius of Tyana.* Translated by Christopher Jones. Vol. 1. Loeb Classical Library. Cambridge, MA: Harvard University Press, 2005.

Piccone, Paul. "The Crisis of Liberalism and the Emergence of Federal Populism." *Telos,* no. 89 (1991): 7–44.

Pieper, Josef. *Faith, Hope, Love.* Translated by Richard Winston, Clara Winston, and Mary Francis McCarthy. San Francisco: Ignatius Press, 1997.

Pixley, Jorge. "Exige o deus verdadeiro sacrifícios cruentos?" In *René Girard com teólogos da libertaçao: Um diálogo sobre ídolos e sacrifícios*, edited by Hugo Assmann, 189–220. Petrópolis, Brazil: Vozes, 1991.

Plato. *The Laws of Plato*. Translated by Thomas L. Pangle. New York: Basic Books, 1980.

———. *The Republic*. Translated by Allan David Bloom. 2nd ed. New York: Basic Books, 1991.

Plutarch. *Lives in Eleven Volumes*. Translated by Bernadotte Perrin. Vol. 1. Loeb Classical Library. Cambridge, MA: Harvard University Press, 1967.

Prodi, Paolo. *Das Sakrament der Herrschaft: Der politische Eid in der Verfassungsgeschichte des Okzidents*. Translated by Judith Elze. Schriften des Italienisch-Deutschen Historischen Instituts in Trient. Berlin: Duncker & Humblot, 1997.

Proust, Marcel. *The Past Recaptured*. Translated by Andreas Mayor. New York: Random House, 1981.

———. *Sodom and Gomorrah*. Translated by C. K. Scott-Moncrieff and Terence Kilmartin. New York: Modern Library, 1993.

———. *Swann's Way*. Translated by Lydia Davis. 1st American ed. New York: Viking, 2003.

———. *Within a Budding Grove*. Translated by C. K. Scott-Moncrieff and Terence Kilmartin. Modern Library ed. New York: Modern Library, 1992.

Ramond, Charles. *Le vocabulaire de Girard*. Paris: Ellipses, 2005.

Rasmussen, Knud. *The Netsilik Eskimos: Social Life and Spiritual Culture*. Report of the Fifth Thule Expedition, 1921–24. Vol. 8, no. 1–2. Copenhagen: Nordisk Forlag, 1931.

Rawls, John. *A Theory of Justice*. Cambridge, MA: Belknap Press, 2005.

Regensburger, Dietmar. "Religion(en) und Gewalt: Systematische Reflexionen zu einem aktuellen und brisanten Spannungsfeld im Lichte der mimetischen Theorie René Girards." In *Weltreligionen im Film: Christentum, Islam, Judentum, Hinduismus, Buddhismus*, edited by Joachim Valentin, 15–34. Marburg: Schüren, 2002.

Reineke, Martha J. *Sacrificed Lives: Kristeva on Women and Violence*. Bloomington and Indianapolis: Indiana University Press, 1997.

Rgveda Samhita. Translated by Svami Satya Prakash Saravasvati and Satyakam Vidyalankar. Vol. 13. New Delhi: Veda Pratishthana, 1987.

Robertson-Smith, William. *Religion of the Semites*. New Brunswick, NJ: Transaction Publishers, 2002.

Röder, Brigitte, Juliane Hummel, and Brigitte Kunz. *Göttinnendämmerung: Das Matriarchat aus archäologischer Sicht*. Munich: Droemer Knaur, 1996.

Rougemont, Denis de. *The Devil's Share*. Translated by Haakon Chevalier. New York: Pantheon Books, 1952.

———. *Journal aus Deutschland 1935–1936*. Translated by Tobias Scheffel. Vienna: Paul Zsolnay Verlag, 1998.

———. *Love in the Western World*. Translated by Montgomery Belgion. New York: Schocken Books, 1990.

Rousseau, Jean-Jacques. *Confessions*. Translated by Angela Scholar. Oxford World's Classics. Oxford: Oxford University Press, 2000.

———. *The Discourses and Other Political Writings*. Translated by Victor Gourevitch, Cambridge Texts in the History of Political Thought. Cambridge: Cambridge University Press, 1997.

———. *Emile: Or, on Education.* Translated by Allan Bloom. New York: Basic Books, 1979.

———. *The Plan for Perpetual Peace, On the Government of Poland, and Other Writings on History and Politics.* Translated by Christopher Kelly and Judith Bush. The Collected Writings of Rousseau. Hanover, NH: Dartmouth College Press, 2005.

———. *Reveries of the Solitary Walker.* Translated by Russell Goulbourne. Oxford: Oxford University Press, 2011.

———. *Rousseau, Judge of Jean-Jacques, Dialogues.* Translated by Judith R. Bush, Christopher Kelly, and Roger D. Masters, The Collected Writings of Rousseau. Hanover: University Press of New England, 1990.

———. *The Social Contract and Discourses.* Translated by G.D.H. Cole, J. H. Brumfitt, and John C. Hall. London: Dent, 1990.

Rousseau, Jean-Jacques, and Johann Gottfried Herder. *On the Origin of Language.* Translated by John H. Moran and Alexander Gode. Chicago: University of Chicago Press, 1986.

Safranski, Rüdiger. *Das Böse oder Das Drama der Freiheit.* Munich: Carl Hanser Verlag, 1997.

Sändig, Brigitte. "'. . . Etwas Stärkeres als alle Rechtsprechung': Camus und die Todesstrafe." *Orientierung* 64 (2000): 215–219.

Santa Ana, Julio de. "Sacralizações e sacrifícios nas práticas humanas." In *René Girard com teólogos da libertação: Um diálogo sobre ídolos e sacrifícios,* edited by Hugo Assmann, 121–52. Petrópolis, Brazil: Vozes, 1991.

Sartre, Jean-Paul. *Anti-Semite and Jew.* Translated by George Joseph Becker. New York: Schocken Books, 1948.

———. *Being and Nothingness: A Phenomenological Essay on Ontology.* Translated by Hazel E. Barnes. New York: Pocket Books, 1966.

——— *A Collection of Critical Essays.* Edited by E. Kern. Englewood Cliffs, NJ: Prentice-Hall, 1962.

———. *Existentialism Is a Humanism.* New Haven: Yale University Press, 2007.

———. *No Exit, and Three Other Plays.* Translated by Stuart Gilbert. New York: Vintage International, 1989.

———. *The Transcendence of the Ego: An Existentialist Theory of Consciousness.* Translated by Forrest Williams and Robert Kirkpatrick. New York: Hill and Wang, 1957.

———. *War Diaries: Notebooks from a Phoney War, November 1939–March 1940.* Translated by Quintin Hoare, Verso Classics. London: Verso, 1999.

Scheer, Klaus-Dieter. "Die aufgeschobene Theokratie: Zur politischen Theologie Carl Schmitts." In *Das Heilige: Seine Spur in der Moderne,* edited by Dietmar Kamper and Christoph Wulf, 441–49. Frankfurt am Main: Athenäum, 1987.

Scheler, Max. *Formalism in Ethics and Non-Formal Ethics of Values: A New Attempt toward the Foundation of an Ethical Personalism.* Translated by Manfred S. Frings and Roger L. Funk. 5th rev. ed., Northwestern University Studies in Phenomenology & Existential Philosophy. Evanston: Northwestern University Press, 1973.

———. *On the Eternal in Man.* Translated by Bernard Noble. New York: Harper, 1961.

———. *Ressentiment.* Translated by Lewis B. Coser and William W. Holdheim. Marquette Studies in Philosophy. Milwaukee, WI: Marquette University Press, 1994.

Schickel, Joachim. *Gespräche mit Carl Schmitt.* Berlin: Merve Verlag, 1993.

Schlesier, Renate. *Kulte, Mythen und Gelehrte: Anthropologie der Antike seit 1800.* Frankfurt am Main: Fischer Taschenbuch Verlag, 1994.

Schmitt, Carl. *The Concept of the Political.* Translated by George Schwab. Chicago: University of Chicago Press, 2007.

———. *The Crisis of Parliamentary Democracy.* Translated by Ellen Kennedy. Cambridge, MA: MIT Press, 1988.

———. *Ex Captivitate Salus: Erfahrungen der Zeit 1945/47.* Köln: Greven Verlag, 1950.

———. *Glossarium: Aufzeichnungen der Jahre 1947–1951.* Berlin: Duncker & Humblot, 1991.

———. *The Leviathan in the State Theory of Thomas Hobbes: Meaning and Failure of a Political Symbol.* Translated by George Schwab and Erna Hilfstein. Chicago: University of Chicago Press, 2008.

———. *The Nomos of the Earth in the International Law of the Jus Publicum Europaeum.* Translated by G. L. Ulmen. New York: Telos Press, Ltd., 2006.

———. "A Pan-European Interpretation of Donoso Cortés." *Telos*, no. 125 (2002): 100–115.

———. *Political Theology: Four Chapters on the Concept of Sovereignty.* Foreword by Tracy B. Strong. Translated by George Schwab. Chicago: University of Chicago Press, 2005.

———. *Roman Catholicism and Political Form.* Translated by G. L. Ulmen. Westport, CT: Greenwood Press, 1996.

Schoeck, Helmut. *Der Neid: Eine Theorie der Gesellschaft.* Freiburg: Verlag Karl Alber, 1966.

Schoffeleers, Matthew. "Twins and Unilateral Figures in Central and Southern Africa: Symmetry and Asymmetry in the Symbolization of the Sacred." *Journal of Religion in Africa* 21, no. 4 (1991): 345–372.

Schwager, Raymund. *Banished from Eden: Original Sin and Evolutionary Theory in the Drama of Salvation.* Translated by James G. Williams. Leominster: Gracewing, 2006.

———. "Christ's Death and the Prophetic Critique of Sacrifice." *Semeia: An Experimental Journal for Biblical Criticism*, no. 33 (1985): 109–123.

———. *Der wunderbare Tausch: Zur Geschichte und Deutung der Erlösungslehre.* Munich: Kösel, 1986.

———. "Eindrücke einer Begegnung." In *Gewalt und Gewaltlosigkeit im Alten Testament*, edited by Norbert Lohfink, 214–224. Freiburg: Herder, 1983.

———. *Jesus in the Drama of Salvation: Toward a Biblical Doctrine of Redemption.* Translated by James G. Williams and Paul Haddon. New York: Crossroad Publishing Co., 1999.

———. "Mimesis und Freiheit." *Zeitschrift für Katholische Theologie* 107 (1985): 365–376.

———. *Must There Be Scapegoats? Violence and Redemption in the Bible.* Translated by Maria L. Assad. San Francisco: Harper & Row, 1987.

———. "Rückblick auf das Symposium." In *Dramatische Erlösungslehre: Ein Symposion*, edited by Józef Niewiadomski and Wolfgang Palaver, 338–384. Innsbruck: Tyrolia, 1992.

———. "Schöpfung und Opfer: Roberto Calasso und René Girard." In *Das Opfer—Aktuelle Kontroversen: Religions-politischer Diskurs im Kontext der mimetischen Theorie. Deutsch-Italienische Fachtagung der Guardini Stiftung in der Villa Vigoni 18.-22. Oktober 1999*, edited by Bernhard Dieckmann, 19–35. Münster: LIT, 2001.

Scubla, Lucien. *Lire Lévi-Strauss: Le déploiement d'une intuition*. Paris: Éditions Odile Jacob, 1998.

———. "Réciprocité rituelle et subordination politique." In *Logiques de la réciprocité*," 119–273. Paris: Centre de recherche en épistemologie appliquée, 1985.

Seitter, Walter. "Katechontiken im 20: Jahrhundert nach Christus." *Tumult*, no. 25 (2001): 104–127.

Serres, Michel. *La Traduction*. Hermès. Paris: Éditions de Minuit, 1974.

Serres, Michel. "Receiving René Girard into the Académie Française." In *For René Girard: Essays in Friendship and in Truth*, edited by Sandor Goodhart, Jørgen Jørgensen, Tom Ryba and James G. Williams, 1–17. East Lansing: Michigan State University Press, 2009.

Shakespeare, William. *The Complete Signet Classic Shakespeare*, ed. Sylvan Barnet. New York: Harcourt Brace Jovanovich, 1972.

Shapiro, Michael J. *Reading the Postmodern Polity: Political Theory as Textual Practice*. Minneapolis: University of Minnesota Press, 1992.

Shea, Chris. "Victims on Violence: 'Different Voices' and Girard." In *Curing Violence*, edited by Mark I. Wallace and Theophus H. Smith, 252–265. Sonoma, CA: Polebridge Press, 1994.

Siebers, Tobin. *The Ethics of Criticism*. Ithaca, NY: Cornell University Press, 1988.

———. "Language, Violence, and the Sacred: A Polemical Survey of Critical Theories." In *To Honor René Girard: Presented on the Occasion of His Sixtieth Birthday by Colleagues, Students, and Friends*, edited by Alphonse Juilland, 203–219. Saratoga, CA: Anma Libri, 1986.

Simmel, Georg. *Simmel on Culture: Selected Writings*. Translated by David Frisby and Mark Ritter. Thousand Oaks, CA: Sage, 1997.

———. *Sociology: Inquiries into the Construction of Social Forms*. Vol. 1. Translated by Anthony J. Blasi, Anton K. Jacobs, and Mathew J. Kanjirathinkal. Leiden: Brill, 2009.

Simonse, Simon. *Kings of Disaster: Dualism, Centralism and the Scapegoat King in the Southeastern Sudan*. Studies in Human Society. Leiden: E.J. Brill, 1992.

———. "Mimesis, Schismogenesis, and Catastrophe Theory: Gregory Bateson as a Forerunner of Mimetic Theory: With a Demonstration of His Theory on Nilotic Regicide." *Synthesis: An Interdisciplinary Journal* 1, no. 1 (1995): 147–172.

Sloterdijk, Peter. "Erwachen im Reich der Eifersucht: Notiz zu René Girards anthropologischer Sendung." In *Ich Sah den Satan vom Himmel fallen wie einen Blitz* by René Girard, 241–54. Munich: Carl Hanser Verlag, 2002.

Smith, Adam. *The Theory of Moral Sentiments*. The Glasgow Edition of the Works and Correspondence of Adam Smith. Indianapolis: Liberty Fund, 1984.

Smith, Brian K. "Capital Punishment and Human Sacrifice." *Journal of the American Academy of Religion* 68, no. 1 (2000): 3–25.

Sofsky, Wolfgang. "Das Gesetz des Gemetzels." *Die Zeit*, 2 April 1998, 53–54.

———. *Traktat über die Gewalt*. Frankfurt am Main: S. Fischer, 1996.

Sombart, Nicolaus. *Pariser Lehrjahre 1951–1954: Leçons de Sociologie*. Frankfurt am Main: Fischer Taschenbuch Verlag, 1996.

———. *Wilhelm II: Sündenbock und Herr der Mitte*. Berlin: Verlag Volk & Welt, 1996.

Sophocles. *The Three Theban Plays*. Translated by Robert Fagles. Penguin Classics. New York: Penguin Books, 1984.

Spinoza, Benedict de. *The Chief Works of Benedict de Spinoza*. Translated by Robert Harvey Monro Elwes. 2 vols. London: G. Bell and Sons, 1883.

Stegemann, Wolfgang. "Der Tod Jesu als Opfer? Anthropologische Aspekte seiner Deutung im Neuen Testament." In *Abschied von der Schuld? Zur Anthropologie und Theologie Von Schuldbekenntnis, Opfer und Versöhnung*, edited by Richard Riess, 120–139. Stuttgart: Verlag W. Kohlhammer, 1996.

Steiner, George. *Real Presences*. Chicago: University of Chicago Press, 1989.

Stendhal. *On Love*. Translated by Vyvyan Beresford Holland and C. K. Scott-Moncrieff. New York: Liveright Publishing Corporation, 1947.

———. *The Red and the Black*. Translated by Robert Martin Adams. 2nd ed. A Norton Critical Edition. New York: W.W. Norton, 2008.

Storm, Theodor. *The Dykemaster*. Translated by Denis Jackson. Angel classics ed. London: Angel Books, 1996.

Strauss, Leo. *The Political Philosophy of Hobbes: Its Basis and Its Genesis*. Translated by Elsa M. Sinclair. Chicago: University of Chicago Press, 1963.

Strauss, Leo, and Alexandre Kojève. *On Tyranny*. Rev. and expanded ed. Toronto: Maxwell Macmillan International, 1991.

Tarde, Gabriel de. *The Laws of Imitation*. Translated by Elsie Clews Parsons. Gloucester, MA: P. Smith, 1962.

Taubes, Jacob. "Ästhetisierung der Wahrheit im Posthistoire." In *Streitbare Philosophie: Margherita von Brentano zum 65. Geburtstag*, edited by Gabriele Althaus and Irmingard Staeuble, 41–51. Berlin: Metropol, 1988.

Taylor, Charles. "Notes on the Sources of Violence: Perennial and Modern." In *Beyond Violence: Religious Sources for Social Transformation in Judaism, Christianity and Islam*, edited by James L. Heft, 15–42. Ashland, OH: Fordham University Press, 2004.

———. *A Secular Age*. Cambridge, MA: Belknap Press, 2007.

———. *Sources of the Self: The Making of the Modern Identity*. Cambridge, MA: Harvard University Press, 1989.

Thomas, Keith. *Religion and the Decline of Magic: Studies in Popular Beliefs in Sixteenth- and Seventeenth-Century England*. 3rd ed. Harmondsworth, UK: Penguin, 1985.

Thomas, Konrad. "René Girard: Ein anderes Verständnis von Gewalt." In *Kultur: Theorien der Gegenwart*, edited by Stephan Moebius and Dirk Quadflieg, 325–338. Wiesbaden: VS Verlag für Sozialwissenschaften, 2006.

———. *Rivalität: Sozialwissenschaftliche Variationen zu einem alten Thema*. Frankfurt am Main: Peter Lang, 1990.

Tierney, Patrick. *The Highest Altar: The Story of Human Sacrifice*. New York: Viking, 1989.

Tijmes, Pieter. "Die Intuitionen René Girards." In *Die Macht der Differenzen: Beiträge zur Hermeneutik der Kultur*, edited by Reinhard Düssel, Geert Edel, and Ulrich Schödlbauer, 127–148. Heidelberg: SYNCHRON, Wissenschafts-Verlag der Autoren, 2001.

Tocqueville, Alexis de. *Democracy in America.* Translated by Henry Reeve, Francis Bowen and Phillips Bradley. 2 vols. Vintage Classics. New York: Vintage Books, 1990.

Todorov, Tzvetan. *The Conquest of America: The Question of the Other.* Translated by Richard Howard. 1st ed. New York: Harper & Row, 1984.

——. *Life in Common: An Essay in General Anthropology.* Translated by Katherine Golsan and Lucy Golsan. European Horizons. Lincoln: University of Nebraska Press, 2001.

Tomelleri, Stefano. "Ressentiment und Dekonstruktion." In *Das Opfer—Aktuelle Kontroversen: Religions-politischer Diskurs im Kontext der mimetischen Theorie. Deutsch-Italienische Fachtagung der Guardini Stiftung in der Villa Vigoni 18.-22. Oktober 1999,* edited by Bernhard Dieckmann, 281–292. Münster: LIT, 2001.

Tommissen, Piet. "Kojèves Hegel-Seminar: Hintergrund und Teilnehmer." In *Schmittiana. Beiträge Zu Leben und Werk Carl Schmitts,* Band 6, edited by Piet Tommissen, 75–94. Berlin: Duncker & Humblot, 1998.

Tschuggnall, Peter. *Das Abraham-Opfer als Glaubensparadox: Bibeltheologischer Befund—Literarische Rezeption—Kierkegaards Deutung.* Frankfurt am Main: Peter Lang, 1990.

Ude, Johannes. *"Du sollst nicht töten!"* Dornbirn: Mayer, 1948.

Ulmen, Gary. "Toward a New World Order: Introduction to Carl Schmitt's 'The Land Appropriation of a New World.'" *Telos,* no. 109 (1997): 3–27.

Vattimo, Gianni. *Belief.* Translated by Luca D'Isanto and David Webb. Stanford, CA: Stanford University Press, 1999.

——. *Beyond Interpretation: The Meaning of Hermeneutics for Philosophy.* Translated by David Webb. Stanford, CA: Stanford University Press, 1997.

——. *Tecnica ed esistenza: Una mappa filosofica del Novecento.* Milano: Mondadori, 2002.

Vattimo, Gianni, and René Girard. *Christianity, Truth, and Weakening Faith: A Dialogue.* Translated by William McCuaig. New York: Columbia University Press, 2010.

Voegelin, Eric. *Modernity without Restraints: The Political Religions, the New Science of Politics, and Science, Politics, and Gnosticism,* In *the Collected Works of Eric Voegelin.* Columbia: University of Missouri Press, 2000.

——. *Order and History.* Vol. 3, *Plato and Aristotle.* The Collected Works of Eric Voegelin. Columbia: University of Missouri Press, 2000.

Volf, Miroslav. *Exclusion and Embrace: A Theological Exploration of Identity, Otherness, and Reconciliation.* Nashville, TN: Abingdon Press, 1996.

Vollmer, Antje. "Gibt es Gemeinschaft ohne Sündenböcke?" *Zeitschrift für Missionswissenschaft und Religionswissenschaft* 83 (2001): 263–276.

——. *Heißer Frieden: Über Gewalt, Macht und das Geheimnis der Zivilisation.* Köln: Kiepenheuer & Witsch, 1995.

Waal, Frans de. *Good Natured: The Origins of Right and Wrong in Humans and Other Animals.* 7th ed. Cambridge, MA: Harvard University Press, 2003.

Waldmann, Peter. *Terrorismus: Provokation der Macht.* Munich: Gerling Akademie Verlag, 1998.

Waldschütz, Erwin. "Schöpferischer Verzicht: Überlegungen zu einer Grundkategorie bei René Girard."

In *Ganzheitliches Denken: Festgabe für Augustinus K. Wucherer-Huldenfeld zum 60. Geburtstag,* edited by Johann Figl and Erwin Waldschütz, 161–181. Vienna: WUV-Universitätsverlag, 1989.

Webb, Eugene. "Girard, Sacrifice, and Religious Symbolism." *Journal of European Psychoanalysis,* no. 14 (2002): 59–79.

———. *Philosophers of Consciousness: Polanyi, Lonergan, Voegelin, Ricoeur, Girard, Kierkegaard.* Seattle: University of Washington Press, 1988.

———. *The Self Between: From Freud to the New Social Psychology of France.* Seattle: University of Washington Press, 1993.

Weber, Max. *Ancient Judaism.* Translated by Hans H. Gerth and Don Martindale. Glencoe, IL: Free Press, 1952.

———. *Economy and Society: An Outline of Interpretive Sociology.* Translated by Ephraim Fischoff. Vol. 3. New York: Bedminster Press, 1968.

Weil, Simone. *Waiting for God.* Translated by Emma Craufurd. New York: Perennial Classics, 2001.

Wendland, Paul. "Jesus als Saturnalien-Koenig." *Hermes: Zeitschrift für Klassische Philologie* 33, no. 1 (1898): 175–179.

Werfel, Franz. *"Leben heißt, sich mitteilen": Betrachtungen, Reden, Aphorismen.* Frankfurt am Main: S. Fischer Verlag, 1992.

Widengren, Geo. *Religionsphänomenologie.* Translated by Rosmarie Elgnowski. Berlin: Walter de Gruyter, 1969.

Williams, James G. *The Bible, Violence, and the Sacred: Liberation from the Myth of Sanctioned Violence.* Foreword by René Girard. San Francisco: HarperSanFrancisco, 1991.

———."On Job and Writing: Derrida, Girard, and the Remedy-Poison." *Scandinavian Journal of the Old Testament* 7, no. 1 (1993): 32–50.

Willson, A. Leslie, ed. *German Romantic Criticism.* The German Library. New York: Continuum, 1982.

Wink, Walter. *Engaging the Powers: Discernment and Resistance in a World of Domination.* Minneapolis: Fortress Press, 1992.

Wohlman, Avital. "René Girard et Saint Augustin: Anthropologie et theologie." *Recherches Augustiniennes* 20 (1985): 257–303.

Wolf, Christa. *Medea: A Modern Retelling.* Translated by John Cullen. 1st ed. New York: Nan A. Talese, 1998.

———. *Voraussetzungen einer Erzählung: Kassandra. Frankfurter Poetik-Vorlesungen.* Darmstadt: Luchterhand, 1983.

Wolf, Christa, and Petra Kammann. "Gespräch am 25.1.1996." In *Christa Wolfs Medea: Voraussetzungen zu einem Text,* edited by Marianne Hochgeschurz, 75–89. Munich: Deutscher Taschenbuch Verlag, 2000.

Yamane, David. "Secularization on Trial: In Defense of a Neosecularization Paradigm." *Journal for the Scientific Study of Religion* 36, no. 1 (1997): 109–122.

Zundel, Rolf. "Der schwere Abschied: Vom Leiden der Politiker nach dem Entzug von Macht, Öffentlichkeit, Apparat und Wirkungsmöglichkeiten." *Die Zeit,* 7 April 1989, 45–46.

Index of Terms

The following is a list of the central concepts of Girard's mimetic theory. Although many of these terms appear more than once in this book, only the page number of the definition for each term is provided here.

Christianity
Sacrificial Christianity ("christianisme sacrificiel"), 246

Crisis
Sacrificial crisis ("crise sacrificielle"), 137
Crisis of distinctions ("crise des différences"), 137
Mimetic crisis ("crise mimétique"), 137

Crystallization
Mythological crystallization ("cristallisation mythologique"), 189

Cycle
Mimetic cycle ("cycle mimétique"), 255

Deferral ("différement"), 253

Delusion ("méconnaissance"), 152

Desire
Desire according to Another ("désir selon l'Autre"), 35
Metaphysical desire ("désir métaphysique"), 125
Mimetic desire ("désir mimétique"), 35/36
Imitated desire ("désir imité"), 35
Triangular desire ("désir triangulaire"), 35

Double ("double"), 132
Monstrous double ("double monstrueux"), 148/149

Ignorance ("ignorance"), 152

Imitation
Double imitation, 130
Nonviolent imitation ("imitation non violente"), 219
Negative imitation ("imitation négative"), 68

Mechanism of the surrogate victim ("mécanisme de la victime émissaire"), 152
See: victimage mechanism
See: scapegoat mechanism

Index of Names